COMPUTER SIMULATION IN BUSINESS

COMPUTER SIMULATION
IN BUSINESS

Hugh J. Watson

JOHN WILEY & SONS

New York • Chichester • Brisbane • Toronto • Singapore

Library of Congress Cataloging in Publication Data:

Watson, Hugh J
   Computer simulation in business.

   Includes index.
   1. Business—Data processing.   2. Computer
simulation.   I. Title.

HF5548.2.W326   658'.054   80-20612
ISBN 0-471-03638-2

Printed in the United States of America

10 9 8 7 6 5 4 3

ABOUT THE AUTHOR

Hugh J. Watson is Professor of Management at the University of Georgia. He has also taught at the University of Hawaii and the Florida State University and is an Affiliate Faculty Member of the Japan-America Institute of Management Science. He holds a B.S. in Electrical Engineering from Purdue University and an M.B.A. and D.B.A. in Management from the Florida State University. His articles have appeared in *Management Science, Interfaces, Omega, Academy of Management Journal, Journal of Business Research, Journal of Bank Research, California Management Review, MSU Business Topics*, and others. He is the co-author of several other texts including *Computers for Business: A Managerial Emphasis, Quantitative Methods for Business Decisions* and *Management: Making Organizations Perform*. His interest in simulation began with his doctoral dissertation and continues with research in financial planning systems and the simulation of human decision making.

PREFACE

Computer simulation is one of the most widely used quantitative methods of analysis in the contemporary business world. Through simulation it is possible to analyze the behavior of systems that cannot be analyzed by alternative methods.

Computer simulation is becoming more and more a part of management science, computer science, operations research, and engineering curriculums, therefore reflecting current industrial usage of simulation and its potential for the future.

During twelve years of conducting simulation research and of teaching simulation courses, I have developed strong beliefs as to what should be included in a college of business administration's introductory simulation course. Consequently, this book shows these beliefs and experiences, based on the following philosophy.

1. The level of quantitative sophistication of the introductory simulation course in a college of business administration should match the quantitative background of business administration students.
2. The wide spectrum of simulation applications in the business world should be presented and discussed.
3. Much of the technology of simulation can, and should, be taught in an application atmosphere.
4. The technology that is introduced should be presented in a complete rather than in a summary manner.
5. The role of simulation relative to other methods of analysis should be thoroughly examined.
6. The material presented should be largely programming-language independent.
7. The managerial topics should be discussed as well as the more traditional technical topics.

This book is written with a college of business administration audience in mind. The increasing number of business students taking simulation courses, their background in statistics, mathematics, computer science, and the functional areas of business, and the wide role of simulation in the modern business world all call for a book on simulation specifically written for a college of business administration course.

Instructors in disciplines other than business administration may find the text suitable for their purposes. Although this book is primarily aimed toward business students, a majority of it is of more general interest. Hopefully, the "teachable" nature of the book will give it broad appeal.

Simulation in the business world has applications in all functional areas as well as in specialized areas such as gaming and the simulation of human decision making. All these applications are discussed and illustrated to the extent possible within space limitations.

Generally, students find that new technology is most easily understood and its usefulness appreciated when presented in an application atmosphere. Through simple applications such as a Monte Carlo inventory simulation and probabilistic financial planning, basic simulation concepts are introduced, which set the stage for the more formal presentations of the technology that follow.

Instead of exploring all the technology associated with simulation (e.g., advanced, special-purpose probability distributions and their process generators), attention is directed to that technology which is compatible with business student's previous quantitative training, yet reflecting the basic skills required in building useful simulation models.

Because of factors such as time, cost, and precision, simulation should usually be viewed as a method of last resort. Consequently, simulation is discussed within the context of its role relative to alternative methods of analysis, for not every problem requires a simulation model.

There is a need for students in an introductory simulation course to be aware of the existence of special-purpose simulation languages, and perhaps even code several programs to understand better the languages' strengths, weaknesses, and usefulness. However, to restrict the introductory course to a special-purpose language, and possibly its applications, severely limits the topics covered. Consequently, at the University of Georgia, special-purpose languages are taught in detail only in advanced simulation courses. This book reflects the belief that the introductory simulation course should be language independent. When computer implementation of simulation models is discussed, the examples are coded in FORTRAN, since FORTRAN remains the most commonly taught language for college of business administration students.

The chronic complaint, whether or not accurate, is that management scientists are insensitive to managerial and behavioral considerations in applying their trade. Although this topic can only be covered briefly, nevertheless, it is discussed relative to recent research findings and thinking.

To facilitate teaching from *Computer Simulation in Business*, an *Instructor's Manual* has been prepared. For each chapter there are learning objectives, suggestions for chapter usage, assignment solutions, and possible test questions.

Many people contributed to the creation of this book. Insightful reviews were provided by Fred McFadden of the University of Colorado, Andy Seila of the University of Georgia, Dennis Streveler of the University of Hawaii, and Tom Schriber of the University of Michigan. Helpful suggestions were made by Roscoe Davis of the University of Georgia, Dwight Norris of Auburn University, Paul Greenlaw of the Pennsylvania State University, Ralph Sprague of the University of Hawaii, Mark Simkin of the University of Nevada-Reno, Gary Dickson of the University of Minnesota, Jerry Wagner of EXUCOM Systems Corporation, and Don Kroeber of James Madison University. Special thanks go to Tom Schriber for allowing the use of his FORTRAN-based queuing model, Howard Thompson of the University of Wisconsin-Madison for materials from the Credit Union Management Game, and Ramin Khadem and Alain Schultzki for their description of Teleglobe Canada's corporate simulation model. Henry Fabian, Gary Cumpson, Patricia Gill Marett, Larry Des Jardines, Don Burkhard, Marianne Hill, Tammy Benson, and Wybren Ritsma, my graduate assistants during the past few years, deserve a special word of thanks for the time and effort they spent on this book. As is always the case, however, final responsibility for any deficiencies lies with the author.

Hugh J. Watson

CONTENTS

Preface   vi

Chapter ■   1   ■   Introduction to Computer Simulation in Business   1

Chapter ■   2   ■   Business Applications of Simulation   21

Chapter ■   3   ■   Monte Carlo Inventory Simulation   47

Chapter ■   4   ■   Probabilistic Financial Planning   69

Chapter ■   5   ■   Probability Distributions and Their Process Generators   93

Chapter ■   6   ■   Random Number Generation   129

Chapter ■   7   ■   Simulating Queuing Systems   147

Chapter ■   8   ■   Special-Purpose Simulation Languages: GPSS   171

Chapter ■   9   ■   Simulating Human Decision Making   207

Chapter ■ 10   ■   Management Games   235

Chapter ■ 11   ■   Corporate Simulation Models   267

Chapter ■ 12   ■   Additional Simulation Technology   295

Chapter ■ 13   ■   Developing Successful Simulation Models   319

Appendix   A   ■   Random Number Table   339

Appendix   B   ■   Standard Normal Table   341

Appendix   C   ■   Binomial Table   343

Appendix   D   ■   Poisson Table   345

Appendix   E   ■ χ^2 **Table**   **348**

Appendix   F   ■   **Kolmogorov-Smirnov Table**   **350**

Appendix   G   ■ e^{-x} **Table**   **351**

Appendix   H   ■   **ln x Table**   **352**

Author Index   **353**

Subject Index   **356**

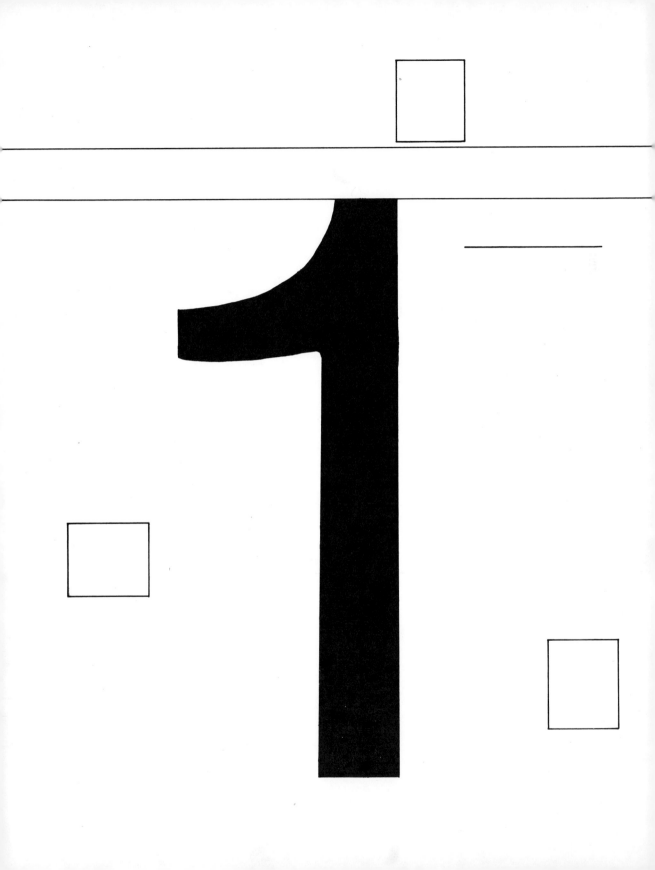

CHAPTER ONE   INTRODUCTION TO COMPUTER SIMULATION IN BUSINESS

What Is Simulation?

Systems Concepts

Types of Models

Characteristics of Mathematical Models

Basic Concepts and Terminology

    Mathematical Models

    Variables in Mathematical Models

    Variables in Simulation Models

    Equations in Simulation Models

The Use of Simulation

Reasons for Simulating

Reasons for Not Simulating

The Model Development Process

Simulation-like Methods

Plan of the Book

Summary

Assignments

References

1

A new recruit to the army of a South American "banana republic" was told that since there were not enough rifles and bayonets to go around, he would have to *simulate* their use. After being given a broomstick, he was shown that by going "bang, bang" or "stab, stab" an enemy would fall down as though dead. And sure enough, during training exercises, if he went "bang, bang" or "stab, stab" the enemy fell down. That is, until an opponent refused to cooperate after repeated "bang, bangs" and "stab, stabs." As the recruit was knocked down and stomped in the dust, he heard the enemy say, "tank, tank."

WHAT IS SIMULATION

Now that is one type of simulation. But a management scientist, being a professional in the use of mathematical models, typically thinks of simulation in different terms. To a management scientist, a *simulation* is a mathematical model that describes the behavior of a system over time. By observing the behavior of the mathematical model over time, the analyst is able to make inferences about the behavior of the real-world system.

SYSTEMS CONCEPTS

Since simulation involves describing the behavior of a system over time, it seems appropriate to discuss briefly what is meant by a system. A *system* can be described as a set of interrelated elements that function in a purposeful manner. A system consists of more than a single element; it is a set of elements that are interrelated and interact with one another. Furthermore, a system's behavior is purposeful; that is, it is goal seeking.

Examples of systems are limitless and vary all the way from large production systems to the mind's system for processing data into information for decision-making purposes. Even though systems vary considerably, most can be visually conceptualized through a diagram such as Figure 1.1.

The most basic observation that can be made about the systems diagram is that *inputs* are being *processed* into *outputs*. For example, a production system includes materials, labor, management, and financial resources as inputs. These inputs are processed or transformed into products, which are sold by the organization. The system is purposeful in that it is designed so as to meet the objectives of the organization. The objectives usually include factors such as output capacity, production efficiency, and product quality.

Figure 1.1   Basic systems relationships.

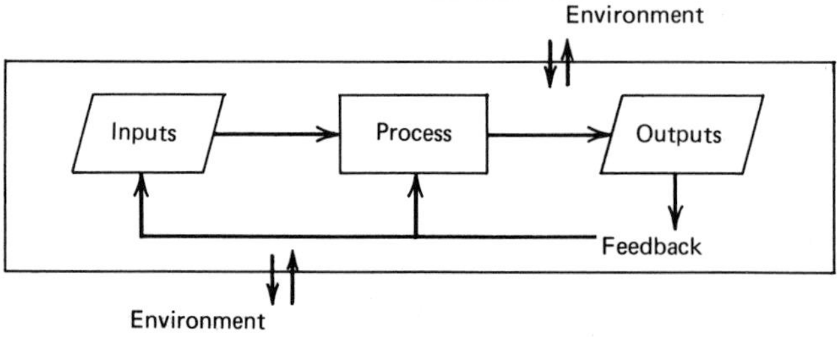

Well-conceived systems contain feedback loops. *Feedback* involves monitoring the actual behavior of a system and comparing its behavior to standards. When there are deviations from standards, this information is transmitted to an appropriate point in the system so that effective action can be taken. For example, in a production system, quality control checks on the final product might reveal that certain raw materials are not up to standards or that important machine settings are incorrect. Hopefully, however, the production system has feedback loops prior to the output stage so that deviations from standards are picked up more quickly. Feedback loops are typically included at many points in a system.

Most systems are not self-contained; they function in an *environment* that affects their behavior. For example, the public's demand for a firm's products affects the organization's production system. On the other hand, the quality of the products produced ultimately influences the buying behavior of consumers. This suggests that there is often a two-way interaction between a system and the environment in which it functions.

Establishing systems *boundaries* for modeling purposes is often difficult, since there can be problems in deciding what should and what should not be conceptualized as being components of the system. There are several reasons for this difficulty.

First, most systems are made up of many subsystems. For example, production systems are comprised of raw materials, materials handling, inventory control, and equipment maintenance systems. It is sometimes difficult to decide at what level the various subsystems should be detailed.

Second, most systems are subsystems of larger systems. For example, a production system is just a subsystem of the total organizational system. Conceptualizing systems in too small a framework can result in problems of suboptimization. *Suboptimization* refers to decisions that optimize the behavior of a subsystem but that are less than optimal for the system as a whole. For example, production runs of a certain length often maximize the efficiency of a production system but can be quite inappropriate given the demand for the product. The analyst must be careful in defining a system for analysis purposes so that possibilities of suboptimization are minimized.

Third, systems tend to *interact* and *overlap* with other systems. In organizations, for example, the marketing system interacts with the production system. Accounting and personnel systems, to mention just two, overlap other systems such as production. Consequently, because of systems overlap and interaction, it is often difficult for the analyst to isolate a single system for analysis.

Fourth, even when systems boundaries have been defined, it is often necessary to have linkages to the *environment*; that is, because most systems are affected by their environment, rarely can it be completely omitted from an analysis. For example, factors such as the condition of the national economy, the availability of labor in the labor force, and actions taken by competitors must be included. Obviously, some of the most important factors influencing a system come from the external environment.

TYPES OF MODELS

Clearly, as seen from our opening discussion, we are limiting our interest in simulation to mathematical modeling efforts. Although this approach is reasonable and practical for our purposes, it seems appropriate to point out that there are other types of models

Figure 1.2 Different types of models.

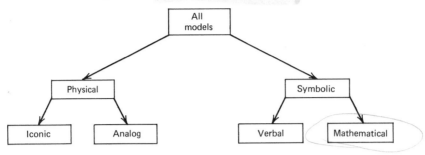

and that there are examples of these types that are sometimes referred to as simulations. Consequently, let us briefly describe a classification system for various types of models and mention a "simulation" example of each type of model.[1]

The classification system in Figure 1.2 first makes a distinction between physical and symbolic models. As the names imply, *physical models* are physical representations of reality, whereas *symbolic models* use symbols to represent reality. Physical models can be further divided into iconic and analog models. An *iconic model* looks like the represented reality; for example, when U.S. astronauts are sent into space, home television viewers are informed as to what is taking place in the space capsule through films that are said to simulate the activities of the astronauts. An *analog model* acts like the represented reality. For example, experiments in wind tunnels, which are used to test airplane designs, are frequently referred to as simulations. Symbolic models can be divided into verbal and mathematical models. *Verbal models* use words to represent reality, whereas *mathematical models* use mathematical symbols. A role-playing exercise where the "actors" assume a specified role is an example of a verbal model. Quite often, role playing is referred to as a simulation.

These examples indicate that models can take many different shapes and forms and that some of them are referred to as simulations. However, our interest in simulation will be confined to the mathematical modeling variety of simulation where mathematical symbols and operators are used to depict the represented reality.

CHARACTERISTICS OF MATHEMATICAL MODELS

Mathematical models can have varying characteristics with differences in their *purpose, mode of analysis, treatment of randomness*, and *generality of application;* see Figure 1.3. Let us consider these characteristics as they apply to simulation.

The purpose of a mathematical model can be either optimization or description. An *optimization model* is one that seeks to identify points of maximization or minimization. For example, in many business problems management wants to know what actions will lead to a profit or a revenue maximization or a cost minimization. Optimization models provide this information.

---

[1] This classification system is suggested by Clifford H. Springer, Robert E. Herlihy, and Robert I. Beggs, *Advanced Methods and Models* (Homewood, Ill.: Irwin, 1965), p. 8.

Figure 1.3   Characteristics of mathematical models.

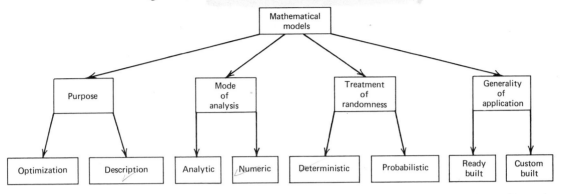

A *descriptive model* describes the behavior of a system. Simulation models are good examples of descriptive models in that they describe the behavior of a system over time. Although simulation models are not directly used for optimization purposes, through intelligent and systematic investigation, one can sometimes learn under what conditions a system operates most effectively and efficiently. This indirect use of a model for optimization purposes is seen in a simulation's ability to answer "what if" questions. For example, a marketing manager might ask the following question: "What will be the effect on profits if advertising expenditures are increased by 10 percent?" By investigating similar "what if" questions, one may obtain optimization information even though the model is basically descriptive.

The mode of analysis for mathematical models can be either analytic or numeric. The *analytic mode* involves using traditional mathematical and statistical techniques to perform the analysis (e.g., differential calculus, matrix algebra, regression analysis). A *numeric mode* of analysis replaces these frequently complex mathematical and statistical operations with a very large number of simple computations. The analytic mode should be used whenever possible, since it is more precise and efficient. However, some systems are either impossible, too cumbersome, or too time consuming to be analyzed by analytic methods and therefore are investigated through numeric techniques. In general, the more complex the system and the more detailed the model, the greater is the likelihood that a numeric mode of analysis will have to be employed.

Simulation models are typically used for the analysis of complex systems. Consequently, numeric modes of analysis are commonly employed. There are some exceptions, however, such as certain econometric models which are based on difference equations.

Regarding randomness, nearly all systems are *probabilistic*. That is, the behavior of the system cannot be predicted with certainty, because a degree of randomness is present. A *probabilistic model* attempts to capture the probabilistic nature of the system by requiring probabilistic data inputs and by generating probabilistic outputs. Even though most systems are probabilistic, most mathematical models are *deterministic*. *Deterministic models* employ single-valued estimates for the variables in the model and generate single-valued outputs. Deterministic models are more popular than probabilistic ones primarily because they are less expensive, less difficult, and less time consuming to build and use, and they often provide satisfactory information to support decision making.

For these reasons, most simulation models are deterministic.[2] However, many simulation models are probabilistic; in presenting and illustrating the available simulation technology in this book, we will see many examples of probabilistic simulations.

In terms of generality of application, a mathematical model can be developed for use with only one system, or a model may be applicable to many systems. A model that is used with only one system is typically *custom built*, while those that can be applied to more than one system are *ready-built* models. In general, custom-built models describe a particular system and, consequently, provide a better description than a ready-built model. However, they are generally more expensive for the organization, because they have to be built "from the ground up."

Most simulation models are custom built. The user of a simulation model normally operates or analyzes complex systems and ready-built models do not provide the descriptive power that is needed. Therefore, custom rather than ready-built models are typically used.

BASIC CONCEPTS AND TERMINOLOGY

It seems useful to introduce some basic concepts and terminology before discussing and describing specific simulation models. This approach sets the stage for introducing many of the simulation models that follow in later chapters. Some of the concepts and terminology are applicable to most types of mathematical models, whereas others are primarily applicable to simulation.

Mathematical Models

Mathematical models involve the use of mathematical symbols and operators to represent items of interest and to capture the nature of the relationship between the items. For example, a familiar accounting model describes the way that total costs accumulate. It recognizes that total costs are a *function* of fixed costs, per unit variable costs, and output.

$$\text{Total costs} = f(\text{fixed costs, per unit variable costs, output})$$

When symbolic notation is added to the functional relationship, the following mathematical model results.

$$TC = FC + VC \times O$$

When values are input for FC, VC, and O, it is possible to estimate TC. These are the *variables* used in the accounting model.

Variables in Mathematical Models

An almost bewildering array of terminology is used to categorize variables found in mathematical models. For example, referring to TC as either an *output*, *dependent*,

---

[2] A 1978 survey found that 65 percent of the simulation models to be deterministic; see Hugh J. Watson, "An Empirical Investigation of the Use of Simulation," *Simulation and Games* (December 1978):477–482.

endogenous, or *response* variable is appropriate depending on the context in which the term is used. There are a large number of terms because mathematical models are used in many disciplines and frequently the favored terminology differs. That is, mathematicians refer to dependent variables, econometricians to endogenous variables, statisticians to response variables, and model builders employ the term output variable in a generic way. Because simulation models are used in many disciplines, terminology varies here, too. Let us now consider some of the terminology employed with the variables used in simulation models.

Variables in Simulation Models

Naylor and Gattis suggest terminology that will often be useful for our purposes. They indicate that variables can be categorized as being *output, lagged output, external, policy,* or *random.*[3] We will also include *deterministic* variables, because many simulation models are not probabilistic. Figure 1.4 illustrates the role of these variables in simulation models by indicating that the values for the lagged output, external, policy, random, and deterministic variables are used in determining the values for the output variables.

Output Variables. Output variables provide either intermediate results or final information of interest to the analyst and/or management. In a production model there might be output variables for the cost of goods sold and work-in-process inventory. A marketing model might output sales and market share. Net income and retained earnings are often output variables in financial models.

Figure 1.4   Variables used in simulation models.

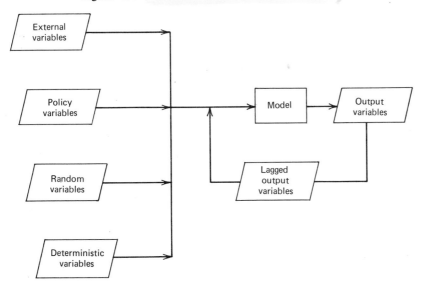

[3] Thomas H. Naylor and Daniel Gattis, "Corporate Planning Models," *California Management Review* (Summer 1976):69–78.

Lagged Output Variables. As previously discussed, simulation models are dynamic and describe the behavior of a system over time. Consequently, the state of a system at the end of some point in time often becomes a required input in the analysis of the system during the next time period. Lagged output variables carry information about the state of the system from time period to time period.

Examples of lagged output variables (sometimes referred to as *serially correlated* variables) can be found in production, finance, and marketing models. End-of-the-period finished goods inventory is an input required in determining the next period's finished goods inventory. Previous orders placed influence future orders and inventory levels. Promotion expenses affect future sales. Last period's market share is related to future market shares. End-of-the-period cash affects cash levels in the next period. Cumulative net earnings is related to the previous periods' net earnings.

External Variables. Those factors affecting the behavior of the system, which in turn are little, if at all, affected by the system, are referred to as external variables. Causality tends to flow in only one direction. X is affected by Y, but Y is not influenced by X. External variables are frequently referred to as *exogenous*, *environmental*, or *uncontrollable* variables.

In a production model, strikes and raw material shortages might be included as external variables. Product recalls or bans might be captured in a marketing model. A financial model might include the state of the economy or the government's current position on income tax credits. In general, the more the modeled system interacts with the environment, the greater is the need for external variables.

Policy Variables. Most systems contain factors that management can exercise control over. For example, in a manufacturing organization, management can decide which machine to buy or under what conditions to authorize overtime. Marketing managers make pricing decisions and develop promotion plans. Financial managers select depreciation methods and establish dividend policies. Factors such as these are included as policy variables in simulation models. Since they are subject to management's decisions and control, policy variables are sometimes referred to as *decision* or *controllable* variables. In most simulation models, the policy variables are systematically investigated in order to determine under what set of policies the system behaves most effectively.

Random Variables. In order to describe the behavior of some systems meaningfully, it is necessary to capture the randomness or probabilistic nature of the system. Random variables serve this role.

In a production model, the time between equipment failures or spoilage rates might be probabilistically (*stochastically*) specified. Sales returns and sales force turnover are sometimes treated as probabilistic variables in marketing models. In financial models, direct labor expense and selling expense might be included as random variables. In all of these instances, the objective is to include the necessary realism to serve the modeler's purposes.

Deterministic Variables. Even though most systems are probabilistic, the analyst may feel that a deterministic model will provide sufficient information for the user's intended purposes. In this case, deterministic variables that require only single-valued estimates are used. Although it is somewhat like mixing apples and oranges, deterministic variables are sometimes used in probabilistic models when the amount of variation they contribute to the system is very small.

In a production model, the lifetime of a machine or scrappage rates may be specified deterministically. Resupply times and back orders may be estimated by single-valued inputs in a marketing model. A financial model might treat raw materials expense and fixed factory overhead as deterministic variables.

It should be emphasized that these classifications are not mutually exclusive. That is, a variable can often be described in several different ways. For example, GNP (gross national product) is typically both an external and a deterministic variable. Also, the classification of a variable depends on the analyst's definition of what represents the system and what is the environment. In a marketing model the production rate might be an external variable, whereas in a production model it would most likely be a policy variable.

Output, lagged output, external, policy, random, and deterministic variables are common components of simulation models. Some of the alternative names to which they are referred by, and several examples of each, are summarized in Table 1.1. Let us now con-

Table 1.1   VARIABLES USED IN SIMULATION MODELS

Type of Variable	Other Names Used	Production Examples	Marketing Examples	Finance Examples
Output	Dependent Response Endogenous	Cost of goods sold Work-in-process inventory	Unit sales Market share	Net income Retained earnings
Lagged Output	Serially correlated Independent Input	Previous finished goods inventory Previous orders placed	Last period's promotion expense Last period's market share	Last period's cash Last period's net earnings
External	Exogenous Environmental Uncontrollable Independent Input	Strikes Raw materials shortages	Product recall Production ban	National economy Investment tax credit
Policy	Decision Controllable Independent Input	Equipment selection decisions Overtime policy	Pricing decisions Promotion decisions	Depreciation methods Dividend policy
Random	Probabilistic Stochastic Independent Input	Equipment failures Spoilage rates	Sales returns Sales force turnover	Direct labor expenses Selling expense
Deterministic	Independent Input	Machine lifetimes Scrappage rates	Resupply times Back orders	Raw materials expense Fixed factory overhead

sider how these different types of variables are put together to form the equations that make up most simulation models.

Equations in Simulation Models

Most simulation models contain many *equations.* Basically, there are two different types—*definitional* and *empirically based.* Let us briefly explore each type.

Definitional Equations. Definitional equations are normally developed from accounting relationships. The following equation is of a definitional nature.

$$ME = DL + RM + FO$$

It indicates that manufacturing expense is equal to the sum of direct labor, raw materials, and factory overhead costs. Accountants have decided that is how manufacturing expense is determined. It is important to recognize that many simulation models contain definitional equations, because so many of an organization's activities are ultimately expressed in financial terms.

Empirically Based Equations. Empirically based equations are formulated by using historical data and attempting to capture important relationships between factors that affect the behavior of the system. The following expression is a realistic example of an empirically based equation.

$$\text{Sales} = a + b \times P + c \times ADV + d \times GNP + e \times RD + f \times P_c + u$$

It suggests that sales of a particular product is functionally related to its selling price, advertising expenditures, the gross national product, research and development expenditures, the selling price of the leading competitor's product, and a random error term. The equation would probably be developed through regression analysis with the contribution of each component being statistically tested to determine its contribution in explaining the sales of the product. Management might then manipulate the policy variables, P, ADV, and RD, in order to develop an effective sales management program. Although the number of empirically based equations in a model might be small, they are important, especially in linking the system to its environment.

THE USE OF SIMULATION

Simulation is a widely used method of analysis. In a 1978 survey of nonacademic, full-time members of The Institute of Management Sciences (TIMS) and the Operations Research Society of America (ORSA), it was found that simulation ranked only behind economic analysis and statistical analysis in frequency of use; see Table 1.2.[4]

The same survey also explored whether simulation was used (1) not at all; (2) some of

[4] Hugh J. Watson and Joan M. Baecher, "A Survey of Industrial Usage of Operations Research Techniques," *Proceedings of the Fifteenth Annual Meeting of the Southeastern Chapter of the Institute of Management Sciences*, Myrtle Beach, S.C. (October 1979).

Table 1.2   FREQUENCY OF USE OF VARIOUS MANAGEMENT SCIENCE METHODS

Rank	Method
1	Economic analysis (payback, breakeven, discounted present value, etc.)
2	Statistical analysis (probability, inference, decision theory, etc.)
3	Simulation
4	Linear programming
5	Inventory models
6	PERT/CPM
7	Other mathematical programming (integer, goal, dynamic, etc.)
8	Search techniques
9	Queuing models
10	Game theory

the time; or (3) often in the respondents' organizations. Table 1.3 presents the study's findings.[5]

These data suggest that simulation is frequently used by organizations, and with good success. Other studies have reported similar findings.[6]

A final question investigated whether simulation was providing (1) poor; (2) fair; (3) good; or (4) uncertain results. Table 1.4 shows the study's findings in this area for those companies that are using simulation models.[7]

Table 1.3   THE EXTENT OF SIMULATION'S USE

Extent	Percentage
Not at all	15
Some of the time	35
Often	50
	100

[5]Ibid.

[6]See, for example, William J. Vatter, "The Use of Operations Research in American Companies," *Accounting Review* (October 1967), pp. 721–730, and R. E. Shannon and W. E. Biles, "The Utility of Certain Curriculum Topics to Operations Research Practitioners," *Operations Research* (July–August 1970): 741–744.

[7]These study findings are reported in Watson, "An Empirical Investigation of the Use of Simulation," op. cit.

Table 1.4   THE RESULTS OF USING SIMULATION

Results	Percentage
Poor	2
Fair	20
Good	73
Uncertain	5
	100

REASONS FOR SIMULATING

As we have seen, simulation is one of the most frequently used management science techniques, and every indication is that its popularity is growing. Let us explore why simulation is being so widely used. A possible starting point for the exploration is to consider alternatives to simulation suggested by Teichroew and Lubin.[8]

1. Use of other kinds of mathematical models.
2. Experimentation with either the actual system or a prototype of the actual system.
3. Reliance on experience and intuition.

In most cases, simulation is used when there are only poor mathematical modeling alternatives. In fact, simulation is often referred to as a "method of last resort." As we will soon discuss and illustrate throughout the book by pointing out alternatives to simulation, the disadvantages of simulation are such that when possible, other modeling alternatives are usually preferable. However, the problem is that there are many systems that do not lend themselves to other modeling approaches and, consequently, simulation must be employed. Consider *queuing*, or *waiting line*, systems as a case in point. For simple systems such as customers arriving at a ticket booth, the behavior of the system can often be explained (or predicted) by mathematical models developed through standard mathematical and statistical methods (the analytic mode of analysis). However, if we are discussing more complex systems such as the flow of a product through a production process (once again a queuing system), the complexity of the system is typically such that simulation is probably the only way to describe the behavior of the system. The complexity of the system is such that no appropriate analytic model currently exists or could be developed.

Another advantage of simulation is that it is possible to experiment on a system without exposing the organization to real-world dangers. For this reason, simulation has been referred to as "the manager's laboratory." By investigating possible changes in a real-world system through a simulation model, we can often learn how to improve on the behavior of a system without actually trying out both good and bad proposals on the system.

---

[8] Daniel Teichroew and John Francis Lubin, "Computer Simulation–Discussion of the Technique and Comparison of Languages," *Communications of the ACM* (October 1966): 723–741.

The previous discussion assumes that the system already exists. In some cases, simulation is used in the initial design of a system. In this case, experimentation on the real-world system is not possible.

Of course, there are instances where an analog model of a system exists and experimentation is made on the analog. For example, in the chemical processing industry it is common to build small-scale working replicas of proposed plant designs. Simulation does not replace all other types of experimentation; it is just a useful and appropriate alternative in some situations.

Experience and intuition have been, and will continue to be, vital ingredients in managerial success. But managers are having to manage increasingly complex systems. Consequently, more and more managers are finding it useful to supplement their experience and intuition with systematic analysis procedures. Simulation is not a replacement for experience and intuition but, rather, an augmentation.

REASONS FOR NOT SIMULATING

The major problem with simulation is that it is sometimes used when there are less expensive, faster, and more precise modeling alternatives. For many management scientists it is very tempting to simulate the behavior of a system instead of searching for or developing an analytic solution. Because simulation models are fun to build and do not require an extensive background in mathematics and statistics, it is not surprising that simulation is so often quickly selected as the modeling approach.

There are, however, several problems with using simulation when there are other options. (1) The model development process can be quite time consuming and costly for the organization; (2) the computer running time for large simulation models can be expensive even with today's fast machines; and (3) the simulation models for probabilistic systems are susceptible to sampling error whereas analytically derived solutions are not.

Simulation is a useful and powerful method of analysis. It is best used, however, after other modeling alternatives have been considered. Throughout this book, we will try to point out and discuss possible alternatives to simulation.

THE MODEL DEVELOPMENT PROCESS

We will be exploring many applications of simulation in this book, as well as learning much of the available technology. It should be kept in mind, however, that simulation modeling requires following a rather well-defined process. The steps in this process can be identified as:

1. Problem and/or information identification.
2. Data collection.
3. Model building.
4. Model validation.
5. Model implementation.
6. Model operation.

A modeling effort is undertaken to provide certain information or to solve a particular problem. Data must be collected in order to build a model. Once a model is built, it must be tested or validated in light of its intended usage. Then the model is implemented in its organizational setting and operated.

The model development process is not so simple or straightforward as it seems when the steps are listed. There are many technical and behavioral considerations that surface with the various steps. These will be discussed throughout and will receive special attention in Chapters 12 and 13.

SIMULATION-LIKE METHODS

A strong effort was made earlier in the chapter to differentiate our conceptualization of simulation from other "simulations" that are based on iconic, analog, or verbal models. We could stop our differentiation at this point and probably have no difficulty talking with other management scientists about simulating the behavior of systems. However, there are other *simulation-like methods* that, depending on one's perspective, might or might not be called simulations. These technologies do involve the use of mathematical models, but differ slightly from the "picture" of simulation that has been "painted" so far. Let us now briefly consider management games, model sampling, Monte Carlo sampling, and the simulation of human decision making as representatives of other simulation-like methods. In later chapters, we will have the opportunity to explore these areas more fully.

Management games are often referred to as simulations. In a management game the participants, or *players*, are placed in a decision-making situation. They are given selected information about a situation and are required to make a set of decisions. The players' decisions are then input to a model, which is at the "heart" of the game. The model transforms the decisions into an output, which reflects the consequences of the players' decisions. Typically, there is a sequence of periods where decisions are made and feedback is given to the players. The purpose of most management games is to improve decision-making skills in specific areas.

A management scientist is most likely to consider the model at the heart of the game to be a simulation. The model may or may not represent an actual real-world system, but it does describe system behavior over time in response to the players' decisions. It is the element of "play" that differentiates management games from simulations in some people's minds.

Monte Carlo sampling is a term which is often used with simulation. It refers to a collection of procedures that are used to sample values randomly from probability distributions. These sampled values are then used in a simulation model. This discussion suggests, then, that Monte Carlo sampling is not simulation at all but a procedure or method used in conjunction with probabilistic simulation models.

Model sampling involves repeated sampling from probabilistic distributions for the random variables in a model in order to approximate the distribution for an output variable that would be difficult or impossible to determine by analytic methods. Suppose, for example, we have two independent distributions that we would like to sum, which are normally distributed with known means and variances. From statistics we know the resultant distribution should be normally distributed with a mean and a variance equal to the sum of the individual means and variances of the component distributions. Suppose, however, that we did not know this important statistical fact. The resultant distribution could still be approximated by randomly sampling values from the two distributions, adding the sampled values together, and repeating the process over and over again until it was felt that a good approximation of the desired distribution had been obtained. Obviously, in a situation as simple as the one just described, model sampling should not be employed; but there are complex models that must use model sampling because an analytic analysis is not possible.

The distinction between model sampling and simulation is that model sampling involves no time dimension. Model sampling is performed upon a static process, and there is no movement of the system over time. If there is a time dimension to the model, the model is best referred to as a probabilistic simulation rather than a model sampling.

An interesting type of modeling is the *simulation of human decision making*. This type of modeling involves duplicating the decisions of a human decision maker in a specific decision-making situation. However, once again there is no time dimension to the model. Consequently, it does not exactly fit our definition of simulation. Still, this type of model is commonly referred to as a simulation.

PLAN OF THE BOOK

Having introduced basic computer simulation concepts, we should now discuss the sequence of the book. Frequently, a "big picture" of what follows is useful in allowing forthcoming component parts to be properly placed.

In Chapter 2 we will examine simulation applications in business; applications from production, marketing, finance, engineering, and industries such as insurance and real estate will be discussed. No attempt will be made to explore simulation technology. Rather, the discussion will be descriptive.

Chapters 3 and 4 both discuss simulation applications, but their primary purpose differs from that of Chapter 2. Through inventory control and probabilistic financial planning applications, some important simulation technology is introduced in a gradual, application-oriented manner.

Chapter 5 is one of the "hard technology" chapters. It explores how probabilistic variables can be incorporated into computerized simulation models. We will learn how to sample values from distributions such as the negative exponential, normal, and binominal.

Probabilistic simulations require random numbers. In Chapter 6 we will discuss desirable properties of random numbers, alternative methods for their generation, and how they can be statistically tested for randomness.

In Chapter 7 our focus returns to a mixture of simulation applications and technology. We will learn how to simulate the behavior of an important type of system—queuing systems.

Special-purpose simulation languages can greatly simplify the modeling of certain types of systems. In Chapter 8 we will look at special-purpose languages in general, and General Purpose Simulation System (GPSS) in particular. GPSS is often used when simulating queuing systems.

Chapters 9 and 10 cover selected simulation-like methods. The simulation of human decision making and management games are discussed.

An increasing number of organizations are developing and using corporate simulation models. Chapter 11 explores this important application of simulation.

In an introductory book there is only so much technology that can, and should, be covered in detail. Chapter 12 discusses some of the more important, additional simulation technology.

This edition closes in Chapter 13, with a look at the model development process. Process, behavioral, and organizational structure considerations are as important to modeling success as are technological factors in most cases.

SUMMARY

A management scientist views a simulation as a mathematical model that describes the behavior of a system over time.

When building models, it is useful to take a systems approach. This approach requires looking at elements in the real world as being interrelated and functioning in a purposeful manner. The model builder focuses his or her attention on the most important elements and the nature of their interrelationships with the intention of ultimately improving on the systems design and operation.

There are many different types of models. Some models are physical whereas others are symbolic. Physical models include iconic and analog models. Verbal and mathematical models are examples of symbolic models.

Mathematical models, our sole interest in this book, have varying characteristics. They can differ in purpose (description versus optimization), mode of analysis (analytic versus numeric), treatment of randomness (deterministic versus probabilistic), and generality of application (custom built versus ready built).

Simulation models contain equations that express relationships between variables of interest. It is possible to categorize the variables found in simulation models as either output, lagged output, external, policy, random, or deterministic. These variables are used in equations that are either definitional or empirically based.

Simulation is one of the most frequently used management science methods. Those organizations that use simulation report favorably on the results of their experiences.

Simulation is a very powerful method of analysis, which undoubtedly accounts for its popularity. It should not be used, however, until alternative methods of analysis have been considered.

Simulation modeling should follow the model development process. This process includes problem and/or information identification, data collection, model building, model validation, model implementation, and model operation.

There are some types of mathematical models, methods of analysis, and instructional methods that are simulation-like. They include simulations of human decision making, model sampling, Monte Carlo methods, and management games. These, as well as the technology and applications of simulation, are discussed in this book.

ASSIGNMENTS

1.1.   What are the vital components of a management scientist's conceptualization of what is a simulation model?

1.2. The following partially completed table indicates the primary inputs, components, functions, and outputs of several systems. Fill in the missing parts.

System	Inputs	Components	Functions	Outputs
Restaurant	Customers	Food, chef, waitresses, building	Good food, well served, pleasant eating environment	Satisfied customers
High school	————	Teachers, books, supplies, classrooms	Imparting knowledge and skills	————
Movie theater	Customers	————	————	————
Penitentiary	————	————	————	————

1.3. Even a simple act such as shaving can be viewed from a systems point of view. Think about shaving for a while and prepare a no more than one page description of shaving using systems terminology and a systems orientation. As a point of demarcation, think about the system's goals, inputs, boundaries, and so on.

1.4. All college students go through their university's registration system. Describe your school's registration system in terms of its inputs, processes, outputs, feedbacks, goals, and so on.

1.5. Hill and Cambre are planning to add a third physician to their family practice clinic and to move to a larger office. Of some concern in selecting a new office is having sufficient space in the waiting room. They want virtually no chance of a patient having to stand while waiting.
  (a) Describe the physician's office from a systems point of view.
  (b) What type of mathematical model might be used in selecting a new office? What should be the output variable(s) in the model? What should be the input variables?

1.6. What is meant by the concept of suboptimization? Suppose that an organization's sales force takes as its objective the maximization of the number of units sold. Is this an example of suboptimization? Why or why not?

1.7. Models can be categorized as being either iconic, analog, verbal, or mathematical. Classify the following models in terms of these categories.
  (a) $E = mC^2$.
  (b) A friend's description of a blind date.
  (c) A Barbie doll.
  (d) A Donald Duck cartoon.
  (e) The game of monopoly.

1.8. Mathematical models can vary in terms of characteristics such as purpose, mode of analysis, treatment of randomness, and generality of application. Identify the characteristics of the following mathematical models.
  (a) Breakeven analysis.
  (b) Linear programming.
  (c) PERT.
  (d) Decision tree analysis.
  (e) Regression analysis.

1.9. The following is a mathematical model used by management in estimating net income after taxes. Management uses the model by entering a proposed selling price, an estimate of the number of units that can be sold at that price, an estimate of fixed and per unit cost of goods sold, selling expense, and general and administrative expense, the amount planned for research and development, and the interest rate on outstanding debt and the amount of that debt. The model uses these inputs and calculates net income before taxes and net income after taxes when supplied with the corporate tax schedule.

Total sales = selling price × units sold

Cost of goods sold = fixed cost of goods sold + variable cost of goods sold × units sold

Selling expense = fixed selling expense + variable selling expense × units sold

General and administrative expense = fixed general and administrative expense + variable general and administrative expense × units sold

Research and development expense = Research and development expense

Interest expense = interest rate × outstanding debt

Total expenses = summation of all expenses

Net income before taxes = total sales – total expenses

Income taxes = tax rate × net income before taxes

Net income after taxes = net income before taxes – income taxes

(a) Is the mathematical model a simulation model? Why or why not?

(b) Identify all of the equations in the model as being either definitional or empirically based.

(c) Identify all of the variables in the model as being output, lagged output, external, policy, deterministic, and/or random.

1.10. Discuss the frequency of use of simulation relative to other management science methods and the results organizations have had using simulation.

1.11. Discuss some of the conditions when simulation should and should not be used.

REFERENCES

Lewis, T. G., and B. J. Smith, *Computer Principles of Modeling and Simulation* (Boston: Houghton Mifflin, 1979).

McMillan, Claude, and Richard F. Gonzalez, *Systems Analysis*, 3rd ed. (Homewood, Ill.: Irwin, 1973).

Meier, Robert C., William T. Newell, and Harold L. Pazer, *Simulation in Business and Economics* (Englewood Cliffs, N.J.: Prentice-Hall, 1969).

Naylor, Thomas H., and Daniel Gattis, "Corporate Planning Models," *California Management Review* (Summer 1976): 69–78.

Shannon, R. E., and W. E. Biles, "The Utility of Certain Curriculum Topics to Operations Research Practitioners," *Operations Research* (July–August 1970): 741–744.

Shannon, Robert E., *Systems Simulation* (Englewood Cliffs, N.J.: Prentice-Hall, 1975).

Springer, Clifford H., Robert E. Herlihy, and Robert I. Beggs, *Advanced Methods and Models* (Homewood, Ill.: Irwin, 1965).

Teichroew, Daniel, and John Francis Lubin, "Computer Simulation-Discussion of the Technique and Comparison of Languages," *Communications of the ACM* (October 1966): 723–741.

Thomas, George, and Jo-Anne DaCosta, "A Sample Survey of Corporate Operations Research," *Interfaces* (August 1979): 102–111.

Vatter, William J., "The Use of Operations Research in American Companies," *Accounting Review* (October 1967): 721–730.

Watson, Hugh J., "An Empirical Investigation of the Use of Simulation," *Simulation and Games* (December 1970): 477–482.

Watson, Hugh J., and Joan M. Baecher, "A Survey of Industrial Usage of Operations Research Techniques," *Proceedings of the Fifteenth Annual Meeting Southeastern Chapter The Institute of Management Sciences*, Myrtle Beach, S.C. (October 1979).

CHAPTER TWO   BUSINESS APPLICATIONS OF SIMULATION

Simulation Applications in the Functional Areas

Finance: A Cash Budget Simulation

Production: Machine Shop Planning and Scheduling

Marketing: Selecting Advertising Schedules

Engineering: Simulation of Tar Sands Mining Operations

Personnel: Affirmative Action Planning

Insurance: Valuing a Property-Liability Insurance Agency

Real Estate: Investment Analysis

Government: Fire Department Deployment Policy Analysis

Econometric Models: The Georgia Model

Systems Dynamics: *The Limits to Growth*

Summary

Assignments

References

Computer simulation is a widely used method of analysis. Its flexibility permits applications in all of the functional areas of business, in different industries, in government, and in a variety of other areas. Before we turn to the technology used in building simulation models, it seems appropriate to describe some of the more interesting, recent, and important applications of simulation. Some benefits of this approach are: (1) it creates a consciousness-expanding awareness of the possible applications of simulation and hopefully (2) it develops a stronger motivation for learning the technology presented in later chapters.

We will begin by considering data that show how frequently simulation is used in the various functional areas of business. Then we will briefly explore some specific simulation models that have been developed. The emphasis will be on business simulations, but several other related applications will also be discussed. For example, we will consider a cash budgeting simulation, a simulation model for analyzing alternative oil extraction methods, the world dynamics model of *The Limits to Growth* fame, and other interesting real-world simulation models.[1] Subsequent chapters will take up the technology required in building simulation models and how this technology can be applied in various types of modeling situations.

SIMULATION APPLICATIONS IN THE FUNCTIONAL AREAS

The 1978 survey of TIMS/ORSA members mentioned in Chapter 1 provides interesting information on the use of simulation in the various functional areas of business. The survey's findings are shown in Table 2.1.[2]

As can be seen, in those organizations that use simulation, its application spans the functional areas. Finance leads the way, however, with 46 percent of simulation users having models in this area. There are also many simulation models being used in produc-

Table 2.1 USE OF SIMULATION IN THE VARIOUS FUNCTIONAL AREAS OF BUSINESS

Functional Area	Percentage
Finance	46
Production	39
Marketing	29
Engineering	21
Personnel	20
Other	26

[1] Dennis L. Meadows, et al., *The Limits to Growth* (New York: Universe Books, 1972).
[2] Hugh J. Watson, "An Empirical Investigation of the Use of Simulation," *Simulation and Games* (December 1978): 477–582.

tion. Many production systems are so sufficiently complex that to simulate their behavior is the only analysis alternative. The study even found many simulation models in personnel, 20 percent, which is somewhat surprising in light of personnel's traditional reluctance to make use of management science methods. In general, the data clearly show the widespread applicability of simulation.

Let us now move from a general discussion of simulation applications to some specific illustrations, beginning in the finance area.

FINANCE: A CASH BUDGET SIMULATION

As the previous data indicated, more companies use financial simulation models than any other kind, since so many aspects of a firm's operations are ultimately expressed in financial terms. Although a variety of financial simulation models are being used by organizations, models for cash management are among the most common. Such a model has been particularly valuable to Air Canada.[3]

Cash management in the airline industry involves a number of complexities. There are a host of cash receipt and disbursement items, interrelationships among cash flow items are not always clear, and a turbulent operating environment leads to uncertainty. These complexities can be seen in the following examples. Credit card payments, advance ticket sales, travel agency ticket sales, and ticket sales by one airline for another all result in fluctuations in the receipt of cash balances. Bad weather further complicates forecasting, as flight cancellations generate cash outflows for dislocation payments to alleviate customer inconvenience. Economic factors such as inflation, fluctuating passenger traffic, labor strikes, increasing payrolls, and inflated fuel prices further contribute to the problem of cash flow forecasting.

Because of cash management difficulties, the management of Air Canada decided to create a new cash forecasting and analysis system. The system was to (1) allow directly for the element of uncertainty that dominates cash forecasting in the airline industry, (2) enhance the accuracy of data inputs used in cash forecasting, and (3) reduce the toilsome computations of previous manual systems.

In response to these specifications, a probabilistic cash budgeting simulation model was created. Its format takes the form of a cash receipts and disbursements statement. For each period's revenue and expenditure sources, three estimates—the lower limit, the most likely value, and the upper limit—are specified in order to quantify the uncertainty that exists. These data inputs are developed from a five-year historical data base and managerial judgment. The cash budget simulator generates probabilistic forecast figures for daily and monthly reports using Monte Carlo sampling procedures as described in Chapter 4.

Air Canada has been pleased with the performance of its cash simulator, although by some statistical standards it has not been very precise. Figure 2.1 graphically presents the actual and forecasted 95 percent confidence margins for the 1975 monthly closing cash balances. With better cash forecasts, the profitability of Air Canada's short-term investing has been enhanced. There has also been a variety of operational improvements. Time is

---

[3]This description is based on David F. Scott, Jr., Lawrence J. Moore, André Saint-Denis, Edouard Archer, and Bernard W. Taylor, III, "Implementation of a Cash Budget Simulator at Air Canada, *Financial Management* (Summer 1979): 46–52.

Figure 2.1   Air Canada Treasury, 1975, monthly closing cash balances, confidence margins, and actuals (in millions of dollars).

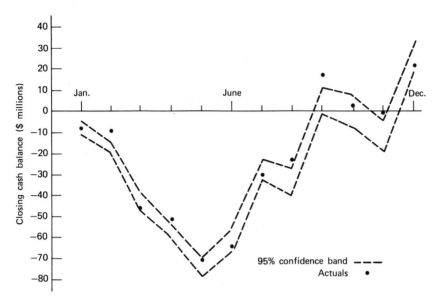

Source.   David F. Scott, Jr., Lawrence J. Moore, André Saint-Denis, Edouard Archer, and Bernard W. Taylor, III, "Implementation of a Cash Budget Simulator at Air Canada," Financial Management (Summer 1979), p. 50.

gained for close examination of the simulation input and output. Staff training has been simplified, because the personnel who operate the system need no special mathematical acumen. Since the simulation model is an on-line computerized system, the forecasts are continuously and rapidly updated as new data become available (a limiting factor in the old methods). The maintenance of historical cash flow data, the analysis of funds flow trends, and the study of actual results have all been improved.

Air Canada's cash simulator is representative of financial simulation models in use today. In Chapter 4 we will explore some of the technology required in building such models. In Chapter 8 there will be a discussion of special-purpose simulation languages that are being used to facilitate the development of financial simulation models, and in Chapter 11, we will see how financial models are key components of corporate simulation models.

PRODUCTION: MACHINE SHOP PLANNING AND SCHEDULING

Simulation models are frequently used to analyze and improve the performance of production systems. As an illustration of this application of simulation, we will consider a machine shop planning and scheduling system developed by the Bethlehem Steel Corporation.[4] It illustrates how a simulation model can be an integral component of a comprehensive information system.

The Cast Roll Manufacturing (CAROM) complex of the Bethlehem Steel Corporation includes foundries and a machine shop important in the production of cast-iron and steel rolls. The machine shop contains over 35 machines that process over 4000 rolls of cast iron and steel each year. Each roll requires an average of ten operations in the machine shop before being shipped to one of about a dozen other Bethlehem Steel plants. Historically, the machine shop has been a bottleneck to meeting production schedules.

On an annual basis each Bethlehem Steel plant transmits its anticipated roll requirements to CAROM, which must quickly decide which rolls it can manufacture and deliver on time during the coming year. Because buying rolls from outside vendors involves foregone profits, it is desirable to make rolls in-house. The objective of making as many rolls as possible in-house and of delivering them on time creates a need for an effective production planning system.

Given the bottleneck problems in the machine shop and the need for an effective production planning system, a decision was made to develop a comprehensive information system composed of three subsystems.

1. A planning subsystem to generate planning schedules and the associated reports for making long- or medium-term planning and operating decisions.
2. A production-scheduling subsystem to generate production schedules in order to determine the day-to-day activities of the machine shop and to monitor the shop's status.
3. An information subsystem to extract information from the planning and production-scheduling subsystems and the permanent data file.

The system that was developed centers around a simulation model that generates both planning and production schedules. Activities of the machine shop are predicted by the model for a period of 10 to 50 weeks. The reports generated by this planning subsystem are shown and described in Table 2.2. The production-scheduling subsystem creates production schedules 9 to 12 days into the future. The reports produced by this subsystem are presented and described in Table 2.3. The reports from the planning and production-scheduling subsystems are major components of the information subsystem. This subsystem is sufficiently flexible to answer management inquiries such as, "How many rolls are due in the Lackawanna plant in June?"

Insights into the functioning of the system can be gained by considering how production schedules are generated. The process of schedule generation is shown schematically in Figure 2.2. Inputs to the scheduling model are prepared by the data generator based on roll orders and a data bank that contains data such as the current status of the machine shop, planned release time for rolls, and manpower availability. These inputs are received by a scheduling model programmed in GPSS (a special-purpose simulation language described in Chapter 8), which captures factors such as processing times for various types of rolls and locally developed scheduling rules. The output generated by the scheduling

---

[4] Suresh K. Jain, "A Simulation-Based Scheduling and Management Information System for a Machine Shop," *Interfaces* (November 1975): 81–96.

Table 2.2   REPORTS GENERATED BY THE PLANNING SUBSYSTEM

Report	Data Arrangement	Contents	Function
Expected machine utilization report	By machine and by week	Manpower available Manpower utilized Work in front of machine at beginning of week	Evaluating alternate manpower strategies Determining suitability of the planning schedules Scheduling maintenance
Group report	By route number and month	1. Number of rolls ordered 2. Number of rolls that can be delivered Cumulative difference between (1) and (2)	Negotiating with individual plants Isolating areas of abnormal demand Testing manpower strategies Evaluating due date performance Determining whether demand will be fulfilled
Summary of expected shipments	By plant and month for iron and steel rolls	Expected roll-tonnage shipment Number of pieces to be shipped	Providing management with a broad overview of schedule
Plant schedules	By plant, mill, and order number	Number of pieces demanded by month Number of pieces to be shipped by month Pieces that cannot be delivered Total pieces on original order Total pieces remaining to be shipped	Informing the plants about the status of their orders
Six-week list	By date on which first operation is scheduled	Full order information. Date on which first operation is scheduled Machine on which first operation is scheduled	Preparing foundry schedules. Informing the foundries about machine shop needs in the immediate future

Source: Suresh K. Jain, "A Simulation-Based Scheduling and Management Information System for a Machine Shop," *Interfaces* (November 1975): 88.

Table 2.3 REPORTS GENERATED BY THE PRODUCTION-SCHEDULING SUBSYSTEM

Report	Data Arrangement	Contents	Functions
Foreman's report	By foreman's area of supervision, machine and scheduled start time of operations	Full order information Roll identification Operation number Starting time of operation Finishing time of operation Operation time Last operation completed Next operation scheduled	Updating machine shop status Scheduling work onto machines Rescheduling shop as needed
Short-term manpower scheduling report	By machine and by turn	Manpower available Manpower utilized Work in front of machine at beginning of turn	Scheduling manpower on a short-term basis
Roll progress schedule	By roll code	Full order information Roll identification Operations to be performed Start, finish, and process times for all operations	Predicting and monitoring progress of rolls Answering queries of plants on specific rolls
Nine-day list	By date on which first operation is scheduled	Full order information Date and machine on which first operation is scheduled	Letting foundries know what to deliver the following week

Source: Suresh K. Jain, "A Simulation-Based Scheduling and Management Information System for a Machine Shop," *Interfaces* (November 1975): 91.

Figure 2.2   Generation of the machine shop schedule.

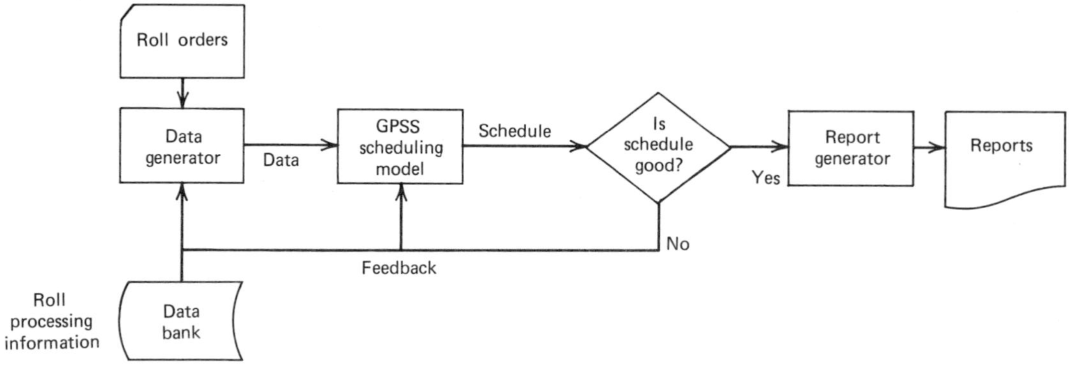

Source.   Suresh K. Jain, "A Simulation-Based Scheduling and Management Information System for a Machine Shop," Interfaces *(November 1975), p. 85.*

model is analyzed by the schedule coordinator who determines the quality of the schedule. If the schedule is considered "good," reports are prepared by the report generator. When the schedule is not satisfactory, this information is fed back in the form of modified data inputs and a new schedule is created. In Chapter 1 the importance of feedback loops in controlling the performance of a system was stressed.

MARKETING: SELECTING ADVERTISING SCHEDULES

An important marketing decision is selecting the best set of national magazines and television programs to communicate a firm's advertising message. Some of the factors influencing this media-selection decision are the availability of time or space in each media vehicle, the firm's advertising budget, whom the firm wishes to reach with a given message, the value of each repeat exposure provided by the media vehicle, the quality of the advertising copy, and the cost of running a selected media package. Obviously, it is not a simple decision.

One approach that has been used is to simulate alternative advertising schedules.[5] As an example of this marketing application of simulation, we will consider the ADvertising MEdia SIMulation (AD-ME-SIM) model.[6] This model requires a number of data inputs: (1) the proposed media schedule, (2) a set of weights for the effectiveness of various media in advertising the product, (3) a set of weights for the effectiveness of alternative size and color advertising forms, (4) a set of weights that show the effectiveness of various patterns of exposure frequency, (5) the costs of advertising through the different media, (6) a set of weights showing the value of an exposure to different types of persons in the target population; and (7) data from the Brand Rating Research Corporation showing the

---

[5]For an early illustration of this simulation application, see "Simulmatics Media Mix: Technical Description," Simulmatics Corporation (New York, October 1962).

[6]Dennis H. Gensch, "A Computer Simulation Model for Selecting Advertising Schedules," *Journal of Marketing Research* (May 1969): 203–214.

reading and viewing patterns over time of a sample of individuals. These inputs as well as the remainder of the model are schematically presented in Figure 2.3.

The model processes the inputs by probabilistically tracking the media exposure experiences of the sample of people described on the tape provided by the Brand Rating Research Corporation. Each individual according to his or her reading and viewing habits are probabilistically simulated as to the frequency and impact with which they are exposed to the proposed advertising schedule. By simulating the experiences of a sample of consumers, one can generate aggregate estimates of the effectiveness of various proposed schedules.

The AD-ME-SIM model provides output on a simulated weekly and cumulative basis. This output includes: (1) the percentage of people in the target audience reached by the proposed advertising schedule; (2) a frequency distribution of the people reached by the proposed schedule; (3) an adjusted percentage figure called the "commercial reach" that measures the overall impact of the proposed media schedule, taking into account all the objective and subjective evaluations of the media and the value of exposures to different members of the target audience; (4) a frequency distribution of the commercial reach; and (5) the number of "impact units," which measures the value of the media package.

In addition to the simulation features, AD-ME-SIM includes a heuristic (rule-of-thumb) routine that generates additional advertising schedules. Although the use of this routine does not guarantee optimal schedules, it can generate better schedules than those that had been proposed.

AD-ME-SIM has been tested using a nationally known soft drink, a nationally known canned dog food, and a regionally known dishwater detergent. These tests have shown that it provides realistic evaluations of proposed advertising schedules. A difficulty with AD-ME-SIM and other models that simulate consumer behavior are their large data requirements. This problem has restricted their real-world usefulness.

Figure 2.3   A schematic of the AD-ME-SIM model.

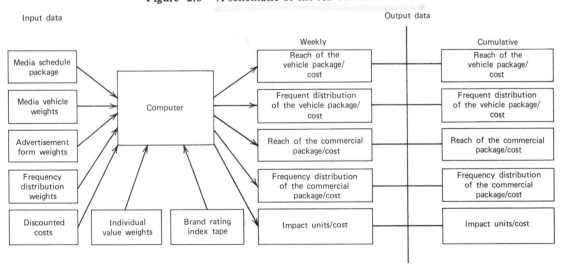

Source. Dennis H. Gensch, "A Computer Simulation Model for Selecting Advertising Schedules," Journal of Marketing Research (May 1969), p. 205.

ENGINEERING: SIMULATION OF TAR SANDS MINING OPERATIONS

For decades it has been known that vast quantities of crude oil are locked in the Athabasca Tar Sands of Canada.[7] It is estimated that the recoverable volume of oil contained there is 300 billion barrels. This figure is roughly one-fourth of Saudi Arabia's presently known oil reserves.

For several decades the tar sands were not developed due to the high cost per barrel relative to ordinary crude. However, in the 1960s this important natural resource began to be tapped for the first time. In 1971 Syncrude Canada Limited, a consortium of government and oil companies, was given authorization to develop a plant to produce up to 125,000 barrels per day of synthetic crude oil. To assist Syncrude in the development of such a plant, Canadian Bechtel Limited, a consulting firm experienced in mining and refining operations, was hired. Bechtel's initial task was to examine Syncrude's mining scheme carefully and to suggest modifications, if necessary, before ordering mining equipment.

The production requirements called for a mining and transportation system capable of high volume and reliability. Syncrude's initial scheme called for a dragline system that functions by dragging a huge bucket into the side of an embankment of ore material; see Figure 2.4. Then the draglines lift and swing the bucket filled with ore to a pile and drop it there. The ore is then moved by conveyors to a train, which transports the ore to an extraction plant.

An alternative approach involves bucket wheel excavation. A bucket wheel excavator uses a large wheel with a bucket attached to the edge. When the wheel revolves, the buckets scoop the material, lift it up, and dump it out on a conveyor moving away from the wheel; see Figure 2.5. Bucket wheel excavation was the only previously proven mining scheme for tar sand.

Although the dragline approach appeared to have good potential, there were also possible problem areas, especially since it was not a proven method. Consequently, a decision was made by Bechtel to expand a simulation model that was being used to analyze the dragline system in order to evaluate proposed design changes. A decision was also made to simulate possible bucket wheel systems as a contingency while the original scheme was being revised, because a delay in the final definition of the mining scheme could have delayed the entire project schedule.

The simulation model contained five interrelated modules: weather, mining, transportation, storage, and extraction. The coded version of the model used 2200 lines of GPSS plus 2100 lines of FORTRAN. Five mining schemes were investigated. Approximately ten runs were made for each scheme in order to analyze factors such as mining procedures, equipment availability, and equipment sizes.

The simulation analysis showed that a feasible scheme existed for meeting production requirements using draglines or bucket wheels. It also showed that the amount of equipment required in the bucket wheel scheme resulted in higher capital and operating costs. Based largely on the simulations, a recommendation was made to implement the dragline scheme even though it was not a proven approach. After this mining scheme was ac-

[7]F. Paul Wyman, "Simulation of Tar Sands Mining Operations," *Interfaces* (November 1977): 6–20.

Figure 2.4   Dragline excavation.

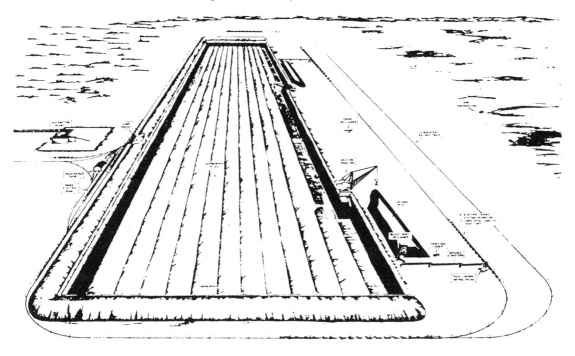

VIEW OF DRAGLINE MINING OPERATION AFTER YEAR 2

Source.   F. Paul Wyman, "Simulation of Tar Sands Mining Operations," Interfaces
(November 1977), p. 9.

cepted, simulation was further used to improve details of the mining design, and continues to be a valuable tool in debottlenecking and the ongoing refinement of the mining
scheme.

PERSONNEL: AFFIRMATIVE ACTION PLANNING

Affirmative action planning has been plagued by ideological conflict and lack of effective
planning techniques. At the center of these difficulties is the fact that in large organizations it is difficult to forecast the effects of equal employment opportunity (EEO) and
affirmative action policy changes on the race and sex composition of the work force.
Consequently, it is difficult to set realistic affirmative action goals. If the organization
agrees to set a certain percentage minority representation as its affirmative action goal for
a certain job category, it may find that it will have to engage in preferential "quota hiring" of minorities in order to attain that goal. Or the organization may find that it cannot attain that goal without terminating current nonminority employees.
    The problem is that the movements of employees of different sex and ethnic groups
into, among, and out of job categories in large organizations is an overwhelmingly com-

Figure 2.5   Bucket wheel excavation.

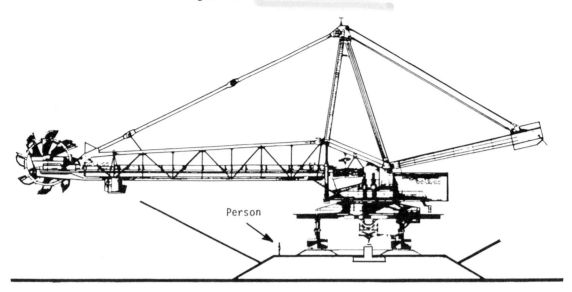

Source. F. Paul Wyman, "Simulation of Tar Sands Mining Operations," Interfaces (November 1977), p. 10.

plex process, which cannot be fully comprehended by the unaided mind. Consequently, the organization is confronted with the task of setting an employment goal without being able to know the hiring and staffing policies it will have to establish in order to attain that goal.

Computer simulations have been developed to aid the organization in setting attainable goals. The model described here and other similar models represent personnel movements as a set of simultaneous probabilistic processes for each sex and ethnic group of concern to management.[8] These movements are simulated in order to forecast movements into and out of each job category for each group.

For example, to determine the number of black females who will occupy first-line supervisory positions next year, the model utilizes last year's data to compute the "transition probabilities" that black females in each other job category will move into such a position and the probability that black female first-line supervisors will remain in those positions. These probabilities are multiplied by the number of black females currently in each job category. The sum of those products is the *internal supply;* the number of black female first-line supervisors forecasted to come from within the organization.

When the forecasts for all race and sex groups are subtracted from next year's anticipated staffing level for first-line supervisors, the result is the number of first-line supervisors who need to be hired from outside the organization; the *external supply.* By examining the internal supply forecasts for black females, the manager can determine how many black females must be hired in order to attain a given affirmative action goal figure.

[8]James Ledvinka, R. Lawrence LaForge, and Thomas G. Corbett, "Test of an Affirmative Action Goal Setting Model," *The Personnel Administrator* (November 1976): 33–38.

If that number is too high, the goal can be lowered. Or the transition probabilities can be changed by instituting training programs or something similar to facilitate the promotion of black females into supervisory positions.

Finally, the impact of these planned programs on the race and sex composition of the organization's work force can be simulated. If the impact is inconsistent with the goals, either the plans or the goals can be adjusted.

In addition to putting affirmative action on a sound footing, the entire procedure does much to dispel the more irrational fears about affirmative action. It clearly shows that affirmative action policymaking is being carried out on a more sensible basis than most employees had been suspecting.

INSURANCE: VALUING A PROPERTY-LIABILITY INSURANCE AGENCY

There are occasions where it is necessary to accurately place a value on a property-liability insurance agency. One such occasion is when there is a merger or acquisition. Another is when an estate is being settled. Since the personal exemption for federal estate taxes is quite low, an agency does not have to be large to create estate tax problems. In dealing with the IRS, one should be able to present an objective valuation method.

The oldest and probably most frequently used valuation method is the gross commission method. With this method, an agency is valued at some proportion of an agency's annual renewal commissions. For example, an agency with $80,000 in renewal commissions might be valued at 1-1/2 times commission or $120,000. Unfortunately, although this method is simple, it frequently does not provide realistic valuations.

An alternative method currently being used involves a probabilistic simulation of the agency's discounted cash flows.[9] The model is a contrast to the models previously described in this chapter in that it is sufficiently small and can be presented completely. It illustrates that simulation models do not have to be large to be useful. The valuation model is shown here

$$\text{Agency value} = \sum_{t=1}^{10} \frac{1}{(1+R)^t} \times (RC_t + UGC_t - \Delta AP_t + \Delta AR_t - SOE_t - ME_t - IT_t)$$

where

RC_t = renewal commissions in time period t
UGC_t = upgraded commissions in time period t
ΔAP_t = change in accounts payable in time period $t (AP_t - AP_{t-1})$
ΔAR_t = change in accounts receivable in time period $t (AR_t - AR_{t-1})$
SOE_t = selling and operating expenses in time period t
ME_t = managerial expense in time period t
IT_t = income taxes in time period t
R = risk-free rate of return

---

[9]James S. Trieschmann, K. Roscoe Davis, and E. J. Leverett, Jr., "A Probabilistic Valuation Model for a Property-Liability Insurance Agency," *The Journal of Risk and Insurance* (June 1975): 289–302.

With the exception of year before purchase commissions (which are known for any agency), the risk-free rate of interest (taken to be the average of 90-day treasury bill rates), the time period of analysis (usually 10 years), and the corporate tax rate, all variables are treated probabilistically. Using the basic model, values for the deterministic variables, and Monte Carlo sampling from the probabilistic variables, one can probabilistically specify an agency's value. From this distribution, a mean value for the agency can be determined as well as a measure of risk from the distribution of possible valuations.

Use of the model has produced interesting findings. The old rule-of-thumb gross commission method of valuation tends to produce valuations that are too high. This is obviously an undesirable situation when dealing with the IRS on the settlement of estate taxes. Sensitivity analysis has also shown that the most important factors for valuation purposes are number of years of upgrading commissions, size of upgrading commissions, selling and operating expenses, and persistency of year before purchase commissions. The factors that have the least effect are change in accounts payable, change in accounts receivable, and the inflation rate. This is useful information when striving to increase the value of an agency.

REAL ESTATE: INVESTMENT ANALYSIS

The most frequent use of simulation in real estate is for investment analysis, and a large number of computerized models have been developed and are available for this purpose. The approaches employed typically fall into one of two categories.

One approach is to calculate the investment value of a property.[10] Data inputs such as net operating income, length of the mortgage, interest rate, conversion periods per year, loan to value ratio, percentage of property appreciation or depreciation during the holding period, and expected or desired equity rate of return are processed through a model to determine the property's value.

The second approach is to simulate the property's cash flows on either a before or after tax basis.[11] This approach is similar to that described for valuing an insurance agency. Typical data inputs include projected rents, expenses, financing terms, depreciation allowances, investor's tax bracket, and the like. Data output often includes cash flow on an annual basis, rates of return on invested capital, and discounted present value of the investment. Most of these models are deterministic; however, probabilistic models have been developed and are in limited use. Such models are most useful for sophisticated investors such as financial institutions, syndicates, builder-developers, and large equity investors. A schematic of a probabilistic model currently used is presented in Figure 2.6.

GOVERNMENT: FIRE DEPARTMENT DEPLOYMENT POLICY ANALYSIS

Local governments must make policy decisions regarding fire fighting systems in their communities. These decisions include how many fire-fighting units to operate, where to

---

[10]See, for example, William M. Shenkel, *Modern Real Estate Appraisal* (New York: McGraw-Hill, 1978), Chapter 13.

[11]Ibid., Chapter 23.

Figure 2.6   A probabilistic real estate investment model.

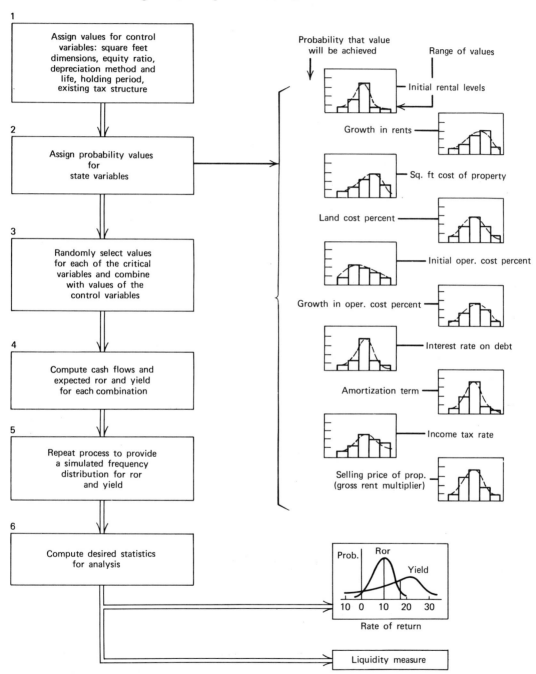

Source. Stephen A. Pyhrr, "A Computer Simulation Model to Measure the Risk in Real Estate Investment," The Real Estate Appraiser (May–June 1973), p. 22.

deploy them, and how to dispatch them. In response to this problem, a simulation model was developed by the New York City-Rand Institute.[12]

The simulation model utilizes three computer programs coded in SIMSCRIPT, a special-purpose simulation language. The first is an "incident generator," which creates a file containing a sequence of alarms. For each alarm, information is generated on when it occurs, where it occurs, what fire-fighting equipment is needed, and for how long. The second is a "simulator" that is a model of the community's fire suppression system. It captures the essence of the system by dispatching vehicles to incidents defined by the incident generator, "servicing" incidents, and returning fire-fighting equipment to the fire station to await the next call. The third program "compares" on an alarm for alarm basis the behavior of the system under varying assumptions of the number of fire stations, their locations, and dispatch rules.

The New York City-Rand Institute model was customized for use in analyzing the fire suppression system of Denver, Colorado.[13] It was employed to test the recommendations of an analytic analysis that suggested it was possible by reconfiguring the existing system to have a net reduction of five fire stations without reducing service levels. The simulation model was used to evaluate the proposal in light of more realistic assumptions. Several simplifying assumptions had been made to make the analytic analysis tractable; however, they had to be relaxed later to provide credibility to the analytic analysis.

The simulation analysis supported the proposed changes. Consequently, it was recommended that the number of fire stations be reduced from 44 to 39. This reduction was to be accomplished by closing obsolete stations and building better houses at new locations. These changes were thought to result in an accumulated net cost reduction of approximately $2.3 million over a 7-year period and a continuing annual cost avoidance of about $1.2 million.

ECONOMETRIC MODELS: THE GEORGIA MODEL

Economists have been concerned for some time on improving methods for analyzing proposed economic policies and forecasting economic trends at the national, regional, state, and local levels. Many of these efforts have focused on the development of *econometric models*, which predict future economic conditions based on historical data, estimates of the future, and governmental policy decisions; see Figure 2.7. Typically, econometric models contain many *recursive equations*, which relate output variables to values for variables in other time periods. The following is a simple equation for predicting population.

$$\text{Population}_t = \text{population}_{t-1} + \text{births}_t - \text{deaths}_t + \text{net migration}_t$$

Values for the output variables are determined by sequentially solving the equations so that the solution values in one time period can be used as inputs to the equations in the next time period.

---

[12] Grace Carter, *Simulation Model of Fire Department Operations: Program Description*, New York: The New York City-Rand Institute, R-118/2-HUD/NYC (December 1974).

[13] David E. Monarchi, Thomas E. Hendrick and Donald R. Plane, "Simulation for Fire Department Deployment Policy Analysis," *Decision Sciences* (January 1977): 211–227.

Figure 2.7   The functioning of an econometric model.

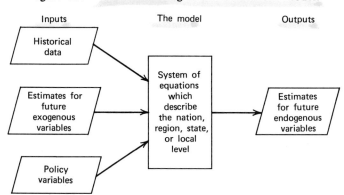

Consider the Georgia model as an example of an econometric model.[14] This regional model forecasts approximately 125 economic variables for the State of Georgia on an annual basis. These equations are segregated into eight blocks or sets of equations.

1. Output by industry.
2. Employment by industry.
3. Wages, income, and prices.
4. State government tax revenues.
5. Manufacturing investment.
6. Population.
7. Banking.
8. Retail trade.

The model is linked to a national econometric model, the famous Wharton model, for inputs of exogenous national variables.[15] Other inputs include additional national projections, past historical data, state projections, and policy decisions (e.g., state tax rates). These inputs are processed through equations that capture relationships among key independent variables. The Georgia model is visually depicted in Figure 2.8.

The Georgia model is used for several purposes. First, it provides a program of ongoing forecasts for the State of Georgia. Short-term forecasts for two years into the future and long-term forecasts for ten or more years are both part of the forecast program. Updated forecasts are made whenever economic developments warrant changing the assumptions or exogeneous variables of the model. For example, the 1974 energy crisis resulted in a rerunning of the model.

Another use of the model is to test the relative impact of alternative economic policy

---

[14] John B. Legler and Terry D. Robertson, "National and Regional Economic Models," *Forecasting Transportation Impacts Upon Land Use*, Paul F. Wendt, ed. (Leiden: The Netherlands, Martinus Nijhoff Social Sciences Division, 1976), pp. 16–31.

[15] M. K. Evans and L. R. Klein, *Wharton Economic Forecast Model*, Economics Research Unit (Philadelphia: University of Pennsylvania, 1968) and A. Ray Grimes, *A Satellite Econometric Model for Georgia* (Athens, Ga.: College of Business Administration, University of Georgia, 1972).

Figure 2.8   The Georgia model.

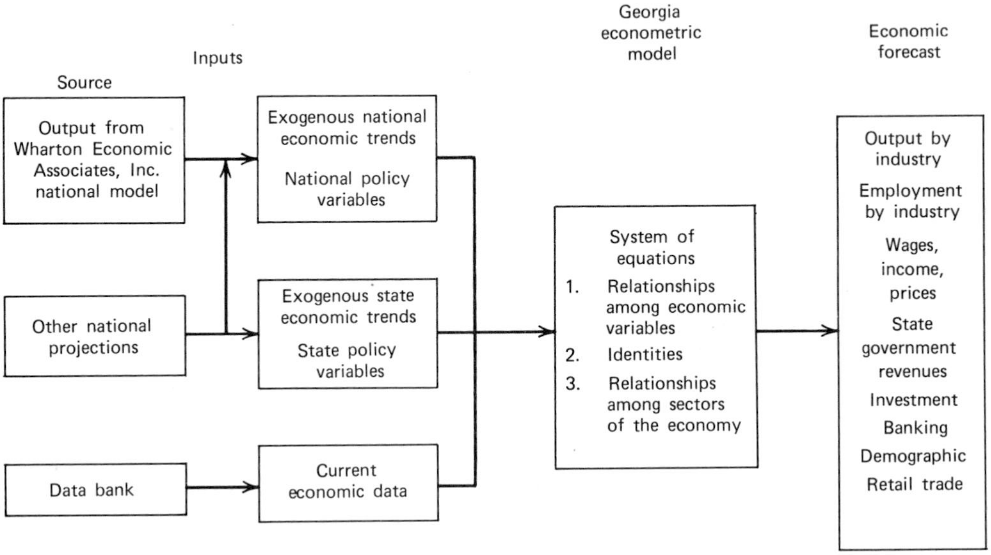

Source. John B. Legler and Terry D. Robertson, "National and Regional Economic Models," Forecasting Transportation Impacts upon Land Use, *Paul F. Wendt, ed. (Leiden: The Netherlands, Martinus Nijhoff Social Sciences Division, 1976), p. 21.*

proposals. For example, the model is used to test the effectiveness of proposed government monetary and fiscal policies in combating inflation and unemployment.

SYSTEMS DYNAMICS: *THE LIMITS TO GROWTH*

Systems dynamics is the name given to a collection of modeling efforts that look at the information-feedback characteristics of systems to show how system structure, amplification (in policies), and time delays (in decisions and actions) interact to affect system behavior. Its origins trace back to Jay Forrester's research into *industrial dynamics*, which has the individual firm as its focus of attention.[16] At a later date Forrester became interested in urban systems, which led to his *urban dynamics* research.[17] The most recent and controversial systems dynamics investigations have dealt with *world dynamics*, which takes the world as the system of interest.[18]

The world dynamics models, because of their startling predictions, have received the most attention. The most famous study was sponsored by The Club of Rome, which is reported in *The Limits to Growth*.[19] The study's objective was to explore some of the underlying assumptions about world subsystems in order to enhance understanding of world behavior. Five subsystems were identified and focused on in the study.

[16] Jay W. Forrester, *Industrial Dynamics* (New York: Wiley, 1961).
[17] Jay W. Forrester, *Urban Dynamics* (Cambridge, Mass.: The MIT Press, 1969).
[18] Jay W. Forrester, *World Dynamics* (Cambridge, Mass.: Wright-Allen Press, 1971).
[19] Dennis L. Meadows, op. cit.

1. Population.
2. Capital investment.
3. Natural resources.
4. Agriculture.
5. Pollution.

The output from the world dynamics model foretold a rather grim future for humankind and planet earth. This is seen in one of the conclusions from *The Limits to Growth*.

If the present growth trends in world population, industrialization, pollution, food production, and resource depletion continue unchanged, the limits to growth on this planet will be reached sometime within the next one hundred years. The most probable result will be a rather sudden and uncontrollable decline in both population and industrial capacity.[20]

There have been numerous criticisms of the world dynamics modeling effort and the conclusions reached. The criticisms have varied from technical modeling considerations to objections to some of the underlying assumptions built into the model. A book entitled, *Models of Doom*, is one of the more interesting critiques of The Club of Rome's study.[21]

In response to criticism, The Club of Rome supported a second study. Taking many criticisms of the first modeling effort into consideration, the club sponsored a second, revised world dynamics model. A major enhancement was to break the world model down into geographical regions. The findings from this second modeling effort can be found in *Mankind at the Turning Point*.[22] The findings remained basically the same as in *The Limits to Growth*. However, the findings were described as they applied to various geographical regions.

Systems dynamics simulation models are particularly interesting because of the size of systems they are sometimes designed to model, the conclusions reached through the modeling effort, and the technology used in developing systems dynamics models. Most systems dynamics models are conceptualized and programmed using DYNAMO, a special-purpose simulation language developed by Forrester. We will have an opportunity to examine this language briefly in Chapter 8.

SUMMARY

Business applications of simulation are found in all the functional areas. Because so much of an organization's activities are eventually expressed in financial terms, more simulation models are found in finance than any other functional area. There are also many simulation models used in production, undoubtedly due to the complexity of many production systems. Even personnel, which has not traditionally been a heavy user of management science methods, is now employing simulation.

---

[20] Ibid., p. 23.
[21] H. S. D. Cole, et al., *Models of Doom* (New York: Universe Books, 1973).
[22] Mihajlo Mesarovic and Edward Pestel, *Mankind at the Turning Point* (New York: Dutton, 1974).

Air Canada's cash budgeting model is typical of financial simulations. Its model allows for the uncertainty that dominates cash forecasting in the airline industry, enhances the accuracy of data inputs used in cash forecasting, and eliminates the toilsome computations of previous manual systems.

The Bethlehem Steel Corporation has employed simulation for machine shop production planning and scheduling at its Cast Roll Manufacturing complex. The system, which has a simulation model as its key component, generates production plans 10 to 50 weeks in advance, creates production schedules 9 to 12 days into the future, and responds to management inquiries.

An important marketing decision involves selecting the best advertising schedule for a product or service. The AD-ME-SIM model was developed for this application and functions by simulating the effectiveness of a proposed advertising schedule on a sample of consumers.

An interesting engineering application of simulation was its use in evaluating alternative excavation schemes for mining the Athabasca Tar Sands of Canada. Based largely on the simulation analysis, the decision was made to employ dragline excavation even though bucket wheel excavation was the only previously proven method.

Affirmative action planning has become an increasingly important organizational concern. Simulation models have been used to describe the movement of personnel into, among, and out of job categories. These models make it possible to evaluate whether proposed policies will result in the realization of affirmative action goals.

For acquisitions and mergers and estate tax settlements, it is important to be able to place a value on a property-liability insurance agency accurately and objectively. Probabilistic simulations have been used for this purpose.

The most important application of simulation in real estate is for investment analysis. A property's cash flows are simulated to provide investment information such as annual cash flow, return on invested capital, and discounted present value.

Simulation is sometimes used by local governments in planning fire-fighting systems. By simulating the occurrence of fire incidents and their servicing by alternative fire-fighting configurations, one can evaluate the effectiveness of alternative configurations.

Econometric models are used to forecast future economic conditions and to evaluate economic policies. The Georgia model is an example of an econometric model, which is useful for planning at the regional level.

Systems dynamics has been employed to model industrial, urban, and world systems. It is the world dynamics models that have captured the public's interest because of their cataclysmic predictions for the future of the world.

ASSIGNMENTS

2.1. As suggested and supported by data, simulation is widely used in business. The journal *Interfaces* frequently contains articles describing simulation models that have been implemented. Look at the last four issues of *Interfaces* for articles describing simulation applications and write a short description of the applications. The call number for this applications-oriented journal is HD28.I455.

2.2. Air Canada has successfully used a cash budget simulator for analyzing its future cash flow position. Based on your knowledge of cash budgeting, the description of Air Canada's model provided in this chapter, and the description of variables used in simulation models from Chapter 1, indicate external, policy, random, deterministic, lagged output, and output variables in Air Canada's model.

2.3 Machine shops such as at Bethlehem Steel often use heuristic scheduling rules. These are logical rules-of-thumb that usually produce reasonably good job-processing schedules. Johnson's method illustrates this type of scheduling. It is applicable when jobs must be processed through two machines in a specific sequence. Johnson's method calls for the application of the following steps.

1. Specify the operation time for each job on both machines.
2. Determine the shortest operation time for any job on either of the two machines.
3. If the shortest time is on the first machine, do that job first; if it is for the second machine, do the job last.
4. Repeat steps 2 and 3 for each remaining job until the schedule is complete.

Assume that the operations times on two machines for three jobs are as follows.

Job	Operation Time on First Machine, hours	Operation Time on Second Machine, hours	TOTAL
A	3	2	5
B	5	3	8
C	4	4	8

Using Johnson's method, schedule the sequencing of jobs. Simulate when each job enters and leaves each of the two machines.

2.4. Models that simulate the effectiveness of alternative advertising schedules must include many factors. For example, for every member of the sample of consumers it is necessary to simulate the media messages received and their impact. Assume that two advertising schedules, A and B, are under consideration, each costing approximately the same. Plan A calls for advertising through media 1, 2, 3, and 4. Plan B is more intensive and involves advertising in only media 1 and 3. The effectiveness of a contact in each of the four media are:

Media	First Contact, units	Second Contact, units
1	2	1
2	3	1
3	5	3
4	2	1.5

If the simulated contacts through a sample of four consumers are as follows, is plan A or B preferable to this point in the simulation?

	Advertising Schedule A		Advertising Schedule B	
	Media	Number of Contacts	Media	Number of Contacts
Consumer 1	1	2	1	2
	2	0	—	—
	3	0	3	1
	4	1	—	—
Consumer 2	1	0	1	0
	2	0	—	—
	3	0	3	1
	4	0	—	—
Consumer 3	1	1	1	1
	2	1	—	—
	3	0	3	0
	4	0	—	—
Consumer 4	1	—	1	0
	2	0	—	—
	3	1	3	2
	4	0	—	—
	⋮	⋮	⋮	⋮

2.5. Engineering simulations such as those employed in tar sands mining operations often require a mixture of talents and backgrounds in developing the model. For the simulation of tar sands mining operations, what types or groups of people would likely have to participate in the development of a model?

2.6. A company's hourly workers are divided evenly between males and females. Percentage wise, however, many more males are in skilled positions than females. The number of males and females in skilled and unskilled positions are given in the state vector shown here. It also indicates the anticipated number of new hires to replace terminating workers.

Unskilled M	Skilled M	Unskilled F	Skilled F	New Hire M	New Hire F
20	40	50	10	6	6

Management has been considering selected policies designed to increase the percentage of females in skilled positions. Before implementing these policies, management wants to evaluate the policies' potential effectiveness. The estimated probabilities of male and female workers moving to unskilled and skilled positions over a 6-month time horizon as a result of the proposed policies is shown in the following transition matrix. It also indicates workers terminating from the organization.

	Unskilled M	Skilled M	Unskilled F	Skilled F	Terminations M	Terminations F
Male unskilled	.60	.30	.00	.00	.10	.00
Male skilled	.00	.90	.00	.00	.10	.00
Female unskilled	.00	.00	.70	.20	.00	.10
Female skilled	.00	.00	.00	.90	.00	.10
Male new hires	1.00	.00	.00	.00	.00	.00
Female new hires	.00	.00	1.00	.00	.00	.00

Having expressed the data in this format, one can simulate the movement of workers among job categories by multiplying the initial state vector times the transition matrix. This multiplication results in a new state vector representing organizational conditions 6 months later. In a similar manner, organizational conditions can be simulated for additional 6-month time periods. Using this analysis approach, evaluate the effectiveness of the proposed policies.

2.7. A model for valuing a property-liability insurance agency was presented. The following table shows deterministic values and sampled values for the independent variables in the model. The only values not shown are for taxes. They can be found by applying the appropriate tax rates to $(RC_t + UGC_t - SOE_t - ME_t)$. Taxes are 0.20 on the first \$25,000, 0.22 on the next \$25,000, and 0.48 on anything over \$50,000.

t	RC_t	UGC_t	ΔAP_t	ΔAR_t	SOE_t	ME_t	IT_t	R
1	\$ 70,000	\$ 5 000	\$3 000	\$2 000	\$ 37,500	\$ 9 000	—	0.06
2	76,000	5 200	3 150	2 100	40,000	9 600	—	0.06
3	80,000	5 300	3 200	2 200	43,000	10,200	—	0.06
4	90,000	6 000	3 400	2 350	47,500	12,000	—	0.06
5	100,000	6 500	3 600	2 500	52,000	13,000	—	0.06
6	112,000	7 000	3 800	2 700	61,000	14,000	—	0.06
7	130,000	7 800	4 100	2 950	70,000	16,800	—	0.06
8	150,000	9 000	4 400	3 200	78,500	18,300	—	0.06
9	175,000	11,000	4 800	3 400	85,000	22,300	—	0.06
10	200,000	13,000	5 500	3 700	101,000	25,100	—	0.06

Using these data, place a value on the agency. Keep in mind that this analysis represents a single sampling from the probabilistic variables.

2.8.   A large real estate company has recently purchased a minicomputer system. One use in mind for the system is to show potential investors in commercial real estate (duplexes, apartment complexes, office buildings) the profitability of such investments. What should, or might be, the input, processing, and output specifications for this application?

2.9.   Springdale and Winterville are neighboring communities that currently operate completely separate fire departments. A proposal has been made, however, to integrate the two systems. Anytime a fire truck is not available in one community, a "hot line" call would be made to a fire station in the other community. If a fire truck is available there, it would answer the call. Because of political considerations, however, the proposal will be seriously considered only if it can be shown that such an arrangement will reduce the amount of time that fires are unattended. The following figure presents the two fire stations (and trucks) in Springdale and the single station in Winterville. Also shown are simulated incidents in each of the two communities. It indicates when the incident occurs and how long it takes to service the incident. The only additional fact needed is that to answer a call in the other community adds a $\frac{1}{2}$ hour to the service time. This time is evenly divided between $\frac{1}{4}$ hour to answer the call and another $\frac{1}{4}$ hour to return to the station. Based on these data, evaluate the proposal for integration of the two fire-fighting systems.

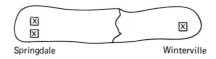

Springdale   Winterville

Springdale Incidents	Service Time, hours	Winterville Incidents	Service Time, hours
8:00 A.M.	1	6:45 A.M.	1
10:00 A.M.	$\frac{1}{2}$	1:30 P.M.	$\frac{1}{2}$
12:30 P.M.	1	6:00 P.M.	1
1:00 P.M.	2	6:30 P.M.	1
6:00 P.M.	$\frac{1}{2}$		
11:00 P.M.	1		

2.10.   The following was given as an example of typical econometric equation.

$$\text{Population}_t = \text{population}_{t-1} + \text{births}_t - \text{deaths}_t + \text{net migration}_t$$

Given the following data (in millions), predict the population in 1984.

t	Population$_t$	Births$_t$	Deaths$_t$	Net Migration$_t$
1980	3 million	—	—	—
1981	—	0.20	0.10	0.05
1982	—	0.18	0.11	0.06
1983	—	0.18	0.11	0.07
1984	—	0.16	0.11	0.07

2.11. Read either *The Limits to Growth* or *Models of Doom* and support or refute the conclusions reached.

REFERENCES

Boere, N. J., "Air Canada Saves with Aircraft Maintenance Scheduling," *Interfaces* (May 1977): 1-13.

Boughey, Arthur S., *Strategy for Survival* (Menlo Park: Cal.: Benjamin, 1976).

Bryant, J. W., "A Simulation of Retail Behavior," *Operations Research Quarterly* (April 1975): 133-149.

Churchill, Neil C., and John K. Shank, "Affirmative Action and Guilt-Edged Goals," *Harvard Business Review* (March-April 1976): 111-116.

Cole, H. S. D. et al., *Models of Doom* (New York: Universe Books, 1973).

Economos, A. M., "A Financial Simulation for Risk Analysis of a Proposed Subsidiary," *Management Science* (August 1969): 675-681.

Field, Al, and Henry J. Cassidy, "Simulation Analysis of Alternative Mortgage Instruments," *Journal of the American Real Estate and Urban Economics Association* (Winter 1977): 411-433.

Forrester, Jay W., *Industrial Dynamics* (New York: Wiley, 1961).

Gensch, Dennis H., "A Computer Simulation Model for Selecting Advertising Schedules," *Journal of Marketing Research* (May 1969): 203-214.

Jain, Suresh K., "A Simulation-Based Scheduling and Management Information System for a Machine Shop," *Interfaces* (November 1975): 81-96.

Ledvinka, James R., Lawrence LaForge, and Thomas G. Corbett, "Test of an Affirmative Action Goal Setting Model," *The Personnel Administrator* (November 1976): 33-38.

Legler, John B., and Terry D. Robertson, "National and Regional Economic Models," *Forecasting Transportation Impacts upon Land Use*, Paul F. Wendt, ed. (The Netherlands: Leiden, 1976): 16-31.

Meadows, Dennis L. et al., *The Limits to Growth* (New York: Universe Books, 1972).

Miller, Peter J., and James S. Burgess, Jr., "Simulating a Municipal Problem," *Journal of Industrial Engineering* (June 1975): 10-14.

Monarchi, David E., Thomas E. Hendrick, and Donald R. Plane, "Simulation for Fire Department Deployment Analysis," *Decision Sciences* (January 1977): 211-227.

Nanda, R., "Simulating Passenger Arrivals at Airports," *Industrial Engineering* (March 1972): 12-19.

Scott, David F. Jr., Lawrence J. Moore, André Saint-Denis, Edouard Archer and Bernard W. Taylor III, "Implementation of a Cash Budget Simulator at Air Canada," *Financial Management* (Summer 1979): 46-52.

Trieschmann, James S., K. Roscoe Davis, and E. J. Leverett, Jr., "A Probabilistic Valuation Model for a Property-Liability Insurance Agency," *The Journal of Risk and Insurance* (June 1975): 289-302.

Wofford, Larry E., "A Simulation Approach to the Appraisal of Income Producing Real Estate," *Journal of the American Real Estate and Urban Economics Association* (Winter 1978): 370-394.

Wyman, F. Paul, "Simulation of Tar Sands Mining Operations," *Interfaces* (November 1977): 6-20.

CHAPTER THREE

MONTE CARLO INVENTORY SIMULATION

Basic Inventory Concepts

A Fixed-Order Quantity Model

The Monte Carlo Inventory Simulation

    Probability Distributions

    A Monte Carlo Method

    The Simulation

The Sample Size

Analysis for Optimization

Adding Greater Realism

Summary

Assignments

References

Our first detailed look at the technology associated with simulation will be through an inventory model, specifically, a *Monte Carlo inventory simulation.* Such an analysis will provide us with an excellent starting point for our examination of simulation because of our intuitive understanding of the role of inventory in organizations and the simplicity of the simulation model itself. But first let us review (or perhaps learn) some basic inventory concepts.

BASIC INVENTORY CONCEPTS

Inventory can best be described as quantities of items that are being held for future use by an organization. Almost all firms maintain inventories of one type or another. Retail stores carry items in inventory that they plan to sell to consumers. Manufacturing firms stock inventories of raw materials that are components of the goods produced. Most organizations find a large proportion of their capital assets tied up in inventory, making inventory control a necessary concern of management.

Because inventory control is a common concern for so many organizations, it has been studied for many years. In fact, inventory control models were developed as early as 1915 by F. W. Harris. The inventory control problem is a well-structured one. That is, the objectives are well known and the means for realizing the objectives are reasonably well defined. Specifically, the objective is to minimize the cost of maintaining an item in inventory. In practice, inventory costs are grouped into one of the following categories.

1. Carrying costs.
2. Ordering costs or setup costs.
3. Stockout costs.
4. Purchasing costs.

Carrying, or holding, costs are the costs associated with physically having the item on hand. Included in this category are warehousing, insurance, spoilage, theft, obsolescence, and tied-up capital costs. The usual range of annual carrying costs is 15 to 40 percent of the inventory investment.[1]

Ordering costs include clerical costs associated with processing the order, shipping costs, and materials handling costs once the order is received. When the item is produced by the organization for inventory rather than being ordered from a vendor, production *setup costs* instead of ordering costs are incurred. Ordering and setup costs are very analogous in their behavior, and for simplicity, we will refer only to ordering costs.

Stockout costs occur when an item is not available on demand. If the item is for final sale to the consumer, the stockout costs include the foregone profits on that particular sale (unless the customer is willing to *back order*, in other words, to wait), plus lost potential future sales when the customer shifts his or her business to a competitor. When the inventory item is for use in a production process rather than for final sale, stockouts disrupt production schedules and, hence, increase costs because of decreased production efficiency. Stockouts are the most difficult of all costs to estimate.

[1] Richard J. Tersine, *Materials Management and Inventory Systems* (New York: American Elsevier, 1976), p. 17.

Purchasing costs are the costs of buying the item and are, of course, very important to the organization. In many cases, however, they can be omitted from the analysis, since they are not incremental with the alternative decisions. That is, they do not vary with the possible courses of action. It is only when there are quantity discounts that purchasing costs must usually be included in the analysis.

What makes the inventory problem difficult is that carrying and ordering costs move in opposite directions with changes in the quantity ordered. Larger order quantities decrease the number of orders placed per time period, thus reducing ordering costs; but larger orders also increase the average inventory balance and, in doing so, increase carrying costs. Stockout costs tend to decrease with larger order quantities, but generally are more closely related to the reorder point rather than to the order quantity decision.

The means through which inventory costs are minimized involve answering the following two fundamental questions.

1. How many items should be ordered?
2. When should the items be ordered?

For items with *dependent demand*, many organizations are turning to materials requirements planning (MRP) systems.[2] Dependent demand refers to situations where the demand for an item depends on the demand for a higher level item. For example, the demand for seat belts in new cars depends on the number of cars produced. Once the estimates for the higher level items have been made and the *product structure* (what components go into making the product) is known, the determination of demand for component parts is relatively straightforward. Of course, in organizations making multiple products composed of many component parts with products being produced in varying numbers and points in time, calculating the quantities and timing of orders for inventory is a complex problem. Consequently, computers are playing a critical role in this area, and when a MRP system is discussed, the person is referring to a computerized system.

Inventory control procedures for items that have *independent demand* are based on different approaches, because inventory requirements are not directly computed based on the demand for a higher level item. Two different approaches are commonly used.[3]

1. Fixed-order quantity methods.
2. Fixed-order period methods.

With the *fixed-order quantity approach*, the quantity to order at a time is fixed (e.g., 100 units) based on prior analysis, but the timing of placing the order varies with demand. Only when the number of units remaining in inventory drops below the reorder, or "trigger," point, is an order placed. With the *fixed-order period* approach, the timing of the placing of an order is fixed (e.g., every 2 weeks) based on prior analysis, but the size of the order placed depends on the number of items remaining in inventory. Both these approaches attempt to get at the "how many" and "when" questions of inventory control. For each approach there are a large number of models that have been developed,

---

[2] For an introductory discussion of MRP systems, see Richard B. Chase and Nicholas J. Aquilano, *Production and Operations Management*, rev. ed. (Homewood, Ill.: Irwin, 1977), pp. 420–451.

[3] Ibid., pp. 368–419.

which vary in the assumptions they make. Some models are deterministic, whereas others are probabilistic; some assume back ordering, whereas others do not; some are for situations where the item is produced for inventory, whereas in other situations it is ordered.

A FIXED-ORDER QUANTITY MODEL

As an illustration of inventory models, we will consider the development and use of a simple fixed-order quantity model. The objective will be to determine an optimal order quantity, Q_{opt}, and reorder point, R. The model will be typical of many models of this type in that it will be deterministic, make many assumptions about the real-world system it models, and be developed through traditional mathematical techniques (simple algebra and differential calculus).

As an illustration, consider a situation where we can assume that the demand for the item is known with certainty (perfect knowledge) and is constant over time (no seasonal demand factors). Furthermore, the delivery, or lead time, is also known with certainty. Although these are admittedly rather strong and in many cases unrealistic assumptions, they are typical of many inventory control models. Granting these assumptions at least for the time being, note that Figure 3.1 depicts the usage and then resupply of the inventory item. At time = 0 an order for Q items arrives, resulting in an inventory balance of Q. This inventory is consumed at a constant known rate over time. Eventually, the reorder point, R, is reached and an order is placed for Q more units. Since the delivery time, L, is known with certainty, the reorder point can be set so that the last item remaining in inventory is used up just as the new order is received. The arrival of the ordered items increases the inventory balance to Q units and the process repeats itself.

Assuming a known demand, D, per unit of time, a carrying cost, K_c, per item per unit of time, and an ordering cost, K_o, per order, one can find the value of Q that minimizes the total inventory costs, *TC*. There is no need to consider stockout costs, because the assumptions of certainty on demand and delivery time rule out the possibility of a shortage. And because there are no quantity discounts, purchasing costs can be ignored as not being incremental to the decision alternatives.

We will first consider the *total carrying costs*. The greatest number of items ever in inventory is Q and the smallest is 0. Since demand is constant, the average inventory level is $(Q + 0)/2$, or $Q/2$. If K_c is the carrying cost per item, the total carrying cost for an average of $Q/2$ items must be:

$$K_c \frac{Q}{2} \qquad (3\text{-}1)$$

Figure 3.1   Amount in inventory as a function of time.

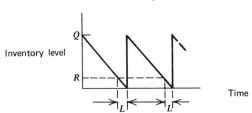

If D is the demand per unit of time, and Q units are ordered at a time, D/Q is the number of orders placed per unit of time. When the cost per order is K_o, the *total ordering cost* is:

$$K_o \frac{D}{Q} \qquad (3\text{-}2)$$

The *total cost of inventory*, TC, is the sum of the carrying and ordering costs.

$$TC = K_c \frac{Q}{2} + K_o \frac{D}{Q} \qquad (3\text{-}3)$$

In order to find the value of Q which minimizes TC, take a first derivative of TC with respect to Q,

$$\frac{dTC}{dQ} = \frac{K_c}{2} - \frac{K_o D}{Q^2} \qquad (3\text{-}4)$$

This expression is then set equal to zero and solved for Q in order to find the value of Q that minimizes TC.

$$\frac{K_c}{2} - \frac{K_o D}{Q^2} = 0$$

$$\frac{K_c}{2} = \frac{K_o D}{Q^2}$$

$$Q^2 = \frac{2 K_o D}{K_c}$$

$$Q_{opt} = \sqrt{\frac{2 K_o D}{K_c}} \qquad (3\text{-}5)$$

The formula just developed can be used to determine the optimum number of items to order for inventory when the demand, carrying costs, and ordering costs are known and the assumptions underlying the model are satisfied. The following example illustrates the use of the model.

$$\text{If} \quad D = 1000 \text{ units per year}$$

$$K_c = \$4 \text{ per item per year}$$

$$K_o = \$20 \text{ per order}$$

$$Q_{opt} = \sqrt{\frac{2(20)(1000)}{4}}$$

$$= 100 \text{ units per order}$$

This order quantity would result in the following average annual costs (excluding of course, purchasing costs).

$$TC = \frac{4(100)}{2} + \frac{20(1000)}{100}$$

$$= \$400$$

In order to determine the reorder point, one must only find the average usage of the item per week, $\bar{d}$, and then multiply this figure by the delivery or lead time, L, expressed in weeks.

$$R = \bar{d}L \tag{3-6}$$

If the delivery time is 2 weeks, the demand is still 1000 units per year, and the firm operates 52 weeks per year, the reorder point should be

$$R = \frac{1000(2)}{52}$$

$$\cong 40 \text{ units}$$

Obviously, the assumptions that underlie the model just developed and illustrated are seldom completely satisfied in the real world. However, there are a number of instances where the assumptions are almost satisfied and use of the model does produce optimum or near-optimum results. In cases where the real-world situation differs significantly from the model's assumptions, possibly models based on the correct assumptions have previously been developed and can be used. If neither of these approaches is viable, it is sometimes possible and appropriate to proceed and use the best model available, and then to apply an intelligently selected adjustment factor. For example, a safety stock is often maintained by firms to adjust for the fact that demand usually varies during the resupply period and delivery time is not always known with certainty.

Ready-built fixed-order quantity and fixed-order period inventory models are commonly used in industry for items with independent demand and generally produce satisfactory results. A completely different approach, however, is to develop a custom-built model that captures most of the real-world complexity associated with maintaining a particular inventory item. The only difficulty in doing so is that in adding more realism and complexity to the model, traditional analytical methods of analysis can quickly become prohibitively difficult to apply, even for professional mathematicians and statisticians. Consequently, if the added complexity is required and justified, the analyst must often switch from an analytic to a numeric mode of analysis. The Monte Carlo inventory simulation, which is presented next, is an example of a numeric approach to the inventory control problem.

A MONTE CARLO INVENTORY SIMULATION

As has been indicated, a common problem with analytic methods of analysis is that the required mathematics and statistics can quickly become prohibitively difficult to apply unless simplifying assumptions are made about the real-world system. In many situations, carefully selected assumptions do not seriously distort the modeling effort. In other cases, however, it is important to capture in the model much of the real-world complexity that actually exists.

For some inventory items it might not be appropriate to assume that demand and delivery time are known with certainty. These variables can sometimes be treated probabilistically using an analytic mode of analysis; however, the analysis does become considerably more complex than what has been illustrated in this chapter. An alternative approach is to simulate the behavior of the inventory system. When this approach is used, a beginning inventory balance for the item is chosen and a demand for the item is simulated. The simulated demand is then subtracted from the existing inventory balance and a decision based on the chosen reorder point is made as to whether or not to reorder. If the decision is "yes," an order is placed for the chosen order quantity, and its delivery time is simulated. After every simulated time period, the appropriate carrying, ordering, and stockout costs are computed. The simulation is conducted for a large number of time periods in order to assure a good estimate of the costs associated with the particular order quantity and reorder point being simulated. Obviously, the simulation approach requires many more calculations than does its analytic counterparts, but all the computations are simple to understand and perform. Let us now examine, in detail, how the simulation would be performed.

Probability Distributions

In the Monte Carlo inventory simulation, demand and delivery time are treated probabilistically, requiring that probability distributions be specified for each variable. The probability distributions can be determined in several ways. One way is to analyze past historical data, because for many inventory items there are ample and reliable data available. For example, assume that the data in Table 3.1 are relevant. These *frequency distributions* show the frequency with which various demand levels and delivery times have been experienced by the organization. When it is believed that the future will be like the past, historical data can be directly used in the formulation of probability statements about the future. What is required is that the *relative frequency* for each variable value be computed and then *treated as a probability*. This transformation is performed by dividing the frequency in each category by the total number of observations, as illustrated in Table 3.2.

This approach to specifying probability distributions assumes that the future will be like the past. When management knows this will not be the case, the probabilities must be adjusted to reflect management's subjective feelings about how the future will differ from the past. Unfortunately, little guidance can be given as to how to make these adjustments. In some instances it may even be possible that the inventory item under

Table 3.1 DEMAND AND DELIVERY TIME DATA

Demand per Week	Frequency	Delivery Time, in weeks	Frequency
0	5	1	4
1	10	2	4
2	15	3	2
3	12		10
4	8		
	50		

Table 3.2 PROBABILITY DISTRIBUTIONS FOR DEMAND AND DELIVERY TIME

Demand per Week	Relative Frequency and Probability	Delivery Time, in weeks	Relative Frequency and Probability
0	$\frac{5}{50} = .10$	1	$\frac{4}{10} = .40$
1	$\frac{10}{50} = .20$	2	$\frac{4}{10} = .40$
2	$\frac{15}{50} = .30$	3	$\frac{2}{10} = \underline{.20}$
3	$\frac{12}{50} = .24$		1.00
4	$\frac{8}{50} = \underline{.16}$		
	1.00		

consideration is new to the list of inventory items maintained by the organization, and all probabilistic estimates will have to be highly subjective. Despite the feelings of discomfort most people have with subjective probabilities, decisions must be made, and carefully reasoned subjective estimates are better than no estimates at all.

A Monte Carlo Method

A Monte Carlo inventory simulation requires the sampling of values from the demand and delivery time probability distributions. The name Monte Carlo was first coined by von Neumann, Ulam, and Fermi while working on the development of the atomic bomb during World War II to describe the set of techniques employed for sampling from probabilistic processes. It is a most appropriate name since the random behavior of the gambling tables at Monte Carlo and the method of sampling values from probability distributions are similar, except that the gambling tables usually provide more excitement and higher costs for the participants.

Monte Carlo methods require the use of random numbers. In a later chapter we will fully discuss random numbers, but for present purposes, we need only say that *random numbers* exhibit no discernible pattern and pass appropriate statistical tests for randomness. The most common source of random numbers for use in simulation studies is from published tables and computerized random number generation routines. Appendix A contains random numbers obtained from the Rand Corporation's book, *A Million Random Digits with 100,000 Normal Deviates*, which is still the best known and most famous published source of random numbers. The random numbers in Appendix A come from the uniform distribution; that is, every number has a uniformly equal chance of appearing next. For example, consider the random numbers in the first two columns of Appendix A (69, 73, 16, . . .). A total of 100 unique numbers, 00 to 99, is possible, and each number has an equal probability of appearing next in the two columns.

In order to perform the Monte Carlo sampling, one should associate random numbers with the possible values for the variable in such a way that the number of random numbers assigned to each variable value is proportional to that value's probability of occurrence. In our inventory example we saw that the probability of experiencing a demand

Table 3.3 RANDOM NUMBERS ASSIGNED TO THE DEMAND AND DELIVERY TIME DISTRIBUTIONS

Demand per Week	Random Numbers	Delivery Time, in weeks	Random Numbers
0	00–09	1	00–39
1	10–29	2	40–79
2	30–59	3	80–99
3	60–83		
4	84–99		

of zero in any particular week was .10. If we are dealing with random numbers that vary from 00 to 99, a total of .10 × 100 or 10 random numbers should be associated with a demand per week of zero. It does not matter which particular random numbers are assigned to each demand value, but for purposes of convenience in locating the random numbers, the consecutive numbers 00 to 09 might be selected for the demand value of 0. Thus, in our inventory simulation, anytime a random number between 00 and 09 appears, a demand per week of zero units will be indicated. In the long run, since 10 of the 100 random numbers are assigned to zero units of demand, we should expect that this will be the demand level $10/100 = .10$ of the time, which is an appropriate frequency of occurrence. Using our previous inventory example, an assignment of random numbers to the possible demand and delivery time values is shown in Table 3.3.

The Simulation

When performing a Monte Carlo inventory simulation by hand, one should prepare a work sheet, as is shown in Table 3.4. Notice that there is a column for keeping track of each week being simulated. Since random numbers are required in simulating weekly demand and delivery time, columns are provided for each. The weekly demand, the placing of an order, the receiving of an order, and the balance of items in inventory are focal points of attention in the simulation and, consequently, each is given a column on the work sheet. The simulation activity results in simulated costs, which includes in this probabilistic environment: carrying, ordering, and stockout costs. Each cost component and the total cost has its own column.

The Monte Carlo inventory simulation framework can be used to investigate the consequences of alternative order quantities and reorder points. However, in any one simulation a particular combination must be selected and simulated. The selection should reflect management's and/or the analyst's thoughts as to which combination might potentially minimize total inventory costs. In our example, a $Q = 6$, $R = 3$ combination will be used. Later we will discuss the results of simulating other Q and R combinations.

Before beginning the analysis, we need to have estimates for the carrying, ordering, and stockout costs. We will assume that carrying costs have been discovered to run $2 per item per week when computed on the basis of the end-of-the-week balance. Conse-

Table 3.4   A MONTE CARLO INVENTORY SIMULATION WORK SHEET

| | Random Numbers | | Simulated Activity[a] | | | | Simulated Costs | | | |
	Demand	Delivery Time	Demand	Order Placed	Order Received	Balance	Carrying	Ordering	Stockout	Total
Time										
0						6				
1	69	64	3	6		3	6	30	0	36
2	73		3			0	0	0	0	0
3	16		1		6	5	10	0	0	10
4	65	39	3	6		2	4	30	0	34
5	01		0		6	8	16	0	0	16
6	71		3			5	10	0	0	10
7	91	19	4	6		1	2	30	0	32
8	99	69	4	6	6	3	6	30	0	36
9	18		1			2	4	0	0	4
10	33		2		6	6	12	0	0	12
11	65	34	3	6		3	6	30	0	36
12	86		4		6	5	10	0	0	10
13	94	91	4	6		1	2	30	0	32
14	39		2		0	0	0	0	20	20
15	38		2			0	0	0	40	40
16	84	42	4	6	6	2	4	30	0	34
17	45		2			0	0	0	0	0
18	91	25	4	6	6	2	4	30	0	34
19	03		0		6	8	16	0	0	16
20	81		3			5	10	0	0	10

[a] $Q = 6$
$R = 3$

quently, if a week ends with 3 items remaining in inventory, the carrying costs for that week are $3 \times \$2 = \$6$. Ordering costs are strictly a function of the number of orders placed, are $30 per order, and are recorded in the week in which the order is placed. Orders are assumed to arrive at the beginning of a week and are available for sale during that week. Stockout costs run $20 for every item not available when demanded, and it is assumed that customers are not willing to back order. Later in the chapter we will consider the inclusion of back ordering in the simulation.

Our simulation begins with an assumed inventory balance of six units being available at the close of week zero. This *starting condition* of six units reflects the order quantity being simulated and is similar to that seen earlier with the fixed-order quantity model where it was assumed that at time = 0 an order for Q units arrives. More will be said about starting conditions in Chapter 12, but the concept involves how the system "looks" when the simulation begins. Here it was judged that an opening inventory balance equal to the order quantity is a reasonable starting condition.

Our simulation uses a *fixed-time increment* time advance. The behavior of the system is observed on a weekly basis. The model moves from week to week. This approach is in contrast to a *next-event* time advance where the model moves from event to event independent of how close or far away the events are in time. In most cases the time advance method is dictated by the nature of the simulation, but in some cases it is at the discretion of the model builder. Time advance methods are discussed at greater length in Chapter 12.

Week 1 opens with a demand for the item. The weekly demand is probabilistic and is determined by drawing a random number from Appendix A, going to Table 3.3, which associates random numbers with various demand levels, and finding the appropriate demand. In our simulation the demand random numbers will be taken from the first two columns of Appendix A. Thus the first random number is 69 and is entered on the work sheet of Table 3.4. Looking back at Table 3.3, one can see that the random number 69 is associated with a weekly demand of 3. This demand level is entered on the simulated activity portion of the work sheet and the previous inventory balance is adjusted for the withdrawal.

Since the inventory balance at the close of week 1 is at the reorder point, $R = 3$, an order for six units is placed. When does the order arrive? This too is a random variable and is determined by drawing a random number. Using the third and fourth columns of Appendix A for delivery time random numbers, one finds the number 64 and enters it on the work sheet. This random number indicates a 2-week delivery time (see Table 3.3), meaning that the order will arrive at the beginning of week 3. The arrows on the work sheet show the arrival of the orders that have been placed.

Given the simulated activity, it becomes possible to calculate the simulated costs. Week 1 closed with an inventory balance of three units, and given carrying costs of $2 per item, the total carrying costs for week 1 are $6. An order was placed during the week, resulting in ordering costs of $30. No shortages occurred, therefore there were no stockout costs. The total inventory cost for week 1 is $6 + 30 + 0 = $36.

Week 2 opens with an inventory balance of three units. The demand during the week is simulated once again by drawing the next random number, 73 in this case. This random number is associated with a demand for three units and, consequently, three units are subtracted from the balance, leaving zero units in inventory.

At this point it is necessary to decide whether or not another order should be placed, because the inventory balance is below the reorder point. One thought might be that since an order was placed last week and is expected at any moment, there is no need to reorder. Another point of view, however, is that the demand for the item is continuing and, consequently, another order should be placed to satisfy the continuing demand. Strong arguments can be made for either position, but perhaps it is better to point out that insights can be gained as to what the organization should follow as a policy by running the simulation both ways and comparing the resultant costs. In our example we will *not* reorder and will refer to this as a "no multiple ordering" policy; leaving the analysis of the "multiple ordering" policy as an assignment at the end of the chapter.

The costs for week 2 are easily computed. No units remained in inventory at the close of the week, no new orders were placed, and all the demand was satisfied, resulting in a total cost of $0.

Week 3 opens with the arrival of the order that was placed in week 1. These six items are available for use during week 3, and the simulated demand of one unit results in a closing inventory balance of 5. Costs for the week include carrying costs of $10, ordering costs of $0, and stockout costs of $0, resulting in a total cost of $10.

The simulated demand of three units in week 4 drives the inventory balance to two, and triggers the placing of an order, because the balance is below the reorder point and no order is outstanding. The order is *prescheduled* to arrive in one week, making the items available for use in week 5. Notice that we have prescheduled the arrival of the order even though in the real world the exact arrival date would be unknown. The simulation could not function without prescheduling and, as will be seen in later chapters, is required in most simulation models. For week 4, we have carrying costs of $4, ordering costs of $30, and no stockout costs, for a total cost of $34.

The simulation continues quite peacefully until week 14 when the first stockout occurs. Setting the stage for the stockout is a condition at the close of week 13 where only one item is in balance and the order that has been placed ultimately takes 3 weeks to arrive. The simulated demand for two units in week 14 exceeds the available supply by one unit and results in a closing balance of zero units (negative inventory levels are not possible), and a resultant stockout cost of $20. Costs for the week are $0 for carrying and ordering costs, $20 for stockout costs, for a total cost of $20.

Week 15 sees the demand for two units being completely unsatisfied, resulting in stockout costs of $40 ($2 \times \$20 = \$40$). No orders are placed because the order from week 13 is still outstanding and, hence, there are no ordering costs. With no units in balance, there are, of course, no carrying costs.

In week 16 the long-outstanding order finally arrives and the activity within the simulation settles down to a more orderly pattern once again.

The work sheet of Table 3.4 carries the simulation through a total of 20 weeks. Based on the 20 weeks of simulated activity, it is possible to estimate the mean weekly cost associated with a policy of ordering six units whenever the inventory level drops to three or below. All that is required is to sum the total weekly cost figures and to divide by 20. For our simulation, the mean cost would be

$$\overline{X} = \frac{422}{20} = \$21.10$$

The Sample Size

Keep in mind that in our simulation we were *sampling* from the demand and delivery time distributions. Had different random numbers been used, the mean weekly cost estimate would have undoubtedly been different. If fewer or more weeks of activity had been simulated, this too would have resulted in a different cost estimate. The question then is, "How good is our estimate?"

Our intuition tells us that we would be more confident in the quality of our estimate had more weeks been simulated. The situation is similar to, but also different from, random sampling from an unknown population. The similarity exists in that a larger number of weeks simulated is analogous to a larger sample size. The difference is that the theory and formulas for random sampling are not directly transferable to the inventory simulation, because the weekly cost figures are not independent observations. That is, the total cost figure in any one week is statistically dependent on those in other weeks. One might expect a negative correlation to exist since low weekly cost figures tend to be associated with low inventory balances, which are sometimes followed in the next week by stockouts that create a high weekly cost. Consequently, because of the correlation, the formulas for simple random sampling are not a perfect fit for our inventory simulation. As a first approximation, however, they frequently can be used in estimating how long to run a simulation in order to achieve a desired degree of precision. More will be said about this topic in Chapter 12.

Analysis for Optimization

In Chapter 1 it was indicated that the purpose of simulation models is *to describe* the system being analyzed; however, by intelligent manipulation of the model, it is sometimes possible to determine points of *optimality*. The Monte Carlo inventory simulation provides a good example. The simulation presented in Table 3.4 was for a $Q = 6$, R = 3 combination. By performing the simulation, one can analyze the cost behavior of the system when an inventory policy of ordering six units whenever the inventory balance fell to three units was followed. Despite this useful information, the simulation still did not reveal what Q and R combination minimizes inventory costs. Only by simulating alternative Q and R combinations can this type of information be gained.

It is useful to visualize the mean weekly cost associated with various Q and R combinations in terms of a response surface, such as that shown in Figure 3.2. Our objective is to find the location of the deepest valley on the surface.

Although it is feasible to simulate one Q and R combination by hand, a computerized analysis becomes almost mandatory when multiple Qs and Rs are to be analyzed. The

Figure 3.2   A cost response surface for alternative Q and R combinations.

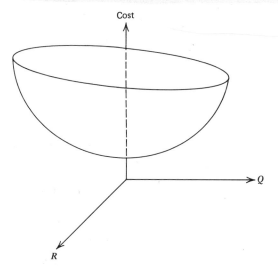

macrologic shown in Figure 3.3 would be appropriate for developing such a computerized model.   After Monte Carlo sampling using the computer is discussed in Chapter 5, an assignment will call for developing a computerized Monte Carlo inventory simulation using the logic of Figure 3.3.   For our example, Table 3.5 presents in matrix form the results of analyzing different Q and R combinations.   The rows in the matrix are the Qs, the columns the Rs, and the matrix elements, the mean weekly cost.   From the matrix it can be seen that for our example a $Q = 10, R = 3$ combination appears optimal.

Note that in developing the cost figures for comparison purposes, the same separate stream of random numbers should be used in sampling from the demand and delivery

Figure 3.3   Macrologic for a Monte Carlo inventory simulation.

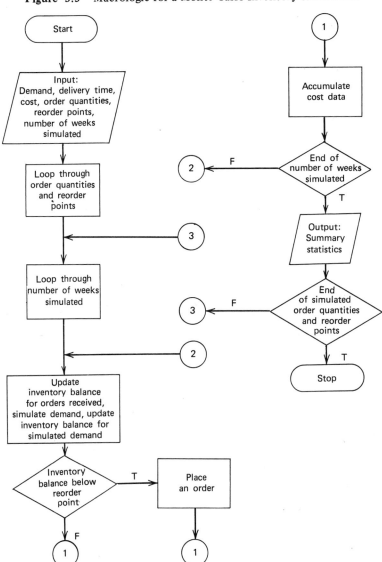

Table 3.5 A MEAN COST MATRIX FOR ALTERNATIVE Q AND R COMBINATIONS

		R			
	1	2	3	4	5
6	22.185	20.76	20.18	20.975	21.465
7	21.415	19.465	18.895	19.56	21.09
8	20.75	19.185	18.935	19.19	19.955
Q 9	20.145	19.315	19.01	19.665	20.27
10	19.56	18.95	18.36	19.635	21.19
11	20.125	18.545	19.57	19.595	21.07
12	20.43	19.14	19.015	20.655	21.01

time distributions. In this way the alternative Q and R combinations are all exposed to the same values for the input variables. This procedure of using the same streams of random numbers for input variables when comparing different configurations of a system or different policy decisions is referred to as *replicating experimental conditions*. This makes it possible to detect differences among alternatives with smaller sample sizes. This subject will be discussed further when correlated sampling is covered in Chapter 12.

Adding Greater Realism

When demand and delivery time were treated as random variables in our Monte Carlo inventory simulation, a more accurate representation of real-world conditions was accomplished. Although a large number of computations was required, all of them were relatively simple to perform. If we are willing to add even more simple computations to our analysis, a still better representation of the real world can be realized.

The Monte Carlo inventory simulation did not include any seasonal demand considerations; every demand level was sampled from the same demand distribution. Obviously, there are many situations where the demand for the inventory item is seasonal. For example, most retail stores experience a heavy demand before and during the Christmas holidays. There is no reason that the same demand (or delivery time) distribution must be used for every week in the simulation. If empirical data or subjective judgment suggests that different distributions are needed for certain times of the year, the simulation framework provides this flexibility without appreciably affecting the complexity of the analysis.

Another real-world possibility is that some of the ordered, incoming items will be defective and, hence, not available for sale or use. In this case it is possible to prepare a probability distribution for the number of defective items in a shipment, and then to sample from this distribution whenever an order arrives. The simulation will reflect the number of items that are actually available for use. Of course, this added realism will increase the number of required computations, but it will not demand any more sophisticated technology than has already been introduced.

As a final example of making our simulation more realistic, consider the possibility of a customer back ordering or, in other words, waiting for an order to arrive after a stockout has occurred. In some instances a customer is willing to back order, depending on factors such as how quickly the item is needed, the availability of alternative suppliers, and so on. If a probability distribution for customers' willingness to back order can be developed, whenever a stockout occurs, the question of whether or not the customer is willing to back order can be simulated and included in the analysis.

From these examples it can be seen that almost any degree of realism can be included in a simulation model. The extent to which a model should capture the richness of the real-world situation depends on, however, many factors, including the intended use of the model, the resources available for model development, the costs of developing, testing and implementing the model, and so on. The major point is that simulation often provides a methodology for modeling complex systems that would be prohibitively difficult or impossible to analyze with alternative approaches.

SUMMARY

Inventory is a quantity of items that are being held for future use by an organization. A primary objective of inventory control is to minimize the cost of maintaining an item in inventory. Inventory costs can be categorized as carrying or holding costs, ordering or setup costs, stockout costs, or purchasing costs. The two fundamental questions that must be answered in inventory control are how many items to order and when should the orders be placed. Solution approaches to these questions depend on whether the inventory item is subject to independent or dependent demand. Materials requirements planning systems are increasingly being used in dependent demand situations. For independent demand, fixed-order quantity and fixed-order period systems are the most popular.

A large number of inventory models have been developed. Most of them are based on simplifying assumptions about the real world. Through standard mathematical techniques such as algebra and differential calculus, cost expressions are manipulated in order to identify optimal order quantities and reorder points. In many instances the resulting models provide effective directional guidance. However, when more realism is desired, the analyst must frequently turn to simulation. A Monte Carlo simulation can be used when key variables such as demand and delivery are expressed probabilistically.

A Monte Carlo inventory simulation describes an inventory system's behavior. In such an analysis, demand, orders placed, orders received, inventory balance, carrying costs, ordering costs, and stockout costs are all simulated.

Simulating probabilistic processes requires the use of the Monte Carlo method. For discrete variables, random numbers are assigned in such a way that the quantity of random numbers assigned to each variable value is proportional to that value's probability of occurrence. Variable values are then sampled by drawing a random number and checking to see which variable value is associated with the random number.

The number of time periods simulated depends on the desired statistical precision. Since the simulated periods of time are not independent observations, the number of weeks simulated is analogous to, but not exactly the same as, the sample size in simple random sampling.

In order to determine points of optimality in a Monte Carlo inventory simulation, one must simulate alternative order quantity and reorder point combinations. The computations required typically demand a computerized analysis.

A simulation model can provide a highly realistic representation of a real-world system. Such a richness of representation is not always possible with an analytic analysis.

ASSIGNMENTS

3.1. In Chapter 1 a classification system for mathematical models was presented. Using this classification system, categorize:
  (a) The fixed-order quantity model.
  (b) The Monte Carlo inventory simulation.

3.2. Williams Hardware is interested in determining the optimal order quantity and reorder point for hammers. Annual demand is 200 hammers per year. Carrying costs are $2 per hammer per year. Ordering costs are $10 per order.
  (a) How many hammers should be ordered at a time?
  (b) If the lead time is two weeks, what should be the reorder point?
  (c) What are the average total annual costs of carrying hammers in inventory?

3.3. The Monte Carlo inventory simulation presented in Table 3.4 drew its demand and delivery time random numbers from columns 1 to 2 and 3 to 4, respectively, of Appendix A. Repeat the simulation in every detail, except now use different random numbers for demand and delivery time. Compare the mean weekly cost figures for the two simulations.

3.4. The Monte Carlo inventory simulation discussed in the text and presented in Table 3.4 employed a "no multiple ordering" policy, wherein no new orders were placed when an order was still outstanding. Repeat the simulation presented in Table 3.4 in every detail, except now place a new order any week the inventory balance is equal to or below the reorder point. Compare the mean weekly cost figures for the two policies.

3.5. Management wants to determine the optimal order quantity and reorder point for an inventory item using the Monte Carlo simulation approach. The following data are available: $K_c = \$1/\text{week}/\text{item}$; $K_o = \$20/\text{order}$; $K_s = \$20/\text{item}$ demanded and not on hand.

Demand per Week	Frequency	Delivery Time, in weeks	Frequency
2	20	1	5
3	20	2	4
4	8	3	1
5	2		
	50		10

Simulate 20 weeks of activity using a $Q = 6$ and $R = 4$ combination. Do not "multiple order"; that is, do not place a new order until all previously placed orders have been received. Compute the mean weekly cost for the $Q = 6$ and $R = 4$ combination.

3.6. Historically, a company has had the following experience with an item carried in inventory.

Demand per Week	Frequency
0	10
1	10
2	25
3	$\dfrac{5}{50}$

Delivery Time, in weeks	Frequency
1	5
2	3
3	$\dfrac{2}{10}$

Number of Unusable Items Received in Ordered Shipment	Frequency
0	8
1	$\dfrac{2}{10}$

The following cost data are available: K_c = \$3/week/item; K_o = \$20/order; K_s = \$30/item demanded and not on hand. Simulate a $Q = 5$ and $R = 3$ combination for 20 weeks of simulated activity. Do not "multiple order." Compute the mean weekly costs for the $Q = 5$ and $R = 3$ combination.

3.7. Old Joe buys doughnuts each morning to sell in the lobby of a large office building. Each dozen doughnuts sold nets Joe \$1.20. Unsold doughnuts can be returned to the bakery, but at a net loss of \$0.60 per dozen. How many dozen doughnuts should Joe buy each morning if the demand for doughnuts is as shown in the following table? Base your analysis on 30 days of simulated activity, buying 12, 13, 14, 15, or 16 dozen doughnuts each day. Replicate experimental conditions as much as possible.

Demand, dozens	Probability
12	.05
13	.20
14	.40
15	.25
16	$\dfrac{.10}{1.00}$

3.8. During the summer a student sells individual roses at a neighborhood shopping center for $1 a rose. She buys the roses from a local florist in lots of a dozen for $8 per dozen. The demand for the roses varies with the weather. On a sunny day the demand is good, whereas on a cloudy or rainy day less people are interested in buying flowers. Unfortunately, it has proven very difficult to forecast whether particular days will be sunny, and orders for flowers to the florist must be turned in several days in advance. The demand for roses on the two types of days is as follows.

Sunny Day		Cloudy or Rainy Day	
Demand, dozens	Probability	Demand, dozens	Probability
6	.10	3	.05
7	.20	4	.15
8	.45	5	.40
9	.25	6	.25
	1.00	7	.15
			1.00

During the summer 75 percent of the days are historically sunny, whereas the other 25 percent are cloudy or rainy. If unsold roses must be thrown away at the close of the day, how many dozen roses should be purchased each day? Base your analysis on 20 days of simulated activity buying 6, 7, 8, or 9 dozen roses each day. Replicate experimental conditions as much as possible.

3.9. In some situations it is difficult to estimate the cost of a stockout. Instead, management specifies some minimum service level. With this approach, some maximum probability of being out of stock is established. The problem is then to find the optimal order quantity and reorder point that satisfies the minimum service level. Describe in detail how this might be done using a Monte Carlo inventory simulation.

3.10. In Chapter 1 it was stated, "Although simulation models are not directly used for optimization purposes, through intelligent and systematic investigation, it is sometimes possible to learn under what conditions a system operates most effectively and efficiently." How does this concept apply to a Monte Carlo inventory simulation?

REFERENCES

Adam, Everette E., Jr., and Ronald J. Ebert, *Production and Operations Management* (Englewood Cliffs, N.J.: Prentice-Hall, 1978).

Buffa, Elwood S., *Modern Production Management*, 5th ed. (New York: Wiley, 1977).

Chase, Richard B., and Nicholas J. Aquilano, *Production and Operations Management*, rev. ed. (Homewood, Ill.: Irwin, 1980).

Dilworth, James B., *Production and Operations Management* (New York: Random House, 1979).

Gallagher, Charles A., and Hugh J. Watson, *Quantitative Methods for Business Decisions* (New York: McGraw-Hill, 1980).

Hillier, Frederick S. and Gerald J. Lieberman, *Operations Research*, 2nd ed. (San Francisco: Holden-Day, 1974).

Lauffer, Arthur C., *Operations Management* (Cincinnati: South-Western, 1979).

Orlicky, J., *Material Requirements Planning* (New York: McGraw-Hill, 1975).

Peterson, Clifford C., "Simulation of an Inventory System," *Industrial Engineering* (June 1973): 35–44.

Plossl, G. W., and O. W. Wright, *Production and Inventory Control* (Englewood Cliffs, N.J.: Prentice-Hall, 1967).

Rand Corporation, *A Million Random Digits with 100,000 Normal Deviates* (Glencoe, Ill.: The Free Press, 1955).

Shore, Barry, *Operations Management* (New York: McGraw-Hill, 1974).

Tersine, Richard J., *Materials Management and Inventory Systems* (New York: North Holland, 1976).

Tersine, Richard J., *Production/Operations Management* (New York: North Holland, 1980).

CHAPTER FOUR

PROBABILISTIC FINANCIAL PLANNING

Financial Planning Generations

First-Generation Financial Planning

Second-Generation Financial Planning

Third-Generation Financial Planning

    The Analytic Mode

    The Numeric Mode

Probabilistic Estimates

A Monte Carlo Method

An Analysis Format

The Analysis

Statistical Analysis of the Output

Computerized Financial Planning Models

Simulation or Model Sampling

A Final Consideration of Financial Planning
Generations

Summary

Assignments

References

In most organizations, especially larger ones, financial planning is a well-established management practice. It is part of the technology that has been developed to assist management in planning and controlling the operations of today's increasingly complex organizations. Without financial planning, it would be virtually impossible to project resource requirements for various organizational undertakings, ensure that scarce resources are being allocated in an appropriate and efficient manner, and control the use of resources in light of plans that have been made. Financial planning adds more science to the art and science mix, which constitutes contemporary management practice.

Today's students of business administration often tend to take for granted the role, use, and importance of financial planning documents such as cash budgets, pro forma income statements and balance sheets, and capital expenditure budgets. It is sometimes difficult to conceive that such financial statements have not always been an integral component of business practice. However, a look at history reveals that comprehensive financial planning is a relatively recent phenomenon.

FINANCIAL PLANNING GENERATIONS

Financial planning, as it has evolved and is currently practiced, varies from rudimentary manual to highly sophisticated computer-based systems. The differences in these systems are sufficiently great to make it useful to think of them in terms of different financial planning generations.[1]

Taking this generations approach to financial planning, *the first generation* can be thought of as *traditional line item budgeting.* With this approach, deterministic estimates are input for the items in the planning document, which in turn are appropriately combined to provide the desired "bottom line" estimate.

Second-generation financial planning sees the introduction of mathematical models to predict the value for the items in the planning document. The analysis is still deterministic, however, in that single-valued estimates are input for the independent variables in the mathematical models, single-valued estimates for the budget items are generated, and a single-valued bottom line figure is ultimately obtained by combining the estimates generated by the models.

Third-generation financial planning can take the basic structure of either first- or second-generation planning, but the analysis switches from being deterministic to being probabilistic. With this approach, probabilistic estimates are input, processed, and a probabilistic estimate is generated for the final item of interest.

This chapter will review and illustrate all three of the financial planning generations, but the third generation will command the majority of our attention, because it is this generation that most fully draws on simulation technology. By the close of the chapter, you should have a greater appreciation and understanding of financial planning systems and be familiar with more of the technology that constitutes the field of simulation. Our progression begins with first-generation financial planning.

---

[1] This conceptualization is used in James E. Walters and Hugh J. Watson, "Building a Budget: 3 Generations," *Hospital Financial Management* (September 1977): 10–17.

Table 4.1   A TRADITIONAL LINE ITEM BUDGET FOR A MEDICAL-SURGICAL DEPARTMENT

Salary and wages	$17,000
Payroll taxes and benefits	1300
Operating supplies	600
Laundry and linen	1300
Dietary transfers	200
Education and travel	100
Maintenance of equipment	100
Equipment rental	300
Total expense	$20,900

FIRST-GENERATION FINANCIAL PLANNING

As previously indicated, first-generation financial planning is associated with what is typically referred to as line item budgeting. With this planning approach, estimates are made for the items in the budget, and these estimates are then combined to obtain the desired financial estimate. The budget shown in Table 4.1 for the Medical-Surgical Department of a hospital provides a good case in point. Single-valued estimates are made for budget items, such as salary and wages, payroll taxes and benefits, and operating supplies. These inputs are then summed to estimate total expenses.

Traditional line item budgeting is without a doubt the most popular form of financial planning in use today. For most managers the basic concepts are easy to grasp, data input and processing requirements are easily satisfied, output from the analysis is useful to management, and the entire process is cost effective.

Despite the popularity and merits of traditional line budgeting, it does have its limitations, which, as a consequence, have led to the development of more sophisticated approaches. One of these approaches involves the use of mathematical models to estimate budget items. This approach to financial planning forms the second generation.

SECOND-GENERATION FINANCIAL PLANNING

Traditional line item budgeting requires the manager to analyze possible interactions among key planning variables subjectively. For example, in the Medical-Surgical Department budget shown in Table 4.1 there is no explicit expression of the relationship between operating supplies and the level of activity within the hospital. In a hospital environment this activity level is commonly expressed in patient-days; that is, the total number of days spent by patients in the hospital. Several of the budget items obviously increase or decrease with rises and falls in patient-days or other explanatory variables. The omission of functional relationships of this type in most budgeting formats requires the manager to add this consideration to his or her already uncertain perception of the future.

A way around the problem of functional relationships among key planning variables is to develop mathematical models that capture and reflect the relationships. For example, consider the models presented in Table 4.2.

As can be seen, many of the budget items (salary and wages, payroll taxes and benefits, etc.) are predicted through a fixed component and variable components related to patient-days and time. The large fixed components reflect what many researchers and administrators have discovered—a large percentage of hospital costs are fixed relative to patient loads. Even the time component reflects the heavy impact fixed costs have on hospital administration, because the time component is included to account for the increase in fixed costs over time. And third, the patient-days' component reflects the impact that patient load has on the Medical-Surgical Department's expenses. These three considerations, (1) fixed costs, (2) increases in fixed costs over time, and (3) cost activity related to patient-days, are used to generate the monthly forecasts for many of the budget items.

The remaining budget items reflect various other types of functional relationships. For example, education and travel is a controllable variable, which is completely within management's discretion. That is, management can allocate funds for education and travel at any desired level. Hence, it is not predicted by an independent variable. In our example, equipment rental is set at $300, which reflects a contractual obligation the department has for the rental of a particular piece of equipment. Equipment maintenance has been found to be related only to time, not to patient-days, and the mathematical model reflects this fact.

The technology for the development of mathematical models, as shown in Table 4.2, is well established and covered in other management science courses. For example, the models that include time or patient-days (or other similar variables) can be determined through the least-squares method of regression analysis. Not so simple an undertaking is

Table 4.2 MATHEMATICAL MODELS FOR A MEDICAL-SURGICAL DEPARTMENT

Salary and wages = $14,000 + 3.00 $\times$ patient-days + 100 $\times$ time

Payroll taxes and benefits = 1000 + .30 $\times$ patient-days + 10 $\times$ time

Operating supplies = 400 + .20 $\times$ patient-days + 5 $\times$ time

Laundry and linen = 800 + .45 $\times$ patient-days + 10 $\times$ time

Dietary transfers = 100 + .10 $\times$ patient-days + 1.00 $\times$ time

Education and travel = education and travel

Maintenance of equipment = 100 + 5 $\times$ time

Equipment rental = 300

**Table 4.3   A FINANCIAL FORECAST FOR THE
MEDICAL-SURGICAL DEPARTMENT**

Salary and wages = $14,000 + 3.00(924) + 100(2)	= $16,972
Payroll taxes and benefits = 1000 + .30(924) + 10(2) =	1297
Operating supplies = 400 + .20(924) + 5(2)	= 595
Laundry and linen = 800 + .45(924) + 10(2)	= 1236
Dietary transfers = 100 + .10(924) + 1(2)	= 194
Education and travel	= 100
Maintenance of equipment = 100 + 5(2)	= 110
Equipment rental	= 300
Total expense	$20,804

---

determining which variables should be used in helping predict the budget items and in obtaining good data for developing the models.

Let us now consider how the mathematical models of Table 4.2 are used to predict total expense. The first requirement is to develop an estimate of patient-days for the planning period. Based on additional models and/or management's subjective beliefs, an estimate, for example, of 924 days is obtained. Furthermore, we will assume that for the planning period being investigated, "time" has a value of 2. The value for time depends on how the time periods were numbered when the mathematical models were developed. The time and the patient-days' predictions are then used to "drive" the mathematical models of Table 4.2, because these factors have been found, through previous analysis, to have the greatest impact on expenses in the Medical-Surgical Department. The total expense forecast for the department is shown in Table 4.3.

Although the mathematical modeling approach to financial planning helps account for important functional relationships among variables, it still does not quantify the administrator's uncertainty about the future. That is, the administrator is not able to make probabilistic statements about the future. The ability to make such statements requires a switch from deterministic to probabilistic financial planning methods and takes us into third-generation financial planning.

THIRD-GENERATION FINANCIAL PLANNING

In their attempts to describe systems of interest better, business organizations have been increasingly turning to probabilistic methods of analysis in order to capture the uncertainty that so frequently exists in real-world situations. Such is the case with financial planning, where it is difficult to predict the future with certainty. By employing a probabilistic method of analysis, one can disclose the nature and extent of real-world uncertainty.

Both analytic and numeric modes of analysis are used in probabilistic financial planning. As indicated in Chapter 1, the *analytic mode* employs standard mathematical and statistical techniques, whereas the *numeric mode* substitutes for these frequently complex techniques a large number of simple numerical computations. Let us now consider these two approaches to financial planning.

The Analytic Mode

The analytic approach to probabilistic financial planning typically draws on a set of formulas in order to describe the result of combining probability distributions according to standard mathematical operations. For example, assume that we want to estimate total cost by adding together fixed and variable cost estimates.

$$\text{Total cost} = \text{fixed cost} + \text{total variable cost} \qquad (4\text{-}1)$$

Furthermore, assume that we have a fixed cost estimate that is normally distributed with a mean of $100,000 and a standard deviation of $9000, and a total variable cost estimate that is normally distributed with a mean of $150,000 and a standard deviation of $20,000. The question is, what can be said about the estimate for total cost?

The theory of the linear combination of variables tells us when two statistically independent probability distributions are summed, the resultant distribution has a mean and a variance equal to the sum of the means and variances of the added distributions. Expressed symbolically,

$$\mu_{A+B} = \mu_A + \mu_B \qquad (4\text{-}2)$$

$$\sigma_{A+B}^2 = \sigma_A^2 + \sigma_B^2 \qquad (4\text{-}3)$$

For our example, then, we can say that

$$\mu_{\text{Total cost}} = \$100,000 + 150,000$$

$$= \$250,000$$

$$\sigma_{\text{Total cost}}^2 = (\$9000)^2 + (20,000)^2$$

$$\sigma_{\text{Total cost}} = \sqrt{(9000)^2 + (20,000)^2}$$

$$\cong \$21,932$$

From statistics we also know that when two normally distributed variables are summed, the resultant distribution is also normally distributed. Consequently, based on our analysis, we can say that our total cost estimate is normally distributed with a mean of $250,000 and a standard deviation of $21,932. This information allows us to make probabilistic statements about what total costs might be. For example, we can say that there is a 95 percent chance that total costs will be between $207,013 and $292,987; see Figure 4.1.

For the simple total cost analysis just presented, the analytic mode of analysis is not difficult to understand and apply. Springer et al. provides an excellent presentation of the analytic approach to probabilistic financial planning, including a summary table, repeated in Table 4.4, of formulas for the basic mathematical operations.[2]

For simple probabilistic financial planning the analytic approach is strongly advocated because of its minimal cost and absence of sampling error. However, in more complex financial planning situations, it may be necessary to turn to a numeric mode of analysis.

[2] Clifford Springer *et al.*, *Probabilistic Models* (Homewood, Ill.: Irwin, 1968), pp. 101–134.

Figure 4.1   Probabilistically adding fixed and variable costs to estimate total cost.

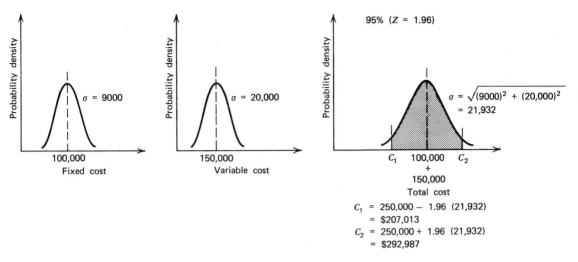

$$C_1 = 250,000 - 1.96 \ (21,932)$$
$$= \$207,013$$
$$C_2 = 250,000 + 1.96 \ (21,932)$$
$$= \$292,987$$

For example, a dividend policy that calls for no dividends until a prespecified income level is reached is easily accommodated in a numeric analysis but is difficult to include in an analytic analysis because the dividend policy requires processing a step function. In this case, even though an analytic analysis of the problem would be preferred, the complexity of the real-world system being investigated probably demands a numeric analysis.

The Numeric Mode

A numeric approach to probabilistic financial planning is normally required when employing sophisticated planning formats. The available technology is such that the analyst can build an almost unlimited amount of detail into the investigation without making the analysis intractable. We will examine some of the numeric technology by continuing with our Medical-Surgical Department example.

Table 4.4   FORMULAS FOR COMBINING PROBABILISTIC VARIABLES

Function	Mean	Variance[a]
Sum $(x + y)$	$\mu_x + \mu_y$	$\sigma_x^2 + \sigma_y^2 + 2r\sigma_x\sigma_y$
Difference $(x - y)$	$\mu_x - \mu_y$	$\sigma_x^2 + \sigma_y^2 - 2r\sigma_x\sigma_y$
Product $(x \cdot y)$	$\mu_x\mu_y + r_{xy}\sigma_x\sigma_y$	$\mu_y^2\sigma_x^2 + \mu_x^2\sigma_y^2 + 2\mu_x\mu_y r\sigma_x\sigma_y$ [b]
Quotient (x/y)	μ_x/μ_y [b]	$\left(\dfrac{1}{\mu_y}\right)^2 \sigma_x^2 + \left(-\dfrac{\mu_x^2}{\mu_y^2}\right)^2 \sigma_y^2 + 2\left(\dfrac{1}{\mu_y}\right)\left(-\dfrac{\mu_x}{\mu_y^2}\right)r\sigma_x\sigma_y$ [b]

[a] r is the correlation coefficient between x and y;
[b] approximate for both independent and dependent x and y

When used deterministically, the mathematical models of Table 4.2 are illustrative of second-generation financial planning. With some modifications, these same models can be used for third-generation probabilistic financial planning. It is possible, however, to employ simpler first-generation planning formats such as shown in Table 4.1, but as previously indicated, relationships between key planning variables are not explicitly expressed. Consequently, for our example, we will make use of a modified version of the mathematical models of Table 4.2.

PROBABILISTIC ESTIMATES

In order to perform probabilistic financial planning (and other types of probabilistic analyses), probabilistic data inputs are required. These inputs are typically supplied by the individual or individuals who are in the best position to provide probabilistic estimates for the variables included in the analysis. Frequently, however, this is more easily said than done, because most individuals are not accustomed to expressing their beliefs about the future in probabilistic terms. Consequently, the analyst must assume a strong role in assisting the manager in preparing and expressing his or her beliefs about the likelihood of future events. Peter Drucker has described what the management scientist can and should expect of the manager.[3]

> To demand of any (management science) tool user that he understand what goes into the making of the tool is admission of incompetence on the part of the tool maker. The tool user, provided the tool is made well, need not, and indeed should not know anything about the tool.

Drucker's statement, taken out of context, might seem rather strong, but it does properly emphasize the role the analyst must often play in applying management science technology.

In our Monte Carlo inventory simulation of Chapter 3 the probabilities were obtained from relative frequencies of past experiences. However, in probabilistic financial planning, many, if not most, of the probabilities will be a reflection of the manager's subjective beliefs. For the manager these are usually the most difficult probabilities to express, and thus pose the greatest challenge to the analyst.

In response to this problem, many methods have been suggested for obtaining probabilistic estimates, ranging from fast, simple approaches to those requiring a skilled interviewer following a highly structured procedure.[4] The approach presented here was suggested by Alderson and Green and involves some structure, is reasonably easy to understand and apply, and seems to produce usable estimates.[5] As an illustration, let us develop a probabilistic estimate for patient-days for use in our hospital example.

---

[3]Peter F. Drucker, *Management* (New York: Harper & Row, 1974), pp. 512–513.

[4]For a simple approach, see Ted F. Anthony and Hugh J. Watson, "Probabilistic Financial Planning," *Journal of Systems Management* (September 1972): 38–41. A more complex procedure is described in Carl S. Spetzler and Carl-Axel S. Stael von Holstein, "Probability Encoding in Decision Analysis," *Management Science* (November 1975): 340–358.

[5]Wroe Alderson and Paul E. Green, *Planning and Problem Solving in Marketing* (Homewood, Ill.: Irwin, 1964), pp. 217–223.

The analysis begins by asking the following questions.

1. What is your most probable estimate of patient-days for the time period under consideration?
2. In line with your best judgment, what probability would you assign to patient-days being equal to or less than that indicated in question 1?
3. Supposing that patient-days decline, at what level do you believe there is only a .10 probability that patient-days will be equal to or less than this level?
4. Now suppose that patient-days increase. At what level do you believe there is a .90 probability that patient-days will be equal to or less than this level?

Assuming that the answers to these four questions are 900, .40, 850, and 1000, respectively, Figure 4.2 is prepared. The points resulting from the questioning procedure can be thought of as most likely, most pessimistic, and most optimistic estimates, respectively. Equidistant points are next plotted between the most pessimistic and most likely estimates, and between the most likely and most optimistic estimates. Then question 5 is asked.

5. What is the probability patient-days will be equal to or less than the points which have just been plotted?

Assuming that probabilities of .25 and .75 are associated with the two equidistant points (875 and 950 patient-days, respectively), the curve shown in Figure 4.3 results from drawing a smooth line through the five points.

Figure 4.2   Points for a cumulative probability distribution for patient-days.

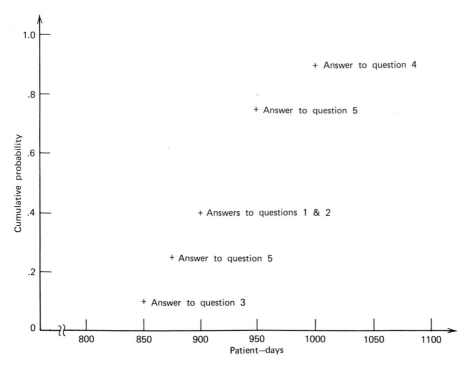

Figure 4.3   A cumulative probability distribution for patient-days.

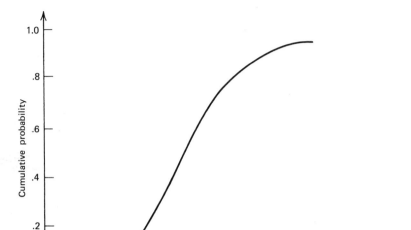

The questioning procedure just described produces a set of data inputs that can be used for the creation of an equal to or less than cumulative probability distribution. Using the curve, one can determine the probability that patient-days will be equal to or less than any particular value. By asking even more questions and, hence, obtaining additional points, the curve can be more carefully described. Furthermore, the additional points can be used to verify the internal consistency of previous estimates.

Some additional comments about Figure 4.3 are in order. First, the variable under study, patient-days, is *continuous* rather than *discrete*. That is, patient-days can take on an infinite instead of a finite number of values. Consequently, sampling from the patient-days' distribution requires a different technology from that used with the discrete demand and delivery time distributions of Chapter 3, because it is impossible to associate a set of random numbers with an infinite number of possible variable values. Also, as we will see, Monte Carlo sampling from continuous distributions normally requires the probabilistic variable to be expressed in cumulative form, which makes our method for obtaining probabilistic estimates quite appropriate. Let us now consider how we will sample from the patient-days' distribution in our probabilistic financial planning example.

MONTE CARLO SAMPLING

In order to sample a value from a continuous probability distribution, one should proceed using the following steps.

1.   Draw a random number, r, that can take on values such that $0 \leq r < 1$.
2.   Treat the random number as a cumulative probability, $r = P(x)$.

3. Find the value from the sampled distribution that corresponds to the cumulative probability.

Just as it was possible to obtain integer random numbers from Appendix A, we can obtain random numbers such that $0 \leq r < 1$. It is necessary, however, for the user mentally to impute a decimal point before the random numbers found. For example, the first numbers in columns 1 to 2 of Appendix A are 69, which are interpreted as 0.69. The careful reader might note that the possibility of $r = 1.00$ has been lost, but this is not critical because, theoretically at least, there are an infinite number of variable values and the loss of one does not create a significant distortion.

Let us now explore how we would sample a value from the cumulative probability distribution for patient-days presented in Figure 4.3. After drawing, for example, the random number 0.39, we would treat it as a cumulative probability and locate its position on the vertical axis. We would then move across to the curve and down to the horizontal axis where the sampled value 894 is found.

AN ANALYSIS FORMAT

As mentioned earlier, our example of the numeric approach to probabilistic financial planning will draw on a modified version of the mathematical models of Table 4.2. These models are shown in Table 4.5.

The most striking difference between Tables 4.2 and 4.5 is the replacement of the constants and coefficients with variables; for example, $14,000, $3 and $100 with fixed salary and wages, variable salary and wages, and variable time$_1$, respectively. Whereas in a

Table 4.5 MODIFIED MATHEMATICAL MODELS FOR A MEDICAL-SURGICAL DEPARTMENT

Salary and wages = fixed salary and wages + variable salary and wages $\times$ patient-days
    + variable time$_1$ $\times$ time

Payroll taxes and benefits = fixed payroll taxes and benefits + variable payroll taxes and
    benefits $\times$ patient-days + variable time$_2$ $\times$ time

Operating supplies = fixed operating supplies + variable operating supplies $\times$ patient-days
    + variable time$_3$ $\times$ time

Laundry and linen = fixed laundry and linen + variable laundry and linen $\times$ patient-days
    + variable time$_4$ $\times$ time

Dietary transfers = fixed dietary transfers + variable dietary transfers $\times$ patient-days
    + variable time$_5$ $\times$ time

Education and travel = education and travel

Maintenance of equipment = fixed maintenance of equipment + variable time$_6$ $\times$ time

Equipment rental = equipment rental

---

deterministic analysis a point estimate can be used for the constants and coefficients, in a probabilistic analysis the constants and coefficients must be treated probabilistically unless they can be closely estimated. Take salary and wages as an example. From least-squares analysis it might be learned that salary and wages are best estimated with a fixed component of $14,000 and variable components of $3 and $100 as coefficients for variable patient-days and time, respectively. But these are only least squares estimates, and unless the error terms are equal to zero, there is no reason to assume they are known with certainty. Therefore they must be treated as probabilistic variables and given variable names. Throughout Table 4.5, variable names are given to what were previously constants and coefficients.

THE ANALYSIS

As has been indicated, the modified mathematical models in Table 4.5 will be used to illustrate the numeric approach to third generation financial planning. As was the case with the deterministic illustration of the use of the models, the assumption will be that the variable "time" has a value of 2. The analysis is presented on the work sheet of Table 4.6.

The first item in the planning document, salary and wages, is functionally related to a fixed component, a variable component involving patient-days, and a time-related component. In order to estimate salary and wages, values must be sampled from the fixed salary and wages, variable salary and wages, patient-days, and variable $time_1$ distributions. The sampling requires that cumulative probability distributions (similar to the one for patient-days in Figure 4.3) be specified for all of the independent variables. However, only the patient-days distribution is shown here, since the sampling from the other distributions is exactly analogous. In our example, we will draw our random numbers in groups of two across the top of Appendix A.

The first four random numbers read from the top of Appendix A are 0.69, 0.64, 0.69, and 0.03. These numbers are entered on to the work sheet of Table 4.6 for use in the analysis. Each of these random numbers is then treated as a cumulative probability in order to find the sampled value. For example, the third random number, 0.69, is associated with 940 patient-days, as can be seen by examining the cumulative probability distribution for patient-days (Figure 4.3). The four sampled values used in estimating salary and wages are shown on the work sheet. When the sampled values and the salary and wages model from Table 4.5 are used, salary and wages are computed to be $17,097.

Salary and wages = fixed salary and wages

+ variable salary and wages $\times$ patient-days

+ variable $time_1$ $\times$ time

= $14,190 + 3.07(940) + 51(2)$

= $17,097

Table 4.6 A WORK SHEET FOR PROBABILISTICALLY ESTIMATING THE EXPENSES OF A MEDICAL-SURGICAL DEPARTMENT

	First Iteration			...	Two-hundredth Iteration		
	Random Number	Sampled Value	Calculated Cost, dollars		Random Number	Sampled Value	Calculated Cost, dollars
Salary and wages							
Fixed salary and wages	0.69	14,910	14,190		0.58	14,080	14,080
Variable salary and wages	0.64	3.07 +	3.07(940) +		0.67	3.08 +	3.08(901) +
Patient-days	0.69	940 +	51(2)		0.26	901 +	87(2)
Variable time$_1$	0.03	51	= 17,097		0.29	97	= 17,029
Payroll taxes and benefits							
Fixed payroll taxes and benefits	0.12	974	974		0.86	1051	1051
Variable payroll taxes and benefits	0.78	0.324 +	0.324(940) +		0.66	0.313 +	.313(901) +
Variable time$_2$	0.61	10.7 +	10.7(2) +		0.29	8.7 +	8.7(2) +
			= 1300				= 1350
Operating supplies							
Fixed operating supplies	0.21	384	384		0.09	364	364
Variable operating supplies	0.62	0.214 +	0.214(940) +		0.29	0.183 +	0.183(901) +
Variable time$_3$	0.26	4.04 +	4.04(2) +		0.27	4.08 +	4.08(2) +
			= 593				= 537
Laundry and linen							
Fixed laundry and linen	0.82	850	850		0.44	795	795
Variable laundry and linen	0.08	0.369 +	0.369(940) +		0.56	0.462 +	0.462(901) +
Variable time$_4$	0.33	9.32 +	9.32(2) +		0.35	9.40 +	9.40(2) +
			= 1216				= 1230
Dietary transfers							
Fixed dietary transfers	0.72	107	107		0.84	112	112
Variable dietary transfers	0.53	0.101 +	0.101(940) +		0.66	0.106 +	0.106(901) +
Variable time$_5$	0.17	0.948 +	0.948(2) +		0.12	0.934 +	0.934(2) +
			= 204				= 209
Education and travel			= 100				= 100
Maintenance of Equipment							
Fixed maintenance of equipment	0.87	119	119		0.25	94	94
Variable time$_6$	0.12	3.48 +	3.48(2) +		0.26	4.04 +	4.04(2) +
			= 126				= 102
Equipment rental	0.76	450	450		0.49	300	300
			$21,086				$20,857

The analysis described to this point is shown under the first iteration heading of Table 4.6. Each "run," "pass," or "time through the model" is commonly referred to as an *iteration.*

The next item in the budget, payroll taxes and benefits, is also functionally related to a fixed component, a variable component involving patient-days, and a time-related component. Using the previously sampled value for patient-days (940), once again a value of 2 for time, and sampled values for fixed payroll taxes and benefits, variable payroll taxes and benefits, and variable $time_2$, one can estimate payroll taxes and benefits. Table 4.6 shows this estimate to be $1300.

Operating supplies, laundry and linen, and dietary transfers are similar to the first two budget items and are computed in an analogous manner to be $593, $1216, and $204, respectively.

The next budget item, education and travel, is treated in our example as a discretionary variable, that is, one that can be set at any desired level by management. Let us assume it has been decided by management to allocate $100 for education and travel and that there is no doubt the total allocated amount will be spent. Consequently, a value of $100 is entered on the work sheet for education and travel.

The maintenance of equipment has been found to be functionally related to a fixed component and time. After sampling values from the fixed maintenance of equipment and variable $time_6$ distributions, its value is computed to be $126.

Equipment rental is the last budget item requiring an estimate. As previously discussed, equipment rental is the result of a fixed contractual agreement. However, let us assume that the equipment rental contract is expiring and we believe there is a 50 to 50 chance that the new contract will require monthly payments of $450 instead of $300. Equipment rental must be treated as a probabilistic variable in order to capture this uncertainty.

The discrete probability distribution for equipment rental can be sampled by employing the Monte Carlo method discussed in Chapter 3. An alternative, however, is to create a cumulative probability distribution for the variable and sample from it using the methods described in this chapter. A cumulative probability distribution for equipment rental is presented in Figure 4.4. The curve shows a discontinuity at a cumulative probability of .50 where the value for equipment rental switches from $300 to $450, reflecting the probabilities that are involved.

Figure 4.4   A cumulative probability distribution for equipment rental.

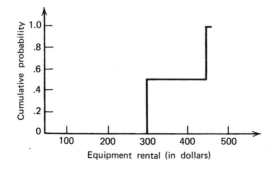

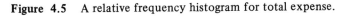

Figure 4.5   A relative frequency histogram for total expense.

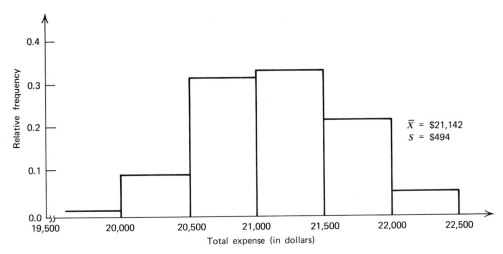

Let us now sample from the equipment rental distribution. After drawing a random number, 0.76 in this case, and examining Figure 4.4, it can be seen that this random number is associated with an equipment rental expense of $450. This figure and the random number used are entered on the work sheet of Table 4.6.

Given estimates for all of the budget items, they can be totaled to provide an estimate of total expense, the item of primary concern and focus of attention in our analysis. A cost figure of $21,086 for total expense is the result of our first iteration.

Quite obviously, however, if different random numbers had been used, different estimates for most of the budget items would have resulted. In order to explore the possible values for total expense more fully, many additional runs through the model must be performed. Table 4.6 shows the results of the first and the two-hundredth iteration. Implied in the numbering of the iterations is the existence of more iterations. Indeed, this is the case, and Figure 4.5 presents a relative frequency histogram for all 200 of the total expense figures generated.

The probabilistic output provides useful information for planning purposes. A close examination of Figure 4.5 shows, for example, that the probability that total expense will be between $20,500 and $21,000 is .315, and the probability that total expense will be greater than $21,500 is .27(.22 + .05). This information allows management to plan for possible expense levels in light of their probability of occurrence. This type of information is not available with deterministic methods of analysis.

STATISTICAL ANALYSIS OF THE OUTPUT

Based on the 200 iterations, a sample mean and standard deviation were computed. These were found to be $21,142 and $494, respectively. Unlike the Monte Carlo inventory simulation where correlated output made the statistical analysis of the output difficult, our example does not pose an analysis problem, because each total expense estimate is an

Figure 4.6   A 95% confidence interval for the mean total expense estimate.

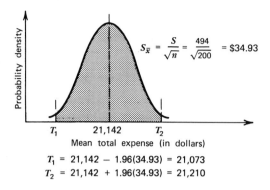

$$S_{\bar{x}} = \frac{S}{\sqrt{n}} = \frac{494}{\sqrt{200}} = \$34.93$$

T_1 21,142 T_2
Mean total expense (in dollars)

T_1 = 21,142 − 1.96(34.93) = 21,073
T_2 = 21,142 + 1.96(34.93) = 21,210

independent observation. For example, we can prepare a confidence interval for mean total expense by drawing on the theory of simple random sampling. A 95 percent confidence interval for mean total expense is shown in Figure 4.6 and ranges from $21,073 – $21,210. The analysis reflects the fact that the sampling distribution for the mean is normally distributed with large sample sizes and has a mean equal to the mean of the population and a standard error of the mean equal to the population standard deviation divided by the square root of the sample size.

The analysis of total expense was arbitrarily based on 200 iterations, rather than on a prior statement of the degree of statistical precision desired. Since our model was quite simple, it was reasonable to set the number of iterations quite high and not worry about computation time. With larger models, this approach is not very desirable. Consequently, for models with high computation time associated with each iteration, it is best to state the degree of confidence desired and the allowed amount of error, estimate the population standard deviation, and solve for the required number of iterations. This may be recognized as the sample size determination problem of simple random sampling, which will be more fully discussed, along with other related considerations, in Chapter 12. To do so now would take us off our present purpose of introducing basic simulation technology and applications.

COMPUTERIZED FINANCIAL PLANNING MODELS

The information presented in Figures 4.5 and 4.6 is the result of a computerized rather than a hand-performed analysis. Even with the simple example presented here, a manual analysis would have been tedious and time consuming. Considering that financial simulations are commonly used to experiment with many different scenerios, it is not surprising that most financial planning systems are computerized.

During the past few years a number of special-purpose languages for financial planning have been developed. Some of the better known ones are SIMPLAN, BUDPLAN, and IFPS. They have built-in features that greatly facilitate the development of financial planning models.

It is not appropriate here to present the computerized model that was developed for the probabilistic financial simulation, because the technology for sampling from prob-

Figure 4.7   Macrologic for probabilistic financial planning.

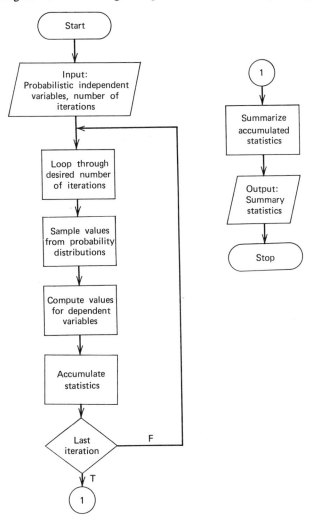

ability distributions in a computerized model will first be discussed in Chapter 5. A flow-chart for the program's logic is shown, however, in Figure 4.7. After the next chapter has been studied, an assignment will call for developing a computerized model using the flow-chart's logic.

SIMULATION OR MODEL SAMPLING

The probabilistic analysis that has been illustrated employed a numeric rather than an analytic mode of analysis. Not mentioned, however, was whether or not it was a simulation. Let us now address this interesting question.

In the strictest sense, the analysis just performed is best classified as *model sampling*, because through multiple sampling trials the characteristics of a probability distribution of interest (total expense) were learned. The analysis did not analyze the behavior of a system over time and, consequently, was not truly a simulation, even though the sampling technology was exactly the same as that used in a probabilistic simulation.

Suppose, however, the analysis was a component of a larger modeling effort. For example, assume we are interested in estimating total expenses in the Medical-Surgical Department over several time periods. Specifically, we might want to sum the individual total expense estimates for each planning period in order to obtain a grand total (monthly estimates to form an annual estimate). In this instance we are looking at the behavior of the system over time as we observe expenses being incurred. Consequently, the analysis is correctly referred to as a simulation. Obviously, then, there is a thin, yet discernible line between model sampling and simulation.

A FINAL CONSIDERATION OF FINANCIAL PLANNING GENERATIONS

Each financial planning generation adds a new dimension to an organization's planning effort, with each succeeding generation providing more accurate or enriched budgeting information. However, from a usefulness point of view, each generation probably provides diminishing marginal returns. That is, the movement from no budgeting to first-generation budgeting provides greater returns than moving from the first to the second, which in turn is more valuable than progressing from the second to the third generation. None of this suggests, however, that decision technology such as third-generation financial planning will not become widespread in the contemporary business world as managers become more comfortable with quantitative aids to decision making.

SUMMARY

Financial planning can be considered in terms of different generations. The first generation, represented by line item budgeting, adds structure to a previously unstructured process. The second generation, which uses mathematical models to predict budget items, captures important functional relationships between key planning variables. The third generation, whether analytic or numeric methods are used, includes real-world uncertainty in the analysis.

Analytic approaches to probabilistic financial planning are the most efficient. Mathematical expressions have been developed, which indicate how probabilistic variables can be combined for simple functional relationships. Unfortunately, numeric approaches must typically be employed with more complex planning formats. Regardless of whether analytic or numeric methods are used, care must be taken in obtaining good probabilistic estimates, because experience has shown that good estimates are not always easily and accurately obtained.

A numeric approach to probabilistic financial planning requires Monte Carlo sampling from the probability distributions for the random variables. With continuous distributions, this sampling is accomplished by drawing a random number between 0 and 1, treating it as a cumulative probability, and finding the associated value. The sampled values are then input to the equations that comprise the planning model and appropriate computations are made for the dependent planning variables of interest. Iterations are performed until the desired degree of statistical precision is obtained. In most cases a computerized rather than a hand-performed analysis is employed. A number of special-purpose languages have been developed for financial planning. When we are being precise in our terminology, some financial planning models are best described as model sampling rather than as simulation.

ASSIGNMENTS

4.1. In Chapter 1 a classification system for mathematical models was presented. Using this classification system, describe the three financial planning generations.

4.2. Contemporary Time Pieces is a new firm that has just introduced a novelty clock into the marketplace. The following financial planning model has been prepared in order to analyze the firm's future profitability.

Total revenue$_t$ = selling price$_t$ $\times$ unit sales$_t$

Cost of goods sold$_t$

$= 1.05 \times$ fixed cost of goods sold$_{t-1}$ + $1.10 \times$ per unit cost of goods sold$_{t-1}$

$\times$ unit sales$_t$

Selling expense$_t$

$= 1.10 \times$ fixed selling expense$_{t-1}$ + $1.10 \times$ per unit selling expense$_{t-1}$

$\times$ unit sales$_t$

General and administrative expense$_t$

$= 1.15 \times$ fixed general and administrative expense$_{t-1}$ + 1.05

$\times$ per unit general and administrative expense$_{t-1}$ $\times$ unit sales$_t$

Profit before taxes$_t$

$=$ total revenue$_t$ $-$ cost of goods sold$_t$ $-$ selling expense$_t$ $-$ general and

administrative expense$_t$

Profit after taxes$_t$ $= 0.52 \times$ profit before taxes$_t$

Current year expenses are as follows:

Fixed cost of goods sold = $500,000
Per unit cost of goods sold = $5
Fixed selling expense = $400,000
Per unit selling expense = $3
Fixed general and administrative expense = $200,000
Per unit general and administrative expense = $1

Managements' planned selling price and matching unit sales estimates for the next three years are given as:

	Year 1	Year 2	Year 3
Selling price	$40.00	$40.00	$50.00
Unit sales	100,000	100,000	100,000

(a)   Using the current data, forecasts, and financial planning model, estimate profit after taxes for the next three years.

(b)   Is the financial planning model a simulation model? Explain.

4.3.   In the chapter, a procedure for obtaining subjective probabilities was illustrated. By following the procedure a cumulative probability distribution can be obtained. Practice the procedure with a friend who is several terms away from graduation by inquiring into what the person believes will be his or her graduation grade point average. Using random numbers from Appendix A, sample 20 graduation grade point averages and prepare a probability distribution.

4.4.   In manufacturing firms, manufacturing expense includes direct labor, raw materials, and factory overhead. Assuming the following mathematical model,

$$ME = DL + RM + FO$$

estimate manufacturing expense given that direct labor, raw materials, and factory overhead are normally distributed with means of $100,000, 50,000, and 20,000 and standard deviations of $10,000, 8000, and 2000, respectively. Also assume that the independent variables are statistically independent. What is the probability that manufacturing expense will be greater than $190,000?

4.5.   A recommended method of financial analysis is net discounted present value analysis. With this approach all cash flows are discounted back to the present. The net discounted present value is equal to the discounted cash inflows minus the discounted cash outflows, including the initial cash outlays.

$$NDPV = DCI - DCO - ICO$$

For a particular project under consideration, probabilistic estimates have been prepared for the three independent variables in the model and are available in the following figure.

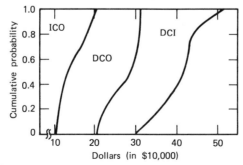

Using the data inputs provided and Appendix A, prepare a probabilistic analysis of NDPV. Your analysis should be based on 20 iterations and include the following:

(a) A histogram for *NDPV*.

(b) The mean and standard deviation for *NDPV*.

(c) A 95 percent confidence interval for the mean of *NDPV*.

4.6. Konzen's Manufacturing Company sells all its output to a large nationwide retail chain. Next year the chain has indicated that it will require 100,000 units of output from the company. For the 100,000 units, $2,000,000 will be received. However, the company is uncertain as to what its profits will be since its fixed and per unit variable costs can only be probabilistically specified. The following table shows points for cumulative probability distributions that describe the fixed and per unit costs.

Fixed Costs	Cumulative Probability	Per Unit Costs	Cumulative Probability
$600,000	.0	$1.00	.0
750,000	.1	2.00	.1
820,000	.2	2.70	.2
860,000	.3	3.20	.3
900,000	.4	3.60	.4
970,000	.5	3.90	.5
1,040,000	.6	4.20	.6
1,100,000	.7	4.60	.7
1,200,000	.8	5.00	.8
1,300,000	.9	5.50	.9
1,440,000	1.0	6.50	1.0

(a) Based on 40 iterations, prepare a probability histogram that forecasts Konzen's profit.

(b) For what range of profit figures is there a .95 probability that Konzen's profit will fall within the range?

4.7. The Happy Feet Dance Shoe Company is preparing its cash budget for the coming year. A scheduled renovation of its production facility will result in probable negative net cash flows during most of the year. Consequently, management wants to begin the year with sufficient cash on hand to weather out the situation. Given the possible cash flow positions and probabilities shown in the following table, use Monte Carlo techniques to simulate the cash flows for the entire year. Repeat the simulation a total of 20 times and analyze the output to determine the minimum cash balance the company must have on hand at the beginning of the year to assure that the probability of emergency borrowing is equal to or less than 20 percent. Repeat the analysis for a 10 percent probability.

	Cash Flow, $1000		
Quarter	Position 1 (.15)	Position 2 (.65)	Position 3 (.20)
1	-650	-500	-395
2	-290	-200	-150
3	-150	0	120
4	175	300	400

4.8.   The following equation describes the monthly net cash flow of the Lipp Paper Products Company.

$$\text{Cash flow} = \text{sales} - .35(\text{sales}) - 12{,}000$$

In the model, sales is the gross sales each month, .35(sales) represents the variable cost of manufacturing and sales, and 12,000 is the monthly fixed cost of the company's operations. When net cash flows are negative, the company plans to borrow short term. More specifically, on a month-to-month basis Lipp will borrow whatever is necessary to cover the cash deficiency. The monthly interest rate on all borrowings will be 1.5 percent. Any borrowings plus the interest owed will be repaid the first possible month when there are positive cash flows. Simulate three years of activity. What is the mean annual interest payments for the three years? Use the cumulative sales distribution given below in your analysis.

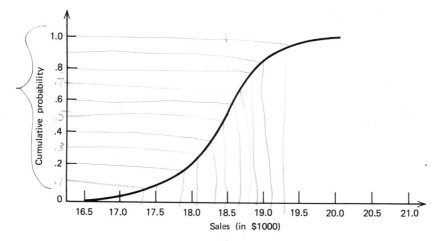

4.9.   A model sampling study employed 100 iterations. The statistical analysis of the model's output reveals a mean cost of $20 and a standard deviation of $4. What is the probability that the actual mean cost is $19.20 or less?

4.10.   The staff assistant to the vice president for production has just completed a model sampling study to explore next year's per unit cost of producing an important company product. Output from the analysis is as follows:

Cost per Unit	Frequency
$2.00–2.10	4
2.10–2.20	18
2.20–2.30	50
2.30–2.40	22
2.40–2.50	6
	100

Continue the analysis by computing a 95 percent confidence interval on the mean per unit cost.

4.11. Not all managers are at ease working with probability concepts, yet desire some indication of the amount of risk associated with a particular situation. For example, in evaluating a new product proposal, management might be interested in learning how great a loss might be experienced if the product fails in the marketplace. How can at least a crude measure of risk be obtained without using a probabilistic model?

REFERENCES

Alderson, Wroe, and Paul E. Green, *Planning and Problem Solving in Marketing* (Homewood, Ill.: Irwin, 1964).

Anthony, Ted F., and Hugh J. Watson, "Probabilistic Financial Planning," *Journal of Systems Management* (September 1972): 38-41.

Cooper, D. O., L. B. Davidson, and W. K. Denison, "A Tool for More Effective Financial Analysis," *Interfaces* (February 1975): 91-102.

Drucker, Peter F., *Management* (New York: Harper & Row, 1974).

Durway, Jerry W., "Sensitivity Analysis and Simulation," *Infosystems* (June 1979): 70-76.

Ferrara, William L., and Jack C. Hayya, "Toward Probabilistic Profit Budgets," *Management Accounting* (October 1970): 23-28.

Fetter, R. B., and J. D. Thompson, "The Simulation of Hospital Systems," *Operations Research* (September-October 1965): 689-711.

Hertz, D. B., "Risk Analysis in Capital Budgeting," *Harvard Business Review* (January-February 1964): 95-106.

Jaedicke, Robert K., and Alexander A. Robichek, "Cost-Volume-Profit Analysis under Conditions of Uncertainty," *Accounting Review* (October 1964): 917-926.

Lord, Robert J., "A Case History of Probability Budgeting," *Management Accounting* (December 1978): 74-78.

McDevitt, Carl D., and Hugh J. Watson, "An Assessment of Probability Encoding Using a Probabilistic, Noninteractive Management Game," *Academy of Management Journal* (September 1978): 451-462.

Scott, David F., Jr., Lawrence J. Moore, André Saint-Denis, Edouard Archer and Bernard W. Taylor, III, "Implementation of a Cash Budget Simulation at Air Canada," *Financial Management* (Summer 1979): 46-52.

Spetzler, Carl S., and Carl-Axel S. Stael von Holstein, "Probability Encoding in Decision Analysis," *Management Science* (November 1975): 340-358.

Springer, Clifford et al., *Probabilistic Models* (Homewood, Ill.: Irwin, 1968).

Walters, James E., and Hugh J. Watson, "Building a Budget: 3 Generations," *Hospital Financial Management* (September 1977): 10-17.

Watson, Hugh J., "Financial Planning and Control," *Management Adviser* (November-December 1972): 43-48.

CHAPTER FIVE

PROBABILITY DISTRIBUTIONS AND THEIR PROCESS GENERATORS

Sampling from Nontheoretical Probability Distributions

Discrete Probability Distributions

Continuous Probability Distributions

A Crude Approximation Method

A Linear Interpolation Method

Sampling from Theoretical Probability Distributions

Continuous Probability Distributions

The Uniform Distribution

The Negative Exponential Distribution

The Normal Distribution

The Triangular Distribution

Discrete Probability Distributions

The Bernoulli Distribution

The Binomial Distribution

The Poisson Distribution

Goodness-of-Fit Tests

Chi-square Test

Kolmogorov–Smirnov Test

Summary

Assignments

References

In the previous two chapters, you have seen the gradual introduction of basic simulation technology. Encouraging to most beginning students is the realization that interesting, challenging, and meaningful problems can be analyzed after only a brief introduction to simulation technology. This success usually leads to a desire to acquire more knowledge, so that increasingly complex systems can be investigated. Hopefully, you are now at this point. In this chapter we will discuss how to incorporate probabilistic factors into simulation models more efficiently. In addition, attention will be given to the computer implementation of simulation models, because the computational demands of simulation models commonly require the use of a computer.

Depending on the real-world situation, we have seen how probabilities can be based either on relative frequencies or subjective judgment. Regardless of the origins of the probabilities, a major factor in computerizing probabilistic models is whether or not *theoretical probability distributions* such as the normal or negative exponential can be used to describe the probabilities. In most cases it is easier to sample from a theoretical distribution, since appropriate sampling procedures have already been developed and only the required parameters for the distribution must be specified. A procedure that generates a sampled value from a specific distribution is referred to as a *process generator* for that distribution. This chapter develops process generators for the distributions that are most commonly employed in simulation studies. In addition, the theoretical groundwork for developing process generators not discussed in the chapter is established. First, let us consider computer-based methods of sampling from distributions that are not theoretical in nature.

SAMPLING FROM NONTHEORETICAL PROBABILITY DISTRIBUTIONS

By a *nontheoretical distribution*, we refer to one that has probabilities not described by a previously developed mathematical expression. For example, in Chapter 3 the demand and delivery time distributions were not described by any theoretical distribution. Rather, the distributions had their own unique properties.

Sampling from nontheoretical distributions requires a good amount of custom building of the sampling procedures, at least more so than sampling from theoretical distributions. There are some general procedures, however, that can be followed and are quite useful. The procedures vary, depending on whether we are dealing with discrete or continuous probability distributions. Let us begin our examination of sampling procedures by considering discrete probability distributions.

DISCRETE PROBABILITY DISTRIBUTIONS

A *discrete probability distribution* is one where the random variable can assume only a finite number of different values. The delivery time distribution from Chapter 3, repeated here, provides a good example. The random variable, delivery time, can only take on the values 1, 2, and 3.

Delivery Time, in weeks	Probability
1	.4
2	.4
3	.2
	1.0

One way to sample from a discrete distribution is to associate integer random numbers with the possible variable values in such a manner that the number of random numbers assigned to each variable value is proportional to its probability of occurrence. When this approach is used, the random numbers 00 to 39, 40 to 79, and 80 to 99 might be assigned to delivery times of 1, 2, and 3 weeks, respectively. This approach is satisfactory with a hand-performed analysis, but a slight change is typically made when the analysis is computerized. Computer generated random numbers almost always have values that fall between 0 and 1. Consequently, it is more convenient to associate decimal rather than integer random numbers with the variable values. For our delivery time distribution the random number ranges 0.00 to 0.40, 0.40 to 0.80, and 0.80 to 1.00 would be associated with delivery times of 1, 2, and 3 weeks, respectively. These ranges are open on the upper end and do not include 1.00, because most random number generating routines do not produce a value of 1.00.

Sampling from a discrete distribution in a computerized model is straightforward. A random number is generated and its value is then used to determine the sampled value. With a programming language such as FORTRAN, a series of IF statements can be used to determine the appropriate value for the variable. For the delivery time example the FORTRAN program segment of Table 5.1 might be used. The program segment first obtains a uniform random number. In Table 5.1 this objective is accomplished by the statement R=RAND. In this and other examples, R=RAND is used to represent a call on the computer's (or your) random number generator. You will have to learn from your instructor or reference manual the specific way to obtain a random number on your computer system. Methods of uniform random number generation are discussed in Chapter 6. For efficiency, the delivery time (DTIME) is first set equal to 1 week. Depending on

Table 5.1   SAMPLING FROM THE DELIVERY TIME DISTRIBUTION

```
INTEGER DTIME
R=RAND
DTIME=1
IF (R.GE.0.40) DTIME=2
IF (R.GE.0.80) DTIME=3
```

the random number generated, DTIME may be reset to either 2 or 3 weeks by the IF statements.

CONTINUOUS PROBABILITY DISTRIBUTIONS

With a *continuous probability distribution* the random variable can assume an infinite number of possible values. As seen in Chapter 4 with the patient-days example, it is possible to sample from a continuous distribution by obtaining a random number between 0 and 1, treating the random number as a cumulative probability, and reading the sampled value from a graph of the variable's cumulative probability distribution. This approach works reasonably well with hand-performed analyses, but must be modified with computerized analyses, because the computer typically does not have the sensory power to read the cumulative probability curve.

A Crude Approximation Method

One solution to the problem involves approximating the continuous distribution with a finite number of discrete points. Logically, the greater the number of discrete points used, the better the approximation. Presented in Figure 5.1 is a cumulative probability distribution that reflects, let us say, a marketing manager's beliefs as to how many units of a new product will be sold. A total of ten points will be used to approximate the marketing manager's subjective beliefs; however, any number of points could be used. The ten points are the unit sales figures that correspond with cumulative probabilities of .05, .15, ..., .95; probabilities that are ten in number and are evenly spaced along the cumulative probability axis. The cumulative probabilities and their associated unit sales figures are indicated in Figure 5.1 and are presented in the following table.

Cumulative Probability	Unit Sales
.05	9375
.15	12,500
.25	14,375
.35	15,625
.45	16,562
.55	17,500
.65	18,750
.75	20,625
.85	23,125
.95	26,250

When sampling from the unit sales distribution, the ten points will be used rather than the entire curve. In other words, the problem has been reduced to sampling from one of ten

Figure 5.1   A cumulative probability distribution for unit sales.

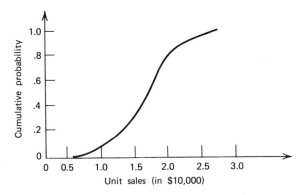

possible points rather than from an infinite number (or nearly so). Table 5.2 shows how the sampling might be performed in a FORTRAN program.

The READ-FORMAT statement pair is used to input the ten-unit sales figures into the array SALES(1), SALES(2), . . . , SALES(10). The sampling of one of the ten figures is performed in the program by obtaining a random number equal to or greater than 0 but *less than* 1, using the random number in the expression 10.*R+1. in order to obtain a subscript between 1 and 10, and then, through indirect addressing, assigning to USALES the appropriately sampled value. The key to understanding the sampling procedure is to realize that the expression I=10.*R+1. results in a value from 1 to 10.999 . . . , but truncation of the decimal portion occurs because it is assigned to the integer variable, I.

A Linear Interpolation Method

An alternative method of sampling from a continuous probability distribution that does not correspond to a theoretical distribution is once again to use a discrete number of points, but this time to perform a linear interpolation between the points. This approach is illustrated in Figure 5.2, which presents a cumulative probability distribution for selling expense. Straight lines are drawn to connect the points that are used in approximating the continuous distribution. Again, the more points used, the better the approximation.

Table 5.2   SAMPLING FROM THE UNIT SALES DISTRIBUTION

```
       READ(5,50)  (SALES(I),  I=1,10)
    50 FORMAT  (10(F5.0,1X))
       ⋮

       R=RAND
       I=10.*R+1.
       USALES=SALES(I)
```

Figure 5.2   A cumulative probability distribution for selling expense.

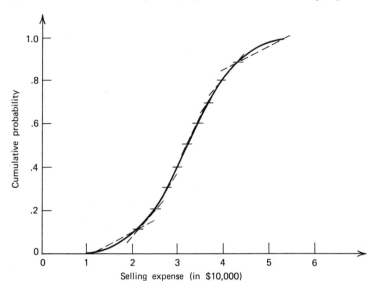

Let us consider how the linear interpolation method works. Suppose that the random number 0.15 is generated. This number is one half, (0.20 - 0.15)/(0.20 - 0.10), of the way between the .10 and .20 cumulative probabilities. It follows then that the sampled value should be 0.50 of the way between the selling expense figures associated with the .10 and .20 cumulative probabilities. The sampled value is computed to be

$$21{,}500 + 0.50 \times (26{,}500 - 21{,}500) \qquad \text{or} \qquad \$24{,}000$$

A FORTRAN program segment for sampling from the selling expense distribution is shown in Table 5.3.

The logic of the program segment is perhaps best understood by taking the previous example and following its step-by-step processing by the program segment. The first two statements input the 11 points that are used to approximate the continuous curve. In order to sample a value from the selling expense distribution, first a random number equal

Table 5.3   SAMPLING FROM THE SELLING EXPENSE DISTRIBUTION

```
       READ(5,50)  (SELL(I), I=1,11)
    50 FORMAT(11(F5.0,1X))
        .
        .
        .
       R=RAND*10+1
       J=R
       VALUE=SELL(J)+(R-J)*(SELL(J+1)-SELL(J))
```

to or greater than 0 but less than 1 is generated, multiplied by 10, and increased by 1, which results in a random number from 1 to 10.999.... Taking our previous example, we would transform the random number 0.15 into 2.5. The integer value of the random number is then found through truncation by setting J=R, which for our example results in a value of 2 for J. The next statement performs the sampling using linear interpolation. The programming statement and the numbers from our example follow.

$$\text{VALUE} = \text{SELL(J)} + (\text{R}-\text{J}) \times (\text{SELL(J}+1) - \text{SELL(J)})$$

$$= 21,500 + (2.5 - 2) \times (26,500 - 21,500)$$

$$= 24,000$$

The amount added to the bottom point of the range is proportional to where the random number falls in the range (in our current example, halfway between the top and the bottom of the range).

Several subtle differences exist between the crude approximation and linear interpolation methods. First, with the crude approximation method the approximating points should not include variable values associated with cumulative probabilities of 0 and 1 unless a large number of points are used. Otherwise, too much emphasis is given to extreme values. In our example, cumulative probabilities of .05 and .95 were the most extreme ones used. In the linear interpolation method the approximating points do include variable values associated with cumulative probabilities of 0 and 1. Second, the multiplier used in the crude approximation method to identify the appropriate subscripted variable value (the 10 in I=10.×R+1.) is the same as the number of points input to approximate the distribution. In the linear interpolation method the multiplier (the 10 in R=RAND×10+1) is one less than the number of points input. This is a consequence of the way the linear interpolation method functions.

We have now seen how to sample from probability distributions that are *not* described by standard theoretical distributions. In general, it can be said that such methods require the custom building of an appropriate sampling procedure. As we will see next, our sampling task becomes somewhat easier when we are able to use theoretical distributions to describe the random variables in our model.

SAMPLING FROM THEORETICAL PROBABILITY DISTRIBUTIONS

Theoretical probability distributions are defined by specific mathematical expressions. For example, probability distributions such as the uniform and normal have unique mathematical expressions that determine their characteristics. When the parameters of these distributions are specified (such as the mean and standard deviation for the normal distribution), the characteristics are uniquely defined.

CONTINUOUS PROBABILITY DISTRIBUTIONS

Let us begin our examination of sampling from theoretical probability distributions by considering continuous distributions. Being more specific, we will investigate the uniform, negative exponential, normal, and triangular distributions. These distributions have high applicability in simulation studies and are relatively easy to use. The first distribution considered will be the uniform.

The Uniform Distribution

The *uniform distribution* is defined by the following mathematical expression (equation).

$$p(x) = \frac{1}{B - A} \quad \text{for} \quad A \leq x \leq B \tag{5-1}$$

$$= 0 \qquad \text{elsewhere}$$

A graph of the uniform distribution is shown in Figure 5.3. With the uniform distribution, all the values between A and B have equal probabilities. Random numbers most often come from the uniform distribution with the parameters A and B set equal to 0 and 1, respectively (except that the random numbers do not include $B = 1$).

At the beginning of the chapter, it was indicated that a procedure for sampling from a specific probability distribution is referred to as a process generator for that distribution. A process generator for the uniform distribution is most easily developed by employing the *inverse method*. Let us now consider how this important method works.

The first step is to develop a mathematical expression for the distribution's cumulative form; specifically, its equal to or less than form. An equal to or less than cumulative probability distribution for the uniform distribution is shown in Figure 5.4. Mathematically, the cumulative distribution is developed from the simple distribution by integrating the simple distribution over its range of possible values. This procedure is shown as

$$P(x) = \int_{-\infty}^{x} p(x)\, dx \tag{5-2}$$

$$= \int_{A}^{x} \frac{1}{B - A}\, dx \tag{5-3}$$

$$= \frac{x}{B - A} + K \tag{5-4}$$

Figure 5.3   The uniform distribution.

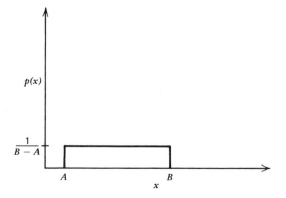

Figure 5.4   A cumulative probability distribution for the uniform distribution.

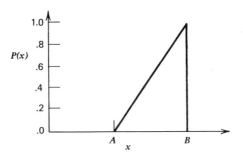

Evaluating the constant of integration, K, in the indefinite integral at $x = A$ where the cumulative probability is known to be 0 reveals that

$$P(x = A) = 0 = \frac{A}{B - A} + K \qquad (5\text{-}5)$$

Therefore

$$\therefore \quad K = -\frac{A}{B - A} \qquad (5\text{-}6)$$

Consequently, the equation for the uniform distribution's cumulative form is

$$P(x) = \frac{x}{B - A} - \frac{A}{B - A} \qquad (5\text{-}7)$$

$$= \frac{x - A}{B - A} \qquad (5\text{-}8)$$

Recall that our sampling from a cumulative distribution was performed by drawing a random number, treating it as a cumulative probability, and finding the associated value. The same procedure is followed in the inverse method by setting r equal to $P(x)$.

$$r = P(x) = \frac{x - A}{B - A} \qquad (5\text{-}9)$$

This equation, which has r as a function of x, is then rearranged to have x defined as a function of r. This "inversing" of variables gives the inverse method its name.

$$r = \frac{x - A}{B - A} \qquad (5\text{-}10)$$

$$x = A + r \times (B - A) \qquad (5\text{-}11)$$

The final Equation 5-11 is easy to use as a process generator for the uniform distribution. Given values for the parameters (A and B) and a random number, a sampled value (a *variate*) is obtained by substituting the appropriate values into Equation 5-11. For example, if the distribution of interest is uniformly distributed with a lower limit of 5 and an

Table 5.4   SAMPLING FROM THE UNIFORM DISTRIBUTION

```
          READ (5,50) A,B
       50 FORMAT (2F8.2)
          .
          .
          .
          R=RAND
          X=A+R*(B-A)
```

upper limit of 10 and the random number 0.75 is generated, the sampled value would be

$$x = 5 + 0.75 \times (10 - 5)$$

$$= 8.75$$

Sampling from the uniform distribution in a FORTRAN program is quite simple and is performed as shown in the program segment of Table 5.4.

Depending on your calculus skills, the derivation of the process generator for the uniform distribution may or may not have been easy to follow. In most instances, however, a knowledge of the final result of the derivation is all that is needed. For example, now that we know that a process generator for the uniform distribution is $A + r \times (B - A)$, it is not tremendously important to understand its development, except from an academic standpoint.

The Negative Exponential Distribution

The *negative exponential* is a very important and useful probability distribution in simulation studies. It is particularly useful for describing the time between occurrences in *queuing*, or *waiting line*, situations. For example, the time between arrivals at a ticket counter is often described by the negative exponential distribution.

The negative exponential distribution is defined by the following mathematical expression.

$$p(x) = \lambda e^{-\lambda x} \quad \text{for} \quad 0 \leq x \leq \infty \qquad (5\text{-}12)$$

The distribution contains a single parameter, λ, which represents the mean number of occurrences per interval; for example, one every 5 minutes. The random variable, x, is the number of intervals. For example, if λ is expressed as an interval of 5 minutes and a period of 10 minutes is our focus of attention, we are talking about 2 time intervals, or $x = 2$.

The negative exponential distribution is shown in Figure 5.5. It intersects the y axis at λ and is asymptotic to the x axis. In order to find the probability of an occurrence by, say, x_1 intervals, we find the area under the curve from 0 to x_1. This area is darkened in Figure 5.5. Obviously, the remaining area must represent the probability of not having an occurrence by x_1.

Figure 5.5   The negative exponential distribution.

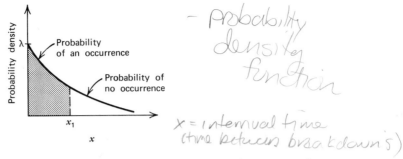

The following equations can be used to find areas under the curve and, consequently, the probability of having or not having an occurrence by x intervals.

$$\text{Probability of an occurrence by } x = 1 - e^{-\lambda x} \tag{5-13}$$

$$\text{Probability of no occurrence by } x = e^{-\lambda x} \tag{5-14}$$

As an example, let us refer to the ticket booth that averages one arrival every 5 minutes. We might ask, what is the probability that there is an arrival within 10 minutes? Using our formulas with $\lambda = 1$ and $x = 2$ (two 5-minute time intervals), we find the probability to be

$$\text{Probability of an occurrence by } (x = 2) = 1 - e^{-1(2)}$$

$$= 1 - 0.135$$

$$= .865$$

Values for e^{-x} can be found in Appendix G.

In simulation models the objective usually is not calculating the probability of an occurrence but, rather, simulating the timing of the occurrence. This requires sampling a value from the negative exponential distribution. The most straightforward method of realizing this objective is to develop a process generator for the negative exponential distribution by the inverse method.

The first step in using the inverse method is to integrate the simple distribution over its range of possible values in order to find its cumulative form.

$$P(x) = \int_0^x \lambda e^{-\lambda x}\, dx \tag{5-15}$$

$$= -e^{-\lambda x} + K \tag{5-16}$$

Evaluating the constant of integration, K, at $x = 0$ where the cumulative area is known to be 0 reveals that K has a value of

$$P(x = 0) = 0 = -e^{\lambda(0)} + K \tag{5-17}$$

$$0 = -1 + K \tag{5-18}$$

Therefore

$$\therefore \quad K = 1 \tag{5-19}$$

Next, the uniform random number, r, is set equal to $P(x)$, and the expression is manipulated in order to express x as a function of r.

$$r = P(x) = -e^{-\lambda x} + 1 \qquad (5\text{-}20)$$

$$e^{-\lambda x} = 1 - r \qquad (5\text{-}21)$$

Taking natural logarithms of each side, we get

$$-\lambda x = \ln (1 - r) \qquad (5\text{-}22)$$

$$x = \frac{-\ln (1 - r)}{\lambda} \qquad (5\text{-}23)$$

Equation (5-23) is our process generator for the negative exponential distribution. Given a mean number of occurrences and a uniform random number, the number of intervals before the next occurrence is easily simulated. Keep in mind, however, that the sampled value is measured in intervals and must usually be transformed into minutes, hours, or whatever the appropriate unit of measurement may be before it can be used in a simulation model. For example, if $\lambda = 1$ occurrence/5 minutes and $r = 0.40$, the sampled value would be:

$$x = \frac{-\ln (0.6)}{1} = 0.51$$

Measured in minutes, this would be

$$(.51 \text{ intervals}) \times (5 \text{ minutes/interval}) = 2.55 \text{ minutes}$$

Values for $\ln (x)$ can be found in Appendix H.

Sampling from the negative exponential distribution in a computer program is relatively easy, as shown in the FORTRAN program segment of Table 5.5. The variable named LAMDA is the mean number of occurrences per interval and LENGTH is the length of an interval.

A final word of caution in regards to working with the negative exponential distribution is required. Frequently, assignments are given and data collected on the basis of the mean time between arrivals; for example, 5 minutes mean interarrival time. Data in this form are just the reciprocal of the units on λ and must be inverted before being

Table 5.5   SAMPLING FROM THE NEGATIVE EXPONENTIAL DISTRIBUTION

```
       REAL  LAMDA,LENGTH,INTVAL
       READ(5,30)  LAMDA,LENGTH
   30  FORMAT(2F8.3)
       .
       .
       .
       R=RAND
       INTVAL=-ALOG(1.-R)/LAMDA
       X=INTVAL*LENGTH
```

used with the negative exponential distribution. For example, a mean interarrival time of 5 minutes/arrival becomes 1 arrival/5 minutes.

It has been indicated that the negative exponential distribution is particularly useful in describing the time between occurrences; for example, the time between the arrival of a customer. Although not shown here, it can be proved that when arrivals are *Poisson distributed*, which is frequently the case, the time between arrivals is negative exponentially distributed. This interesting fact will be mentioned again later when the Poisson distribution is discussed along with other discrete probability distributions.

The Normal Distribution

Perhaps the most useful of all probability distributions is the *normal distribution*, because it can be used to describe so many real-world situations. The distribution is defined by the following equation.

$$p(x) = \frac{e^{-\frac{1}{2}[(x-\mu)/\sigma]^2}}{\sigma\sqrt{2\pi}} \qquad \text{for} \quad -\infty \leqq x \leqq \infty \qquad (5\text{-}24)$$

The distribution contains two parameters, μ, the mean, and σ, the standard deviation; for example, a mean of 25 and a standard deviation of 5. As with our other distributions, x is the random variable.

Figure 5.6 shows the familiar shape of a normal distribution with a mean of 25 and a standard deviation of 5. As with all continuous probability distributions, probabilities are found by finding areas under the curve. For example, in Figure 5.6 the probability that x will take on a value between 25 and 30 is determined by finding the appropriate Z value, turning to the standard normal table in Appendix B, and finding a value of .3413 as the area under the curve (the desired probability).

$$Z = \frac{x - \mu}{\sigma}$$

$$= \frac{30 - 25}{5} = 1$$

$$p(0 \leqq Z \leqq 1) = .3413 \qquad \text{(from Appendix B)}$$

When working with the normal distribution, probabilities are found by using tables rather than by integrating the curve between the points of interest. The reason for this

Figure 5.6   The normal distribution.

practice is more than simple convenience. The mathematical expression for the normal distribution cannot be exactly integrated; rather, its integrated form can only be approximated. Consequently, tables are always used unless "messy" approximations are utilized.

Not being able to integrate the normal curve poses a slight problem when developing a process generator, because the inverse method cannot be readily applied. Therefore, other methods must be used. Let us now consider some of the alternatives.

The Box-Muller Method. Even though the normal distribution cannot be integrated exactly, a number of approximations have been developed that lead to process generators. Box and Muller have developed one that is simple to use, is reasonably fast, and produces normally distributed variates! The method requires two random numbers (r_1 and r_2), which when placed in the appropriate expressions provide two variates ($V1$ and $V2$) from the *standard normal distribution.* The mathematical equations that are used follow

$$V1 = (-2 \ln r_1)^{1/2} \cos (2\pi r_2) \qquad (5\text{-}25)$$

$$V2 = (-2 \ln r_1)^{1/2} \sin (2\pi r_2) \qquad (5\text{-}26)$$

It should be stressed that the values for $V1$ and $V2$ are from the standard normal distribution and have the same properties as the familiar Z statistic. In other words, the values for $V1$ and $V2$ must be treated as Z values. In order to obtain normally distributed variates with means and standards deviations different from 0 and 1, respectively, we must express x, our sampled value, as a function of Z.

$$Z = \frac{x - \mu}{\sigma} \qquad (5\text{-}27)$$

$$x = \mu + Z\sigma \qquad (5\text{-}28)$$

When sampling values from a normal distribution with a specific mean and standard deviation, we substitute appropriate values in Equation 5-28 for μ and σ, along with the sampled value for $V1$ and $V2$. The FORTRAN program segment shown in Table 5.6 illus-

Table 5.6   SAMPLING FROM THE NORMAL
DISTRIBUTION BY THE BOX–MULLER
METHOD

```
      REAL MEAN
      READ(5,60) MEAN,STD
   60 FORMAT(2F8.2)
         .
         .
      R1=RAND
      R2=RAND
      V1=SQRT(-2*ALOG(R1))*COS(6.28*R2)
      X=MEAN+V1*STD
```

[1]G. E. P. Box and M. E. Muller, "A Note on the Generation of Random Normal Deviates," *Annuals of Mathematical Statistics* 29: 610–611.

trates sampling from a normal distribution with a given mean and standard deviation by the Box–Muller method. The program segment, as written, generates only one normally distributed variate.

A Sampling Method. Because of the frequency with which normally distributed variates are needed in simulation studies, some computer systems include a normal random number generator as a library subroutine. For example, on IBM equipment the library subroutine named GAUSS can be used to obtain normally distributed values. This subroutine employs a sampling procedure that can be used on any computer system.

The *sampling method* is based on the fact that the *sampling distribution for the sum* tends to be normally distributed with large sample sizes. Furthermore, the sampling distribution has a mean equal to the mean of the population times the sample size, and a standard deviation (*standard error of the sum*) equal to the population standard deviation times the square root of the sample size.

$$\mu_\Sigma = \mu n \tag{5-29}$$

$$\sigma_\Sigma = \sigma \sqrt{n} \tag{5-30}$$

When the sampling method is used, the uniform distribution is convenient to sample from, since uniform random numbers are easily obtained and the characteristics of the uniform distribution are well known. Being more specific about the uniform distribution's characteristics, it has a mean equal to 0.50, and a standard deviation of $1/\sqrt{12}$ when $A = 0$ and $B = 1$. Consider now how this information can be used to develop a useful method for generating standard normal values.

The sampling procedure functions by obtaining 12 uniformly distributed variates, computing their sum, and then subtracting 6. Mathematically, this is expressed as

$$Z = \sum_{i=1}^{12} (r_i) - 6 \tag{5-31}$$

The output from this sampling procedure are sample sums that are normally distributed with a mean of 0 and a standard deviation of 1 as follows.

$$\mu_\Sigma = 0.50(12) - 6 = 0 \tag{5-32}$$

$$\sigma_\Sigma = 1/\sqrt{12}\,(\sqrt{12}) = 1 \tag{5-33}$$

These output characteristics are the same as the Z statistic of the standard normal distribution. When the outputs from the sampling procedure are adjusted for the required mean and standard, the variates are appropriate for use in simulation studies. The FORTRAN program segment of Table 5.7 illustrates how the sampling method might function in a computerized model. At the beginning of the program the appropriate mean and standard deviation are input, a DO loop accumulates the 12 sampled values, 6 is subtracted from the sum, and the normally distributed value of interest is determined by adjusting for the desired mean and standard deviations.

The sampling method for generating normally distributed variates is easy to program and is reasonably fast, because there are no logarithms or trigonometric functions to evaluate. However, because 12 random numbers are required to generate a single normal variate, in large simulation models it is possible that the supply of random numbers will

Table 5.7 SAMPLING FROM THE NORMAL
DISTRIBUTION BY THE SAMPLING METHOD

```
      REAL MEAN
      SUM=0.
      READ(5,70) MEAN,STD
   70 FORMAT(2F8.2)
      ⋮
      DO 100 I=1,12
      R=RAND
      SUM=SUM+R
  100 CONTINUE
      Z=SUM-6.
      X=MEAN+Z*STD
```

be insufficient. Furthermore, the sampling distribution for the sum is not exactly normally distributed for sample sizes of only 12. Consequently, beyond $\mu \pm 2\sigma$ the values generated can deviate from the normal distribution's characteristics.

The Rejection Method. The third and final method we will discuss for generating normally distributed variates is the *rejection method*. It is particularly interesting because it can be used with the normal distribution as well as with any continuous distribution.

The first step in using the rejection method is to enclose the continuous distribution in a rectangle. Since the standard normal distribution is asymptotic to the Z axis, it is necessary to truncate the distribution at some reasonable point; see Figure 5.7. Points that are 5 standard deviations from the mean include virtually all of the area under the normal curve and will be used in our illustration. By inserting a value of $Z = 0$ in the expression for the standard normal distribution, it can be seen that the maximum height of the curve (its *ordinate*) is 0.3989. Consequently, a rectangle with a height of 0.40 includes the entire distribution.

Figure 5.7 The standard normal distribution.

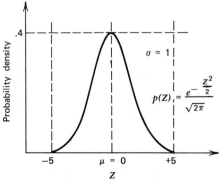

The next step is to select randomly a Z value between +5 and -5. In other words, we want to select at random a value along the length of the rectangle. Our uniform process generator can be used for this task with $A = -5$ and $B = +5$.

$$Z = -5 + 10r_1$$

After the Z value has been randomly selected, it is inserted in the equation for the standard normal distribution in order to determine the height of the curve at that point. Then a second random number is generated. It is transformed, using the uniform process generator, so that it randomly selects a point along the height of the rectangle.

$$H = 0.4r_2$$

And now comes the rejection part of the rejection method. If the value of H falls below (is less than) the computed height of the curve at the randomly selected Z value, the Z value is treated as if it comes from the standard normal distribution and is used in the simulation model. If, however, the value of H falls above the curve, the Z value under consideration is rejected, and the process is repeated until an appropriate value is found.

Because it is easy to get lost in the details of the rejection method, let us consider the big picture of what is taking place. Essentially, the two random numbers are randomly locating a point within the rectangle. If the point falls on or below the curve, we accept the associated Z value as coming from the standard normal distribution. If it falls above the curve, the Z value is rejected as coming from the distribution. It should be apparent that the rejection method can be used with any continuous distribution, since what we are doing is rejecting points that do not generate a distribution of the desired shape.

The FORTRAN program segment shown in Table 5.8 generates values from the standard normal distribution by the rejection method. As was the case with our other methods for generating normal variates, the values must be transformed to have the desired mean and standard deviation.

Table 5.8 SAMPLING FROM THE NORMAL
DISTRIBUTION BY THE REJECTION METHOD

```
      REAL MEAN
      READ(5,70) MEAN,STD
   70 FORMAT(2F8.2)
       ⋮
   80 R1=RAND
      R2=RAND
      Z=-5+10*R1
      H=0.4*R2
      C=(2.72**(-(Z*Z)/2))/SQRT(6.28)
      IF(H.LE.C) GO TO 90
      GO TO 80
   90 X=MEAN+Z*STD
```

The Triangular Distribution

When probability distributions skewed to the right or to the left are needed, the *triangular distribution* is often convenient to use. Although there are other distributions that can be skewed (gamma, log normal), none of them are as easy to understand and work with as the triangular. The following equation defines the triangular distribution.

$$p(x) = \frac{2(x - O)}{(L - O)(P - O)} \qquad \text{for} \quad O \leq x \leq L \qquad (5\text{-}34)$$

$$= \frac{2(p - x)}{(P - L)(P - O)} \qquad \text{for} \quad L \leq x \leq P \qquad (5\text{-}35)$$

The triangular distribution is shown in Figure 5.8.

A major reason for using the triangular distribution is that its parameters $(O, L, \text{and } P)$ are easy for nonquantitatively trained personnel to understand. For example, if we are considering the time to complete an activity, the parameters O, L, and P can be thought of in terms of most optimistic, most likely, and most pessimistic estimates, respectively. This usage is somewhat analogous to that of PERT analysis, which employs three inputs to estimate a subjective probability distribution. The only difference is that in PERT the underlying distribution is assumed to be the beta rather than the triangular distribution.

A common use of the triangular distribution is in providing probabilistic cost and revenue estimates. However, caution must be exercised in this application, since most optimistic and most pessimistic estimates mean different things depending upon whether it is a cost or a revenue. An optimistic estimate for a cost means a very low figure while for a revenue it is a high figure. Just the opposite applies for a pessimistic estimate.

A process generator for the triangular distribution can be developed by using the inverse method. Because of the discontinuity of the function, however, (at $x = L$), two separate generators must be developed; one for $x \leq L$ and one for $x \geq L$. Let us first develop the process generator for $x \leq L$.

$$P(x) = \int_o^x \frac{2(x - O)}{(L - O)(P - O)}\, dx \qquad (5\text{-}36)$$

$$= \frac{x^2 - 2Ox}{(L - O)(P - O)} + K \qquad (5\text{-}37)$$

Figure 5.8   The triangular distribution.

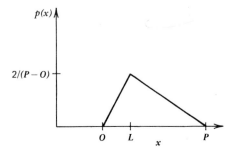

Evaluating the constant of integration, K, at $x = O$, where it is known that the cumulative area under the curve is 0, reveals that

$$P(x = O) = 0 = \frac{O^2 - 2O^2}{(L - O)(P - O)} + K \tag{5-38}$$

Therefore

$$\therefore \quad K = \frac{O^2}{(L - O)(P - O)} \tag{5-39}$$

The uniform random number, r, is then set equal to $P(x)$ and the equation is manipulated so that x is expressed as a function of r.

$$r = P(x) = \frac{x^2 - 2Ox + O^2}{(L - O)(P - O)} \tag{5-40}$$

$$r = \frac{(x - O)^2}{(L - O)(P - O)} \tag{5-41}$$

$$(x - O)^2 = r(L - O)(P - O) \tag{5-42}$$

$$x = O + \sqrt{r(L - O)(P - O)} \tag{5-43}$$

This process generator is used whenever $r < (L - O)/(P - O)$, since the ratio of $(L - O)$ to $(P - O)$ is the area under the triangular distribution from $x = O$ to $x = L$.

Let us now develop the process generator for $x \geq L$.

$$P(x) = \int_{L}^{x} \frac{2(P - x)}{(P - L)(P - O)} dx \tag{5-44}$$

$$= \frac{2Px - x^2}{(P - L)(P - O)} + K \tag{5-45}$$

Evaluating the constant of integration, K, at $x = P$ where the cumulative area is 1, we find that

$$P(x = P) = 1 = \frac{2P^2 - P^2}{(P - L)(P - O)} + K \tag{5-46}$$

Therefore

$$\therefore \quad K = 1 - \frac{P^2}{(P - L)(P - O)} \tag{5-47}$$

The uniform random, r, is set equal to $P(x)$ and the equation is manipulated until x is expressed as a function of r.

$$r = P(x) = \frac{-x^2 + 2Px - P^2}{(P - L)(P - O)} + 1 \tag{5-48}$$

$$\frac{(x - P)^2}{(P - L)(P - O)} = 1 - r \tag{5-49}$$

$$x - P = -\sqrt{(1 - r)(P - L)(P - O)} \tag{5-50}$$

$$x = P - \sqrt{(1 - r)(P - L)(P - O)} \tag{5-51}$$

Table 5.9 SAMPLING FROM THE TRIANGULAR DISTRIBUTION

```
      REAL L
      READ(5,40) O,L,P
 40   FORMAT(3F8.2)
      ⋮
      R=RAND
      IF(R.LT.(L−O)/(P−O)) GO TO 60
      X=P−SQRT((1−R)*(P−L)*(P−O))
      GO TO 70
 60   X=O+SQRT(R*(L−O)*(P−O))
 70   CONTINUE
```

Figure 5.9 A distribution not frequently used.

BI-GNOMIAL DISTRIBUTION

Source. Interfaces (November 1977), p. 69.

Equation 5-51 is used as the process generator for the triangular distribution whenever $r \geq (L - O)/(P - O)$.

Sampling from the triangular distribution in a computerized model is a relatively straightforward process as illustrated in the FORTRAN program segment of Table 5.9.

The material on the triangular distribution concludes our treatment of continuous theoretical probability distributions. There are additional distributions that have varying degrees of usefulness in simulation studies (see Figure 5.9); however, the scope of the book and space limitations preclude their coverage.[2] Instead, our attention now turns to discrete theoretical probability distributions.

DISCRETE PROBABILITY DISTRIBUTIONS

The most important discrete probability distributions for simulation modeling are the binomial and Poisson distributions. We will investigate both of these distributions, but first of all, we will consider the Bernoulli distribution, because it is a building block for the binomial distribution.

The Bernoulli Distribution

The *Bernoulli distribution* can be used to describe situations where there are *two mutually exclusive outcomes*, often categorized as success or failure. For example, when auditing an accounts payable, the account can be found to be either correctly (failure) or incorrectly (success) recorded (no connotations of good or bad are implied by the terms success and failure).

The Bernoulli distribution is defined by the following equation.

$$p(x) = p \qquad \text{for} \quad x = 1$$
$$ = 1 - p \qquad \text{for} \quad x = 0 \tag{5-52}$$

The probability of an outcome being in state 1 is p, whereas the probability of state 0 occurring is $1 - p$. For example, if 2 percent of the accounts payable are incorrectly recorded and an incorrect account payable is recorded as state 1, we can say that

$$p(x = 1) = .02$$
$$p(x = 0) = .98$$

Sampling from the Bernoulli distribution in a computerized model is very simple; for example, consider the FORTRAN program segment of Table 5.10. All that is required is generating a random number, comparing it to the probability that separates the two states, and recording the appropriate outcome.

The Binomial Distribution

The *binomial distribution* can be used to describe the outcome of a series of independent Bernoulli trials. For example, assume we are interested in knowing the probability of

---

[2] A more comprehensive coverage of process generators is provided in George S. Fishman, *Concepts and Methods in Discrete Event Digital Simulation* (New York: Wiley, 1973), pp. 197–241.

Table 5.10 SAMPLING FROM THE
BERNOULLI DISTRIBUTION

```
      INTEGER X
      READ(5,10) PROB
   10 FORMAT(F4.3)
      .
      .
      .
      R=RAND
      X=0
      IF(R.LT.PROB) X=1
```

finding 1 incorrect account payable in a sample of size 5, if we know that 2 percent of all the accounts payable are in error. The binomial distribution can be used to answer such questions.

The mathematical expression (equation) defining the binomial distribution is

$$p(x) = \frac{n! p^x (1-p)^{n-x}}{x!(n-x)!} \qquad \text{for} \quad 0 \leq x \leq n \qquad (5\text{-}53)$$

In the binomial formula, n is the number of trials (the sample size), p is the probability of success on any one trial, and x is the random variable that represents the number of successes in the n trials. Picking up on our accounts payable example, we see that the probability of finding 1 incorrect account payable in a sample of size 5 would be

$$p(x = 1) = \frac{5!(0.02)^1(0.98)^4}{1!4!}$$

$$= .092$$

This and similar probabilities can be found either by using the binomial formula or a table of binomial values, as provided in Appendix C.

The process generator for the binomial distribution involves performing n Bernoulli trials and summarizing the outcome of the n trials. Table 5.11 presents a FORTRAN

Table 5.11 SAMPLING FROM THE BINOMIAL
DISTRIBUTION

```
      INTEGER X
      READ(5,90) N, PROB
   90 FORMAT(I3,F4.3)
      .
      .
      .
      X=0
      DO 95 I=1,N
      R=RAND
      IF(R.LT.PROB) X=X+1
   95 CONTINUE
```

program segment for sampling from the binomial distribution. The DO loop performs the *n* Bernoulli trials with X accumulating the number of successes (state 1's) found in the *n* trials.

The Poisson Distribution

The *Poisson distribution* was mentioned briefly earlier in conjunction with the negative exponential distribution. Specifically, it was stated that if arrivals can be described by the Poisson distribution, then the time between arrivals is described by the negative exponential distribution. Although in most instances the time between arrivals is of more interest in simulation studies, there are instances in which the number of arrivals (or occurrences) captures our attention, rather than their timing.

The Poisson distribution is defined by the following equation.

$$p(x) = \frac{\lambda^x e^{-\lambda}}{x!} \qquad \text{for} \quad 0 \le x \le \infty \qquad (5\text{-}54)$$

It contains one parameter, λ, the mean number of occurrences per interval, and the random variable x, the number of occurrences in an interval. It is important that the interval for x and λ be the same.

Many real-world situations can often be described by the Poisson distribution—arrivals at a ticket booth, scratches on furniture, printing errors in a book. To illustrate the use of the Poisson distribution, let us assume that incoming telephone calls to a switchboard are Poisson distributed with a mean of two calls every 5-minute interval. We might ask, "What is the probability of receiving 3 calls in any particular 5-minute interval?" The Poisson formula can be used to answer this question by setting $x = 3$ and $\lambda = 2$. The probability is found to be .180.

$$p(x = 3) = \frac{2^3 e^{-2}}{3!}$$

$$= .180$$

This same probability could also have been obtained by consulting the Poisson table in Appendix D.

The best way to simulate the number of Poisson arrivals in a particular interval is to use the negative exponential distribution to simulate the timing of the arrivals, and then to count the number of arrivals that take place. Table 5.12 illustrates this. For our ex-

Table 5.12   SIMULATING POISSON ARRIVALS

Random Numbers	Time Between Arrivals, in intervals	Total Elapsed Time, in intervals
0.45	0.30	0.30
0.23	0.13	0.43
0.71	0.62	1.05

Table 5.13   SAMPLING FROM THE POISSON DISTRIBUTION

```
        INTEGER X
        REAL LAMDA, INTVAL
        READ(5,15) LAMDA
    15  FORMAT(F8.3)
        ⋮
        X=0
        TOTAL=0.
    20  R=RAND
        INTVAL=-ALOG(1.-R)/LAMDA
        TOTAL=TOTAL+INTVAL
        IF(TOTAL.GT.1) GO TO 25
        X=X+1
        GO TO 20
    25  CONTINUE
```

ample we will continue to use the incoming telephone calls that average two every 5 minutes. Using the negative exponential process generator, first with the random number 0.45, results in the first incoming call 0.30 into the interval. The second call occurs 0.13 intervals later, for a total elapsed time of 0.43 intervals. The third call does not come in until 0.62 intervals later, which places it outside the interval being simulated. Consequently, two incoming calls were received during the simulated time period.

The FORTRAN program segment of Table 5.13 illustrates how the number of Poisson occurrences might be simulated in a computerized model. Each occurrence is simulated by the negative exponential process generator until the interval has elapsed. The number of arrivals is accumulated by the random variable X.

GOODNESS-OF-FIT TESTS

It should now be apparent that sampling from theoretical probability distributions is usually easier than sampling from nontheoretical distributions. Let us now investigate when we can use theoretical distributions in our simulation models.

Rather than relying on our intuition, *goodness-of-fit tests* are commonly employed to decide whether or not to use a theoretical distribution. We test to see how good our subjective benefits or data fit the theoretical distribution. Two goodness-of-fit tests will be presented; the χ^2 and the Kolmogorov–Smirnov.

Chi-square Test

The χ^2 distribution is used in the following mathematical form for goodness-of-fit tests.

$$\chi^2 = \sum \frac{(f_0 - f_e)^2}{f_e} \tag{5-55}$$

In this equation, f_0 is the *observed* number of observations in each category and f_e is the *expected* number of observations. The χ^2 distribution is completely defined by the number of degrees of freedom (df). The number of *degrees of freedom* can be defined as the number of observations that are free to vary after certain restrictions have been placed on the data. For most goodness-of-fit tests, the number of degrees of freedom is equal to the following.

$$df = \text{Number of categories} - \text{number of parameters} - 1 \qquad (5\text{-}56)$$

As an example, let us assume that the data in the first two columns of Table 5-14 are available on the number of incoming calls to an insurance company's switchboard. Based on what we have said previously, we might expect the Poisson distribution to describe the distribution of incoming calls. In order to test this hypothesis, one must obtain an estimate of λ from the data. From column 3 of Table 5.14 we see there were a total of 100 calls during the 100 one-minute intervals. Therefore the mean number of calls per minute is best estimated as $100/100 = 1$. If $\lambda = 1$, what is the expected frequency of calls in each category? Let us consider the first category, which is 0 calls/minute, since all of the expected frequencies are found in the same manner. Consulting Appendix D with $x = 0$ and $\lambda = 1$, we find the probability of 0 calls in any particular 1 minute interval to be .368. And because there were 100 intervals, the expected frequency is $100 \times .368$ or 36.8. The expected frequencies are shown in column 4 of Table 5.14.

The χ^2 goodness-of-fit test usually requires that there are at least a total of 50 observations and that the expected frequency in every category be at least five. In order to have five observations in every category, the categories of 3, 4, and 5 or more must be collapsed into a single category, which results in a new category called 3 or more. This category has an observed frequency of 11 and an expected frequency of 8. It is now possible to compute the χ^2 value for this situation, and the calculation is shown in column 5 of Table 5.14.

The null hypothesis, H_0, in our goodness-of-fit test is that the distribution of incoming calls is Poisson distributed. The alternative hypothesis, H_1, is that the distribution of incoming calls is *not* Poisson distributed. If we fail to reject the null hypothesis, we will continue to assume that the incoming calls are Poisson distributed and use the Poisson process generator with $\lambda = 1$ in our simulation.

Table 5.14 INCOMING CALLS TO AN INSURANCE COMPANY SWITCHBOARD

Number of Calls per Minute	Observed Frequency, f_0	Total Calls	Expected Frequency, f_e	$(f_0 - f_e)^2/f_e$
0	40	$0 \times 40 = 0$	36.8	0.28
1	35	$1 \times 35 = 35$	36.8	0.09
2	14	$2 \times 14 = 28$	18.4	1.05
3	8 ⎫	$3 \times 8 = 24$	6.1 ⎫	
4	2 ⎬ 11	$4 \times 2 = 8$	1.5 ⎬ 8	1.12
5	1 ⎭	$5 \times 1 = 5$	0.4 ⎭	
	100	100	100	$\chi^2 = 2.54$

Figure 5.10   A χ^2 goodness-of-fit test.

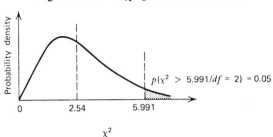

The number of degrees of freedom in this particular hypothesis test is 2, since there are four categories and the Poisson distribution has one parameter; $(4 - 1 - 1) = 2$. For our test we will use an $\alpha = .05$. In order to find the χ^2 that goes with df = 2 and $\alpha = .05$, we turn to Appendix E and find $\chi^2 = 5.991$. Since our value for χ^2 computed from the data is less than 5.991, we continue to accept the null hypothesis that the incoming calls are Poisson distributed; see Figure 5.10.

Kolmogorov–Smirnov Test

The Kolmogorov-Smirnov goodness-of-fit test is another popular method for comparing a data set to a theoretical distribution. It has two advantages over the χ^2 : (1) it is a more powerful test and (2) it can be used with small sample sizes.

The Kolmogorov-Smirnov test involves working with two cumulative distributions. The first is an observed cumulative relative frequency distribution developed from sample data. The other is a cumulative probability distribution for the theoretical distribution being tested. The point at which these two distributions show the greatest divergence is determined, and a decision is made to accept or reject the null hypothesis depending on the probability that the observed difference would occur if the observations were really a random sample from the theoretical distribution.

To demonstrate the use of the Kolmogorov-Smirnov test, assume that we wish to simulate activities at an auto repair shop. In the auto repair shop, one of the service bays is set aside for engine tune-ups and the shop foreman has collected data on how long it takes to do a tune-up. Based on 60 random observations, a mean of 50 minutes and a standard deviation of 5 minutes have been calculated. The observations appear to come from a normal distribution. The data have also been placed in an equal to or less than cumulative relative frequency distribution; see Table 5.15. Each observed cumulative relative frequency, F_0, represents the cumulative values of f_0 (the same observed frequencies used in the χ^2) expressed as a proportion of the total. In other words, each F_0 is calculated by dividing the cumulative observations in each class, n, by the total number of observations, N, in the sample, that is, n/N. For example, in Table 5.15 it can be seen that 20 percent of the tune-ups included in the sample were completed in less than 45 minutes.

The null hypothesis in the Kolmogorov-Smirnov test is that the observed distribution does not differ significantly from the theoretical distribution. In our auto shop example the null hypothesis is that the tune-up times can be described by a normal distribution with a mean of 50 minutes and a standard deviation of 5 minutes. In order to perform

Table 5.15   TIME REQUIRED FOR AN ENGINE TUNE-UP AT AN AUTO REPAIR SHOP

Service Time, minutes	Observed Cumulative Relative Frequency, F_0	Expected Cumulative Frequency, F_e	$D = \|F_0 - F_e\|$
Less than 35	0.01	0.0013	0.0087
Less than 40	0.04	0.0228	0.0172
Less than 45	0.20	0.1387	0.0413
Less than 50	0.48	0.5000	0.0200
Less than 55	0.75	0.8413	0.0913 ⇐ maximum
Less than 60	0.98	0.9772	0.0028
Less than 65	1.00	0.9987	0.0013

the Kolmogorov–Smirnov test, one must calculate a cumulative expected frequency, F_e, for each class that has been created. Table 5.15 shows the expected cumulative frequencies for a normal distribution with a mean of 50 minutes and standard deviation of 5 minutes. The computation of the F_e, the expected cumulative frequency, for the less than 45 minutes class is illustrated here.

$$Z = \frac{45 - 50}{5} = -1.00$$

$$p(Z < -1.00) = .5000 - .3413 = .1387 \qquad \text{(Appendix B)}$$

The Kolmogorov–Smirnov test uses the maximum absolute difference, D, between the F_0's and the F_e's.

$$D = \text{maximum } \|F_0 - F_e\|$$

The differences for our auto shop illustration are shown in column four of Table 5.15. The maximum difference is 0.0913. But is this difference significantly large so that we reject the null hypothesis and the contention that the tune-up times come from a normal distribution? The answer to this question is obtained by using a Kolmogorov–Smirnov table such as that provided in Appendix F. The table requires that the sample size and the level of significance (e.g., the α value) be specified. In our example, the sample size is 60 and let us assume $\alpha = .05$ is appropriate. Because our N is over 35, the D value from the table must be calculated and is $1.36/\sqrt{60} = 0.176$. Since the value from the table is greater than the maximum D found from calculating $D = \|F_0 - F_e\|$, we continue to accept H_0 and assume that tune-up times can be simulated by sampling from a normal distribution with a mean of 50 minutes and a standard deviation of 5 minutes.

SUMMARY

An important component of many simulation models is sampling from probabilistic processes. A procedure that performs this sampling is referred to as a process generator.

Sampling procedures for nontheoretical probability distributions usually require more effort than from theoretical distributions, because the process generator must typically be custom built. Process generators for theoretical distributions, on the other hand, have been developed in a generalized form, which requires the analyst only to input appropriate parameters. Differences in process generators also exist depending on whether the probability distributions are discrete or continuous.

Sampling from discrete nontheoretical distributions is performed through a table lookup procedure. When the distribution is continuous, either an approximation or linear interpolation routine can be used.

For continuous theoretical distributions such as the uniform, negative exponential, and triangular distributions, a process generator can be obtained by the inverse method. With this method, the simple distribution is integrated to obtain its cumulative form, the resulting equation is set equal to r (the random number), and the equation manipulated until the random variable is stated as a function of r. Because the cumulative form of the normal distribution cannot be obtained in exact form through integration, other methods such as the Box–Muller, the sampling method, and the rejection method are used to generate normally distributed variates. Discrete theoretical distributions such as the Bernoulli, binomial, and Poisson distributions are sampled from in ways that count the value for the random variable.

Before theoretical distributions are used to describe real-world processes, goodness-of-fit tests should be employed to decide whether the distribution provides a good description of the real world. Two popular tests are the χ^2 and the Kolmogorov–Smirnov.

ASSIGNMENTS

5.1. Distinguish between the following:
   (a) Probabilities based on subjective judgment and relative frequencies.
   (b) Probabilities that do and do not correspond with theoretical probability distributions.
   (c) Continuous and discrete probability distributions.

5.2. The following probability distribution reflects the number of equipment failures experienced per week by a company during the past year.

Number of Failures	Frequency
0	5
1	10
2	20
3	8
4	7
	50

   (a) Simulate 10 weeks of equipment failure experience using random numbers from Appendix A.

(b) Simulate 10 weeks of equipment failure experience using a computerized model.

5.3. In the chapter, Figure 5.1 presented a cumulative probability distribution for unit sales.

(a) Sample 5 values from this distribution using random numbers from Appendix A. Employ the noncomputerized graphical method.

(b) Using a computerized crude approximation method, sample 50 points from the unit sales distribution. Estimate the unit sales distribution with 5 points. Compute the mean of the 50 sampled points.

(c) Using a computerized linear interpolation method, sample 50 points from the unit sales distribution. Estimate the unit sales distribution with 6 points. Compute the mean of the 50 sampled points.

5.4. The amount of time to service a customer at a particular checkout counter is uniformly distributed with a lower limit of 2 minutes and an upper limit of 7 minutes.

(a) Simulate 10 checkouts using the uniform process generator with random numbers drawn from Appendix A.

(b) Simulate 50 checkouts using the uniform process generator in a computerized model.

5.5. The time between arrivals at a barber shop is negative exponentially distributed with a mean of 5 minutes.

(a) Simulate the arrival (in minutes) of 10 customers with the negative exponential process generator using random numbers from Appendix A.

(b) Simulate the arrival (in minutes) of 50 customers with the negative exponential process generator in a computerized model. Calculate the mean inter-arrival time.

5.6. The weight of items produced by a production process is normally distributed with a mean of 2 lbs and a standard deviation of 0.05 lbs. Simulate in a computerized model the weight of 25 items produced by the production process using the Box–Muller, sampling, and rejection methods. Compute the mean weight associated with each sampling method.

5.7. The time between failures of a particular computer system can be described by the negative exponential distribution with a mean of 2 failures per 200 hours. Using the rejection method, simulate the timing of 3 equipment failures. Truncate the distribution of 800 hours. Use the random numbers in Appendix A.

5.8. White Manufacturing has a particular machine with a time to failure distribution defined as

$$p(t) = .25e^{-.25t} \qquad 0 < t < \infty$$

In this distribution, t is the time to failure expressed in weeks. When the machine fails, a repairman immediately begins repairs on the machine. The repair time distribution is

$$p(r) = 4e^{-4r} \qquad 0 < r < \infty$$

In this distribution, r is the repair time expressed in days. Develop a simulation model to estimate the mean downtime per week in days. Simulate 10 machine failures and repairs. Use random numbers from Appendix A.

5.9.   A manager is uncertain as to how long it will take to complete an activity that he is supervising. He does think, however, that it will not take less than 3 weeks or more than 6 weeks, but that 4 weeks is his best guess.
(a)   Simulate the completion of the activity 10 times using random numbers from Appendix A.
(b)   Simulate the completion of the activity 50 times using a computerized model. Compute the mean of the 50 observations.

5.10.   Using the inverse method, develop process generators for the following probability distributions:

(a) $p(x) = x + 1$ for $-1 \leq x \leq 0$

$= 1 - x$ for $0 \leq x \leq 1$

(b) $p(x) = (\frac{1}{2}) e^x$ for $-\infty < x \leq 0$

$= (\frac{1}{2}) e^{-x}$ for $0 \leq x < \infty$

(c) $p(x) = \frac{1}{6}$ $0 \leq x < 2$

$= \frac{1}{3}$ $2 \leq x < 3$

$= \frac{1}{12}$ $3 \leq x \leq 7$

5.11.   In the ABC Company, 4 percent of the accounts receivable are in error. Simulate the results of an audit of 5 accounts receivable. Use random numbers from Appendix A. Repeat the sampling experiment 5 times.

5.12.   As a part of a larger simulation model, it is necessary to simulate whether a particular machine is "up" or "down," (e.g., running or not running). Assuming that the machine is "up" 98 percent of the time, write and run a computer program that simulates whether the machine is "up" or "down." Check the status of the machine 50 times and output the number of times that it is "up."

5.13.   The job-related accidents in a factory can be described by the Poisson distribution with a mean of 2 accidents per week. In a computerized model, simulate the number of accidents in a 2-week period. Repeat the simulation 5 times.

5.14.   Students arrive at Professor Goodguy's office during his 10:00–11:00 A.M. office hours in a Poisson manner with a mean arrival rate of 1 student/5 minutes. Unfortunately, Professor Goodguy had to take his daughter to the hospital and does not return until 10:20 A.M. Write and run a computer program that simulates the number of students who are waiting when Professor Goodguy returns.

5.15.   The number of defects in a roll of cloth produced in a textile mill can be described by the Poisson distribution with a $\lambda = 2$ defects per roll.
(a)   Find the probability of finding 0 defects in a roll selected at random.
(b)   What is the probability of finding 1 or more defects in a roll selected at random?
(c)   Management is considering doubling the length of a roll of cloth. If this development occurs, find the probability of finding 0 defects in a roll selected at random.
(d)   What is the probability of finding at least one defect?

(e)   Develop an expression for finding the probability of 0 defects in a roll of cloth t times the length of the original roll mentioned.

(f)   What is an appropriate expression for at least one defect occurring?

(g)   Instead of using $\lambda = 2$, develop a general expression for part (f) that is appropriate for any λ.

(h)   Your answer to part (g) is the cumulative density function for the negative exponential distribution. It can be used directly to find the probability of an occurrence by time t.

(i)   Take the derivative of the expression developed in part (g) in order to obtain the density function for the negative exponential distribution.

5.16.   A study has been conducted on the arrivals at a tool crib. The frequency of arrivals in 5-minute time periods is as follow.

Number of Arrivals	Frequency
0	35
1	40
2	17
3	6
4	2
	100

Using a χ^2 goodness-of-fit test with $\alpha = .10$, test whether or not the arrivals at the tool crib can be described by the Poisson distribution.

5.17.   Data have been collected on the time customers spend at a bank's drive-in teller. An analysis of 20 observations reveals a mean of 4 minutes and a standard deviation of 1 minute. A look at the cumulative frequency distribution that follows suggests the possibility that the times may be normally distributed. Investigate this possibility using a Kolmogorov–Smirnov goodness-of-fit test with an α of .10.

Time at Drive-in Teller, in minutes	Observed Cumulative Relative Frequency
Less than 2	0.03
Less than 3	0.30
Less than 4	0.52
Less than 5	0.60
Less than 6	0.94
Less than 7	0.98
Less than 8	1.00

5.18.   The Lewis Manufacturing Company wants to simulate the behavior of its production system. In building the simulation model, the question has come up as to whether the number of defective end products is uniformly distributed throughout the days of the week or whether there are more defective products on certain days. In order to investigate this concern, the company collected the following data.

Day of the Week	Number of Defective Products
Monday	23
Tuesday	18
Wednesday	10
Thursday	25
Friday	24

(a) Using a χ^2 goodness-of-fit test with an α of .05, decide how the number of defective products should be included in the simulation model.

(b) Repeat the analysis of part (a) except employ a Kolmogorov–Smirnov test.

5.19. In Chapter 4, assignment 4.6 called for an analysis of Konzen's profit using a manual approach. Repeat the analysis required in 4.6, except this time use a computerized analysis based on 100 iterations.

5.20. In Chapter 4, probabilistic financial planning using a numeric mode of analysis was presented. A work sheet shown in Table 4.6 illustrated how the analysis for the Medical-Surgical Department would be performed by hand. A computerized analysis was not described, however, since appropriate Monte Carlo sampling technology had not been introduced. Figure 4.7 did show the macrologic for such an analysis. After studying this chapter, you should be able to perform a computerized analysis. Using the following data inputs, the equations presented in Table 4.5., and the logic expressed in Figure 4.7, perform 100 iterations through the model. Compute the mean and standard deviation for total expenditures in the Medical-Surgical Department. Prepare a 95 percent confidence interval on the estimate of the mean.

Variable	Distribution	Parameters
Fixed salary and wages	Normal	$\mu = \$20{,}000$ $\sigma = \ \ \ 2000$
Variable salary and wages	Normal	$\mu = \$ \ \ \ \ \ 4.00$ $\sigma = \ \ \ \ \ \ 0.40$
Patient-days	Triangular	$O = \ 12{,}000$ patient-days $L = \ \ \ \ 9000$ $P = \ \ \ \ 8000$
Variable time$_1$	Uniform	$A = \$ \ \ \ \ 45.00$ $B = \ \ \ \ \ 55.00$
Fixed payroll taxes and benefits	Normal	$\mu = \$ \ 1000$ $\sigma = \ \ \ \ \ 100$

Variable	Distribution	Parameters	
Variable payroll taxes and benefits	Normal	$\mu = \$$ $\sigma =$	0.40 0.04
Variable time$_2$	Uniform	$A = \$$ $B =$	8.00 12.00
Fixed operating supplies	Normal	$\mu = \$$ $\sigma =$	500.00 50.00
Variable operating supplies	Normal	$\mu = \$$ $\sigma =$	0.20 0.03
Variable time$_3$	Uniform	$A = \$$ $B =$	4.00 6.00
Fixed laundry and linen	Triangular	$O = \$$ $L =$ $P =$	500.00 700.00 1000.00
Variable laundry and linen	Triangular	$O = \$$ $L =$ $P =$	0.30 0.40 0.55
Variable time$_4$	Uniform	$A = \$$ $B =$	9.00 12.00
Fixed dietary transfers	Normal	$\mu = \$$ $\sigma =$	100 10
Variable dietary transfers	Normal	$\mu = \$$ $\sigma =$	0.15 0.02
Variable time$_5$	Uniform	$A = \$$ $B =$	1 1.5
Education and travel	Deterministic	$\$$	300
Fixed maintenance of equipment	Normal	$\mu = \$$ $\sigma =$	100 50
Variable time$_6$	Uniform	$A = \$$ $B =$	1 2
Equipment rental	Discrete	$p =$ $(1 - p) =$	.4; $400 .6; $500

5.21. A computerized model for the Monte Carlo inventory simulation in Chapter 3 was never presented because the appropriate sampling technology had not been introduced. Only the macrologic for a computerized model was shown. Prepare and run a computerized Monte Carlo inventory simulation using the macrologic of Figure 3.3 and the following data. Simulate 100 weeks of activity and output the mean cost and standard deviation. Try to make your program as general as possible.

Demand/Week	Frequency	Delivery Time (in weeks)	Frequency
0	6	1	4
1	14	2	4
2	20	3	2
3	8		
4	2		
	50		10

K_c = \$2/item/week   Policies: no "multiple ordering"
K_0 = \$20/order   : simulate Q = 4 to 8
K_s = \$20/item not available R = 2 to 6

REFERENCES

Box, G. E. P., and M. E. Muller, "A Note on the Generation of Random Normal Deviates," *Annuals of Mathematical Statistics*, 29: 601–611.

Clark, Charles T., and Lawrence L. Schkade, *Statistical Methods for Business Decisions* (Cincinnati: South-Western, 1969).

Fishman, George S., *Concepts and Methods in Discrete Event Digital Simulation* (New York: Wiley, 1973).

McMillan, Claude, and Richard F. Gonzalez, *Systems Analysis*, 3rd ed. (Homewood, Ill.: Irwin, 1973).

Meier, Robert C., William T. Newell, and Harold L. Pazer, *Simulation in Business and Economics* (Englewood Cliffs, N.J.: Prentice-Hall, 1969).

Mize, Joe H., and J. Grady Cox, *Essentials of Simulation* (Englewood Cliffs, N.J.: Prentice-Hall, 1968).

Naylor, Thomas H. et al., *Computer Simulation Techniques* (New York: Wiley, 1968).

Schmidt, J. W., and R. E. Taylor, *Simulation and Analysis of Industrial Systems* (Homewood, Ill.: Irwin, 1970).

Shannon, Robert E., *Systems Simulation* (Englewood Cliffs, N.J.: Prentice-Hall, 1975).

Springer, Clifford et al., *Probabilistic Models* (Homewood, Ill.: Irwin, 1968).

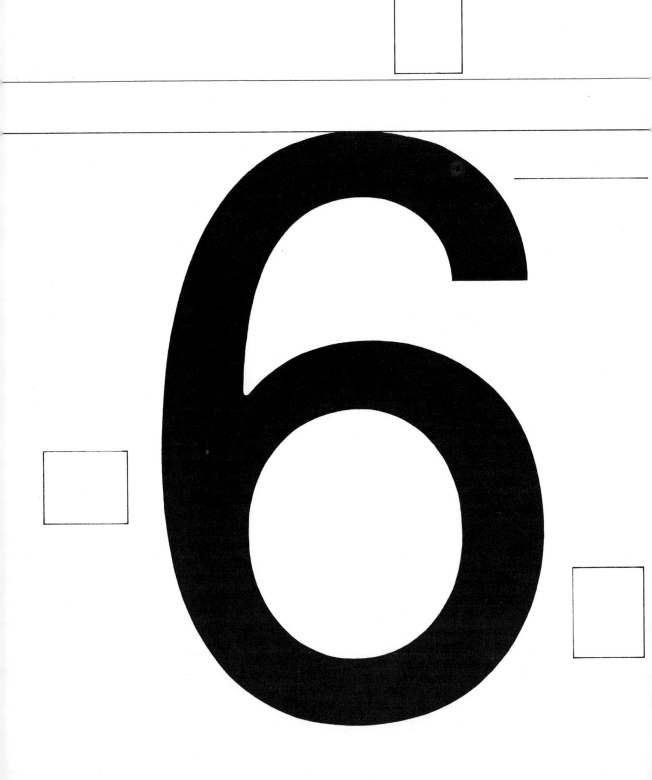

CHAPTER SIX   RANDOM NUMBER GENERATION

Properties of a Good Random Number Generator

Random Number Generation Methods

Digital Computer Methods

    The Midsquare Method

    Congruential Methods

    Examples of Congruential Generators

Statistical Tests for Randomness

    Uniformity Test

    Runs Up and Down Test

    Other Tests

    Applying the Tests

Assignments

References

In previous chapters we have seen numerous occasions where uniform random numbers were needed. In fact, any time a value was sampled from a probability distribution, a random number was required. However, until now our focus has been on how to use random numbers rather than on how to generate them. We have always assumed that usable random numbers could be obtained easily from a table or provided by the computer. Although this orientation is basically correct, there are instances where the model builder must create the means for generating random numbers. Consequently, it seems appropriate to discuss the properties of good random number generators, methods that can be used to generate random numbers, and how the numbers can be statistically tested for randomness. These considerations provide the major focus for this chapter.

PROPERTIES OF A GOOD RANDOM NUMBER GENERATOR

There are numerous ways to generate random numbers and some of the more interesting ways will be explored later. However, for most meaningful real-world applications the generator should possess the following properties.

1. It should produce numbers that are random.
2. It should be fast.
3. It should not require much computer storage.
4. It should have a long period before cycling.
5. It should not degenerate.
6. It should generate random numbers that can be reproduced.

Obviously, the random numbers should be random, or at least have *the appearance of randomness*. Actually, whether any numbers are truly random is a philosophical question, because it may simply be that we are currently unable or uninterested in predicting the pattern with which a sequence of numbers is occurring. Even drawing numbered chips from a bowl might not be considered truly random if the hand motions used in selecting the chips could be predicted.[1] For our purposes, as long as the numbers pass appropriate statistical tests, they will be considered random, even when they can be predicted with certainty.

Large-scale simulation models often require many random numbers. Consequently, their generation method *should be fast*, not requiring much computer time. Furthermore, the method *should not demand much computer storage*.

Nearly all commonly used generation methods produce random numbers that ultimately begin cycling at some point. In other words, the sequence of random numbers begins repeating itself. The objective is to select a generation method that *produces all of the random numbers that are needed* before the cycling occurs. This suggests that what is a satisfactory generation method depends at least somewhat on the application. If only 50 random numbers are needed, cycling after producing 100 numbers creates no problems.

---

[1]Claude McMillan and Richard F. Gonzalez, *Systems Analysis*, 3rd ed. (Homewood, Ill.: Irwin, 1973), p. 237.

It is also important that the generation method *does not degenerate*. That is, the method should not begin repeating the same number over and over. For example, it is not uncommon for some generation methods to degenerate to a value of 0.

It is often useful to *be able to repeat a sequence of random numbers*. This capability is important in replicating experimental conditions, that is, subjecting different configurations of a system to the same conditions and then observing the behavior of the system. For example, in our inventory simulation it was useful to experiment with different Q and R combinations under the same demand and delivery time patterns. This requires that the same sequence of random numbers be repeated.

RANDOM NUMBER GENERATION METHODS

Having discussed the properties of good generation methods, let us now explore some of the alternatives that are open to the model builder. Some of the options are mentioned only to provide a historical perspective to the topic, whereas others are in wide use today. In general, the methods fall into one of the following categories.

1. Manual methods.
2. Random number tables.
3. Analog computer methods.
4. Digital computer methods.

Manual methods are typically used for classroom demonstrations rather than for actual simulation modeling. These methods include the drawing of numbered chips from a bowl, balls from an urn, slips of paper from a hat, and the like. As long as manual methods are carefully performed, a limited supply of random numbers can be obtained. The major drawback of these methods is that they are too slow to generate the quantity of random numbers that are typically needed. Furthermore, the numbers are not reproducible.

Many different *tables of random numbers* have been developed, the earliest being prepared by Tippett in 1927. As mentioned in a previous chapter, the Rand Corporation's *A Million Random Digits with 100,000 Normal Deviates* is one of the largest and best known tables.[2] Although random numbers tables are highly satisfactory for hand-performed simulations, they are less desirable for computerized modeling, because the numbers have to be stored in the computer. If they are maintained in primary storage, precious storage capacity is used. If the random numbers are stored on magnetic tape, the relatively slow transfer times from tape to the central processing unit increases computer running time. Consequently, given other alternatives, tables are infrequently used with computerized modeling.

The Rand table was developed using an *analog computer method*. Observations were made off an electronic pulse generator driven by a noise source. Similar types of devices have been used in developing random number tables and are described elsewhere.[3]

Although analog computer methods provide a fast source of a large quantity of random

[2]Rand Corporation, *A Million Random Digits with 100,000 Normal Deviates* (Glencoe, Ill.: The Free Press, 1955).

[3]Granino A. Korn, *Random Process Simulation and Measurements* (New York: McGraw-Hill, 1966).

numbers, there are problems with this approach—the random number devices are not easily connected to digital computers and the numbers generated are not reproducible. Thus we are left with only methods that have been developed specifically for use with digital computers when we are working with computerized simulation models.

Methods for generating random numbers on *digital computers* vary from the midsquare method proposed by von Neumann and Metropolis in 1946 to the congruential methods employed today.[4] These methods are frequently referred to as *pseudo* random number generators, since each number is developed from a *recursive* mathematical relationship. That is, the mathematical relationship provides a link between any number generated and the next one in the sequence. Because the numbers in the sequence can be predicted with certainty, the term "pseudo" is sometimes used. From our point of view this distinction is not important, since our criterion for randomness requires only the passing of appropriate statistical tests. As we will see, the digital computer generation methods satisfy our properties for good random number generation better than alternative methods.

DIGITAL COMPUTER METHODS

A considerable number of digital computer-oriented methods for generating random numbers have been suggested. We will consider only two of the alternatives, the *midsquare* and *congruential methods*. The first is discussed to provide historical perspective, whereas the latter is explored because of its current popularity.

The Midsquare Method

The midsquare method is very simple to understand and use, which undoubtedly led to its early popularity. The steps to follow when using the midsquare method are:

1. Select a number of n digits (usually even) where n is the number of digits desired in the random number.
2. Square the number from step 1 and add zeros to the left as necessary in order to form a number of $2n$ digits.
3. Extract the middle n digits from the number in step 2. This is the random number.
4. Square the random number obtained from step 3, adding once again zeros to the result as needed to form a number of $2n$ digits.
5. Repeat steps 3 and 4 in order to obtain additional random numbers.

As an example, assume that 25 is selected as the starting number for generating two-digit random numbers. The starting number is commonly referred to as the "seed number." This selection of 25 as the seed number results in the following sequence of random numbers.

$$(25)^2 = 06\underset{\vee}{2}5$$

therefore, $r_1 = 62$

$$(62)^2 = 38\underset{\vee}{4}4$$

[4]N. Metropolis, "Phase Shifts-Middle Square-Wave Equation," *Symposium on Monte Carlo Methods*, Herbert A. Meyer, ed. (New York: Wiley, 1956).

therefore, $r_2 = 84$

$$(84)^2 = 7056$$

therefore, $r_3 = 05$

$$\vdots$$

Despite the ease and simplicity of the midsquare method, its use is no longer recommended for several reasons: The method, depending on the initial number selected, (1) can produce random numbers with exceptionally short periods before cycling occurs; (2) the numbers generated may not pass statistical tests of randomness; (3) the method has a tendency to degenerate; and (4) the method is not very fast when compared to alternative methods.

Congruential Methods

Congruential methods for generating random numbers were first suggested by Lehmer in 1949.[5] These methods are based on what is mathematically referred to as a *congruence relationship*. Although there are many variations, *multiplicative congruential generators* are perhaps the most popular. They are based on the following congruence relationship.

$$r_{i+1} = ar_i \pmod{m} \qquad (6\text{-}1)$$

The relation reads, "r_{i+1} is congruent to ar_i modulo m." Any number in the random number sequence is found by multiplying the preceding number by a constant and then "reducing the product by modulo m." The *modulo m* operation calls for dividing ar_i by m and keeping *only the remainder* as the value for r_{i+1}. Assume, for example, that $a = 5, r_0 = 3$, and $m = 32$. The value of r_i is found to be 15, as shown here.

$$r_1 = 5 \times 3 \pmod{32}$$

$$
\begin{array}{r}
0 \\
32 \overline{\smash{)}15} \\
0 \\
\hline
\end{array}
$$

(15)   the remainder

therefore, $r_1 = 15$
The value for r_2 is found to be

$$r_2 = 5 \times 15 \pmod{32}$$

$$
\begin{array}{r}
2 \\
32 \overline{\smash{)}75} \\
64 \\
\hline
\end{array}
$$

(11)   the remainder

therefore, $r_2 = 11$.

[5]D. H. Lehmer, "Mathematical Methods in Large Scale Computing Units," *Proceedings of a Second Symposium on Large Scale Calculating Machinery*, The Annals of the Computation Laboratory of Harvard University, Vol. XXVI (Cambridge, Mass.: Harvard University Press, 1951), pp. 141–146.

The distribution of r_{i+1}'s are uniformly distributed and provide the source of random numbers.

Design Criteria. Two points about congruential random number generators need to be made. First, at some point they all begin to cycle. Consider, for example, the preceding illustration. If r_i ever takes on a previous value, for example, $r_i = 3$, the same sequence has to be repeated, since the next numbers are computed in exactly the same manner as before. The only question is when the cycling will begin and what can be done to provide reasonably long periods. Second, some approaches are more computationally efficient than others.

These concerns have led to considerable thinking and research on various types of congruential generators (e.g., mixed, additive) and as to what values for a, r_0, and m are best. These investigations take one into the field of number theory and are beyond the scope of this book. Our interest, instead, will be limited to the results of these explorations.

The development of a multiplicative generator is highly machine dependent. Values for a, r_0, and m should be selected so as to (1) produce sequences of numbers with long periods and (2) create computationally efficient generators. For a binary computer, these objectives are achieved with r_0 odd and $a = 8t \pm 3$ for $t = 1, 2, 3, \ldots$. For some time it was also thought that a should be selected so that $a = 2^{b/2}$, where b is the number of bits in a word *exclusive of the sign bit*. However, current research casts doubts on this last criterion.[6] Shannon concludes that a "... should be chosen such as to be five or more digits and not contain long strings of zeros or ones."[7]

The value for m is selected largely on the basis of maximizing computational efficiency. For this reason, m is commonly chosen to be $m = 2^b$. When a and r_0 are selected as described, random numbers with a maximum period of $m/4$ are generated.

Examples of Congruential Generators

Let us now see how these criteria can be applied when developing a multiplicative congruential generator. First, we will consider a hypothetical computer, one whose structure is sufficiently simple that the development of the generator is easy to follow and understand. The logic underlying the generator will be patterned after the design criteria just described. Next, after the logic of the simple computer has been discussed, SUBROUTINE RANDU will be examined. This subroutine is available on most IBM System 360 and 370 computers. This two-step process should serve to illustrate how many random number generators are developed and function.

A Simple Computer. Our hypothetical computer will be a very small one. It has only four bits to a word and one of them is a sign bit. Consequently, 111_2 or 7 is the largest integer number that can be stored. The value of a is selected as 5, since it satisfies $a = 8t \pm 3$, where $t = 1$ and the minus portion of the ± 3 is chosen. Of course, other choices for a could have been made.

---

[6] A. Van Gelden, "Some New Results in Pseudo-Random Number Generation," *Journal of the Association for Computing Machinery* (October 1967), pp. 785–792 and R. R. Coveyou and R. D. MacPherson, "Fourier Analysis of Uniform Random Number Generators," *Journal of the Association for Computing Machinery* (January 1967), pp. 100–119.

[7] Robert E. Shannon, *Systems Simulation* (Englewood Cliffs, N.J.: Prentice-Hall, 1975), p. 351.

Table 6.1 SUBROUTINE RANDUX FOR A HYPOTHETICAL FOUR BIT WORD SIZE COMPUTER

```
SUBROUTINE RANDUX(IX,IY,YFL)
  IY=IX *5
  IF(IY) 5,6,6
5 IY=IY+7+1
6 YFL=IY
  YFL = YFL* 0.125
  RETURN
  END
```

The value for m in the generator should be 2^3 or 8. As will be seen, this selection for m greatly simplifies the modulo m operation. Our generator will have a maximum period of only 2 before cycling. This is seen by dividing the value for m, which is 8 in this case, by 4.

These choices for a and m result in the following random number generator.

$$n_{i+1} = 5 \times n_i \ (\text{mod } 8) \tag{6-2}$$

Let us now consider how this generator might function when placed in a subroutine; see Table 6.1.

On the surface it is not apparent that RANDUX functions as a multiplicative congruential random number generator because the generator is designed around the characteristics of a particular computer and much of its functioning is not clear until the characteristics of the machine are considered.

The IX and IY in RANDUX correspond with n_i and n_{i+1}, respectively, in Equation 6-2. IX is initialized in the main program with a seed number and IY is computed from it. When subsequent calls on RANDUX are made, IX must first be set equal to IY (i.e., IX=IY) in the main program so that the next number in the sequence is generated.

The most interesting and not obvious thing about the statement IY=IX*5 is that the (mod 8) operation is being performed as well as the multiplication of IX by 5. In order to see this point, visualize how an integer number is stored in a four-bit word size computer. As an example, assume that the odd number 3 has been selected as the seed number for IX. Computer memory would then appear as shown in Figure 6.1. The rightmost three bits store in binary form the number 3. The left bit is the sign bit and stores a 0 for positive numbers and a 1 for negative values. Now let us consider what happens when the

Figure 6.1. The integer number 3 stored in a four bit word size computer.

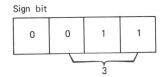

Figure 6.2.   The result in computer memory of multiplying 3 by 5.

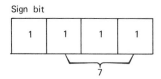

seed number 3 is multiplied by 5. This product is 15, which is the binary number 1111_2. But consider what happens within the computer's memory because of this multiplication; see Figure 6.2. The multiplication causes an overflow with 7 being the number stored and a 1 being stored in the sign bit. It turns out in this case, and in every case, that the number in storage is the result of mod 8.

$$
\begin{array}{r}
1 \\
8\,\overline{)\,15} \\
8 \\
\hline
\textcircled{7}
\end{array}
\;\leftarrow \text{the result of mod 8}
$$

By selecting m to be 2^b, we see that what remains is always the result of a mod 2^b operation. This result is true regardless of the number of bits to a word. It also creates a very efficient random number generator.

Our concern now turns to the 1 that has overflowed to the sign bit, since only positive random numbers are desired. RANDUX attacks this problem by first testing whether IY is negative. If this test proves true, IY is made positive by the statement IY=IY+7+1. The first number that is added to IY is the largest number than can be stored in IY, which is 7 for our hypothetical computer ($2^3 - 1 = 7$). Figure 6.3 shows the result of adding 7. It causes the leftmost digit to be lost due to even more overflow, and the sign bit is changed back from 1 to 0, indicating a positive number. The number that is stored (here the number 6) becomes the desired number (7 in this case), when the number 1 is added. In other words, by adding the largest integer value that can be stored and then 1 more, negative numbers are made their positive equivalents.

The next step is to transform the IYs, which are random between 0 and 7 (the largest integer number that can be stored) into uniform random numbers between 0 and 1. The statement YFL=IY changes the random number from integer to real mode (and also the way that the number is stored in memory). In subroutine RANDUX, YFL ultimately stores and communicates back to the main program the uniform random numbers that have been generated. The next statement, YFL=YFL*0.125, transforms YFL into a number between 0 and 1. The multiplier for YFL is always selected to be $1/2^b$. In our

Figure 6.3.   The result in computer memory of adding 7 to -7.

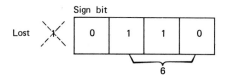

example, the multiplier is found to be $1/2^3$ or 0.125. Since the initial value for YFL has to be between 0 and $2^b - 1$, multiplying by $1/2^b$ always results in a number between 0 and up to but excluding 1. Continuing with our specific example, multiplying 7 by 0.125 results in the first uniform random number 0.875. This, by the way, is the largest random number that will ever be generated by our computer. The random number 0.875 is carried back to the main program for use in a simulation model by YFL. Subsequent calls on RANDUX (with IX=IY preceding the call in the main program) results in the following string of random numbers: 0.375, 0.875, 0.375, ... The sequence of random numbers is obviously cycling with a period of two. This result is as expected because the maximum period for this small computer is $m/4$ or $8/4 = 2$.

IBM System 360 and 370 Computers. Most computers have many more bits to a word than four. For example, the popular IBM System 360 and 370 series of computers features 32 bits, including a sign bit. SUBROUTINE RANDU is based on the same logic as our hypothetical RANDUX subroutine.[8] When a random number is needed, it is only necessary to CALL RANDU(IX,IY,YFL). Table 6.2 presents the RANDU subroutine. The variables in the argument list, IX, IY, and YFL, serve the same role as with our simple computer. The statement IY=IX* 65539 involves both multiplication by a and the modulo m operation. The value for a, 65539, satisfies the $a = 8t \pm 3$ for $t = 1, 2, 3, \ldots$ criterion by using $t = 8192$ and taking the plus portion of the ± 3. The value for m is 2147483648 and was found by setting $m = 2^b$ or 2^{31}. Using odd values for IX and the previous values for a and m results in a maximum period of $m/4$ or 536870912.

Because of the possibility of an overflow due to the multiplication process, IY is checked for its sign. If found to be negative, $(2^{31} - 1) + 1$ or 2147483647 + 1 is added in order to change the sign but not the value of the random number.

The random number that has been stored in integer mode in IY is then changed to real mode and stored in YFL by the statement YFL=IY. The value for YFL is then multiplied by $1/2^{31}$ or 0.4656613E-9 in order to make it uniform between 0 and 1.

Table 6.2   SUBROUTINE RANDU WHICH IS
AVAILABLE ON MANY IBM COMPUTERS

```
      SUBROUTINE RANDU(IX,IY,YFL)
      IY=IX*65539
      IF(IY) 5,6,6
    5 IY=IY+2147483647+1
    6 YFL=IY
      YFL=YFL* .4656613E-9
      RETURN
      END
```

[8]IBM Corporation, *System/360 Scientific Subroutine Package* (360A-CM-03X), Form H20-0205-0 (White Plains, N.Y., 1966).

The random number generation routine for the hypothetical computer was easier to follow than RANDU, because it was easier to describe the computer's memory at any point and the numbers were of a smaller magnitude. However, RANDU uses exactly the same logic as the hypothetical computer. Employing the same logic, one can develop a multiplicative congruential uniform random number generator for a binary computer of any word size.

STATISTICAL TESTS FOR RANDOMNESS

Before using an unknown or untested generator, one should test the generator for randomness. There are many ways in which a generator can fail to be random—the numbers produced may not come from the uniform distribution; the sequence of numbers may not be random; the digits within the numbers may not be random. In response to these potential problems a large number of statistical tests have been developed. We will consider in detail only a uniformity test and a runs up and down test and briefly describe several other tests, since complete discussions are available in many other sources.[9] A reasonable understanding should be gained, however, as to the nature of tests for randomness.

Uniformity Test

Random numbers should come from the uniform distribution and several tests have been developed to test for this condition. We will consider the χ^2 goodness-of-fit test, although the Kolmogorov–Smirnov test is also frequently used.[10]

The χ^2 goodness-of-fit test, as you will recall from Chapter 5, requires that there be at least 50 observations in total with an expected frequency of at least five in each class. Table 6.3 shows the results of placing a total of 100 observations in 10 evenly spaced classes. The observations in each class vary from 7 to 12, although the expected frequency in each class is 10. The question is, do these numbers come from the uniform distribution? Calculating the χ^2 statistic from the data using the equation

$$\chi^2 = \sum \frac{(f_0 - f_e)^2}{f_e}$$

finds a value of $\chi^2 = 2.40$. In testing the null hypothesis that the random numbers come from the uniform distribution, one compares the calculated χ^2 to the χ^2 value obtained from Appendix E based on $(10 - 1) = 9$ degrees of freedom (10 classes - 1) and an appropriate α value, say, $\alpha = .05$. This χ^2 value is found to be 16.919, which is much greater than the calculated χ^2 value. Consequently, we continue to accept the null hypothesis, and continue to find our random number generator acceptable.

Runs Up and Down Test

Numbers can pass a uniformity test and still not be random. For example, the numbers 0.00, 0.10, 0.20, 0.30, 0.40, 0.50, 0.60, 0.70, 0.80, 0.90, 0.00, . . . obviously are not ran-

[9]J. W. Schmidt and R. E. Taylor, *Simulation and Analysis of Industrial Systems* (Homewood, Ill.: Irwin, 1970), Chapter 6.
[10]Ibid., pp. 230–234.

Table 6.3   100 RANDOM NUMBERS PLACED IN TEN CLASSES

Classes	Observed Frequency	Expected Frequency	$(f_0 - f_e)^2/f_e$
0.00–0.10	9	10	0.10
0.10–0.20	12	10	0.40
0.20–0.30	10	10	0.00
0.30–0.40	11	10	0.10
0.40–0.50	8	10	0.40
0.50–0.60	10	10	0.00
0.60–0.70	10	10	0.00
0.70–0.80	7	10	0.90
0.80–0.90	12	10	0.40
0.90–1.00	11	10	0.10
	100	100	2.40

dom. The numbers must also be random in their sequencing in order to be judged truly random. A variety of runs tests can be used for this purpose. We will consider a runs up and down test.

In a sequence of numbers, if a number is followed by a larger number, this is an upward run. Likewise, a number followed by a smaller number is a downward run. If the numbers are truly random, one would expect to find a certain number of runs up and down.

Consider the following sequence of numbers:

$$0.30, 0.46, \quad 0.14, \quad 0.49, 0.83, \quad 0.64, 0.41, \quad 0.96$$
$$+ \qquad\qquad - \qquad\qquad + \qquad\qquad - \qquad\qquad +$$

The random number 0.30 is the first number in the sequence and sets the stage for either an upward or downward run. Since the second number, 0.46, is larger than the first, the first run is an upward run and is marked by a (+). The third number, 0.14, is less than the second and, consequently, ends the first run and begins a downward run. This run is indicated by a (-). Using similar logic, we find the sequence of numbers to contain a total of five runs.

In a sequence of N numbers, one should expect to find runs equal to that calculated from Equation 6-3. The variance in the number of runs is given by Equation 6-4.

$$\mu = \frac{2N - 1}{3} \tag{6-3}$$

$$\sigma^2 = \frac{16N - 29}{90} \tag{6-4}$$

As an example, assume that the following 40 numbers have been generated.

$$0.43, 0.32,\ \ 0.48,\ \ 0.23,\ \ 0.90,\ \ 0.72,\ \ 0.94,\ \ 0.11,\ \ 0.14, 0.67,$$
$$-\ \ +\ \ -\ \ +\ \ -\ \ +\ \ -\ \ +$$

$$0.61, 0.25,\ \ 0.45, 0.56, 0.87,\ \ 0.54, 0.01,\ \ 0.64, 0.65,\ \ 0.32, 0.03,$$
$$-\qquad\qquad +\qquad\qquad -\qquad\qquad +\qquad\qquad -$$

$$0.93,\ \ 0.08,\ \ 0.58,\ \ 0.41, 0.32, 0.03,\ \ 0.18, 0.90,\ \ 0.74, 0.32,$$
$$+\qquad -\qquad +\qquad\qquad -\qquad\qquad\qquad +\qquad\qquad -$$

$$0.75,\ \ 0.42,\ \ 0.71,\ \ 0.66, 0.03,\ \ 0.44, 0.99,\ \ 0.40,\ \ 0.51$$
$$+\qquad -\qquad +\qquad\qquad -\qquad\qquad +\qquad -\qquad +$$

One should expect to find 26.33 runs.

$$\mu = \frac{2 \times 40 - 1}{3} = 26.33$$

The variance in the runs for 40 random numbers is 6.79.

$$\sigma^2 = \frac{16 \times 40 - 29}{90} = 6.79$$

Actually, however, 26 runs were observed, which is as close as possible in this case, because the number of runs must be integer valued. For the sake of completeness, let us continue with the formal test of randomness.

For sample sizes of 20 or more the sampling distribution for the number of runs is normally distributed with a mean and variance given by Equations 6-3 and 6-4, respectively. Figure 6.4 depicts the testing of the null hypothesis at the $\alpha = .05$ level that the runs exhibited by the data are random. Since there can be more or less runs than expected, the test is two tailed.

Figure 6.4. Testing the number of runs up and down.

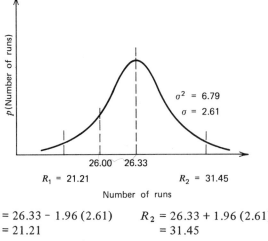

$$R_1 = 26.33 - 1.96 (2.61) \qquad R_2 = 26.33 + 1.96 (2.61)$$
$$= 21.21 \qquad\qquad\qquad\qquad = 31.45$$

There were 26 runs in the sequence of numbers and this falls within R_1 and R_2, the points at which we would reject the null hypothesis. Consequently, we continue to accept the numbers generated as being random.

Other Tests

As mentioned, there are many possible tests for randomness. These tests are described elsewhere and we will only briefly describe some of the more important ones.[11] Each examines a particular characteristic of randomness.

Tests for Autocorrelation. Numbers are autocorrelated when the numbers in the sequence tend to be followed by other numbers in some specific way. For example, if starting with the fifth number, every tenth number is correlated, the sequence would be said to be autocorrelated. Obviously, autocorrelation is a deviation from randomness and is a possible reason for rejecting a set of random numbers for use in a simulation model.

Gap Test. One would expect to find "gaps" between repetitions of a number. For example, in the sequence 83, 13, 19, 46, 83, there is a gap of 3 between the number 83. The gap test ensures that the spacing between particular numbers is random.

Poker Test. The poker test is used to test randomness within random numbers. It considers the likelihood that certain combinations of digits should occur against actual occurrences. It is analogous to evaluating the likelihood of certain poker hands being dealt. For example, the random number 0.44334 is analogous to a full house. Similar numbers should not occur too often if the generator is truly random.

Runs Above and Below the Mean Test. In addition to the runs up and down test described previously, it is also possible to analyze the number of runs above and below some constant, usually the mean. For example, the random numbers 0.83, 0.92, 0.63, 0.60, 0.43, 0.48, 0.18, . . . might pass a runs up and down test, but certainly do not appear random based on their sequencing above and below a mean of 0.50. The runs above and below the mean test detects this deviation from randomness.

Applying the Tests

Obviously, just from the tests described, there are many possible statistical tests for randomness that can be applied. How many and what particular tests should be used depend on factors such as how much is known about the generator, what deviations from randomness are most likely, what are the costs associated with performing the tests, and what are the possible errors and costs associated with deviations from randomness.

In most instances a uniformity test is the first one applied. Lack of uniformity is a fairly common and potentially serious deviation from randomness. Even if the numbers are uniformly distributed, their sequencing may not be random. This possibility suggests the use of runs up and down, autocorrelation, gap and/or runs above and below the mean tests. And finally, the digits within the random numbers can be analyzed by tests such as the poker test.

[11] Ibid., pp. 241–254.

Even when a generator fails a particular test, this does not necessarily mean that the generator is "bad." Rather, the failure itself may be due to randomness. For example, if three tests on a "good" generator at an $\alpha = .05$ level are performed, the probability of failing one or more tests is, $1 - (.95)^3$, or approximately 16 percent. The failure of a test should usually be followed by a reapplication of the test with a larger sample size to determine whether the generator is truly good or bad.

SUMMARY

Random numbers are important to any probabilistic simulation study. In most instances random numbers can be obtained from a table or packaged computer software. There are instances, however, where random numbers are not available and the analyst must be able to generate and test the numbers.

There are important properties associated with a good random number generator. The generator should produce numbers that are random, be fast, not require much computer storage, have a long period before cycling, not degenerate, and provide numbers that are reproducible.

There are a number of methods for generating or obtaining random numbers. They include manual methods, random number tables, analog computer methods, and digital computer methods.

Most real-world applications of simulation rely on digital computer methods as the source of random numbers. An early method of this type was the midsquare method, but it is no longer used. The most common methods employed today are congruential methods.

Congruential methods meet the properties of good random number generators. Most medium to large computer systems have callable congruential random number generation routines as part of their software. For example, SUBROUTINE RANDU is available on many IBM computers. The design of a congruential random number generator is highly machine dependent in order to achieve computational efficiency.

A random number generator should be able to pass statistical tests for randomness. There are a large number of tests that can be applied. These tests include: uniformity tests, runs up and down tests, tests for autocorrelation, gap tests, poker tests, and runs above and below the mean tests. The failure to pass any one test, however, should not result in automatic rejection of the random number generator.

ASSIGNMENTS

6.1. Discuss the following methods of random number generation in terms of the properties of good generation methods.
(a) Manual methods.
(b) Random number tables.
(c) Analog computer methods.
(d) Midsquare methods.
(e) Congruential methods.

6.2.   Design and use a manual method for generating 100 random numbers. Test the randomness of the numbers generated by subjecting them to a uniformity test.

6.3.   Using 84 as the starting pointing, generate ten random numbers by the midsquare method.

6.4.   Using 4301 as the starting point, generate ten random numbers by the midsquare method.

6.5.   Using $a = 55$, $r_0 = 3$ and $m = 32$, generate ten random numbers by means of a multiplicative congruential generator.

6.6.   Using $a = 19$, $r_0 = 15$ and $m = 128$, generate ten random numbers by means of a multiplicative congruential generator.

6.7.   Develop a multiplicative congruential random number generation subroutine for a computer with 6 bits to a word, including a sign bit.

6.8.   Develop a multiplicative congruential random number generation subroutine for a computer with 8 bits to a word, including a sign bit. Using 31 as a seed number, generate 5 random numbers using the logic expressed in your subroutine.

6.9.   Consult the reference manual for your computer system. Find a listing of its subroutine for generating random numbers. Explain the logic behind its design.

6.10.   The following sequence of random numbers should be read across the rows from left to right. Test the sequence of numbers for randomness at an $\alpha = .05$ level using a uniformity and a runs up and down test. Based on your analysis, what should be done next?

0.81, 0.44, 0.58, 0.71, 0.33, 0.53, 0.89, 0.58, 0.49, 0.78,
0.80, 0.73, 0.76, 0.64, 0.65, 0.32, 0.86, 0.34, 0.43, 0.04,
0.93, 0.04, 0.20, 0.66, 0.44, 0.66, 0.95, 0.97, 0.60, 0.36,
0.50, 0.02, 0.81, 0.11, 0.24, 0.58, 0.76, 0.52, 0.75, 0.07,
0.88, 0.53, 0.34, 0.90, 0.25, 0.89, 0.87, 0.44, 0.12, 0.21

6.11.   Taking 3865 as the seed number, generate 50 random numbers using the random number generation subroutine on your computer system. Test the randomness of the numbers generated with a uniformity and a runs up and down test at the $\alpha = .05$ level.

6.12.   Consider the last four digits of telephone numbers as a possible source of random numbers. Test their suitability using a uniformity and a runs up and down test at the $\alpha = .05$ level.

REFERENCES

Coveyou, R. R., and R. D. MacPherson, "Fourier Analysis of Uniform Random Number Generators," *Journal of the Association for Computing Machinery* (January 1967).

IBM Corporation, *Random Number Generation and Testing*, Form C20-8011 (White Plains, N.Y., 1959).

IBM Corporation, *System/360 Scientific Subroutine Package* (360A-CM-03X), Form H20-0205-0 (White Plains, N.Y., 1966).

Jansson, B., *Random Number Generators* (Stockholm: Almquist and Witsell, 1966).

Korn, Granino A., *Random Process Simulation and Measurements* (New York: McGraw-Hill, 1966).

Lehmer, D. H., "Mathematical Methods in Large Scale Computing Units," *Proceedings of a Second Symposium on Large Scale Digital Calculating Machinery*, The Annals of the Computation Laboratory of Harvard University, Vol. XXVI (Cambridge, Mass.: Harvard University Press, 1951), pp. 141–146.

McMillan, Claude, and Richard F. Gonzalez, *Systems Analysis*, 3rd. ed. (Homewood, Ill.: Irwin, 1973).

Metropolis, N., "Phase Shifts-Middle Square-Wave Equation," *Symposium on Monte Carlo Methods*, Herbert A. Meyer, ed. (New York: Wiley, 1956).

Schmidt, J. W., and R. E. Taylor, *Simulation and Analysis of Industrial Systems* (Homewood, Ill.: Irwin, 1970).

Shannon, Robert E., *Systems Simulation* (Englewood Cliffs, N.J., 1975).

Teichroew, Daniel, "A History of Distribution Sampling Prior to the Era of the Computer and Its Relevance to Simulation," *American Statistical Association Journal* (March 1965): 36–37.

Tippett, L. H. C., *Tracts for Computers*, No. XV (Cambridge, Eng.: Cambridge University Press, 1927).

Van Gelden, A., "Some New Results in Pseudo-Random Number Generation," *Journal of the Association for Computing Machinery* (October 1967).

CHAPTER SEVEN

SIMULATING QUEUING SYSTEMS

Basic Terminology

A Simple Queuing System: A Tool Crib

Approaches to Queuing Problems

Applying the Analytic Approach to the Tool Crib Operation

    Applicable Formulas

    Adding Cost Considerations

An Important Characteristic of Queuing Systems

Simulating the Tool Crib Operation

    A Solution Approach

    Model Start-up

    Model Shutdown

No Scheduled Service Completion

Simultaneous Events

The Data Inputs

The Data Output

The FORTRAN-based Model

Program Output

Varying the Run Time

Comparing Solution Approaches

Summary

Assignments

References

Queuing, or *waiting line*, systems are exceptionally common. Customers queue up before tellers at a bank. Unfinished goods wait at work stations for further processing. Students line up at registration to sign up for courses. Any system that is characterized by elements possibly having to wait in line to receive service can be conceptualized as being a queuing system.

The design of any queuing system should take into consideration two different sets of costs. The first set involves the costs of providing service. The second set involves the costs of having elements waiting in line. Take the checkout lanes at a grocery store as an example. The service costs include the costs of the cash registers, counters, and checkout clerks. The costs to the store of having people wait in line reflect the possibility of people laying down their merchandise and walking out of the store and of customers not returning because of long waiting lines. Optimal system design should attempt to minimize the sum of service and waiting costs. However, in some instances it is difficult to estimate waiting costs, and systems are designed to satisfy minimum service level requirements.

This chapter discusses the analysis of queuing systems by (1) trial-and-error, (2) analytic, and (3) simulation methods. Through the example of a tool crib operation, we will see how simple systems can be investigated through analytic methods. The major thrust of the chapter, however, will be to illustrate how simulation can be used to describe the behavior of queuing systems. In the next chapter it will be shown how General Purpose Simulation System (GPSS), a special-purpose simulation language, can be used to analyze queuing systems.

BASIC TERMINOLOGY

When describing queuing systems, certain terminology is commonly used. For example, a distinction is made between the queue and the system. The *queue* is made up of those elements waiting in line to receive service. The *system* includes the queue, the server, and any element currently being served. In our grocery checkout example, the customers waiting in line constitute the queue whereas the system also includes the customer currently being served and the checkout clerk; see Figure 7.1.

Queues are also described by their number of channels and phases. The number of *channels* describes the number of lines that are in the system. Queuing systems are

Figure 7.1   A basic queuing system.

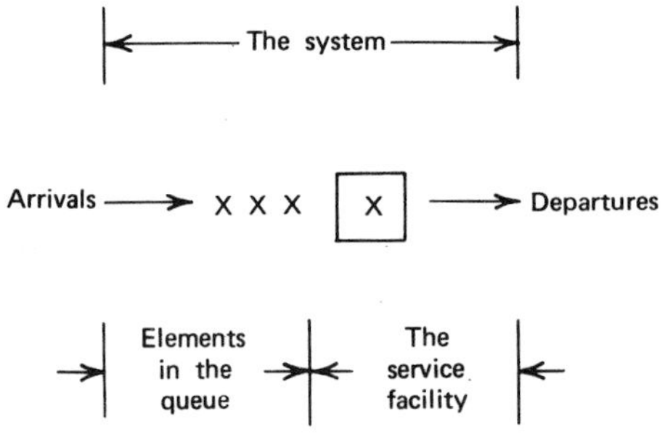

Figure 7.2   Different queuing configurations.

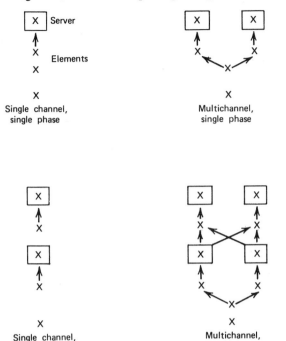

Single channel,
single phase

Multichannel,
single phase

Single channel,
multiphase

Multichannel,
multiphase

either single or multichannel. The number of *phases* refers to the number of service facilities an element must pass through before completing service. Queuing systems are either single or multiphase; see Figure 7.2.

Let us consider some common examples of different types of queuing systems. A toll booth on a bridge is a single-channel, single-phase queue. Most large discount store checkout facilities are multichannel, single phase. An assembly line is commonly single-channel, multiphase. University registration systems are often multichannel, multiphase. Examples of other queuing systems are presented in Table 7.1.

Queuing systems differ in their arrival and service time distributions. The *arrival distribution* describes the pattern by which the elements arrive for servicing. For example, uniform, Poisson, and normal arrival rates are all common. Likewise, the *service distribution* describes the pattern by which the server provides service. Again, many different service distributions are found in the real world.

Waiting lines are also characterized by their *queue discipline.* This concept refers to the order in which elements waiting in line are served. Most of us are accustomed to first-come, first-served queue disciplines. But, for example, in a job shop the queue discipline may be based on promised delivery dates rather than on when orders are received. Those with earlier due dates are said to have higher *priorities* than the others.

Balking is often encountered in queuing systems. Whenever an element turns away from a queue, usually because of its length, the element is said to have balked. All people balk at queues at one time or another.

Table 7.1   EXAMPLES OF QUEUING SYSTEMS

Single Channel, Single Phase	Single Channel, Multiphase	Multichannel, Single Phase	Multichannel, Multiphase
1. A theater ticket booth	1. A bus route	1. Cashiers at a bank	1. Landing and picking up luggage at a major airport
2. Car repairs in a one-man garage	2. Customers passing through a cafeteria	2. Customers awaiting service in a multi-pump filling station	2. Orders being received, filled, and billed in a large mail order house
3. Trucks arriving at a single warehouse dock for unloading	3. Patients in a dentist's office having their teeth cleaned and checked	3. Telephone operators providing directory assistance	3. Stoplights on the streets in a city
4. An automatic car wash	4. Inspection stations in a manufacturing system	4. Judges in a judicial system hearing cases	4. A large public health clinic

A SIMPLE QUEUING SYSTEM: A TOOL CRIB

In production facilities it is common to find a tool crib where expensive tools are kept. Workers needing tools present an appropriate authorization to the tool crib clerk, who in turn issues the required tools. The workers return to their work station, use the tools, and ultimately return them to the tool crib.

Figure 7.3   Service, waiting, and total costs in a queuing system.

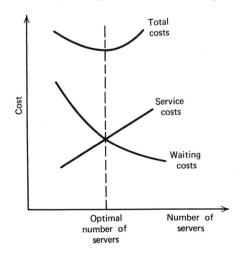

There are two obvious sets of costs in this situation: (1) the cost of having workers wait in line and (2) the cost of providing one or more servers. Providing more servers decreases waiting costs but increases service costs. The problem is to design the system so as to minimize the sum of all costs; See Figure 7.3.

APPROACHES TO QUEUING PROBLEMS

Three approaches to the queuing problem are possible. First, a system design can evolve on a trial-and-error basis. For simple systems this approach is often cost effective. An optimal design is often identified after only a few alternatives have been explored. However, as more complex systems are explored, it becomes less likely that an optimal design will be discovered by trial-and-error procedures.

Another approach involves the use of the analytic mode of analysis. Through standard mathematical and statistical methods, expressions are developed that describe the behavior of the system. Numerous books and articles have been devoted to the derivation of formulas for various queuing systems.[1] When these expressions are combined with cost considerations, the analyst is able to make recommendations about the system's design. Whenever possible, this approach should be used. In the next section an illustration of this type of analysis is presented.

There are many queuing systems, however, that are too complex to analyze by analytic methods. In this case, the analyst must turn to a numeric mode of analysis—more specifically, a simulation approach. Later we will see how a queuing system can be simulated. Let us now turn our attention to an analytic analysis of the tool crib operation.

APPLYING THE ANALYTIC APPROACH TO THE TOOL CRIB OPERATION

As described, the tool crib operation is an example of a very simple queuing system. It exemplifies a single-channel, single-phase queue. We will assume that the arrival distribution is Poisson, the service distribution is negative exponential, there is no balking, and the queue discipline is first come, first served. Although these are possibly slight simplifications, they are reasonable.

Applicable Formulas

The formulas that describe the tool crib operation are derived in many sources and will not be repeated here.[2] Instead, let us just consider the resulting expressions that describe *steady-state* conditions. This implies that the formulas are appropriate for describing the system when the initial effect of having no workers in the queue at the beginning of the day has passed. For our problem we should be looking at steady-state conditions even though there are situations where transient conditions are the focal point of attention.

---

[1] Thomas L. Saaty, *Elements of Queuing Theory* (New York: McGraw-Hill, 1961).
[2] Ibid. and J. W. Schmidt and R. E. Taylor, *Simulation and Analysis of Industrial Systems* (Homewood: Ill.: Irwin, 1970).

all steady state results

apply 1 channel 1 phase — poisson arrivals — expon. serv. time — only.

152   SIMULATING QUEUING SYSTEMS

The following symbols are used in the formulas for the tool crib operation.

λ = the *arrival* rate (the mean number of elements arriving per unit of time) — load

μ = the *service* rate (the mean number of elements served per unit of time) — service capacity

One characteristic of interest is the probability of various numbers of workers being in the system. The probability of no workers is given by Equation 7-1.

$$\text{Probability of zero in the system} = 1 - \frac{\lambda}{\mu} \qquad (7\text{-}1)$$

The probability of n workers is given by Equation 7-2.

$$\text{Probability of } n \text{ in the system} = \left[1 - \frac{\lambda}{\mu}\right]\left[\frac{\lambda}{\mu}\right]^n \qquad (7\text{-}2)$$

Let us assume that the arrival rate is 15 workers per hour and the service rate is 18 workers per hour. Using Equations 7-1 and 7-2, one can calculate the probability of zero and 2 workers in the system

$$\text{Probability of zero workers in the system} = 1 - \tfrac{15}{18} \cong .17$$

$$\text{Probability of 2 workers in the system} = [1 - \tfrac{15}{18}] \times [\tfrac{15}{18}]^2 \cong .12$$

The percent utilization of the server or, in other words, the percentage of time the clerk is processing workers' requests is given by Equation 7-3.

$$\text{Percent utilization of the server} = \frac{\lambda}{\mu} \qquad \text{— server utilization} \qquad (7\text{-}3)$$

For example,

$$\tfrac{15}{18} \cong 0.83$$

The expected number of workers in the *system* is given by Equation 7-4.

$$\text{Expected number in the system} = \frac{\lambda}{(\mu - \lambda)} \qquad (7\text{-}4)$$

For example,

$$\frac{15}{(18 - 15)} = 5 \text{ workers}$$

The expected number in the *queue* is given by Equation 7-5.

$$\text{Expected number in the queue} = \frac{\lambda^2}{\mu(\mu - \lambda)} \qquad (7\text{-}5)$$

For example,

$$\frac{(15)^2}{18(18 - 15)} \cong 4.17 \text{ workers}$$

The expected time spent in the *system* is given by Equation 7-6.

$$\text{Expected time spent in the system} = \frac{1}{(\mu - \lambda)}$$

For example,

$$\frac{1}{(18 - 15)} \cong 0.33 \text{ hours}$$

The expected time spent in the *queue* is given by Equation 7-7.

$$\text{Expected time spent in the queue} = \frac{\lambda}{\mu(\mu - \lambda)} \qquad (7\text{-}7)$$

For example,

$$\frac{15}{18(18 - 15)} \cong 0.28 \text{ hours}$$

A good description of the tool crib operation is provided by these formulas. However, if, for example, the arrival pattern were to change from Poisson to uniform, different formulas would apply.

Adding Cost Considerations

By adding cost considerations to the analysis, one can decide how many clerks to place in the tool crib. Let us assume that workers earn $6 per hour, whereas clerks are paid $4 per hour. From these data and previous information, it is possible to calculate the total hourly cost of the tool crib operation with a single attendant. We know that the average time in the queue is 0.28 hours. Multiplying this time by the average number of workers arriving per hour gives total waiting time, which is $0.28 \times 15 = 4.2$ hours in this case. Each hour wasted costs $6, so the total waiting costs are $4.2 \times 6 = \$25.20$. Adding the clerk's wages of $4 results in a total hourly tool crib cost of $\$25.20 + \$4.00 = \$29.20$.

One Clerk	
Hourly cost of lost worker time	$0.28 \times 15 \times 6 = \$25.20$
Clerk's hourly wage	4.00
Total hourly costs	$29.20

Adding another clerk (assuming they do not get in one another's way) has the effect of doubling the service rate. Consequently, Equation 7-7 can be used with a μ of 36 rather than 18. This changes the average waiting time to

$$\text{Expected time spent in the queue} \cong 0.02$$

With this information and the realization that two clerks' wages must be paid, it is possible to once again calculate the total hourly costs of operating the tool crib.

Two Clerks	
Hourly cost of lost worker time	$0.02 \times 15 \times 6 = \$1.80$
Clerks' hourly wages	$2 \times 4 = 8.00$
Total hourly costs	$9.80

Obviously, having two clerks is better than having only one. The cost of the extra clerk's wages is more than offset by reductions in waiting costs.

But what about hiring three clerks? This question can be answered very quickly. Even if waiting time is reduced to zero, the hourly cost of employing three clerks exceeds the total costs associated with having two clerks. Consequently, we are better off with only two attendants.

AN IMPORTANT CHARACTERISTIC OF QUEUING SYSTEMS

It is not unusual for people unfamiliar with the behavior of queuing systems to be surprised when waiting lines suddenly turn to near chaotic conditions. This situation tends to occur when the arrival rate approaches the service rate. Managers and other personnel fail to appreciate that queuing characteristics such as average waiting time and queue length increase in a nonlinear fashion with increases in the arrival rate. Figure 7.4 illustrates this point for expected time in the queue. It is based on Equation 7-7 for Poisson arrivals and negative exponential service times. In Figure 7.4 the service rate is held con-

Figure 7.4   Expected time in the queue as the arrival rate approaches the service rate.

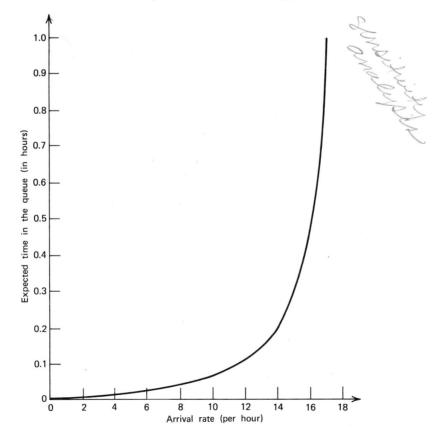

stant at 18 per hour, whereas the arrival rate is allowed to vary from 0 to 17. When the arrival rate equals the service rate, theoretically at least, the system degenerates completely; see Equation 7-7. In practice, however, balking typically begins much before this point.

SIMULATING THE TOOL CRIB OPERATION

The analytic approach served our tool crib analysis quite well and, as previously discussed, should be used whenever possible. However, it does not take much added complexity before a simulation approach is required. We will now consider how the operation of the tool crib might be simulated.

The tool crib simulation is based on a modified version of a FORTRAN-based model developed by Thomas J. Schriber at the University of Michigan. Some of the narrative that describes the program was also written by Schriber.[3] However, modifications have been made to describe the tool crib operation better and to be compatible with other chapter materials. The logic of the model is appropriate for any single-channel, single-phase queue. Extensions can be made to the model to describe more complex systems.[4]

A Solution Approach

The task involved here is to move a system forward in simulated time. This means that the various events that can occur in the tool crib operation must be identified, and their potential effect on the system's status must be articulated. The model must be "taught" how to allow these events to occur. Their occurrence must be faithful to the independent variables (in this case, arrival and service rates) that affect the system's behavior.

It is convenient to divide all possible events into two categories—primary and secondary events. *Primary events* are those whose time of occurrence is prescheduled by sampling from distributions provided as data. *Secondary events* are those that occur at the same time as primary events, and as a direct consequence of the primary events. When primary and secondary events occur, then it is usually necessary to preschedule other primary events.

Primary events are said to be prescheduled. This concept was introduced in the Monte Carlo inventory simulation when prescheduling the arrival of orders that had been placed was necessary. Now, however, let us consider more closely what this means. The arrival of a customer is a primary event. When a customer arrives, his or her successor's time of arrival is predetermined by sampling from the arrival time distribution, then adding the sampled value to the current clock reading. It is this need to preschedule arrivals that makes them, by definition, primary events.

---

[3] Much of the material presented here was contained in a prepublication version of Schriber's book, *Simulation Using GPSS* (New York: Wiley, 1974). Prior to printing the GPSS book, the decision was made to exclude the FORTRAN model, but it is now presented here. Schriber's original FORTRAN model does appear in "Three Computer Models for Probability Applications," *FORTRAN Applications in Business Administration*, Volume II, Thomas J. Schriber and Laurence A. Madeo, eds. (Ann Arbor, University of Michigan, 1971), pp. 349–422.

[4] See, for example, Schmidt and Taylor, op. cit.

To illustrate prescheduling, suppose a worker arrives at simulated time 21. A sample is then drawn from the arrival time distribution. The sampled value is, say, 4. Then the next worker is scheduled to arrive at future time 21 + 4, or 25. When he comes at time 25, the time of his or her successor's arrival will then have to be prescheduled. In short, a "boot-strapping" technique is used to arrange for worker arrivals.

In this example, occurrence of a primary event called for prescheduling the next primary event of the same kind. Now consider the other primary event in the system—completion of a service. Service completion is prescheduled at the time a worker goes into service. That is, when service is begun on a worker, the time of service completion is predetermined by sampling from the service time distribution, then adding the sampled value of the current clock reading. If a service begins at simulated time 52, and a service time of 3 is drawn, completion of that service is then scheduled to occur at future time 52 + 3, or 55.

Note that a service completion does not necessarily call for prescheduling the next service completion. Service completions can logically be prescheduled only when (1) a service completion has just occurred *and* there is another customer waiting to be put into service or (2) a customer arrives at the system and finds the server idle.

A listing of primary events and their consequences in the tool crib operation is shown in the following table.

Primary Event	Consequences (Secondary Events and Prescheduling)
Arrival of a worker	1. Preschedule time of successor's arrival
	2. Is the server currently available?
	No: Put worker in waiting line.
	Yes: Put worker into service. This requires:
	(a) Updating the server's status, and
	(b) Prescheduling the time of the service completion.
Completion of a service	1. Is there a worker waiting to go into service?
	No: Update the server's status.
	Yes: Put the worker into service. This requires:
	(a) Updating the length of the waiting line, and
	(b) Prescheduling the time of the service completion.

With the exception of prescheduling, these consequences of the primary events can be thought of as secondary events. For example, joining a waiting line is a secondary event.

It is worthwhile to note that we are describing a *next-event* rather than a *fixed-time increment* simulation. The clock is advanced to the time of the next event rather than by some predetermined amount. Recall that the Monte Carlo inventory simulation moved through time on a week-to-week basis. Consequently, it was a fixed-time increment simulation.

Now that the basic logic for the computer model has been presented, several final points need to be discussed.

Model Start-up

At model start-up, the simulation clock is initially set to a reading of zero. There are no workers in the system, and the server is idle. The arrival of the first worker is prescheduled by sampling from the arrival time distribution and adding the sampled value to a copy of the current clock reading (which is 0). The logic of the system does not call for any additional prescheduling at simulated time zero. The next (and only) event scheduled to occur, then, is arrival of the first worker. The simulation clock is advanced to the time of this primary event, and its consequences are carried out.

There are now two events prescheduled for future occurrence: time of the second worker's arrival and time of the first worker's service completion. The event times are tested to determine which of these events is the next to occur. The clock is then advanced to the earliest event time, and consequences of the event are carried out. The process is continued, event after event. The result is to move the system forward in simulated time.

Our model differs from the analytic analysis presented previously. The simulation includes both transient and steady-state conditions. A discussion of this point will be taken up later when the data output is presented.

Model Shutdown

Eventually, as simulated time elapses, the time of model shutdown is reached. Model shutdown can itself be thought of in the spirit of a primary event. Its time of occurrence is scheduled at model start-up when the desired running time of the simulation is input to the model. In general, then, there can be *three* events prescheduled for future occurrence. Whenever it is time to advance the simulation clock, all three events can be tested to determine which occurs next. Ultimately, the next event will be to shut off the model.

No Scheduled Service Completion

If the server is idle, no service completion is scheduled for future time. When testing to find the next event, then, only worker arrival and model shutdown should be considered. Rather than providing a special test for this situation, it is more convenient always to use a single test that scans the event times for all three potentially prescheduled events (worker arrival, service completion, and model shutdown). But if, as hypothesized, no service is in progress, care must be taken to see that "service completion" is not the indicated next event. This can be done by setting service completion time to some arbitrarily large value. Any large value could be used. One convenient choice is to have the "large value" be the shutdown time. When the shutdown time is actually reached, the model goes directly into the shutdown phase anyway. Hence, no attempt is ever made to bring about a nonexistent service completion.

Simultaneous Events

Consider what happens when two primary events are scheduled to occur at the same reading of the simulated clock. The clock is first advanced to the time in question. The consequences of one of the primary events are carried out. (The particular primary event selected depends on the way testing for the "next event" is conducted. In the single-channel, single-phase system without balking, it does not matter which of the two events is selected first.) As usual, the prescheduled events are then tested to find which is imminent. By hypothesis, the "other" primary event is next to occur. The simulation clock is now "advanced" to the corresponding time. But the effect of the "advance" is null; the new time is identical to the previous clock reading, so simulated time has not really changed. Hence, both events are caused to occur at the given reading of the simulated clock.

The Data Inputs

Four data inputs are required for the model. First is the arrival rate. For the tool crib operation, arrivals are Poisson distributed with a mean of 15 per hour. As discussed in Chapter 5, when occurrences are Poisson distributed the time *between* arrivals follows the negative exponential distribution. Consequently, the FORTRAN-based model includes sampling using the negative exponential process generator in order to simulate worker arrivals.

The service rate is another required data input. It too is negative exponentially distributed. The mean service rate for the tool crib operation is 18 workers per hour. The negative exponential process generator is used to simulate the clerk's service times. The length of the simulation (in hours) also has to be input. For our simulation, an eight-hour working day is used. The final input is the seed number for the random number generator. SUBROUTINE RANDU is used in the model and is input with a value of 53745 for IX.

The four input variables, their required format, and the data used are all summarized in Table 7.2.

The Data Output

The FORTRAN-based model has been programmed to provide the following output.

1. Duration of the simulation.
2. Server utilization.
3. Average length of the waiting line.
4. Average number of workers in the system.
5. Average time in the waiting line.
6. The fraction of workers who had to wait for service.

Table 7.2   DATA INPUTS FOR THE FORTRAN-BASED MODEL

Variable Name	Card Number	Columns	Format	Data Input
ARATE	1	1–6	F6.2	15.0
SRATE	2	1–6	F6.2	18.0
HOURS	3	1–6	F6.2	8.0
IX	4	1–5	I5	53745

Table 7.3   COMBINING LINE LENGTH AND DURATION

Length of Line	Clock Reading When Line Became That Length	Duration of Length	Product of Length and Its Duration
0	21	4	0
1	25	2	2
2	27	1	2
3	28	11	33
2	39	8	16
1	47	4	4
2	51	—	—
—	—		

Time Spanned (51-21): 30   Total: 57

Average Line Length = 57/30 = 1.90 workers

The duration of the simulation is how long the simulation ran before it shutdown. The duration is specified by a data input. Server utilization is determined by dividing the total time the server is engaged by the total time the simulation ran.

In order to calculate the average length of the waiting line, one must consider not only the line length, but also the duration of the length. For example, consider the numeric situation tabulated in Table 7.3.

As the calculation indicates, the average line length for the data shown is 1.9 workers. The average length is not simply the sum of the entries in the first column, divided by the number of entries. That value ($\frac{11}{7} = 1.571+$), which is meaningless, fails to take into account how long the line was at its various lengths.

The average number of workers in the system is similar to the average length of the waiting line, but it also includes any worker being served. It can be found by adding the percent utilization of the server to the average length of the waiting line.

The average time in the waiting line is found by dividing the total time spent by the workers in the waiting line by the total number of workers who enter the system. Again, as with the previous two data outputs, the calculation must consider both the length of the queue and its duration.

The fraction of workers who had to wait for service is determined by dividing the number of workers who go immediately into service on arrival by the total number of arrivals.

These are the data outputs. When the model is run with the same numbers used in the analytic analysis, interesting comparisons can be made.

The FORTRAN-based Model

A complete description of the variables used in the FORTRAN-based model is provided in Table 7.4. The macrologic for the model is shown in Figure 7.5. The program itself is presented in Table 7.5 and functions according to the previously described logic.

Table 7.4 A SYMBOL TABLE FOR THE FORTRAN-BASED MODEL

Program Variable	Definition	Mode
ALWL	Average length of the waiting line	Real
AMIN1	An open FORTRAN function returning a copy of the smallest entry in its list of arguments; see any FORTRAN primer for further details	Real
ARATE	Arrival rate; mean number of Poisson arrivals per time interval	Real
ARRTOT	Arrival total; number of workers arriving at the system	Integer
ATWL	Average time in the waiting line; mean time that workers spent in the waiting line	Real
AWIS	Average workers in system; equal to average length of the waiting line, plus server utilization (i.e., average number of workers at the server)	Real
CLOCK	Simulated clock	Real
DOWAIT	Number of workers who cannot go immediately into service on arrival	Integer
EVENTT	Event time; time of next event scheduled to occur	Real
IDLE	A variable recording the status of the server; when IDLE = 0, the server is engaged; when IDLE = 1, the server is idle	Integer
IX	The seed number for the random number generator	Integer
IY	Resets the random number generator to produce the next number in the sequence	Integer
LWL	Length of the waiting line	Integer
PRWAIT	Probability of waiting; the probability that a worker cannot immediately go into service on arrival	Real
SRATE	Service rate; mean number of Poisson service completions per time interval	Real
STOPT	Stop time; simulated time at which the model is to be shutdown	Real
SUBROUTINE RANDU	The library subroutine used to generate uniformly distributed random numbers over the open 0–1 interval; see Chapter 6	Real
TIDT	Total idle time; total time the server is idle	Real
TOA	Time of arrival; time the next worker is scheduled to arrive at the system	Real
TOSC	Time of service completion; time the worker now in service will be done with service; equal to STOPT in value if no customer is in service	Real
TWE	Total waiting experience; accumulated product of waiting line length and duration of length	Real

Table 7.4 *(Continued)*

Program Variable	Definition	Mode
UTIL	Utilization of the server; fraction of the time that the server is engaged	Real
YFL	Stores the uniform random number over the open 0–1 interval, which has been produced by the random number generator	Real

Figure 7.5 Flow diagram for the queuing system model.

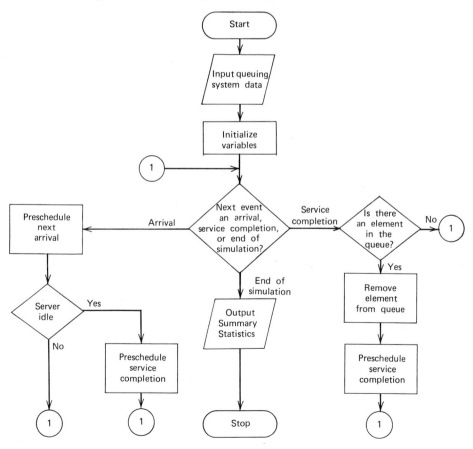

Table 7.5   THE FORTRAN-BASED MODEL

```
C      ***THIS PROGRAM SIMULATES A SINGLE CHANNEL, SINGLE PHASE
C         QUEUING SYSTEM. ARRIVAL RATES OF DEMANDS FOR SERVICE ARE
C         POISSON DISTRIBUTED. SERVICE TIMES ARE NEGATIVE EXPONEN-
C         TIALLY DISTRIBUTED. SERVER UTILIZATION, AVERAGE LENGTH OF
C         THE WAITING LINE, AVERAGE NUMBER OF CUSTOMERS IN THE SYS-
C         TEM, AVERAGE TIME IN THE WAITING LINE, AND THE PROBABILITY
C         THAT AN ARRIVAL WILL HAVE TO WAIT FOR SERVICE ARE ESTI-
C         MATED BY THE MODEL. THE ESTIMATES ARE BASED ON A SIMULA-
C         TION OF DURATION SPECIFIED AS DATA***
C
C      ***PROVIDE MODE INFORMATION***
       INTEGER ARRTOT,DOWAIT,LWL
C
C      ***INPUT MEAN ARRIVAL RATE ('ARATE'), MEAN SERVICE RATE
C         ('SRATE'), THE NUMBER OF SIMULATED TIME UNITS (HOURS) FOR
C         WHICH THE MODEL IS TO BE RUN ('STOPT'), AND THE SEED NUMBER
C         ('IX')
    10 READ(5,20) ARATE,SRATE,STOPT,IX
    20 FORMAT(F6.2/F6.2/F6.2/I5)
C      ***INITIALIZE PERTINENT VALUES BEFORE STARTING THE SIMULATION***
    30 ARRTOT=0
       CLOCK=0.
       DOWAIT=0
       IDLE=1
       TIDT=0.
       TWE=0.
       LWL=0
C
C      ***COMPUTE THE TIME OF ARRIVAL TO THE SYSTEM OF THE FIRST
C         SERVICE DEMAND***
       CALL RANDU(IX,IY,YFL)
       IX=IY
       TOA=-ALOG(1.-YFL)/ARATE
C      ***BECAUSE THERE IS NOT NOW ANYONE 'IN SERVICE', SET THE TIME
C         OF NEXT SERVICE COMPLETION TO AN ARBITRARILY LARGE VALUE.
C         A CONVENIENT CHOICE OF AN 'ARBITRARILY LARGE VALUE' IS THE
C         TIME THE MODEL IS SCHEDULED TO SHUT OFF***
       TOSC=STOPT
C
C      ***SET TIME OF NEXT EVENT TO THE MINIMUM OF TIME OF ARRI-
C         VAL, TIME OF SERVICE COMPLETION, AND TIME OF STOPPING THE
C         SIMULATION***
    60 EVENTT=AMIN1(TOA,TOSC,STOPT)
C
C      ***UPDATE TOTAL IDLE TIME OF THE SERVER AND TOTAL WAITING
C         EXPERIENCE OF THOSE WAITING FOR SERVICE. THEN ADVANCE THE
C         CLOCK TO THE TIME OF THE NEXT EVENT***
       TIDT=TIDT+IDLE*(EVENTT-CLOCK)
       TWE=TWE+LWL*(EVENTT-CLOCK)
       CLOCK=EVENTT
C
```

Table 7.5 (*Continued*)

```
C     ***GO TO 90 IF THE NEXT EVENT IS TO STOP THE SIMULATION; OR GO
C         TO 80 IF THE NEXT EVENT IS A SERVICE COMPLETION***
      IF (EVENTT .EQ. STOPT) GO TO 90
      IF (EVENTT .EQ. TOSC) GO TO 80
C
C     ***IF NEITHER TRANSFER WAS TAKEN, THE NEXT EVENT IS ARRIVAL
C         OF A DEMAND FOR SERVICE. UPDATE THE TOTAL ARRIVALS TO
C         DATE, THEN PRESCHEDULE THE TIME WHEN THE ARRIVAL'S SUC-
C         CESSOR WILL ARRIVE***
      ARRTOT=ARRTOT+1
      CALL RANDU(IX,IY,YFL)
      IX=IY
      TOA=CLOCK-ALOG(1.-YFL)/ARATE
C
C     ***TRANSFER TO 70 IF THE SERVER IS IDLE; OTHERWISE, UPDATE
C         BOTH THE NUMBER OF THOSE WHO HAVE HAD TO WAIT FOR SER-
C         VICE, AND THE NUMBER OF THOSE WHO ARE NOW WAITING. THEN
C         RETURN TO DETERMINE THE NEXT EVENT***
      IF(IDLE .EQ. 1) GO TO 70
      DOWAIT=DOWAIT+1
      LWL=LWL+1
      GO TO 60
C
C     ***UPDATE THE STATUS OF THE SERVER, PRESCHEDULE THE TIME OF
C         SERVICE COMPLETION, AND THEN RETURN TO DETERMINE THE
C         NEXT EVENT***
   70 IDLE=0
      CALL RANDU(IX,IY,YFL)
      IX=IY
      TOSC=CLOCK-ALOG(1.-YFL)/SRATE
      GO TO 60
C     ***A SERVICE COMPLETION IS THE EVENT OCCURRING. TRANSFER TO
C         85 IF SOMEONE IS WAITING FOR THE SERVER WHO HAS JUST BE-
C         COME AVAILABLE***
   80 IF(LWL.GT.0) GO TO 85
C
C     ***WHEN NO ONE IS WAITING, RECORD THAT THE SERVER IS IDLE,
C         AND SET THE TIME OF NEXT SERVICE COMPLETION TO AN ARBI-
C         TRARILY LARGE VALUE. THEN RETURN TO DETERMINE THE NEXT
C         EVENT***
      IDLE=1
      TOSC=STOPT
      GO TO 60
C
C     ***REMOVE A WAITING SERVICE DEMAND FROM THE WAITING LINE,
C         PRESCHEDULE THE TIME OF SERVICE COMPLETION, THEN RETURN
C         TO DETERMINE THE NEXT EVENT***
   85 LWL=LWL-1
      CALL RANDU(IX,IY,YFL)
      IX=IY
      TOSC=CLOCK-ALOG(1.-YFL)/SRATE
```

Table 7.5   (*Continued*)

```
        GO TO 60
C       ***THE END OF THE SIMULATION HAS BEEN REACHED. COMPUTE
C       PERTINENT STATISTICS, THEN OUTPUT THE SYSTEM PERFORMANCE
C       INFORMATION***
  90    UTIL=(STOPT-TIDT)/STOPT
        ALWL=TWE/STOPT
        AWIS=ALWL+UTIL
        ATWL=TWE/ARRTOT
        PRWAIT=1.*DOWAIT/ARRTOT
        WRITE(6,100) STOPT,UTIL,ALWL,AWIS,ATWL,PRWAIT
 100    FORMAT('1DURATION OF SIMULATION, HOURS:',F16.2/
     1           ' FRACTIONAL UTILIZATION OF SERVER:',F16.3/
     2           ' AVERAGE LENGTH OF THE WAITING LINE:',F14.3/
     3           ' AVERAGE NUMBER OF WORKERS IN THE SYSTEM:',F11.3/
     4           ' AVERAGE TIME IN THE WAITING LINE:',F16.4/
     5           ' PROBABILITY OF HAVING TO WAIT FOR SERVICE:',F5.2)
        STOP
        END
        SUBROUTINE RANDU(IX,IY,YFL)
        IY=IX*65539
        IF(IY) 5,6,6
   5    IY=IY+2147483647+1
   6    YFL=IY
        YFL=YFL*.4656613E-9
        RETURN
        END
```

PROGRAM OUTPUT

The data inputs that were presented in Table 7.2 were processed through the FORTRAN-based model. The output from the model is presented in Table 7.6.

It is interesting to compare the output from the simulation with that from the analytic approach. The summary statistics on pages 152 and 153 are strikingly close to those in

Table 7.6   OUTPUT FROM THE FORTRAN-BASED MODEL

DURATION OF SIMULATION, HOURS:	8.00
FRACTIONAL UTILIZATION OF SERVER:	0.820
AVERAGE LENGTH OF THE WAITING LINE:	4.147
AVERAGE NUMBER OF WORKERS IN THE SYSTEM:	4.968
AVERAGE TIME IN THE WAITING LINE:	0.2765
PROBABILITY OF HAVING TO WAIT FOR SERVICE:	0.84

Table 7.6. Of course this is to be expected. Other than a careless error, there are only two reasons that they might differ. (1) With simulation there is the possibility of sampling error. The shorter the period of time simulated, the greater is the likelihood of sampling error. (2) The simulation included both transient and steady-state conditions, whereas the equations for the analytic solution were only for steady-state conditions. In our simulation model, however, it did not take long for the steady-state conditions to take over and "swamp" any data collected while the system was moving from an empty state.

VARYING THE RUN TIME

Insights into how long it takes for steady-state conditions to take over and dominate output statistics such as "average time in the waiting line" can be gained by varying the run time. Because our simulation starts with the queue empty and the clerk free, we would expect average waiting time to get larger with longer run times until steady-state conditions finally take over. The results of this type of comparison are shown in Figure 7.6. Run time was increased by increments of 0.5 hour until average time in the waiting line approximated its steady-state value. Average time in the waiting line increased gradually with some fluctuation until finally reaching a steady-state value of 0.2766 after six hours of simulated time.

Figure 7.6   Comparing average time in the waiting line with run time.

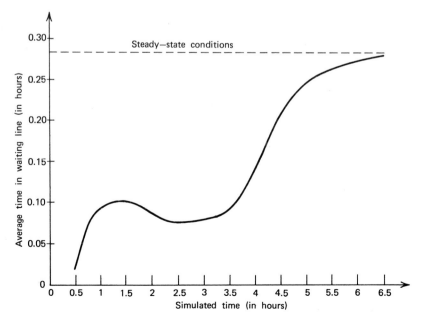

COMPARING SOLUTION APPROACHES

In conclusion, it seems appropriate to compare the analytic and simulation approaches to analyzing queuing systems. Whenever possible the analytic approach should be used. It is usually faster and less expensive and does not involve the possibility of sampling error. Unfortunately, many queuing systems deviate in important ways from the underlying assumptions of the analytic models that have already been developed. And if a model is not already available, the time, difficulty, or cost of developing an appropriate model may be prohibitive. By using simulation, one can capture virtually any peculiarities of a system in a model. Although in a FORTRAN-based model this capturing process may not always be a simple accomplishment, by using a special-purpose simulation language for queuing systems such as General Purpose Simulation System (GPSS), this process is facilitated. The majority of the next chapter is devoted to GPSS and it will be interesting to compare the FORTRAN and GPSS programs for a single-channel, single-phase queue.

SUMMARY

Queuing systems are very common and it is important to understand their characteristics and to be able to model them. They vary in terms of their number of channels and phases, arrival and service patterns, queue discipline, and priorities in processing new arrivals. Ideally, the objective in designing and operating a queuing system is to minimize the sum of waiting and service time costs. Since waiting time costs are frequently difficult to estimate, attention sometimes focuses on satisfying minimum service level requirements.

An analytic analysis of queuing systems should always be considered first. This approach is often fast, simple, cost effective, and does not involve the possibility of sampling error. For many standard queuing systems, equations have already been developed that describe the system's characteristics. All the analyst must do is enter appropriate data and generate the output through simple calculations. By adding cost considerations to the analysis, one can move to optimal system design.

When an analytic approach is not feasible, simulation is a powerful alternative. Simulation can be used to capture the unusual features of a system that often preclude the possibility of employing an analytic analysis. When simulating a queuing system, attention must focus on moving the system through time. Care must be taken in generating arrivals to the system, keeping track of their progress in the system, generating service times, and moving elements out of the system.

Even after a computerized model of a queuing system has been developed, additional factors must be considered. The analyst must think about appropriate starting conditions, how long to run the simulation, and the possible impact of transients on the model's output.

ASSIGNMENTS

7.1. Give an example of a queuing system found in the following functional areas. Using queuing terminology, describe the system.

(a) Production.
(b) Personnel.
(c) Marketing.
(d) Accounting-Finance.
(e) Data Processing.

7.2. Using the characteristics of mathematical models described in Chapter 1, classify the following models:
(a) Analytic models of queuing systems.
(b) Simulation models of queuing systems.

7.3. Trucks arrive at a warehouse for unloading in a Poisson manner at a rate of ten trucks per hour. Idle trucks have an opportunity cost of $30 per hour. Materials handlers at the warehouse earn $6 per hour and provide service at a negative exponential rate of five trucks per hour. Using an analytic analysis, how many materials handlers should be employed?

7.4. A toll booth is located on a bridge connecting a newly developed summer resort island to the mainland. This past summer cars arrived at the toll booth in a Poisson manner with a mean arrival rate of one car per minute. The woman in the toll booth is able to serve cars in a negative exponential manner at a rate of two cars per minute. Simulate 8 hours of activity at the toll booth. Collect statistics on toll booth activity.

7.5. The developer of the resort island discussed in assignment 7.4 is concerned about the consequences of an increase in the number of visitors to the island this summer. He both hopes and fears that the arrival rate at the toll booth could approach two cars per minute. Simulate three hours of activity at the toll booth using arrival rates of 1.0, 1.2, 1.4, 1.6, 1.8, and 2.0 cars per minute. Prepare a graph based on your simulations with mean arrival rate on the horizontal axis and average length of the waiting line on the vertical axis. Should the developer be concerned about possible developments at the toll booth?

7.6. A conveyor belt brings an item to a work station at the rate of one every 5 minutes. This means that arrivals are deterministically rather than probabilistically determined. Service is performed on the item at a negative exponentially distributed rate. Which of the following service rates is required if the average time in the waiting line is not to exceed 3 minutes? Base your analysis on 8 hours of simulated activity.
(a) $\mu = 30$/hour.
(b) $\mu = 20$/hour.
(c) $\mu = 15$/hour.
(d) $\mu = 12$/hour.

7.7. An ice cream stand is operated by a single server who provides service in a negative exponential manner with a mean service rate of 15 customers per hour. Customers arrive according to the Poisson distribution with a mean arrival rate of 10 per hour. However, if there is a queue, potential customers may balk. More specifically, if n customers are in the queue, the probability that an arriving customer will balk is $n/4$ for $n = 1, 2, 3, 4$. Simulate 8 hours of activity at the ice cream stand and output the number of potential customers who balked.

7.8. A small grocery store uses a single checkout lane. The cashier provides service in a normally distributed manner with a mean of 4 minutes and a standard deviation of 1 minute. However, when the system contains three or more customers, the cashier rings a bell that signals the stockboy to come help bag groceries. This practice reduces service time to a mean of 3 minutes and a standard deviation of 0.50 minutes. When the system is empty, the stockboy returns to stocking shelves. Customers come to the checkout lane in a Poisson manner with a mean arrival rate of 10 per hour. What is the average length of the queue based on 8 hours of simulated activity?

7.9. A drive-in bank teller facility has room for only four cars in line before the cars back up into the street. Once the line is in the street, the probability of a potential arriving customer balking is $\frac{1}{2}$. Assuming Poisson arrivals with a mean of 15 customers per hour and negative exponential service time with a mean of 18 customers per hour, what is the percentage of time that customers are backed up into the street? Simulate 8 hours of activity.

7.10. A travel agency has an agent who handles incoming calls. The agent can place a single caller on "hold" if she is currently engaged. If both the agent's line and the hold line are "busy," there is a 50 to 50 chance that the caller contacts another agency rather than waiting to call again. The agent provides service in a negative exponential manner with a mean service rate of 12 customers per hour. Incoming calls are Poisson distributed with a mean of eight calls per hour.

(a) Simulate 8 hours of activity. How many potential customers are lost?

(b) The travel agency is considering hiring an additional agent to handle calls. This addition would make it possible to handle two callers at a time and to place a third caller on hold. The hourly wage of the additional agent would be $6 per hour. The cost of a "lost" customer is estimated to be $25. Simulate the proposed system over 8 hours of time. Do you recommend hiring the second agent?

REFERENCES

Bhat, V. Narayan, "Sixty Years of Queuing Theory," *Management Science* (February 1969): B280–B294.

Cook, Thomas M., and Robert A. Russell, *Introduction to Management Science* (Englewood Cliffs, N.J.: Prentice-Hall, 1977).

Cooper, Robert B., *Introduction to Queuing Theory* (New York: MacMillan, 1972).

Cosmetatos, George P., "The Value of Queuing Theory—A Case Study," *Interfaces* (May 1979): 47–51.

Foote, B. L., "A Queuing Case Study of Drive-In Banking," *Interfaces* (August 1976): 31–37.

Gallagher, Charles A., and Hugh J. Watson, *Quantitative Methods for Business Decisions* (New York: McGraw-Hill, 1980).

Gilliam, Ronald R., "An Application of Queuing Theory to Airport Passenger Security Screening," *Interfaces* (August 1979): 1–8.

Gross, D., and C. N. Harris, *Fundamentals of Queuing Theory* (New York: Wiley, 1974).

Hillier, Frederick S., and Gerald J. Lieberman, *Operations Research*, 2nd. ed. (San Francisco: Holden-Day, 1974).

Kleinrock, Leonard, *Queuing Systems*, 2 vols., (New York: Wiley, 1975).

Levin, Richard I., and Charles A. Kirkpatrick, *Quantitative Approaches to Management*, 4th ed. (New York: McGraw-Hill, 1978).

McMillan, Claude, and Richard R. Gonzalez, *Systems Analysis*, 3rd. ed. (Homewood, Ill.: Irwin, 1973).

Morse, Philip M., *Queues, Inventories, and Maintenance* (New York: Wiley, 1962).

Naylor, Thomas H., *et al*, *Computer Simulation Techniques* (New York: Wiley, 1966).

Panico, J. A., *Queuing Theory: A Study of Waiting Lines for Business, Economics and Science* (Englewood Cliffs, N.J.: Prentice-Hall, 1969).

Saaty, Thomas L., *Elements of Queuing Theory* (New York: McGraw-Hill, 1961).

Schmidt, J. W., and R. E. Taylor, *Simulation and Analysis of Industrial Systems* (Homewood, Ill.: Irwin, 1970).

Vogel, Myles A., "Queuing Theory Applied to Machine Manning," *Interfaces* (August 1979): 1–8.

White, J. A., J. W. Schmidt, and G. K. Bennett, *Analysis of Queuing Systems* (New York: Academic Press, 1975).

CHAPTER EIGHT

SPECIAL-PURPOSE SIMULATION LANGUAGES: GPSS

Advantages of Simulation Languages

Disadvantages of Simulation Languages

Selecting a Language

Simulation Languages

    DYNAMO

    GASP

    SIMSCRIPT

    IFPS

The Popularity of Various Languages

General Purpose Simulation System: GPSS

    GPSS Features

    Block Diagrams

    The GENERATE Block

    The QUEUE and DEPART Blocks

The SEIZE and RELEASE Blocks

The ADVANCE Block

The TERMINATE Block

Stopping the Simulation

The Punched Card Program

Program Output

Parallel Servers

The ENTER and LEAVE Blocks

Negative Exponential Processes

Modeling More Complex Systems

Summary

Assignments

References

171

A *language-independent* approach to computerized simulation modeling is employed in this book. This means that the computerized models are not limited to any particular programming language. Although FORTRAN has been used in the textual materials and illustrations, many other *general-purpose languages* such as BASIC, PL/1, or COBOL could have been employed. Given the widespread knowledge of FORTRAN and its popularity for simulation studies, it is a logical, but not necessary, choice.

As the popularity of simulation as a method of analysis has risen with the availability of digital computers, so has the emergence of *special-purpose simulation languages* that are particularly well suited for simulation studies. Originally, the languages were little more than existing languages with special features to facilitate simulation modeling. Over time, completely new languages with powerful description and analysis capabilities have been developed.

This chapter begins with a broad survey of simulation languages. Included are topics such as the advantages and disadvantages of simulation languages, how to select a language for a particular modeling effort, a brief look at some of the major simulation languages in use today, and consideration of the relative popularity of various languages. Most of the chapter, however, is devoted to an introduction to General Purpose Simulation System (GPSS), a powerful simulation language for modeling queuing systems. It will be seen how easily the queuing systems discussed in the preceding chapter can be described in a GPSS program. Thus an increased appreciation should be gained as to the potential value of simulation languages.

ADVANTAGES OF SIMULATION LANGUAGES

A programmer often has the option of using either a general- or a special-purpose language. General-purpose languages such as FORTRAN do have certain advantages. The following list suggests some of the reasons for their use.

1. Maximum flexibility is offered in mathematically describing the modeled system. There are no inherent limiting structures to general-purpose languages.
2. The programmer can select the type and format of the output reports. Only time and programming ability limit the reports that can be generated; see Figure 8.1.
3. Maximum flexibility is allowed in terms of the type of experiments that can be performed on the modeled system.
4. The analyst is typically already skilled in the use of one or more general-purpose languages. Such is not always the case with special-purpose languages.

Obviously, there are advantages to special-purpose languages or they would not have been developed and used. Simulation languages typically include at least several of the following desirable features.

1. Easy description of the modeled system.
2. Automatic movement of the model through time.
3. Automatic gathering of statistics that are later output in fixed-format reports.
4. Easy generation of probabilistic processes.
5. Diagnostic capabilities that check for logic as well as for syntax errors.

Figure 8.1   Programming the model can be a painful experience.

DOONESBURY   by Garry Trudeau

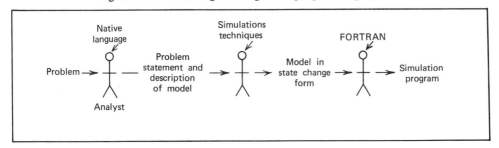

Source.   Copyright 1972 G. B. Trudeau, distributed by Universal Press Syndicate. Reprinted by permission.

These features result in the following advantages.

1. Reduced programming time and effort.
2. Conceptual guidance in formulating a model, describing a system, and analyzing the system.

Emshoff and Sisson illustrate these advantages through two figures. Figure 8.2 shows how computerized simulation models are developed with a general-purpose language. The analyst thinks about the problem in his or her native language. The result is a problem statement and description of the model. Drawing on simulation technology, the analyst develops an appropriate mathematical model. Knowing a general-purpose language such as FORTRAN, the analyst uses it in coding the model into a simulation program.

An analyst who knows an appropriate simulation language follows a slightly different process; see Figure 8.3. The language itself provides conceptual guidance in defining the problem and creating a model. Because the model is formulated in the analyst's mind in terms of the simulation language, it eliminates the step in Figure 8.2 where a native lan-

Figure 8.2   Modeling with a general-purpose language.

Source.   James R. Emshoff and Roger L. Sisson, Design and Use of Computer Simulation Models *(New York: Macmillan, 1970), p. 116.*

Figure 8.3   Modeling with a special-purpose simulation language.

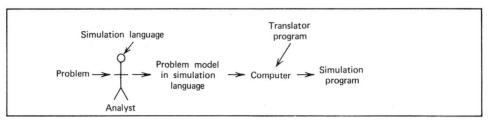

Source.   James R. Emshoff and Roger L. Sisson, Design and Use of Computer Simulation Models *(New York: Macmillan, 1970), p. 117.*

guage description is used in developing a mathematical model, which in turn must be programmed.

The advantages offered by special-purpose simulation languages vary from language to language.   For example, simulation languages that are heavily *problem oriented* provide considerable conceptual guidance, because they are typically designed to model a *specific type of problem or system.*   Consequently, the entire structure of the language focuses one's attention on required model concepts, relationships, and details.

Many problem-oriented simulation languages are also *flowchart oriented.*   With such languages, a set of symbols is used to describe a problem or a system during the model development stage, and these symbols later lead to a relatively straightforward coding of a program.

Procedure-oriented simulation languages are similar to general-purpose languages in that an algorithm, or procedure, for performing the simulation must be programmed. Normally, however, the language contains features, often as subroutines and functions, which facilitate the modeling effect.   These simulation languages offer a weakened mixture of the advantages of both general- and special-purpose languages; however, such languages may be appropriate for certain applications.

Figure 8.4, which is patterned after a similar one suggested by Emshoff and Sisson, shows the characteristics of different programming languages.[1]   The horizontal axis pre-

Figure 8.4   A classification of languages used in computerized simulation modeling.

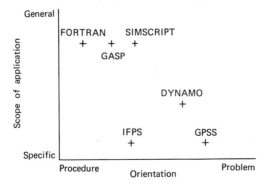

[1] James R. Emshoff and Roger L. Sisson, *Design and Use of Computer Simulation Models* (New York: Macmillan, 1970), p. 140.

sents *orientation* and varies from procedure to problem-oriented languages, whereas the vertical axis presents the *scope of application* and varies from specific to general. Plotted by their approximate location are the languages discussed in this chapter.

DISADVANTAGES OF SIMULATION LANGUAGES

There are also potential disadvantages or limitations to special-purpose simulation languages. Some of the major disadvantages are identified here. Obviously, they vary somewhat depending on the language.

1. The language may not be available on the user's computer system. In general, simulation languages are available only on larger systems. Also, some languages are limited to particular manufacturer's computers. Over time, however, simulation languages are becoming more widely available.
2. The language may not already be known by the programmer. This condition frequently leads to use of a general-purpose language.
3. The language may not be suitable for the modeled system. For example, a language designed for simulating a queuing system is not appropriate for most financial planning applications.
4. The processing costs can be high. Overhead and running time costs are typically higher than with general-purpose languages.
5. The model may be more difficult to validate, because most languages place the model builder at a higher level of abstraction.

SELECTING A LANGUAGE

There is no single language that is best for all applications. Each application should be evaluated on its own. Although in many instances a language is chosen because the programmer is familiar with the language and it is available on the organization's computer system, a less closed selection process is recommended.

Shannon conceptualizes an appropriate selection process as consisting of two phases.[2] The first phase is concerned with questions of the availability of references, documentation, and software compatibility. The following types of questions should be answered.

1. Are intelligibly written user's manuals available?
2. Is the language translator compatible with available computer systems?
3. Is this language available on other computer systems where the user's problem might be run?
4. Does the language translator provide documentation and extensive error diagnostics?
5. When the organizing, programming, and debugging times are combined with the translating and execution times, does the efficiency appear attractive?

[2] Robert E. Shannon, *Systems Simulation* (Englewood Cliffs: N.J.: Prentice-Hall, 1975), pp. 107–109.

6. What is the cost of installing, maintaining, and updating the software for the language? (Because some languages are proprietary, there may be an explicit charge for these services.)
7. Is the language already known or easily learned?
8. Are a sufficient number of simulation studies anticipated for the future to justify the cost of learning and installing the new language?

Based on phase one, several languages should emerge for further consideration.

The second phase deals with characteristics of the problem under investigation. Shannon suggests that questions similar to the following be asked.

1. For what types of real-world systems is the language appropriate?
2. How easily can data that describe a system be stored and retrieved?
3. What is the flexibility and power provided by the language to modify the state of the system?
4. How easily can it be used to specify dynamic behavior?
5. What are the available output forms and what statistical analyses can be performed on the data?
6. How easy is it to insert user-written subroutines?

The selection of an appropriate language should follow from phase two.

SIMULATION LANGUAGES

More special-purpose simulation languages have been developed than can possibly be described here. Consequently, we will only briefly discuss several important ones—DYNAMO, GASP, SIMSCRIPT, and IFPS. More extensive coverages are provided elsewhere for the interested reader.[3] Our discussion will focus on the general characteristics of the languages rather than on their detailed functioning. Only to a limited extent will an effort be made to differentiate between different versions or generations of the same language; for example, GASP and GASP IV. A general appreciation should be gained as to the nature of special-purpose simulation languages. Let us begin our explorations with DYNAMO.

DYNAMO

In Chapter 2 when systems dynamics models were discussed, it was mentioned that DYNAMO is typically the programming language used. DYNAMO was created in the late 1950s by Phyllis Fox and Alexander Pugh.[4] Many of the more famous applications that employ DYNAMO were developed by Jay Forrester.

---

[3]Ira M. Kay, "Digital Discrete Simulation: A Discussion and an Inventory," *Fifth Annual Simulation Symposium*, Kenneth W. Gohring, Newton D. Swain and Richard L. Sanders, eds. (New York: Gordon and Breach, 1972).

[4]Alexander L. Pugh, III, *DYNAMO User's Manual*, 5th ed. (Cambridge, Mass.: The MIT Press, 1976), p. viii.

Figure 8.5   Basic structure of a DYNAMO programmed systems dynamics model.

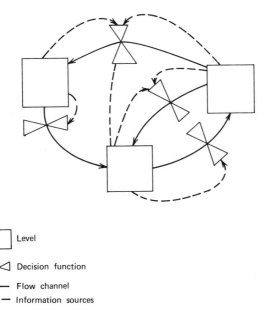

☐ Level

▷◁ Decision function

─── Flow channel

── ── Information sources

DYNAMO is employed with continuous rather than discrete models. A continuous model is appropriate when the behavior of the system depends more on aggregate flows than on the occurrence of discrete events. As Pugh states it:

> *The problems of top management generally do not involve individual orders or particular machines. The mayor of a major city does not solve the city's problems on an individual-by-individual basis. An engineer is not concerned with the behavior of an individual molecule. All of these problems can be studied by aggregating the "events" into a continuous flow and setting this flow in the context of the (continuous) variables that affect it and are affected by it.*[5]

The basic structure of a DYNAMO-programmed systems dynamics model is shown in Figure 8.5. There are four essential features to such a model.

1. Several *levels* of interrelated variables. These are accumulators and could represent inventories, employees, or bank balances in the case of industrial models. In a world model they might represent populations, resources, or even pollution. Levels always represent the accumulated difference between inflows and outflows.
2. *Flows* into or out of the levels. Examples are rates of capital expenditures, hire and fire rates, and birth and death rates. These flows are expressed as rates and represent the instantaneous flow between levels in any given time period.
3. *Decision functions.* These are controls for the rates of flow and represent policy decisions. Examples include inventory policies, school districting decisions, and abortion laws.

[5] Ibid., p. 1.

4. *Information channels* that connect the decision functions to the levels. These channels trigger decisions regarding the flows based on the levels of the variables.

In developing a DYNAMO-based model, the analyst must describe the system using first-order difference equations to approximate the continuous processes in the modeled system. Equations are required to describe the levels at a given time, the flows into and out of the levels, and policy decisions. The equations are FORTRAN-like and employ a fixed-time increment time advance.

It is also necessary to supply other inputs. These include, for example, the number of time periods to simulate, starting conditions for variables in the model, values for constants in the model, and output specifications for variables to be printed or plotted.

GASP

The GASP language was created at U.S. Steel by Philip Kiviat. At a later date GASP II was developed at Arizona State University. The most recent version is GASP IV.[6] GASP and GASP II are discrete simulation languages. GASP IV has been expanded to permit continuous and combined discrete–continuous simulations. This capability makes GASP suitable for systems dynamics-type modeling.

All versions of GASP are FORTRAN based. Since most analysts are familiar with FORTRAN, GASP is a relatively easy simulation language to learn. The most difficult challenge is initially learning the required interfaces between the main program, subroutines, and required files. GASP does not require a separate compiling system, because FORTRAN is the host language.

Every GASP-based model contains the following.[7]

1. A set of event programs or state variable equations, or both, which describe a system's dynamic behavior.
2. Lists and matrices that store information.
3. An executive routine that directs the flow of information and control within the model.
4. Support routines.

Items (1), (2) and sometimes portions of (4) are user written. The GASP language provides item (3) and many useful routines as part of (4).

GASP has the following functional capabilities, which greatly simplify the modeling effort.[8]

1. Event control.
2. State variable updating using integration if necessary.
3. Information storage and retrieval.
4. System state initialization.
5. System performance data collection.

[6] A. Alan B. Pritsker, *The Gasp IV Simulation Language* (New York: Wiley, 1974).
[7] Ibid., p. 16.
[8] Ibid., p. 17.

6.   Program monitoring and event reporting.
7.   Statistical computations and report generation.
8.   Random deviate generation.

The analyst has responsibilities for initializing certain variables, calling the GASP executive subroutine, specifying event conditions, and bringing appropriate process generators into use.

SIMSCRIPT

The SIMSCRIPT programming language was developed in the early 1960s at the Rand Corporation.[9] Based on FORTRAN, it has all of FORTRAN's capabilities plus terminology and features designed specifically for the simulation of discrete systems. In developing the language, the user was given top priority, and as a result the language is free form and English-like. The SIMSCRIPT compiler is even "forgiving" in that it corrects certain types of user syntax errors and forces execution of every program which considerably shortens user "debugging" time.

Over the years several versions of SIMSCRIPT have evolved. Originally, a translator was used to convert a SIMSCRIPT program to FORTRAN statements that were then compiled and assembled. Later SIMSCRIPT I.5 evolved and eliminated the translation step by providing equivalence between SIMSCRIPT I.5 statements and assembly language. SIMSCRIPT II and II.5, which are considerably different and more powerful than SIMSCRIPT I and I.5, are the most recent versions of the language and can be conceptualized as consisting of five levels.

1.   A simple teaching language designed to introduce programming concepts to nonprogrammers.
2.   A language roughly comparable in power to FORTRAN, but departing greatly from it in specific features.
3.   A language roughly comparable in power to ALGOL or PL/1, but again with many specific differences.
4.   The part of SIMSCRIPT that contains the entity-attribute-set features of SIMSCRIPT.
5.   The simulation-oriented part of SIMSCRIPT, containing statements for time advance, event processing, generation of statistical variates, and the accumulation and analysis of simulation-generated data.

A SIMSCRIPT-based model has five major parts.

1.   Definition section.
2.   Event routines list.
3.   Event routines.
4.   Initialization section.
5.   Exogenous event list.

SIMSCRIPT is built on the concept of entities, attributes, and sets. Entities denote objects of a system; attributes denote characteristics of the entities; and sets define entity

---

[9]F. Paul Wyman, *Simulation Modeling: A Guide to Using SIMSCRIPT* (New York: Wiley, 1970).

groupings. An example might be

ENTITY	SHIP
ATTRIBUTES	CARGO, PASSENGERS
SET	TRANSPORTATION

In the definition section the entities, attributes, and sets are defined. If an entity is expected to remain in the system it is designated permanent, otherwise it is temporary and flows through the system.

The event routine list labels the routines that perform system activities. Events may be exogenous or endogenous; for example,

EXOGENOUS	LOW TIDE
	HIGH TIDE
	CURRENT SHIFT
ENDOGENOUS	SHIP LEAVES PORT
	SHIP DOCKS
	SHIP TAKES ON CARGO

Part 3, event routines, contains a separate event subroutine for each different kind of event. The initialization section provides initial values for variables. The last section, the exogenous event list, consists of records that each have a number corresponding to an exogenous event routine. The record also contains a time at which the corresponding event routine will be executed.

IFPS

Over 40 different financial planning languages are currently being used. These languages vary from simple pro forma statement generators to systems with extensive modeling and analysis capabilities. One of the most sophisticated systems is the Interactive Financial Planning System (IFPS) developed by EXECUCOM.[10] It is a terminal-oriented system that employs an English-like modeling language and is designed for use by management-type personnel in support of their planning responsibilities.

IFPS consists of five subsystems.[11]

1. Executive.
2. Modeling language.
3. Report generator.
4. Data file.
5. Command file.

---

[10]*EXECUCOM IFPS Tutorial* (Austin, Tex.: EXECUCOM System Corporation, 1980).

[11]"EXECUCOM System Corporation, Interactive Financial Planning System (IFPS)," *Auerbach Corporate EDP Library* (Pennsanken, N.J.: Auerbach, 1977).

The executive subsystem serves a number of roles. It is used to specify permanent files, list models and reports, delete models and reports, combine models, consolidate models and data files, copy models and reports, and call other subsystems.

The modeling language subsystem is used to describe and analyze the situation of interest. It includes capabilities for creating models; editing models, model solution, and analyses; asking "What if" questions; performing goal seeking; and conducting probabilistic analyses.

The report generator subsystem allows the user to create or edit reports. This capability results in customized reports.

The data file subsystem is used to create, edit, and maintain data files. With this subsystem, data that have multiple modeling uses can be quickly retrieved for any particular analysis effort.

The command file subsystem permanently stores IFPS commands and directives. These stored commands are executed by commands from the executive subsystem.

An IFPS model is shown in Table 8.1. Model CASHFLOW calculates a monthly cash flow, borrowing money whenever cash falls below $10,000 and paying off loans when-

Table 8.1   A CASH FLOW MODEL PROGRAMMED IN IFPS

```
MODEL CASHFLOW  VERSION OF  02/16/80  10:49
10 COLUMNS JAN, FEB, MAR, APR, MAY, JUNE
20 BEGINNING BALANCE = 10000, PREVIOUS ENDING BALANCE
30 *
40 COLLECTIONS ON RECEIVABLE = 500, 60%*SALES+38%*PREVIOUS SALES
50 OTHER INCOME = 0,5000,0,20000,0,70000
60 CASH AVAILABLE = COLLECTIONS ON RECEIVABLES+OTHER INCOME
70 *
80 *
90 TRADE PAYABLES = 10000,0,12000,2000,5000,0
100 DIRECT LABOR = 400
110 MFG OVERHEAD = 400
120 GEN AND ADMIN = 400
130 INCOME TAXES = 0 FOR 4,4000
140 TOTAL DISBURSEMENTS = SUM(TRADE PAYABLES THRU INCOME TAXES)
150 INDICATED BALANCE = BEGINNING BALANCE+CASH AVAILABLE – TOTAL DISBURSEMENTS
160 LOAN PAYMENTS = MAXIMUM(0,MINIMUM(INDICATED BALANCE–20000,
170               PREVIOUS LOAN BALANCE))
180 INTEREST=INTEREST RATE*PREVIOUS LOAN BALANCE
190 ADJUSTED BALANCE=INDICATED BALANCE–LOAN PAYMENTS–INTEREST
200 LOANS=IF ADJUSTED BALANCE.GT.10000 THEN 0 ELSE
210       ROUNDUP (ADJUSTED BALANCE–10000/10000)*10000
220 ENDING BALANCE = ADJUSTED BALANCE+LOANS
230 SALES=400
240 LOAN BALANCE=MAXIMUM, PREVIOUS LOAN BALANCE+LOANS–LOAN PAYMENTS
250 INTEREST RATE=XPOWERY(1.10,1/13)–1
END OF MODEL
```

Table 8.2   OUTPUT FROM AN IFPS CASH FLOW MODEL

	JAN	FEB	MAR	APR	MAY	JUNE
BEGINNING BALANCE	10000	19300	19841	16901	19789	13482
COLLECTIONS ON RECEIVABLES	500	392	392	392	392	392
OTHER INCOME	0	5000	0	2000	0	70000
CASH AVAILABLE	500	5392	392	20392	392	70392
TRADE PAYABLES	10000	0	12000	2000	5000	0
DIRECT LABOR	400	400	400	400	400	400
MFG OVERHEAD	400	400	400	400	400	400
GEN AND ADMIN	400	400	400	400	400	400
INCOME TAXES	0	0	0	0	400	0
TOTAL DISBURSEMENTS	11200	1200	13200	3200	6600	1200
INDICATED BALANCE	−700	23492	7033	34093	13581	82674
LOAN PAYMENTS	0	3492	0	14093	0	12415
INTEREST	0	159.5	131.6	211.4	99.00	99.00
ADJUSTED BALANCE	−700	19841	6901	19789	13402	20160
LOANS	20000	0	10000	0	0	0
ENDING BALANCE	19300	19841	16901	19789	13482	70160
SALES	400	400	400	400	400	400
LOAN BALANCE	20000	14508	26508	12415	12415	0
INTEREST RATE	.0000	.0000	.0080	.0080	.0080	.0080

ENTER SOLVE OPTIONS
?

ever the available cash exceeds $20,000. The output from CASHFLOW is presented in Table 8.2.

THE POPULARITY OF VARIOUS LANGUAGES

It seems interesting and useful to discuss the languages that are being used in organizations for simulation modeling. The findings of a 1978 survey of a sample of TIMS/ORSA members as to the percentage of simulation models programmed in various languages is shown in Table 8.3.[12]   By far the most frequently used language is FORTRAN. Other popular general-purpose languages are BASIC and PL/1. GPSS is the most frequently used special-purpose language. Financial planning languages are also used rather frequently. In general, however, it appears that general-purpose languages dominate in most organizations.

GENERAL PURPOSE SIMULATION SYSTEM: GPSS

Our consideration of simulation languages now turns to GPSS, the most popular of all special-purpose simulation languages. It was developed in the early 1960s by Geoffrey

[12] Hugh J. Watson, "An Empirical Investigation of the Use of Simulation," *Simulation and Games* (December 1978): 477–482.

Table 8.3   THE USE OF VARIOUS PROGRAMMING LANGUAGES
IN SIMULATION MODELING

Programming Language	Percentage
APL	6
Assembler	2
BASIC	9
COBOL	6
DYNAMO	2
FORTRAN	35
GPSS	13
PL/1	10
SIMSCRIPT	4
Special financial planning (PSG, BUDPLAN SIMPLAN, etc.)	9
Other	4
	100

Source: Hugh J. Watson, "An Empirical Investigation of the Use of Simulation,"
Simulation and Games (December 1978): 481.

Gordon and others working at IBM. Over the years, many different versions of GPSS
have evolved (GPSS II, GPSS III, and GPSS/360), with GPSS V being the most recent
version. The successive versions of GPSS have continued to add to its descriptive and
analysis capabilities. These enhancements become apparent and important, however,
only as one requires advanced capabilities of the language. There are a number of excellent books available that provide a detailed description of the entire language.[13] The
basic capabilities that we will discuss in this chapter are available in all versions of GPSS.

GPSS Features

GPSS is a powerful simulation language; rich in its descriptive and analysis capabilities.
Its use is limited, however, to queuing systems. It is interesting, though, how many systems can be conceptualized as being a queuing system.

   The language has a number of features that facilitate simulation modeling. Because
of its problem and flowchart orientation, describing a system is relatively simple. The
language includes an automatic timing routine that moves the system through time from
event to event. Certain types of statistics are automatically gathered and are later output
in a number of reports. The GPSS translator detects syntax errors and some inherently
illogical conditions. Of all of the desirable features of a simulation language that were
mentioned previously, GPSS is weakest in its generation of probabilistic variates. With
the exception of sampling from the uniform distribution, obtaining variates from different distributions is relatively cumbersome.

---

[13] See, for example, Thomas J. Schriber, *Simulation Using GPSS* (New York: Wiley, 1974).

Block Diagrams

GPSS is a flowchart-oriented language. The flowchart that is developed for a GPSS modeled system is referred to as a *block diagram.* Figure 8.6 provides an illustration of a block diagram for the single-channel, single-phase queuing system discussed in Chapter 7. A comparison of the GPSS block image program with the FORTRAN program provides interesting insights into the power of GPSS in particular, and simulation languages in general.

A GPSS model builder must conceptualize a system in terms of *transactions* moving through the system. For example, in the tool crib operation the workers (other than the tool crib clerk) are the transactions. They enter the system, are processed by the system, and ultimately leave the system.

A model should introduce transactions into a system with the same timing that they appear in the actual system. That is, if workers enter a system with a Poisson arrival pattern, transactions must be placed into a GPSS model in the same manner. These transactions then move through the system as they would the real-world system. They join a queue, receive service, and ultimately leave the system. In GPSS, an automatic

Figure 8.6   A block diagram for a single-channel, single-phase queuing system.

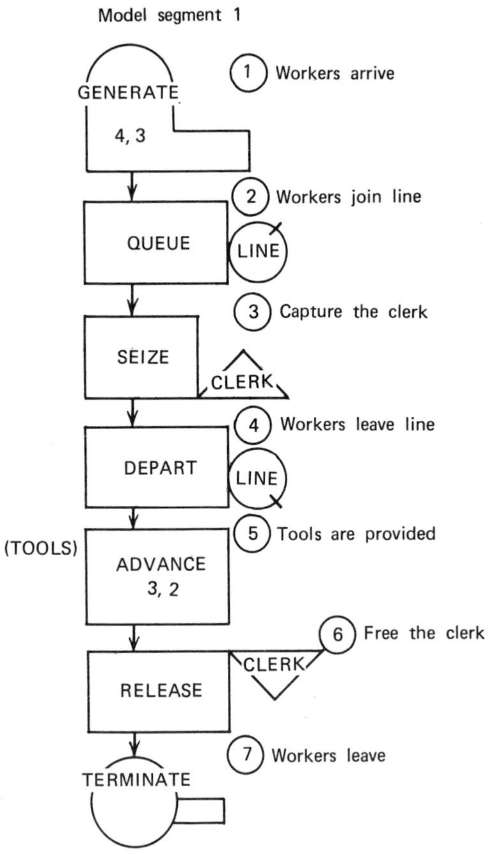

timing routine keeps track of which events are scheduled to occur next. After each arrival event occurs, its successor is scheduled. In other words, GPSS employs the by now familiar concept of prescheduling of events. It also uses a next-event time advance mechanism.

Given these introductory comments, consider Figure 8.6 once again. For now, focus attention on model segment 1, which describes the tool crib operation. Model segment 2 controls the duration of the simulation and will be discussed later. In GPSS there can be many free-standing model segments.

The "source" of transactions in the model is the block numbered 1. With a prespecified arrival time pattern, it introduces transactions into the system. For our example, these transactions are equivalent to workers approaching the tool crib. Once a transaction appears, it enters block 2, where it either temporarily stays or immediately moves on. If held, the transaction is equivalent to a worker having to wait in line for the tool crib operator. At some point in time the server becomes free. Block 3 is used to record the "capture" or "seizing" of the server by the transaction. In this case the worker gains the attention of the tool crib clerk. By seizing the server the transaction leaves the queue. Block 4 records this departure. Blocks 2 and 4 are matched pairs and record the passing of workers through the waiting line. Block 5 holds the transaction while service is being performed. The amount of time the transaction spends in the block is equal to the service time. When service is completed, the transaction passes through block 6, which releases the server for the next transaction. Matching blocks 3 and 5 record the seizing and freeing of the server. The transaction finally leaves the system as it moves into the "sink" represented by block 7.

Although portions of the program will not be clear at this point, it is useful to take a "sneak look" at the GPSS program for the tool crib operation; see Table 8.4. Our purpose is to see how easily the blocks are coded into punched card block images.

Each block in the block diagram has a specific *location*, an *operation* that it performs, and *operands* that provide specific information about the block's functioning.

Blocks are assigned a location number by the GPSS translator, but can also be given a symbolic location name by the programmer. The translator numbers the blocks in the same order that they are placed in the card deck. As an example of a *symbolic location name*, block 5 has been symbolically called TOOLS. Whenever a block is referenced from elsewhere in a program (not illustrated in our example), symbolic location names are a convenience. Symbolic names must be from three to five alphanumeric characters in length, with the first three characters being alphabetic. Table 8.5 shows examples of valid and invalid symbolic location names. When symbolic location names are used, they are placed in columns 2 to 6 of the punched card program.

GPSS has in excess of 40 blocks, each with its own distinctive shape. Each block performs a specific operation. The operations are selected by the analyst as needed to describe the modeled system. For example, Figure 8.6 shows operations such as GENERATE, QUEUE, SEIZE, and so on. The block's operation is specified in columns 8 to 18. As the chapter progresses we will describe some of the basic GPSS operations.

A block's operands provide specific information about the block's functioning. The various operands are referred to as the A operand, the B operand, and so on. The number of operands varies, depending on the block being used. We will not always discuss all of a block's operands, only those most useful in simulating simple queuing systems. Operands are placed in columns 19 to 71, with each operand separated by a comma.

Table 8.4 A GPSS PROGRAM FOR A SINGLE-CHANNEL, SINGLE-PHASE QUEUING SYSTEM.

IBM GPSS/360 — CODING FORM

LOCATION	OPERATION	A,B,C,D,E,F	
	SIMULATE		
*	MODEL SEGMENT 1		
*			
	GENERATE	4,3	WORKERS ARRIVE
	QUEUE	LINE	WORKERS JOIN LINE
	SEIZE	CLERK	CAPTURE THE CLERK
	DEPART	LINE	WORKERS LEAVE LINE
TOOLS	ADVANCE	3,2	TOOLS ARE PROVIDED
	RELEASE	CLERK	FREE THE CLERK
	TERMINATE		WORKERS LEAVE
*			
*	MODEL SEGMENT 2		
*			
	GENERATE	480	THE 8 HOURS PASS
	TERMINATE	1	THE TOOL CRIB CLOSES
*			
	START	1	START THE SIMULATION
	END		LOGICAL END OF PROGRAM

GX20-1701-1 U/M 025*
Printed in U.S.A.
*No. of forms per pad may vary slightly.

SHEET ____ OF ____

Table 8.5   EXAMPLES OF VALID AND INVALID SYMBOLIC LOCATION NAMES

. Valid	Invalid
WAIT	2QUE
LINE3	A
TED23	TELLER

The GENERATE Block

Transactions are introduced into a model through the GENERATE block. The operands on the block define the manner in which the transactions enter. Obviously, they are defined in such a way so as to describe the modeled system. Figure 8.7 shows the GENERATE block's characteristic shape and defines its A and B operands.

GPSS permits a straightforward sampling from the uniform distribution, and permits with additional effort sampling from other distributions. For now we will work only with a situation where the introduction of transactions is described by the uniform distribution, and later in the chapter will discuss how to sample from other distributions.

The A operand communicates the mean arrival time. The B operand provides the half-width of the arrival time. The A and B operands must be integer valued and define a unique uniform arrival time distribution, as shown in Figure 8.8.

The GENERATE block introduces transactions at integer-valued points in time. For example, the GENERATE block in Figure 8.6 has A and B operands of 4 and 3, respectively. These specifications result in possible arrivals at 4 ± 3 or 1, 2, 3, 4, 5, 6, or 7 minutes. After each transaction is entered into the model, its successor is prescheduled. It is possible to *default* on the B operand; that is, specify no value. In this case the GPSS translator assumes its value to be zero. The consequence of setting the B operand equal to zero is to make the process deterministic rather than probabilistic. This feature is necessary, of course, for there are deterministic (or nearly so) processes in the real world.

Figure 8.7   The GENERATE block.   **Figure 8.8**   A uniform arrival-time distribution.

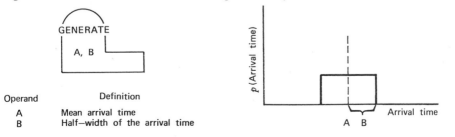

Operand	Definition
A	Mean arrival time
B	Half-width of the arrival time

Figure 8.9   The QUEUE and DEPART blocks.

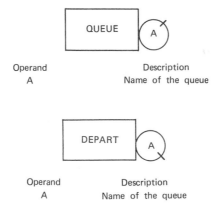

The QUEUE and DEPART Blocks

Our earlier discussion of Figure 8.6 described how a transaction moves from the GENER-ATE to the QUEUE block. This block records any possible waiting in line by the transaction. Later, as the transaction moves through the DEPART block, its passage out of the queue is noted. The QUEUE and DEPART blocks are used in tandem to gather statistics on how long transactions have to wait at various points in the system. For our tool crib operation, statistics are collected on how long the workers are waiting in line to seize the tool crib operator.

The characteristic symbol and A operand for the QUEUE and DEPART blocks are shown in Figure 8.9. The A operand can be given either a numeric or a symbolic name. A numeric name can be any integer value between one and the maximum number of queues permitted by the GPSS translator. Symbolic names that meet the same requirements as for symbolic location names can also be used. That is, the names must be three to five alphanumeric characters in length with the first three characters being alphabetic. A matched pair of QUEUE and DEPART blocks must have the same name, because that is how the GPSS translator identifies which pairs go together. In our example, the only queue was given the symbolic name LINE.

QUEUE and DEPART blocks are not actually needed to have queues in a system. That is, the GPSS translator will allow queues to form even without QUEUE and DEPART blocks. They are used solely for gathering statistics. This point was obscured previously in order to keep the discussion on a straightforward path. However, given this new interpretation of the role of QUEUE and DEPART blocks, we see that they can actually be placed anywhere in the model that the analyst wants statistics gathered. For our example, it was useful to have information on how long the workers were waiting in the *queue*. If the DEPART block had been placed after the RELEASE block, statistics would have been gathered on waiting time in the *system*.

The SEIZE and RELEASE Blocks

A transaction may or may not be able to capture the server at once. The SEIZE block stops movement of the transaction until the server is free. When the server becomes free,

Figure 8.10   The SEIZE and RELEASE blocks.

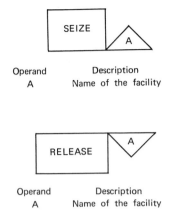

Operand	Description
A	Name of the facility

Operand	Description
A	Name of the facility

the transaction that has been waiting the longest moves into the SEIZE block. After the server has completed service on the transaction, the RELEASE block sets the transaction free and allows another transaction to capture the server, if one or more are waiting. Single servers (as opposed to multiple servers) are referred to as *facilities* in GPSS terminology. Statistics are automatically gathered on the activities of facilities. We will see the format in which they are output later.

Figure 8.10 shows the characteristic symbol and defines the A operand for the SEIZE and RELEASE blocks. As with the QUEUE and DEPART blocks, the A operand on the SEIZE and RELEASE blocks can be given either numeric or symbolic names. A numeric name can be any integer value between one and the maximum number of facilities permitted by the GPSS translator. Symbolic names must be three to five alphanumeric characters in length with the first three characters being alphabetic. The symbolic name CLERK was given to the only facility in our example.

The ADVANCE Block

The ADVANCE block is used to "freeze" a transaction and advance the clock while the transaction receives service. The block holds the transaction until service is completed. Its characteristic shape and A and B operands are presented in Figure 8.11.

The ADVANCE block is similar to the GENERATE block in its functioning. Unless special provisions are made, integer values are sampled from a uniform distribution with a mean specified by the A operand and a half-width given by the B operand. The sampled

Figure 8.11   The ADVANCE block.

Operand	Description
A	Mean service time
B	Half—width of the service time

values are used in simulating how long it takes the server to provide service. In our tool crib example, mean service times of 3 ± 2 or 1, 2, 3, 4, or 5 minutes are used. Defaulting on the B operand causes the translator to assign a value of zero, which creates a deterministic service time.

The TERMINATE Block

The TERMINATE block is used to remove transactions from the system. It also plays a vital role in controlling the duration of the simulation. Its characteristic shape and A operand are presented in Figure 8.12.

When a transaction enters the TERMINATE block, a special variable known as the *termination counter* is decremented by the value specified as the A operand. This A operand is known as a *termination counter decrement*. The initial value of the termination counter is set by the START card, which is described next. It is possible to default on the terminate block's A operand and the GPSS translator will assign a value of zero to it. Consider Table 8.4 once again. Notice that there is a START card with the number 1 in the A operand field. The START card is not a block but, rather, an internal control card. It tells the translator to begin program execution and to assign to the memory location for the termination counter a value equal to that specified on the START card. In our example, the termination counter is initialized with a value of 1. The TERMINATE block in model segment 1 does not have an A operand specified. Consequently, the translator assigns it a value of zero. Everytime a transaction enters the TERMINATE block in model segment 1, nothing happens to the value of the termination counter, because the termination counter decrement has an assigned value of zero. It is only the TERMINATE block in model segment 2 that affects the termination counter. It is here that the length of the simulation is controlled.

Stopping the Simulation

The A operand for the TERMINATE block in model segment 2 has a value of 1. When a transaction enters this block, the termination counter is decremented by 1, which causes it to take on a value of zero. *This condition causes the simulation to stop.* Anytime the termination counter's value becomes zero, the translator shuts off the simulation. In fact, this is the only way to terminate a GPSS simulation.

When does the simulation stop in our tool crib example? A transaction is brought into the model by the GENERATE block in model segment 2 exactly 480 simulated minutes after the run begins. This figure corresponds to an 8-hour work shift (60 minutes/ hour × 8 hours = 480 minutes). The transaction in model segment 2 does not actually

Figure 8.12   The TERMINATE block.

Operand	Description
A	A termination counter decrement

Table 8.6 AN ALTERNATIVE METHOD FOR
STOPPING THE SIMULATION

```
        :
    MODEL SEGMENT 2

    GENERATE  1
    TERMINATE 1

    START      480
        :
```

---

correspond to a worker going to the tool crib. Instead, it is just a way to terminate the simulation.

Although the way we chose to end the simulation was the most efficient, it was not the only choice. For example, model segment 2 could have been set up as shown in Table 8.6. With this approach a transaction enters the system every simulated minute. Each transaction that enters the TERMINATE block decreases the termination counter by 1. Since the counter is initialized with a value of 480, after 480 minutes the termination counter is finally decreased to zero and the simulation ends.

This method does terminate the simulation at the desired point in time. It is inefficient, however, in that it requires 480 transactions rather than one.

The Punched Card Program

Now we are ready to discuss the punched card version of the block diagram for Figure 8.6. It is useful to consider the various cards as being for *external control, comments, block diagram images*, and *internal control*.

The external control cards are not shown in Table 8.4. They vary with the computer facility being used. In general, they communicate information such as the user's account number, the language translator to be used, the required storage capacity, and so on. The required cards and their format can be obtained either from your instructor or computer center personnel.

Comments can be included with a GPSS program by placing an asterisk in column 1. The asterisk tells the translator to ignore the card. Asterisks are used in Table 8.4 to identify the model segments and to improve the model's readability through spacing.

To a large extent the punched card images on the block diagram have already been discussed. The fields in which the block information is placed are summarized in Table 8.7. The only additional necessary comment is that the translator stops its scan when it encounters a blank in the operands field. Consequently, comments can be placed after leaving a space.

The final cards that need to be discussed are internal control cards. At the beginning of a program the SIMULATE card with the single word SIMULATE is placed in the operation field. At the end of the program is the START card. Its use has already been de-

Table 8.7 PUNCHED CARD FIELDS IN
WHICH BLOCK INFORMATION IS
ENTERED

Columns	Block Information
2–6	Location
8–18	Operation
19–71	Operands

scribed. The final card is an END card with the word END placed in the operation field. It identifies the logical end of the program.

Program Output

The GPSS translator outputs summary statistics collected during the running of the simulation. The output that results from executing the sample GPSS program is presented in Table 8.8.

The first report (Table 8.8a) is referred to as an *extended program listing*. It provides all the information punched on cards, plus additions made by the translator. Specifically,

Table 8.8a EXTENDED PROGRAM LISTING FOR THE SINGLE-CHANNEL, SINGLE-PHASE QUEUING SYSTEM

BLOCK NUMBER	*LOC	OPERATION	A,B,C,D,E,F,G	COMMENTS	CARD NUMBER
		SIMULATE			1
	*	MODEL SEGMENT 1			2
	*				3
1		GENERATE	4,3	WORKERS ARRIVE	4
2		QUEUE	LINE	WORKERS JOIN LINE	5
3		SEIZE	CLERK	CAPTURE THE CLERK	6
4		DEPART	LINE	WORKERS LEAVE LINE	7
5	TOOLS	ADVANCE	3,2	TOOLS ARE PROVIDED	8
6		RELEASE	CLERK	FREE THE CLERK	9
7		TERMINATE		WORKERS LEAVE	10
	*				11
	*	MODEL SEGMENT 2			12
	*				13
8		GENERATE	480	THE 8 HOURS PASS	14
9		TERMINATE	1	THE TOOL CRIB CLOSES	15
	*				16
		START	1	START THE SIMULATION	17
		END		LOGICAL END OF PROGRAM	18

Table 8.8*b*   CLOCK VALUES AND BLOCK COUNTS

RELATIVE CLOCK			480 ABSOLUTE CLOCK			480		
BLOCK COUNTS								
BLOCK	CURRENT	TOTAL	BLOCK	CURRENT	TOTAL	BLOCK	CURRENT	TOTAL
1	0	109						
2	0	109						
3	0	109						
4	0	109						
5	1	109						
6	0	108						
7	0	108						
8	0	1						
9	0	1						

descriptive column headings are provided and all of the blocks are numbered as well as the cards in the program deck.

The second report (Table 8.8*b*) presents the *clock values and block counts*. At the top of the report is the *relative clock* and *absolute clock* readings at the end of the simulation. Each clock shows a value of 480, the time when the simulation terminated. For our purposes, the difference between the relative and absolute clocks is unimportant.

The block counts record the condition of the blocks at the end of the simulation. The *current count* shows the number of transactions that were in each block when the simulation shut off. The *total count* reveals the number of transactions that entered each block during the running of the simulation.

The third report (Table 8.8*c*) presents *information on each facility*. The name given to each facility is shown, and the percentage of time that the facility (the server) was utilized is reported. The number of transactions that engaged the facility during the simulation is indicated, and the average time the server spent with each transaction is shown. Two other items are reported but they need not concern us.

The final report (Table 8.8*d*) presents *information on each queue*. The queue names are shown first. This information is followed by the maximum number of transactions that were ever in the queue. The average number of transactions in each queue is also reported, as well as the total number of transactions that entered each queue during the simulation. "Zero entries" and "percent zeroes" refer to transactions that entered a queue, but spent zero units of simulated time there. The first average (AVERAGE) provides the average time spent in the queue by all transactions, whereas the second average

Table 8.8*c*   INFORMATION ON EACH FACILITY

FACILITY	AVERAGE UTILIZATION	NUMBER ENTRIES	AVERAGE TIME/TRAN	SEIZING TRANS. NO.	PREEMPTING TRANS. NO.
CLERK	.674	109	2.972	4	

Table 8.8d INFORMATION ON EACH QUEUE

QUEUE	MAXIMUM CONTENTS	AVERAGE CONTENTS	TOTAL ENTRIES	ZERO ENTRIES	PERCENT ZEROS	AVERAGE TIME/TRANS	$AVERAGE TIME/TRANS	TABLE NUMBER	CURRENT CONTENTS
LINE	2	.191	109	‑70	64.2	.844	2.358		

$AVERAGE TIME/TRANS = AVERAGE TIME/TRANS EXCLUDING ZERO ENTRIES

($AVERAGE) excludes zero entries in its computation. The table number information is beyond our current interest. The current content figures show the number of transactions in each queue when the simulation ended.

Parallel Servers

In addition to single-server systems, servers working in parallel are common. Although it is not possible to discuss the entire spectrum of parallel server systems, a basic system is within our scope. This system is shown in Figure 8.13. The arrivals form a single line before the servers, in contrast to systems where the elements chose a particular server to queue up before. The elements in the single queue are served on a first-come, first-served basis. The servers themselves are *homogeneous*. That is, they provide service in exactly the same manner. More specifically, they provide service at the same rate.

An example of a parallel server system might be our tool crib illustration with two clerks in the tool crib. This system would be described by the block diagram presented in Figure 8.14.

The ENTER and LEAVE Blocks

The block diagram in Figure 8.14 has new blocks replacing the SEIZE and RELEASE blocks. These are ENTER and LEAVE blocks and are used to depict servers working in parallel. In GPSS terminology they represent a *storage*. Their characteristic shape and A operand are presented in Figure 8.15. The A operand has the same naming requirements as those for block location names, queues, and facilities.

The ENTER and LEAVE blocks do not define their *storage capacity*, that is, how many servers are in parallel. This information is placed on a *storage capacity definition card*. This card is typically placed at the beginning of the program and functions as an internal control card. One card is required for each storage in the system. The name of

Figure 8.13 A parallel service queuing system.

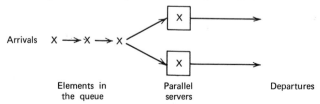

Arrivals   X → X → X

Elements in the queue   Parallel servers   Departures

Figure 8.14 A block diagram for parallel servers.

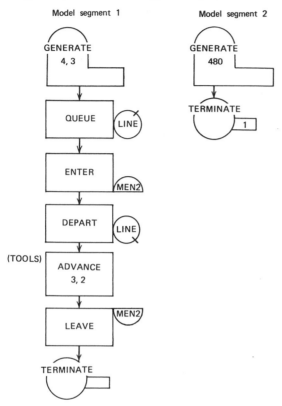

Figure 8.15 The ENTER and LEAVE blocks.

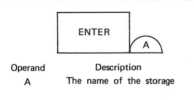

Operand	Description
A	The name of the storage

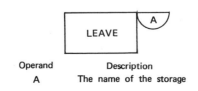

Operand	Description
A	The name of the storage

Table 8.9 A GPSS PROGRAM FOR TWO PARALLEL SERVERS.

IBM

GPSS/360 — CODING FORM

NAME				DATE		PROBLEM NO.	PHONE NO.	PROGRAM TITLE	GX20-1701-1 U/M 025 Printed in U.S.A. "No. of forms per pad may vary slightly" SHEET ___ OF ___

LOCATION	OPERATION	A,B,C,D,E,F Comments
	SIMULATE	
MEN2	STORAGE	2 TWO TOOL CRIB CLERKS
		MODEL SEGMENT 1
*		
*		
	GENERATE	4,3 WORKERS ARRIVE
	QUEUE	LINE WORKERS JOIN LINE
	ENTER	MEN2 CAPTURE ONE OF THE CLERKS
	DEPART	LINE WORKERS LEAVE LINE
TOOLS	ADVANCE	3,2 TOOLS ARE PROVIDED
	LEAVE	MEN2 FREE ONE OF THE CLERKS
	TERMINATE	WORKERS LEAVE
*		
*		MODEL SEGMENT 2
*		
	GENERATE	480 THE 8 HOURS PASS
	TERMINATE	1
*		
	START	1 START THE SIMULATION
	END	LOGICAL END OF PROGRAM

196

Table 8.10 A STORAGE REPORT

STORAGE	CAPACITY	AVERAGE CONTENTS	AVERAGE UTILIZATION	ENTRIES	AVERAGE TIME/TRAN	CURRENT CONTENTS	MAXIMUM CONTENTS
MEN2	2	.706	.353	111	3.054	1	

the storage whose capacity is being defined is placed in the location field. The word STORAGE is in the operation field. The number of servers working in parallel is entered in the operand field. Table 8.9 shows the GPSS program for the tool crib operation with two parallel servers. Take special notice of the use of the ENTER and LEAVE blocks and the storage capacity definition card.

When parallel servers are modeled in a GPSS program, a *storage* report is provided. The report that resulted from running the GPSS program just discussed is presented in Table 8.10. The report provides the names of the storages and their maximum content. The average number of transactions in the storages during the simulation is indicated. Also provided is the average percentage of time that the servers were engaged. The number of transactions that entered the storages during the simulation is reported as well as how long on average their servicing required. The current contents reveals how many transactions were in the storages when the simulation ended. The maximum content of the storages during the running of the simulation is also shown.

Negative Exponential Processes

In general, nonuniform processes are beyond the scope of our GPSS coverage. As indicated earlier, sampling from probabilistic processes is cumbersome in GPSS. However, one of our objectives in this chapter is to contrast a GPSS program with its FORTRAN equivalent. Consequently, it seems necessary to present the treatment of Poisson arrivals and negative exponential service times even though most of what is discussed must be taken at face value rather than being fully understood. Working only with the end result should permit making at least interesting comparisons with the FORTRAN model and allow a broader, more realistic set of queuing systems to be modeled in GPSS.

In order to sample from nonuniform distributions, *functions* must be defined. These functions can be for either discrete or continuous variables. An appropriate function for the negative exponential distribution is shown in Table 8.11.

The function has been symbolically named XPDIS. The name of a GPSS function is specified by the programmer. As seen in Table 8.11, a function-defining statement is identified by the word FUNCTION in the operation field. The RN1 in the first operand field indicates that this function is to be sampled from by using the first random number generator. In GPSS there are a total of eight different random number generators. This feature is convenient for replicating experimental conditions, because specific generators can be dedicated to important probabilistic processes. The C24 in the second operand field communicates that the continuous (hence the C) function named XPDIS is being represented by 24 points. The ordered pairs that are separated by slashes indicate points from XPDIS's cumulative density function and their associated cumulative probabilities.

Table 8.11 A FUNCTION FOR THE NEGATIVE EXPONENTIAL DISTRIBUTION

IBM GPSS/360 — CODING FORM

```
LOCATION  OPERATION  A,B,C,D,E,F
XPDIS     FUNCTION   RN1,C24
0,0/.1,.104/.2,.222/.3,.355/.4,.509/.5,.69/.6,.915/.7,1.2/.75,1.38
.8,1.6/.84,1.83/.88,2.12/.9,2.3/.92,2.52/.94,2.81/.95,2.99/.96,3.2
.97,3.5/.98,3.9/.99,4.6/.995,5.3/.998,6.2/.999,7/.9998,8
```

Figure 8.16   The GENERATE and ADVANCE blocks with negative exponential processes.

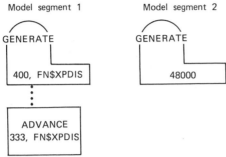

When random numbers that do not correspond exactly with the listed cumulative probabilities are generated, a linear interpolation is performed.

Function XPDIS is set up so that it can be used with any mean arrival or service time. It is only necessary to multiply the desired mean by the sampled value from XPDIS. But how is this multiplication performed in GPSS? A special feature of the language allows the multiplier to be specified as the A operand for the GENERATE and ADVANCE blocks with the function name preceded by FN$ as the B operand. In the FORTRAN model from Chapter 7, a mean interarrival time of 4 minutes and a mean service time of 3.33 (15/hour and 18/hour, respectively) were used. However, for reasons that we need not mention here, multipliers this small for the A operand violate an assumption that underlies the Poisson distribution. It is recommended that the multiplier be at least 50. We can satisfy this requirement by changing our interval time from minutes to hundredths of a minute. This change indicates that mean arrival and service times of 400 and 333, respectively, should be used. Using these times, we would set up the GENERATE and ADVANCE blocks as shown in Figure 8.16.

The function-defining cards are placed early in the program deck, before the function is referenced elsewhere in the program. The GENERATE and ADVANCE blocks are placed in the same locations as earlier. The GPSS program, which is the equivalent to the FORTRAN program presented in Table 7.5, is shown in Table 8.12.

Modeling More Complex Systems

Our discussion of GPSS has barely scratched the surface. We have only minimal information as to how the GPSS translator functions. Only 9 of the more than 40 blocks have been discussed, and even then, some of their capabilities have been omitted. In conclusion, let us consider some of the real-life aspects of queuing systems that can be modeled in GPSS, but not with our current knowledge of the language.

Elements do not always mindlessly line up in queues. They tend to balk with increasing frequency as lines become longer. Elements often do not stay in the queue they originally join. Instead, they move from queue to queue in search of a shorter, faster moving line. Serving rules are not always first come, first served. Some elements typically have higher service priorities. Servers do not function at a constant rate. They may slow down as they become fatigued, or speed up as queues becomes longer. These exam-

Table 8.12 A GPSS PROGRAM FOR THE TOOL CRIB OPERATION WITH NEGATIVE EXPONENTIAL ARRIVAL AND SERVICE TIMES.

IBM

GPSS/360 — CODING FORM

LOCATION	OPERATION	A,B,C,D,E,F	
XPDIS	FUNCTION	RN1,C24	
		0,0/.1,.104/.2,.222/.3,.355/.4,.509/.5,.69/.6,.91/.7,1.2/.75,1.38	
		.8,1.6/.84,1.83/.88,2.12/.9,2.3/.92,2.52/.94,2.81/.95,2.99/.96,3.2	
		.97,3.5/.98,3.9/.99,4.6/.995,5.3/.998,6.2/.999,7/.9998,8	
*	MODEL SEGMENT 1		
*			
	GENERATE	400,FN$XPDIS	WORKERS ARRIVE
	QUEUE	LINE	WORKERS JOIN LINE
	SEIZE	CLERK	CAPTURE THE CLERK
	DEPART	LINE	WORKERS LEAVE LINE
	ADVANCE	333,FN$XPDIS	TOOLS ARE PROVIDED
	RELEASE	CLERK	FREE THE CLERK
	TERMINATE		
*			
*	MODEL SEGMENT 2		
*			
	GENERATE	48000	THE 8 HOURS PASS
	TERMINATE	1	STOP THE SIMULATION
*			
	START	1	START THE SIMULATION
	END		LOGICAL END OF PROGRAM

GX20-1701-1 U/M 025
Printed in U.S.A.
No. of forms per pad may vary slightly

SHEET ___ OF ___

200

ples illustrate just some of the complexities associated with real-world queuing systems, but complexities that can be accommodated in GPSS.

SUMMARY

Simulation models can be programmed in either general- or special-purpose languages. General-purpose languages offer advantages in terms of maximum flexibility in mathematically describing the real-world system, selecting the type and format of output reports, and experimenting on the modeled system. The programmer is also usually knowledgeable in a suitable general-purpose language. Special-purpose languages, on the other hand, normally possess features that facilitate simulation modeling. These features include easy description of the modeled system, automatic movement of the model through time, automatic gathering and outputting of summary statistics, easy generation of probabilistic processes, and good logic and syntax diagnostics. Consequently, special-purpose simulation languages tend to reduce programming time and effort, provide conceptual guidance in formulating a description of the modeled system, and facilitate description and analysis of the modeled system.

Problem-oriented simulation languages are designed to model a particular type of problem or system. Procedure-oriented simulation languages are similar to general-purpose languages in that an appropriate procedure or algorithm must be developed to describe the modeled system. However, the language can often be used for a variety of applications. Flowchart-oriented simulation languages use special symbols that simplify system modeling and the later coding of a program.

Simulation languages do have several potential disadvantages. These disadvantages include considerations such as the language may not be available on the user's computer system, the language may have to be learned, the language may not be appropriate for the application, and processing costs can be high.

A two-phase selection process is recommended when choosing a language. The first phase investigates the availability of references, documentation, and software compatibility. The second phase explores the suitability of the languages for the intended application.

A large number of simulation languages have been developed. DYNAMO is used to simulate large-scale continuous systems. GASP is a FORTRAN-based language that has callable subroutines and functions that facilitate simulation modeling. SIMSCRIPT has a number of levels including levels that are designed for simulation modeling. IFPS is one of many languages that have recently been developed for financial planning purposes. Despite the growing availability of special-purpose simulation languages, recent studies have found FORTRAN to be the most popular by a wide margin.

General Purpose Simulation System, GPSS, has evolved through many versions with GPSS V being the most recent version. With the exception of easy generation of probabilistic processes, it has all the desirable features of a simulation language. GPSS is a problem-oriented language used to model queuing systems. The modeled system is described in a flowchart known as a block diagram. A GPSS program is later easily coded from the block diagram. The modeled system must be conceptualized as transactions flowing through the system. Transactions enter the system, are processed by the system, and finally leave the system.

Each block in a block diagram has a location, operation, and operands. The location, whether numeric or symbolic, identifies the block in a GPSS program. The operation communicates the block's function. The operands provide detailed information about the block's characteristics.

The GENERATE block is used to enter transactions into the modeled system. Its basic structure is for uniformly distributed arrival times.

Statistics are automatically gathered by placing QUEUE and DEPART blocks around a subsystem of interest.

The SEIZE and RELEASE blocks are used for capturing and freeing the server. In GPSS, a single server is referred to as a facility.

The ADVANCE block is used to simulate the passage of time while service is being provided. Its basic structure is for uniformly distributed service times.

The TERMINATE block is the "sink" for all transactions. It also plays, along with the START card, an important role in controlling the duration of a simulation.

Parallel servers can be depicted through ENTER and LEAVE blocks. A storage capacity definition card is used to indicate the number of servers in parallel.

Nonuniform processes can be generated in GPSS. Required, however, are functions and function definition cards.

A punched card GPSS program contains external control cards, comment cards, block diagram image cards, and internal control cards.

GPSS outputs many summary statistics in fixed-format reports. These reports include an extended program listing, clock values and block counts, information on each facility, each queue and each storage.

GPSS is a rich and powerful simulation language. It has the capability for modeling much more complex systems than were discussed here.

ASSIGNMENTS

8.1. Programming languages differ in their characteristics. Describe the following types of languages.
     (a) Procedure-oriented languages.
     (b) General-purpose languages.
     (c) Flowchart-oriented languages.
     (d) Problem-oriented languages.
     (e) Special-purpose languages.

8.2. General- and special-purpose simulation languages were discussed in this chapter. For the following situations, would you suggest using FORTRAN, IFPS, SIM-SCRIPT, GASP, GPSS, or DYNAMO? More than one language might be appropriate in some situations.
     (a) A large automobile manufacturer wants to develop a simulation model of its assembly line. The model will be developed by the company's staff and run on the company's IBM 370 Model 158.
     (b) A student in a banking class wants to build a model of a single-teller drive-in window system as a class project. His previous programming experience has been in FORTRAN.

(c) A group of newly graduated MBAs has formed a consulting firm to develop financial planning systems. The group has extensive backgrounds in finance, accounting, and computer science. The systems they develop will run on the sponsoring companys' computer systems.

8.3. In Chapter 7 a number of assignments requiring the writing of FORTRAN programs for queuing systems were given. Several of these queuing systems can be modeled in GPSS with our current knowledge of the language. Write and run GPSS programs for the following Chapter 7 assignments.

(a) Assignment 7.4.

(b) Assignment 7.5.

(c) Assignment 7.6.

8.4. Customers arrive at a single-server pastry shop in a manner that is uniformly distributed with a mean arrival time of 5 minutes and a variability of ±3 minutes. Service time is uniformly distributed at 3 ± 2 minutes. Gather statistics in a GPSS program on the system's performance.

(a) What was the average time that all customers spent in the queue?

(b) How many customers entered the shop?

(c) Describe the system as it appeared at the close of the day.

(d) What percentage of time was the server engaged?

(e) How many customers did not have to wait in line?

8.5. A small amusement park sells tickets at one booth and collects them at another. Customers arrive at the park in a uniformly distributed manner with an arrival time of 3 ± 1 minutes. Tickets are sold and later collected with uniformly distributed service times of 2 ± 1 and 0.3 ± 0.1 minutes, respectively. Write and execute a GPSS program that collects statistics on time spent in the two queues. Simulate one hour of activity. What time unit did you use in the model?

8.6. Ships arrive at a harbor in a Poisson manner with an arrival rate of 2 per day. The ships are unloaded at one of three docks in a negative exponential manner. Each dock has a mean service time of one ship per day. Simulate 360 days of activity at the harbor using a GPSS program. Collect statistics on average time spent waiting for service.

8.7. A university registration system has a single table where students' course cards are checked, and three tables in parallel where registration fees are paid. Students approach the first table in a uniform manner with an arrival time of 2 ± 1 minutes. Students' cards are checked in a uniform manner with a mean service time of 2 ± 0.5 minutes. Fees are paid according to the negative exponential distribution with a mean service time of 5 minutes. Simulate 3 hours of activity in a GPSS program collecting data on time spent in the two queues and the total system.

8.8. Workers come to a supply room in a uniform manner with an arrival time of 4 ± 2 minutes. The two supply room clerks fill the requisitions in an exponentially distributed manner with a mean service rate for each clerk of 1 requisition/ 5 minutes. How many requisitions will be filled in the first hour of simulated time?

8.9. The owner of Robbins Ice Cream Shoppe is trying to decide how many employees to have on a typical Saturday afternoon. Customer arrivals tend to be Poisson distributed with a mean arrival rate of 1 customer/minute. Service rates are negative exponentially distributed with a mean service rate of 1 customer/minute/ employee. The owner wants to keep the mean waiting time in the queue below 5 minutes. How many employers should be on duty? Base your analysis on 6 hours of simulated activity.

8.10. A company is trying to decide how many clerks to put in a tool crib. Workers going to the tool crib average $9 per hour, whereas clerks earn $4.50 per hour. Arrival rates are Poisson distributed with an average of 15 per hour. Service times are uniformly distributed at 5 ± 3 minutes. Base your analysis on a GPSS program that simulates 8 hours of activity. Attempt to replicate experimental conditions as much as possible. What assumptions have your made in your modeling efforts?

REFERENCES

Bobillier, P. A., B. C. Kahan, and A. R. Prolist, *Simulation with GPSS and GPSS V* (Englewood Cliffs, N.J.: Prentice-Hall, 1976).

Emshoff, James R., and Roger L. Sisson, *Design and Use of Computer Simulation Models* (New York: Macmillan, 1970).

Fishman, George S., *Concepts and Methods in Discrete Event Digital Simulation* (New York: Wiley, 1973).

Forrester, Jay W., *Industrial Dynamics*, (Cambridge, Mass.: Massachusetts Institute of Technology Press, 1961).

Gordon, Geoffrey, *The Application of GPSS V to Discrete System Simulation* (Englewood Cliffs, N.J.: Prentice-Hall, 1975).

IBM Corporation, *General Purpose Simulation System–V*, *User's Manual*, Form SH20-0351 (White Plains, N.Y.).

Kay, Ira M., "Digital Discrete Simulation Languages. A Discussion and an Inventory," *Fifth Annual Simulation Symposium*, Kenneth W. Gohring, Newton D. Swain, and Richard L. Sander, eds. (New York: Gordon and Breach, 1972).

Kiviat, P. J., R. Villanueva, and H. M. Markowitz, *The SIMSCRIPT II Programming Language*, R-360-PR (Palo Alto, Cal.: Rand Corp., 1968).

Kwak, N. K., P. J. Kuzdrall, and Homer H. Schmitz, "The GPSS Simulation of Scheduling Policies for Surgical Patients," *Management Science* (May 1976): 982–989.

Lewis, T. G., and B. J. Smith, *Computer Principles of Modeling and Simulation* (Boston: Houghton Mifflin, 1979).

McMillan, Claude, and Richard F. Gonzalez, *Systems Analysis*, 3rd. ed. (Homewood, Ill.: Irwin, 1973).

Meadows, Donella H., Dennis L. Meadows, Jorgen Randers, and William S. Behrens, III, *The Limits to Growth* (New York: Universe Books, 1972).

Meier, Robert C., William T. Newell, and Harold L. Pazer, *Simulation in Business and Economics* (Englewood Cliffs, N.J.: Prentice-Hall, 1969).

Naylor, Thomas H., Joseph L. Balintfy, Donald S. Burdick, and Kong Chu, *Computer Simulation Techniques* (New York: Wiley, 1966).

Naylor, Thomas H., and Daniel R. Gattis, "Corporate Planning Models," *California Management Review* (Summer 1976): 69–78.

Pugh, Alexander L. III., *DYNAMO User's Manual*, 2nd ed. (Cambridge, Mass.: Massachusetts Institute of Technology Press, 1963).

Schriber, Thomas J., *Simulation Using GPSS* (New York: Wiley, 1974).

Shannon, Robert E., *Systems Simulation* (Englewood Cliffs, N.J.: Prentice-Hall, 1975).

Wyman, F. Paul, and Gerald Creaven, "Experimental Analysis of a GPSS Simulation of a Student Health Center," *Socio-Economic Planning Science* (October 1972): 489–499.

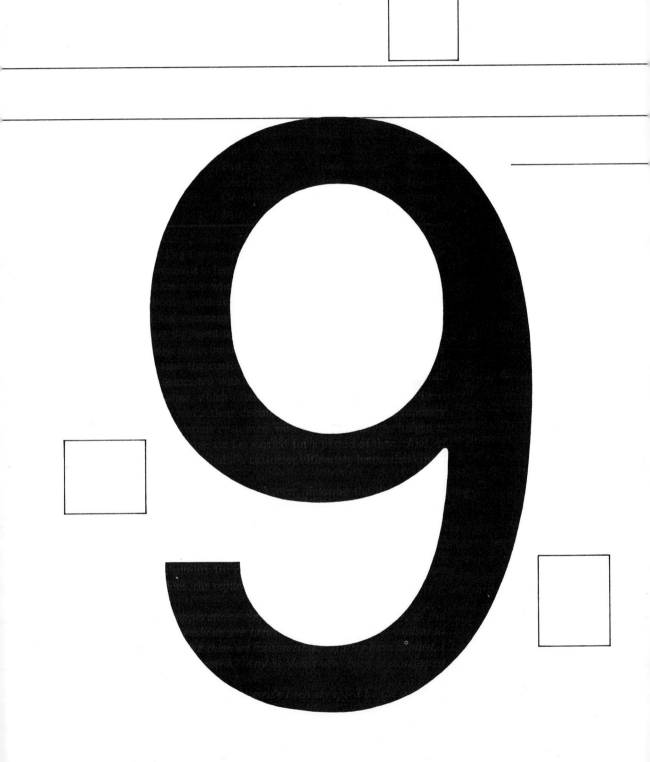

CHAPTER NINE

SIMULATING HUMAN DECISION-MAKING

Artificial Intelligence

A Brief History

Illustrations of Models that Simulate Human Decision-Making

    Clarkson's Trust Investment Model

    Dickson's Vendor Selection Model

    Smith and Greenlaw's Personnel Selection Model

Potential Benefits

A Methodology for Simulating Human Decision Making

Conditions Conducive to Modeling

An Illustration of Simulating Human Decision Making: Processing Overdrafts

    Background Material

    Building the Model

    The Model

Closing Remarks

Summary

Assignments

References

As already seen, many types of systems can be simulated. These systems vary from physical to financial systems and, as will be seen in this chapter, the mind's system for arriving at decisions. A model of this latter type of system will be referred to as a *simulation of human decision-making*. Such models attempt to duplicate the decisions made by real-world decision makers, and represent some of the most interesting applications of simulation.

This chapter covers a variety of topics associated with the simulation of human decision making—a brief history, with a presentation of some of the most significant contributions; a discussion of the potential of this type of modeling; a description of the methodology for developing models; a discussion of the conditions that are conclusive to modeling; and an application is presented in depth.

ARTIFICIAL INTELLIGENCE

Any discussion of the simulation of human decision-making must include its relationship to artificial intelligence. *Artificial intelligence* (AI) is concerned with the development of models that act in an "intelligent" manner. That is, models that produce output similar to that generated by human beings, who by definition are deemed intelligent.

The classic test for AI was provided by the noted, eccentric British mathematician Alan Turing.[1] Turing's test calls for questions to be submitted by an interrogator to both a human and a computer. If based on the responses to the questions it is impossible for the interrogator to determine whether the human or the machine has provided the response, it is said that AI has been realized. Obviously, Turing's test is very demanding and only limited progress has been made in developing generalized computer programs that can respond to several categories of questions. Being able to "intelligently" respond to any type of question is still far, if not forever, in the future.

Most AI research has been conducted in areas with only limited immediate real-world usefulness. For example, some of the most famous AI studies have dealt with chess-playing programs and programs that prove simple logic and calculus theorems. In the long run, however, this type of research is leading to a better understanding of the functioning of the human mind and models more useful to the business world. In fact, models are currently being implemented that, although not intelligent in Turing's use of the word, are capable of making simple decisions that formerly could only be made by humans.

The field of AI contains many subsets, including the simulation of human decision-making. While there is much overlap among the subsets, reference is frequently made to *heuristic problem solving or programming*, *pattern recognition*, *game playing*, and *robotology*.[2] Our interest will be primarily limited to the simulation of human decision-making, for it is of immediate potential value to organizations and this book is on simulation. Heuristic problem solving does merit brief mention, however, because of its close relationship to the simulation of human decision-making and its practical business applications.

---

[1] Alan M. Turing, "Can a Machine Think," *The World of Mathematics*, ed. James R. Newman (New York: Simon & Schuster, 1956), pp. 2099–2123.

[2] Earl B. Hunt, *Artificial Intelligence* (New York: Academic Press, 1975).

This problem-solving approach uses algorithms composed of a series of *heuristics* (rules-of-thumb, decision rules) which, when sequentially applied, intelligently explore the possible solutions to the problem until one is identified. It is typically applied to problems where there exists an extremely large number of possible solutions that cannot be effectively explored by alternative methods of analysis. For example, Tonge has investigated the line-balancing problem,[3] Gere the job-shop-scheduling problem,[4] and Keuhn and Hamburger the warehouse location problem.[5] The systematic application of heuristics is often analogous to how a human might intelligently search through possible solutions if possessed with the computational speed and storage capacity of a computer. It should be pointed out that heuristic problem-solving methods do not always generate optimal solutions. In fact, a satisfactory solution is often all that can be expected. However, this is also true of human decision-making.

We have now reached the point of considering the relationship of the simulation of human decision-making to AI. It is partially differentiated in that the decision-making task being studied is of a real-world decision-maker in an actual organization environment. The focus of attention tends to be on the application, rather than on gaining insights about human decision-making behavior, even though this too might be of some interest. Although it is more characteristic of recent modeling efforts than of earlier exploratory work, analysts develop models to simulate human decision-making in order to realize organization benefits rather than as a pure research effort.

A distinction is often made between a simulation and a replication.[6] A *simulation* need only duplicate the output of a process, whereas a *replication* must duplicate the input, process, and output. Consequently, replications are more difficult to achieve than simulations. Much of the work done in AI involves replications, because the process is the focus of attention as researchers strive to learn more about human cognitive processes. The output in the research settings is often of little interest except in that it provides some indication of how well the process has been modeled. Not surprisingly, in business applications it is usually unimportant whether the model is a simulation or a replication, since a duplication of the output is all that is typically required. In other words, a "black box" model of the decision-making process often has as much usefulness to the organization as a "white box" model.

Another differentiating characteristic of models for simulating human decision-making is that the decisions that the models are expected to cover are much narrower in scope than those of most AI models. Typically, the models in which we will be interested will be for a single decision-making task. Later we will explore some of the conditions that make specific decision-making tasks amenable to modeling efforts. Let us now, however, consider some of the past events that have led to our current state of the art.

---

[3] Fred M. Tonge, *A Heuristic Program for Assembly Line Balancing* (Englewood Cliffs, N.J.: Prentice-Hall, 1961).

[4] William S. Gere, "Heuristics in Job Shop Scheduling," *Management Science* (November 1966): B167–B190.

[5] Alfred A. Keuhn and Michael J. Hamburger, "A Heuristic Program for Locating Warehouses," *Management Science* (July 1963): B643–B666.

[6] See Frederick J. Crosson and Kenneth M. Sayre, "Modeling: Simulation and Replication," *The Modeling of Mind*, eds. Kenneth M. Sayre and Frederick J. Crosson (South Bend, Ind.: University of Notre Dame Press, 1963), pp. 3–24.

A BRIEF HISTORY

Because the simulation of human decision-making evolved from AI research, its roots are found there. Artificial intelligence itself is largely a post-World War II development. Its intellectual foundations do trace back earlier, however, finding contributions in psychology and formal logic.[7] The development and availability of the digital computer in the mid-1950s did much to spur AI research.

Many of the earliest studies involved the use of relatively simple games such as tick-tack-toe and checkers. However, in 1954 Newell set out to develop a good chess-playing program for a digital computer. Such an undertaking was, and still is, a difficult task because of the large number of moves that exist. Consequently, it is necessary to build in value systems (such as knights are more valuable than pawns) and logical rules-of-thumb (heuristics) to guide play. The difficulty of this task is still seen today in that a chess-playing program, even with a computer's speed and storage capacity, can be beaten. This is in contrast to the simpler game of checkers where computers have been unbeatable for several years.

In 1955, Allan Newell, Herbert Simon, and J. C. Shaw began their now classic work at the Rand Corporation and the Carnegie Institute of Technology (now Carnegie–Mellon University) on the Logical Theorist (LT). The Logical Theorist was a computer program designed to prove logic and calculus theorems. In 1957 their research efforts switched to another program, the General Problem Solver (GPS).[8] This program differed from the LT in that it attempted to incorporate the types of heuristics employed by humans. In other words, it was designed along lines to replicate human cognitive processes. In addition to changes in design philosophy, it had advanced capabilities that allowed it to be used for a broader set of tasks, including solving puzzles (such as the cannibals and the missionaries), high school algebra word problems, and answering questions phrased in somewhat ambiguous English. Research continues today on extensions and improvements to the original GPS design.

The Rand–Carnegie group was not the only one making significant progresss in AI research. Marvin Minsky and John McCarthy at the Massachusetts Institute of Technology took a highly mathematical approach to the study of AI. Later, McCarthy and E. A. Feigenbaum, a member of the original Carnegie group, moved to Stanford and created the third major center for the study of AI. These three research centers continue to lead the way in AI research today. Although there has been progress in the study of AI, doubts have been recently expressed by both insiders and outsiders as to its ultimate potential.[9] A large part of the problem seems to be that the mind receives and processes information in ways that are currently poorly understood. Possibly, advances in psychology and physiology will be required before the full potential of AI is understood and realized.

The early 1960s also saw the beginning of what we are referring to as the *simulation of human decision-making.* Probably the best known study was Clarkson's simulation of the

[7]See Allen Newell and Herbert A. Simon, *Human Problem Solving* (Englewood Cliffs, N.J.: Prentice-Hall, 1972).

[8]See G. W. Ernst and Allen Newell, *GPS: A Case Study in Generality and Problem Solving* (New York: Academic Press, 1969).

[9]See, for example, Hubert L. Dreyfus, *What Computers Can't Do: A Critique of Artificial Reason* (New York: Harper & Row, 1972).

decisions of a bank trust investment officer.[10]   The modeling objective was to reproduce the behavior of a trust investor in selecting investments for a given client. The methodology employed utilized the *protocol method* wherein the decision-maker verbalizes his or her thought processes while performing the decision-making task under study. Based on the protocol method, Clarkson developed heuristics from the protocol similar to those used by the bank officer. Clarkson concluded that the model did in fact duplicate the trust officers' decisions to a great degree. More will be said about Clarkson's model later.

Another important simulation of human decision-making model was developed by Dickson.[11]   The objective was to develop a model that would duplicate the vendor selection decisions of a purchasing agent. Dickson's study differed from Clarkson's, however, in that simulation of the output was the objective rather than the replication of the entire decision-making process. Dickson's model will also be discussed subsequently.

A still later 1960s simulation of human decision-making model was developed by Smith and Greenlaw who simulated the decisions of a psychologist charged with the responsibility of evaluating applicants for clerical and clerical-administrative positions.[12]   Basing their model on the protocols expressed by the decision-maker, Smith and Greenlaw were able to effectively replicate the decisions and the interpretive comments made by the psychologist. Their study will also be described in this chapter.

The models of Clarkson, Dickson, and Smith and Greenlaw demonstrated the feasibility of simulating a wide range of decision-making tasks. In the 1970s even more progress was made. As in the past, some of the research dealt with intelligent game playing.[13]   For example, in 1978 a chess grand master won a 10-year-old bet that no computer could beat him by 1978. It is interesting to note, however, that he won only three out of five games and declined to renew the bet for another 10 years.

Research in the 1970s did not exclude practical applications.[14]   Recent developments include models that can talk, listen, or read, or do combinations of all three, in an effort to interact with human decision-makers. People are now telling computers to sort packages, fill out forms, and keep track of stock and bond transactions. A system now being tested will enable pilots to talk with in-flight computers. Applications such as these will become more widespread in the 1980s as AI researchers increasingly turn their attention to practical applications of their work.

ILLUSTRATIONS OF MODELS THAT SIMULATE HUMAN DECISION-MAKING

Several of the models that simulate the decision-making behavior of a real-life decision maker in a typical organizational setting are described next. The models should illustrate

---

[10] Geoffrey P. E. Clarkson, *Portfolio Selection: A Simulation of Trust Investment* (Englewood Cliffs, N.J.: Prentice-Hall, 1962).

[11] Gary W. Dickson, "Decision-Making in Purchasing: A Simulation Model of Vendor Selection," unpublished Ph.D. thesis (Seattle: University of Washington, 1965).

[12] Robert D. Smith and Paul S. Greenlaw, "Simulation of a Psychological Decision Process in Personnel Selection," *Management Science* (April 1967): B409–B419.

[13] Art Robinson, "His Master's Voice," *Science 80* (March–April, 1980): 52–53.

[14] Ibid.

the potential of this type of modeling and impart a "feel" for how such models can be developed and tested.

Clarkson's Trust Investment Model

Clarkson's objective was to replicate the actions of a trust investment officer charged with the responsibility for selecting portfolios of stocks for clients. The trust investment process was conceptualized as consisting of three parts.

1. The analysis and selection of a list of stocks suitable for current investment—the "A" List.
2. The formulation of an investment policy for the client.
3. The selection of the portfolio.

This process is depicted in Figure 9.1.

The "A" List, from which a portfolio was actually selected, was based on a subset of another list, called the "B" List. The "B" List was made up of stocks that were considered to be suitable for trust investment by a particular bank. This list remains fairly stable over time, with changes being mainly in the form of additions. Given the "B" List and information on the general economy, industries, and companies, the model calculated expectations of future performance. Based on this analysis, a "scanner-selector" chose the "A" List.

The formulation of an investment policy depended, of course, on the client's personal characteristics and goals. Given this information, the "scanner-selector" chose either a (1) growth account, (2) growth and income account, (3) income and growth account, or (4) income account as an appropriate investment policy for the client.

Once the investment policy was formulated, a list of industries compatible with that policy was selected. The "scanner-selector" then selected specific companies from the list of acceptable industries for inclusion in the portfolio. Mechanisms were included to ensure sufficient diversification and to determine the number of companies and shares of each stock to purchase.

Since Clarkson's model was a replication, both the output and the decision-making process were tested. To test the output, portfolios of stocks were generated for selected test cases by both the trust officer and the model. Although the portfolios selected were not identical, they were more similar than portfolios generated by various random and naïve models.

Tests of the process involved a comparison of the bank officer's *protocols* with *traces* from the "scanner-selector" mechanism. Excerpts of the comparison for a sample account follow.[15]

Trace of Simulation	Trace of Trust Officer's Decision Process
Goal: High income with possible price appreciation	Goal: High income with possible price appreciation
Funds available: $37,500	Funds available: $14,000
Number of Companies: 9	Number of Companies: 3

---

[15] Clarkson, op. cit., p. 83.

Figure 9.1 Clarkson's model of the trust investment process.

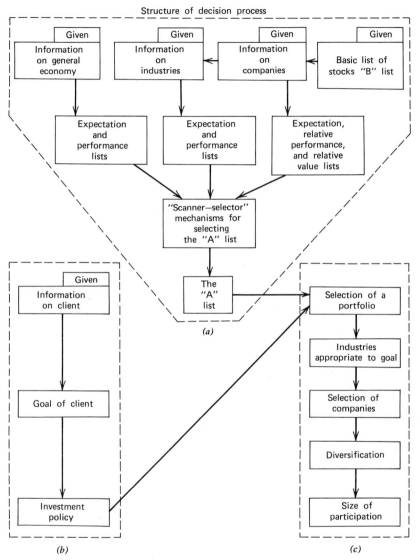

Source. *Goeffrey P. E. Clarkson*, Portfolio Selection: A Simulation of Trust Investment *(Englewood Cliffs: New Jersey: Prentice-Hall, 1962), p. 29.*

Although it was not possible to conclude that the processes were identical, Clarkson felt that "the evidence does support the hypothesis that these mechanisms ("scanner-selector") have captured a considerable portion of the trust investment process."[16]

Dickson's Vendor Selection Model

Dickson's objective was to simulate the decisions made by a purchasing agent when selecting a vendor. Based on a survey of purchasing agents, Dickson concluded that the factors

[16]Clarkson, op. cit., p. 89.

considered when arriving at a purchasing decision vary with the purchasing agent and the item being purchased. The four items for purchase used in the study were:

1. Paint that would be subjected to severe chemical fumes.
2. Desks to be used by faculty in a soon-to-be-completed office building.
3. Computers to be placed in orbital laboratories.
4. Preparation of artwork for training manuals for the company's supervisory and engineering personnel.

For each item, descriptions of the characteristics of alternative vendors were provided as well as the price bid. The characteristics described varied with the item depending on what characteristics were important in selecting a vendor for that item. For each item the number of characteristics described were limited to five. Table 9.1 shows the characteristics of vendor A who was a potential supply source for paint. Table 9.2 presents the coded descriptions of all the potential paint vendors.

Data for building the vendor selection model was gathered by having purchasing agents make vendor-selection decisions when presented with descriptions, as illustrated in Table 9.1. No attempt was made to replicate the complete decision-making process, rather, only to simulate the decisions that were made. A mathematical model was developed for each purchasing agent that functioned by relating subjective costs to the characteristics of the various vendors.

Table 9.1   A DESCRIPTION OF VENDOR A–CASE A (PAINT)

Vendor A's Characteristics

The most outstanding characteristics of Vendor A are his ability to meet delivery schedules and his compliance with this company's bidding and operating procedures. It is expected that A will be able to deliver on the specified date with no appreciable difficulty. In addition, it is expected that he will comply completely with all operating procedures. With regard to the technical capability, Vendor A is expected to be able to provide technical assistance if any problems arise regarding the paint; however he will not be able to provide any basic research and development of new paint types.

Unfortunately Vendor A is doubtful in regard to his ability to meet quality standards. The best knowledge available indicates that Vendor A will only have a fair chance of supplying paint that will last three years with no defects or only minor defects. If serious defects occur, it is expected that they may be major and will require re-painting of a wall or more. Making up somewhat for the quality difficulty is Vendor A's warranty policy. It is expected that he will refund 50 per cent of the cost of the paint and the associated labor if any major defects occur within two years of the application.

Price bid by vendor A: $175 per barrel

Source. Gary W. Dickson, "Decision Making in Purchasing: A Simulation Model of Vendor Selection," unpublished PhD thesis (Seattle: University of Washington, 1965), p. 127.

Table 9.2   A POTENTIAL VENDOR LEVEL DEFINITION USED IN CASE A (PAINT)

Potential Vendor	Factors					Price, dollars
	Quality	Guarantees	Delivery	Procedural Compliance	Technical Capability	
A	3	2	1	1	2	175/barrel
B	1	3	3	1	1	190/barrel
C	2	2	1	1	1	170/barrel
D	1	1	2	3	3	180/barrel

Source. Gary W. Dickson, "Decision Making in Purchasing: A Simulation Model of Vendor Selection," unpublished PhD thesis (Seattle: University of Washington, 1965), p. 127.

The model's predictive powers were tested by comparing the model's predictions to various random selection and naïve models. Dickson concluded that:

the vendor selection model was much more able to account for the influence of the individual on the vendor-selection decision than was any other method. In addition, with the exception of case B (desks), the vendor selection model was better able to reflect the influence of the purchased item on the decision than were the other models.[17]

Smith and Greenlaw's Personnel Selection Model

Smith and Greenlaw's model was designed to simulate the decision making of a psychologist employed by a large consulting firm specializing in personnel selection. The applicants being screened by the psychologist were all females applying for clerical and clerical-administrative positions such as billing clerk, statistical clerk, and executive secretary.

Inputs to the psychologist's decision-making process were: (1) test scores, (2) personal information about the applicants, and (3) indications as to the relative importance of job requirement variables for the specific position for which the individual was being considered. These inputs were processed by the psychologist into output, which consisted of (1) a written description of the applicant's skills, abilities, and personality characteristics as related to the requirements of the job under consideration and (2) a recommendation regarding the advisability of hiring (or promoting) the individual. This decision-making process is depicted in Figure 9.2.

The model was developed using the protocol method. Sixteen cases were selected from the files and the psychologist verbalized his thoughts while processing the cases. The following edited excerpts are from one of the case verbalizations. The italicized words and phrases were considered to be reflections of the basic decision rules used in the process.[18]

[17] Dickson, op. cit., p. 140.
[18] Smith and Greenlaw, op. cit., pp. B411–B412.

Figure 9.2   Smith and Greenlaw's model of the personnel selection process.

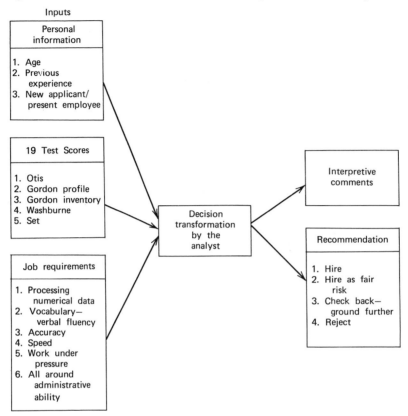

Source.   Robert D. Smith and Paul S. Greenlaw, "Simulation of a Psychological Decision Process in Personnel Selection," Management Science *(April 1967), p. B412.*

Here is a woman age 50 being considered for the position of *Branch Office Clerk.* This is a job involving *general office work*, a *relatively routine office job.* No analysis of complex problems is involved. Her *score on the general intelligence test indicates* that she is *above average in intelligence.* She also has a score *just above average for intellectual curiosity*, which means that although she is of above average intelligence, she's *not likely to feel unchallenged in her job.* Consequently, we say that she is *readily trainable, mentally alert, and a bright woman.* Her *intelligence test* performance is *all the more healthy* since she is *age 50* and in our experience we find that as people approach their later maturity, they tend to slow down on time tests. Next question, of course, is whether she has specific *ability for handling general office work.* Consequently, I must *look at her performance* in the *clerical area.* Now she is at the *32nd percentile.* So *immediately* I must raise the question—*"What is this performance due to?"* Is it *slowness* on the test or *lack of accuracy?* I find that there is *nothing wrong with accuracy.* She just didn't cover too much ground. All I would say is that although *she moves slow when it comes to handling clerical problems*, her accuracy is quite good.

The resulting model took the form of a tree diagram where each branch captured a decision rule employed by the psychologist. In all 16 cases the model's branches led to the same hiring recommendation as the psychologist's. When eight new test cases were considered, the model and the psychologist were in agreement in seven of the eight cases.

The branches in the tree diagram also resulted in computer-generated interpretive comments. A sample of the output for one applicant follows.[19]

APPLICANT IS ABOVE AVERAGE IN INTELLIGENCE, WOULD CALL HER VERY
    BRIGHT AND MENTALLY ALERT

APPLICANT POSSESSES GOOD CLERICAL ABILITIES

IS NOT ACCURATE WHEN WORKING WITH NUMBERS

APPLICANT IS VERY PROFICIENT IN EXPRESSING HERSELF VERBALLY

APPLICANT IS CONTENT

GOAL ORIENTED

SOMEWHAT BELOW AVERAGE IN SOCIAL ADJUSTMENT, MAY TEND TOWARD THE
    SHY SIDE

PUTS FIRST THINGS FIRST

IS SENSITIVE TO FEELINGS AND PROBLEMS OF OTHER PEOPLE

HAS SELF-CONTROL, SHOULD BE ABLE TO MAKE AND EXECUTE PLANS

WILL NOT TAKE THE LEAD IN GROUP SITUATIONS

PASSIVE, LACKS SELF-CONFIDENCE

OVERLY DEPENDENT

PERSEVERING, DETERMINED AND RELIABLE

HOWEVER, BASED UPON SPECIFIED JOB REQUIREMENTS, IT APPEARS THAT THIS
    APPLICANT MAY BE HIRED WITHOUT SERIOUS RESERVATIONS.

A second psychologist employed with the consulting firm was shown the 16 cases and the computer-generated interpretive comments and indicated that 273 of the 290 comments (94 percent) were psychologically sound. Smith and Greenlaw concluded that "the simulated interpretations were highly congruent with the psychological thinking of the firm, at least as so perceived by the evaluator (the second psychologist)."[20]

As with other 1960s simulation of human decision-making studies, Smith and Greenlaw's was more of a pure research effort instead of an attempt to develop a model that would be used in a real-world setting. They did point the way, however, for the 1970s with a rather comprehensive discussion of the potential organizational benefits that might accrue from actually developing and using such models.

POTENTIAL BENEFITS

There are many potential benefits that can result from developing models that simulate human decision-making. Although any single modeling effort will not typically generate

---

[19] Smith and Greenlaw, op. cit., p. B416.
[20] Smith and Greenlaw, op. cit., p. B417.

the entire spectrum of possible benefits, each successful effort will usually result in some combination of the following.

1.   Freeing personnel for other activities.
2.   Saving time spent on the decision-making activity.
3.   Saving money spent on the decision-making activity.
4.   Providing decision-making skills that are in short supply.
5.   Moving toward more nearly optimal decision-making.
6.   Increasing decision-making consistency.
7.   Providing a model for training new personnel in decision-making.
8.   Providing a standard of performance for control purposes.

A model that simulates the actions of a human decision-maker can, at least partially, substitute for the decision-maker, and thus free the person for other productive activities. In some decision-making situations the model can substitute for the decision-maker completely. In others, the model can be used to identify those decision cases that are best handled by a human, while the remainder of the decisions are processed automatically by the model.

In a computerized environment, a completely, or partially, automated decision-making process will clearly result in time reductions between when data inputs are available for processing and when decisions are made. This is a natural outcome given the computational speed of the computer. It does not mean, however, that the time spent on the preparation of data inputs or the implementation of decisions made through automation will necessarily be reduced. These important decision-making components may or may not be affected by the existence of a model.

Both the freeing of personnel for other productive activities and the reduction of time spent on decision-making can result in incremental savings for the organization.

In some situations, requisite decision-making skills are in short supply. The field of medicine, in particular, has seen the development of diagnostic programs that simulate the diagnosis of experienced physicians when presented with lists of symptoms and test results. In fact, some models have been found to be superior to the average physician with limited experience in the problem area.[21]

Models that are replications reflect the most salient features of the human's decision-making process. When captured in a model, the decision-maker's heuristics become available for examination. Thus it may be discovered that certain heuristics are not compatible with organizational objectives and therefore should be modified. What is being suggested, of course, is that the descriptive model of the decision-making process can serve as a vehicle for moving toward optimality in decision making.

Human decision makers and their decisions suffer from the typical dysfunctions associated with anger, fatigue, hunger, and the like. Obviously, a model does not suffer from these problems and will make the same decisions given the same data inputs unless specifically designed to do otherwise. As a result, a model that simulates human decision-making will in the long run make more internally consistent decisions than the human after

[21] N. E. Betaque and G. A. Gorry, "Automating Judgmental Decision-Making for a Serious Medical Problem," *Management Science* (April 1971): 421–434.

which the model is patterned. This condition is desirable both for the organization and individuals impacted by the decisions.

A model can also be used for training personnel in appropriate decision-making behavior. For example, the model can be shown to a novice decision-maker to illustrate the decision-making heuristics that have been employed in the past. In a training program the novice can be given structured decision cases, asked to make decisions, and presented with the decisions made by the model, and the process can be repeated until the decisions made by the novice and the model converge.

A model for simulating human decision making can also be used to monitor decisions made by humans. The decisions made by the model can be compared to the human's with exception reports being generated when deviations are noted. This procedure might be desirable with novice decision-makers or when there are multiple decision-makers acting according to prescribed guidelines.

Having considered the potential benefits associated with simulating human decision-making, let us now consider an appropriate methodology for model development.

A METHODOLOGY FOR SIMULATING HUMAN DECISION-MAKING

As the author has gained experience in developing models of human cognitive processes, a methodology has evolved and been successfully applied. This methodology is reflected in the following steps.

1. Gain an understanding of the information flows and the decisions that are made.
2. Generate a list of variables that are possibly used in the decision-making process.
3. Analyze the decision-making process using the protocol method.
4. Collect appropriate data for developing the model.
5. Develop the model for the decision-making process.
6. Test the model that has been built.
7. Iterate steps 3 to 6 until an appropriate model is developed.
8. Implement the model in the organization.

Before the modeling effort can begin, the information flows and decision alternatives must be thoroughly understood. The information flows can originate from both formal and informal sources and can be either objective or subjective in nature. There are also decision-making situations where much of the information comes from the decision-maker's memory. The decision alternatives can be either categorical or continuous. Furthermore, the decision alternatives can either result in the final disposition of the case or be preparatory to further processing.

In attempting to include in the final model all the key variables involved in the decison-making process, we should start with an all-inclusive list and then eliminate variables as they are discovered to be irrelevant or unimportant. The all-inclusive list is best generated by having the decision-maker and the analyst separately prepare lists that are later discussed and combined. Such an approach is consistent with the procedures and benefits associated with the Delphi method and nominal grouping. Unimportant or irrelevant variables can be eliminated in later stages of the model-building process.

The decision-making process can be analyzed through the protocol method in order to gain an understanding of what variables are actually being employed by the decision-maker and how the variables are being interrelated. In practice, the protocol method is seldom ever applied in a "pure" form. The analyst typically has to ask the decision maker for explanations, clarifications, or even about heuristics that are obviously being used but are not being articulated.[22]

Appropriate data must be collected for those variables that appear to be used. For this purpose it is useful to prepare a coding sheet on which the values for the input variables and the decisions made by the decision-maker are recorded.

The model can be developed in several possible ways. One approach is to develop a model that processes inputs into outputs in a manner analogous to the methods employed by the human. This approach results in a replication-type model and is based on the following assumptions.[23]

1. Humans, in making decisions, break down complex problems into numerous simpler but interrelated subproblems.
2. Individuals also develop and follow with some degree of consistency, decision rules—which can be identified and isolated—to handle these subproblems, and that consequently,
3. Complex thought processes can be represented by networks of relatively simple decision branches, reflecting these rules.

The models of Clarkson and Smith and Greenlaw used this approach.

Another alternative is to develop a "black box" model based on multivariate techniques such as regression and discriminate analysis. With this approach the protocol method is used solely to identify the variables employed in the decision-making process. Models developed by multivariate techniques tend to be simulations rather than replications.

A hybrid model can also be developed which partially draws on the decision-maker's heuristics and partially on standard statistical analyses. As an example, the author participated in the development of a screening model for applicants to the University of Georgia's law school.[24] The model contained an initial three-way branch based on the applicant's undergraduate grade point average, Law School Aptitude Test score, and undergraduate school attended. However, off each branch a linear, weighted model including additional variables was used to compute a score for each applicant, and the applicants were rank ordered based on this score. No claim was made that this latter procedure was followed by the admissions officer; and, in fact, it is unlikely that he used this procedure. The model of Dickson is similar in that it employed some heuristic-like procedures, but not exactly those used by the purchasing agent.

It is rare when the initial modeling effort results in an acceptable final version of a model. Usually it is necessary to iterate the modeling-building and testing process. The

---

[22] For an example of this point, see John A. Howard and William Morgenroth, "Information Processing Model of Executive Decision," *Management Science* (March 1968): A416–A428.

[23] Smith and Greenlaw, op. cit., p. B410.

[24] Hugh J. Watson, Ted F. Anthony, and William S. Crowder, "A Heuristic Model for Law School Admissions Screening," *College and University* (Spring 1973): 195–204.

Figure 9.3   A confusion matrix for comparing the models and the human's decisions.

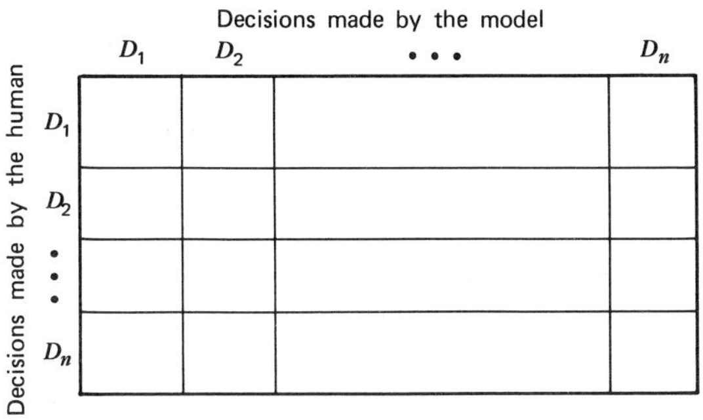

procedures used for testing the model depend on whether it is a replication or a simulation. Replications require that the trace from the model be similar to the heuristics used by the decision-maker. Such a test was illustrated in the discussion of Smith and Greenlaw's model. The comparison of the trace and the heuristics can be made by the decision maker and/or an outside expert.

Simulations and replications both demand that the decisions of the model and the human be in agreement. A convenient format for making this test involves the preparation of a *confusion matrix*, as shown in Figure 9.3. When the decisions, the D_i's, are ordinally scaled in the matrix, a model with perfect predictive powers places all the test cases along the major diagonal of the matrix. Observations that fall far off the diagonal indicate serious deficiencies in the model's predictive power, or inconsistencies on the part of the human decision-maker.

Implementing models that simulate human decision-making encounter more, if not all, of the usual problems associated with bringing about organizational change. Human fears of the consequences of the change must be alleviated, training programs for learning how to encode data inputs may have to be conducted, computer programs and appropriate documentation most likely will have to be prepared, and so on.

CONDITIONS CONDUCIVE TO MODELING

Not all decision-making situations lend themselves to the development of operational models. Experience has shown that certain organizational conditions and characteristics of the decision-making task are important when considering the possible development of a model that simulated human decision-making. Being more specific, the author has found that most of the following must exist in order to make the modeling possible and cost effective.

1. Top-to-bottom managerial support.
2. Heavy commitment of organizational resources being devoted to the decision-making task.
3. Consequences of a "bad" decision are not too great.
4. Computerized environment with many of the data inputs already contained in the organization's data base.

5. Lower paid personnel being able to encode most of the required data inputs.
6. Decision-making process being relatively stable over time.

As with most new technology that brings about organizational change, top management support is mandatory to ensure cooperation. When simulating human decision-making, it is also imperative that the human being modeled be supportive of the effort, because that individual's decision-making process is being modeled. Such support is far from certain if the modeling effort is perceived as being threatening to job security; see Figure 9.4.

Modeling efforts should be undertaken only when the expected benefits to be received exceed the expected costs. In order to justify the costs of developing, implementing, and operating the model, one must realize substantial cost savings. This condition demands the decision-making task have characteristics such as a high volume of activity, requires a substantial number of man-hours, and is reasonably important to the organization.

It is unlikely that managers will turn over decision-making responsibilities to a computer when the consequences of a bad decision are great. There is always the belief that certain intuitive feelings are held by the human but not by the machine. Even if this intuition comes into use only occasionally, in order to avoid potentially serious consequences, a computerized model will not be employed.

Although not mandatory, the attractiveness of the modeling effort is enhanced appreciably when the final model can be computer implemented. Adding to the desirability is when most of the requisite data inputs for the model are already contained in a computerized data base. Some of the greatest cost savings can be realized when these conditions are met.

It is rare when any model for simulating human decision-making is able to operate exclusively with information contained in a data base—especially when human judgment is involved in the decision-making process. If the human decision-maker is required to encode many of the data inputs for the model, many of the benefits of automating the decision-making process are lost. This suggests that employing lower paid and trained personnel to encode requisite data inputs is beneficial. It has been the author's experience that this substitution is often possible, even for inputs requiring subjective judgment.

A common problem with almost all decision models is that they become out-of-date as the environment around them changes. In other words, it is difficult to keep decision

Figure 9.4 Computerized models have a great potential for affecting routine, repetitive decision-making.

Source.   Used by the permission of Newspaper Enterprise Association, Inc.

models relevant in a highly dynamic environment. This problem is particularly acute with models that simulate human decision making. In order to update the model, one must re-analyze the decision-making task as performed by the human. Because this requirement can be costly and time consuming, situations where the decision-making process remains relatively stable over time are most desirable. The author has found this to be the greatest problem area in implementing and operating this type of model.

Given this background on a methodology and conditions conducive for simulating human decision-making, let us consider a detailed, final illustration.

AN ILLUSTRATION OF SIMULATING HUMAN DECISION-MAKING: PROCESSING OVERDRAFTS

Banks engage in many repetitive, high volume decision-making activities. Examples include decisions on loan applications, issuing charge cards, and processing overdrafts ("bad" checks).[25]   Many of these activities are potential candidates for automation through models that simulate human decision-making. The following discussion describes a model-building project the author participated in with the First National Bank of Athens for the development of a computerized model for processing overdrafts.

Background Material

There are a number of ways that have been developed for handling overdrafts. A common way is to have a bank officer decide on the final disposition of all bad checks. The bank officer decides which checks to pay immediately or not to pay, and which checks require a personal call to the depositor before a decision is made. In the bank participating in this study, an average of several hundred checks a day are processed by one of its vice presidents. Up to one half of his day is consumed by the routine task of handling bad checks.

The bank officer who deals with these checks on a day-to-day basis develops a sensitivity to the appropriate disposition of any particular check. Some checks, because of the integrity of their writers, are payed almost routinely. Other checks, say, from notoriously careless depositors, may not be payed. In other words, the bank officer accumulates a wealth of information about his bank's depositors. In addition, he develops an efficient set of heuristics that defines how he will probably act in any given situation. Any replacing system should maintain the professional expertise gathered by the bank officer over time.

Building the Model

The building of the model began with the Athens bank's officer and the author listing those variables thought to be the most important in the decision-making process. The initial list contained 14 variables, some of which were the dollar amount of the check, to whom the check was written, and the credit worthiness of the depositor. The initial list

---

[25] This illustration is adapted from Hugh J. Watson and H. William Vroman, "A Heuristic Model for Processing Overdrafts," *Journal of Bank Research* (Autumn 1972): 186–188.

of variables even indicated that the bank officer was more likely to pay a check written by a University of Georgia coed than a male.

The next step in the model-building process was to observe the bank officer at work and record appropriate empirical data. It was found that a number of variables that were originally considered to be important, were actually not and could be discarded (e.g., to whom the check was written). From the empirical data a model that simulated the bank officer's thought processes was built. Not surprisingly, because the model was built from the data, it accurately predicted the actions taken by the bank officer.

The author then collected more data to validate the model further. The validation employed was to compare the bank officer's decisions with those predicted by the model. During the validation process it became clear that parts of the model had to be changed (e.g., a procedure for handling multiple overdrafts was needed). This data collection, model validation, model improvement process was repeated until a model was developed that closely described the bank officer's actions. The final testing of the model revealed that it predicted correctly the bank officer's actions over 95 percent of the time.

An analysis of the remaining 5 percent resulted in the conclusion that some of the factors responsible for the errors were inherent in the human variable—the bank officer. It was noticed that the bank officer became weary and distracted by customer calls toward the end of his task and tended to adopt a harsher attitude toward overdrafts. In this regard the model was more internally consistent than the bank officer.

Even when the model was in error, it did not do so diametrically. There were no instances, for example, where the model predicted the bank officer would pay a check and he actually did not. The errors that occurred were the type where the officer decided to pay the check, whereas the model predicted that he would call the depositor.

The Model

The final model that was built contained five variables. The *type of account*, regular or special, was one of the factors considered by the Athens bank's officer. Another variable was whether the *existing balance was positive or negative.* This consideration was necessary for handling multiple overdrafts. The bank officer's subjective evaluation of the person's *general credit worthiness* was also important—whether it was good, bad, or unknown. To the extent it was known, this factor included the depositor's past history of overdrafts, his or her place of residence in the city, property ownership, employment record, savings account balance, and so on. Another variable was the *magnitude of the overdraft compared to the current balance.* This consideration was quantified by dividing the difference between the check's amount and the account's balance by the account's balance (check-balance/balance). The final variable was the *amount of the check.* Overdrafts for small amounts are usually paid.

The model that contained the five variables was formulated as a tree diagram, which showed all the possible combinations of values for the variables and the resultant courses of action. For example, one branch of the tree diagram is shown in Figure 9.5. (The tree diagram contained many similar branches.) This branch shows that a regular check, which is not a multiple overdraft, and is written by a depositor with a good credit rating, for $50 or less, is paid by the Athens bank's officer. The model does not claim that the bank officer should act this way; rather, it indicates that he does act in this manner.

Figure 9.5   A sample branch of the tree diagram for processing overdrafts.

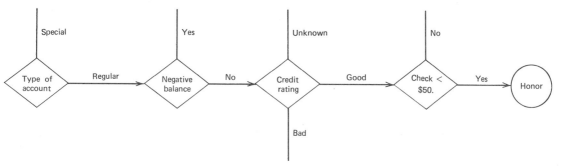

The model developed for the Athens bank is probably appropriate only for that bank. Other bank officers presumably employ a different set of decision criteria in judging overdrafts. Even if the same variables are used, the tree diagram formulated would probably be different. This likelihood is not surprising, because people perceive things differently, operating conditions vary from bank to bank, and the implications of the social milieu vary from community to community.

Computerization of this task did not completely release the officer's time. There were some customers categorized as "to call" by the model and these still had to be handled by this officer or some lesser official. In addition, regardless of how their checks are handled, there are some customers who feel their overdraft is a result of a unique situation and should be handled specially. The bank officer can then treat these individuals in an unhurried manner, thus avoiding the typical customer complaint of bureaucratic dysfunctions such as categorization and impersonality. In addition, the officer's "psychological set" is to treat customers as individuals, whereas before he was alternating his overdraft task with customer relations, which required the mental chore of switching "psychological sets." This is costly to the individual because it is tiring, and costly to the organization because as time progresses the switching becomes inconsistent.

The model developed for the Athens bank was easily computerized. The equivalent of a week's overdrafts were processed in less than a minute. The only information required by the model, which was not readily available in the bank's accounting system, was the depositor's credit worthiness. Over time this information could be built into the system. In the meantime, the "unknown" branches of the tree diagram still allowed the computer to process the checks.

CLOSING REMARKS

Models of the type described in this chapter are not as widely used as one might first expect. One can summarize the reluctance of practicing managers to accept operational models of complex decision-making behavior as the "Tin Woodman" syndrome.[26] The following discussion took place between the Tin Woodman and the Scarecrow.[27]

[26] The Tin Woodman analogy was created by Michael S. Parks of the University of Houston.
[27] Lyman F. Baum, *The New Wizard of Oz* (New York: Bobbs Merrill, 1941), p. 41.

"I don't know enough," replied the Scarecrow cheerfully. "My head is stuffed with straw, you know, and that is why I am going to Oz to ask him for some brains."

"Oh, I see," said the Tin Woodman. "But after all, brains are not the best things in the world."

"Have you any?" inquired the Scarecrow.

"No, my head is quite empty," answered the Woodman, "but once I had brains and a heart also; so, having tried them both I should much rather have a heart."

Management personnel over the years have willingly used the computer for routine data processing tasks such as payroll, inventory control, and production scheduling. However, there has been little utilization of computer technology to perform tasks involving judgment, intuition, sensitivity, and creativity. Just as the Tin Woodman might be an efficient machine for cutting wood, because he has no heart, many would hesitate to employ him for tasks involving the characteristics we assume to be strictly human. To demonstrate the existence of technology capable of performing tasks involving "heart" will be much more difficult for model builders.

SUMMARY

The simulation of human decision-making involves duplicating through a model the decisions made by a human in a real-world decision-making situation. It finds its ancestral roots in artificial intelligence (AI), which is concerned with the development of models that act in an "intelligent" manner. Contributions from AI researchers such as Alan Turing and his Turing's test, Newell, Simon, and Shaw and their work on the Logical Theorist and the General Problem Solver, and the research of Minsky and McCarthy did much to set the stage for the recent efforts in simulating human decision.

Although the differences between AI and the simulation of human decision are not clear-cut, we tend to think of the latter as involving an actual decision-maker functioning in a real-world environment, a focus on possible application rather than gaining insights into human decision-making behavior, and a much narrower range of decisions being simulated.

A number of 1960s studies demonstrated the feasibility of simulating human decision-making. Clarkson replicated the actions of a trust investment officer charged with the responsibility for selecting portfolios of stocks for clients. Dickson simulated the vendor selection decisions made by purchasing agents. Smith and Greenlaw simulated the decisions of a psychologist charged with the responsibility for making hiring and promotion recommendations. These studies set the stage for developing models that would actually be implemented and operated in organizations. Such models can free personnel, save time, save money, provide decision-making skills that are in short supply, provide a basis for moving to more optimal decision-making, increase decision-making consistency, be used for training new personnel, and be employed for control purposes.

When simulating human decision-making, one should gain an understanding of the information flows and decisions that are made, generate a list of variables that are possibly used in the decision-making process, analyze the process using the protocol method, collect appropriate data, develop the model, test the model, and repeat the process until an appropriate model has been obtained.

Not all decision-making tasks and situations lend themselves to simulation modeling. There must be top-to-bottom managerial support, heavy commitment of resources being devoted to the task, consequences of bad decisions cannot be too great, many of the data inputs should already be in a computerized data base, lower paid personnel should be able to encode most of the required data inputs, and the decision-making process should be relatively stable over time. At the heart of this type of modeling is the belief that a computer can be used for subjective decision-making tasks as well as for more routine applications.

ASSIGNMENTS

9.1. Describe what distinguishes the simulation of human decision-making from the general field of artificial intelligence.

9.2. Decision-making responsibilities tend to vary with the managerial level. Robert Anthony in his book, *Planning and Control Systems: A Framework for Analysis*, discusses the strategic planning, management control, and operational control responsibilities of top, middle, and lower management, respectively. Anthony defines these responsibilities in the following way.

> Strategic planning *is the process of deciding on objectives of the organization, on changes in these objectives, on the resources used to obtain those objectives, and on the policies that are to govern the acquisition, use, and disposition of these resources.*

> Management control *is the process by which managers assure that resources are obtained and used effectively and efficiently in the accomplishment of the organization's objectives.*

> Operational control *is the process of assuring that specific tasks are carried out effectively and efficiently.*

    (a) Which of these decision-making responsibilities is the easiest to simulate? the most difficult? Explain.

    (b) Categorize Clarkson's trust investment model, Dickson's vendor-selection model, Smith and Greenlaw's personnel-selection model, and the overdraft-processing model as being applicable for strategic planning, management control, or operational control.

9.3. A large insurance company is considering developing a model to simulate the initial screening of applicants for clerical positions. What would be the advantages and disadvantages of such a model? Would you recommend the development of a model?

9.4. Union Grove Federal Savings and Loan is considering developing a model to automate the mortgage granting decision. Depending on factors such as the time of the year and economic conditions, Union Grove Federal receives between 5 and 60 mortgage applications a week. Each application contains information such as the applicant's name, income, place of employment, financial status, and the like. On receipt of an application, a credit report is obtained from the credit bureau and an appraiser is sent out to appraise the property. When all this information is assembled, the Executive Loan Committee makes the mortgage granting decision.

(a)   Is it possible to develop a model that simulates the mortgage granting decision? Discuss.

(b)   Would you recommend developing such a model? Explain.

9.5.   The following protocol of an admissions officer processing applicants' folders for possible admission to law school was recorded.

Case 1:   John James is a University of Georgia graduate. His grade point average (GPA) was 3.25 and his Law School Aptitude Test (LSAT) score was 610. He would probably be a good law school student.

Case 2:   Shirley Farmer graduated from Valdosta State University with a 3.87. Her LSAT score was only 485. The high GPA perhaps should be discounted.

Case 3:   Barbara Samuels is finishing at Stanford University. Her GPA was 3.10 with a 540 LSAT. She might be a good addition to the incoming law school class.

Case 4:   Bill Williams graduated from the University of Alabama several years ago with a 3.10 GPA and a 620 LSAT. He probably should be accepted.

Case 5:   Alan Hill graduated with a 2.90 GPA from Harvard and had an LSAT of 620. The competition for grades at Harvard is keen and more attention should be paid to the LSAT score than the GPA.

Based on the protocol, what variables are important to the admissions officer? What type of model structure would you suggest if you wanted to simulate the admissions officer's decision-making process?

9.6.   A local bank officer spends a substantial portion of each working day processing charge card applications. He has expressed an interest in the possibility of computerizing his decision-making process. Based on your discussions with him, it appears that three variables are of critical importance in the decision-making process: (1) previous credit record—excellent, good, fair, or bad; (2) income—over $10,000 or under $10,000; and (3) whether the applicant is a homeowner—yes or no. The bank officer has three decision alternatives available to him. (1) He can issue no card; (2) issue a card with a $300 credit limit, or (3) issue a card with a $700 credit limit. Using the sample data, prepare a tree diagram that describes the bank officer's decision-making process.

Case	Previous Credit Record	Income, dollars	Homeowner	Decision
1	Fair	Over 10,000	Yes	Card–$300
2	Poor	Under 10,000	No	No Card
3	Fair	Over 10,000	No	Card–$300
4	Excellent	Over 10,000	Yes	Card–$700
5	Good	Under 10,000	No	Card–$300
6	Good	Over 10,000	Yes	Card–$700
7	Poor	Over 10,000	Yes	No Card
8	Fair	Under 10,000	No	No Card

Case	Previous Credit Record	Income, dollars	Homeowner	Decision
9	Fair	Under 10,000	Yes	Card—$300
10	Good	Over 10,000	No	Card—$700
11	Excellent	Over 10,000	No	Card—$700
12	Excellent	Under 10,000	Yes	Card—$700
13	Good	Under 10,000	Yes	Card—$700
14	Excellent	Under 10,000	No	Card—$700

Prepare a computer program for your tree diagram. Process the following charge card applications through your program. The program output should be the applicant's name and the decision made.

Name	Previous Credit Record	Income, dollars	Homeowner
Hall	Good	Over 10,000	No
Lee	Poor	Over 10,000	No
Case	Excellent	Under 10,000	Yes
Hill	Fair	Over 10,000	Yes
Mix	Fair	Under 10,000	Yes
Page	Good	Over 10,000	Yes

9.7. A large credit union is considering the development of a model to simulate an experienced loan officer's processing of loan applications. Based on the protocol method and conversations with the loan officer, three variables are identified as being important.

1. Loan purpose—necessity, luxury, frivolous.
2. Ability to repay the loan—good or bad.
3. Past loan repayment record—good, slow, or poor.

The three variables and the resulting decision as whether to grant or deny the loan seem to be related through a series of branches. Based on the following data, develop the best possible model.

Case Number	Loan Purpose	Ability to Repay	Past Repayment Record	Loan Officer's Decision
1	Frivolous	Bad	Good	Grant
2	Necessity	Good	Good	Grant
3	Frivolous	Bad	Slow	Deny
4	Luxury	Good	Good	Grant

Case Number	Loan Purpose	Ability to Repay	Past Repayment Record	Loan Officer's Decision
5	Necessity	Bad	Good	Grant
6	Necessity	Good	Poor	Deny
7	Luxury	Good	Poor	Deny
8	Necessity	Good	Slow	Grant
9	Luxury	Bad	Poor	Deny
10	Necessity	Bad	Slow	Deny
11	Luxury	Bad	Good	Grant
12	Luxury	Good	Slow	Grant
13	Luxury	Good	Slow	Grant
14	Luxury	Bad	Slow	Grant

From the data used in building the model, prepare a confusion matrix to validate the model. Can you recommend a better validation procedure?

9.8.   Consider what typically takes place when a potential customer contacts an insurance company's agent about automobile insurance. If the customer elects to purchase insurance from the company, the agent fills out forms entering the required data. At this time the agent is empowered to grant temporary coverage to the customer, even though the company's underwriters at the home office may ultimately choose not to take the customer on as an insurance risk. There are several potential problems associated with this procedure. First, agents are notoriously poor at filling out forms, which often have to be returned for corrections before the underwriters can make their decision. Second, granting temporary coverage can be costly because some customers who will ultimately be judged as being too risky for permanent coverage are carried for a period of time. And, of course, considerable ill will is generated if a customer ultimately learns that coverage is not going to be provided.

Based on the materials presented in this chapter, describe the development, testing, and implementation of an alternative, computerized system.

9.9.   The Office of Graduate Studies at a large university's College of Business Administration is considering automating some of the routine decision-making activities of its overworked administrative coordinator. One of the tasks performed by the coordinator is determining eligibility for graduate assistantships. When asked how she goes about making decisions, she replied:

A lot of our assistantship applications come from incoming students, so the first group of applications I evaluate are theirs. If they haven't yet applied to the graduate school, I can't give them an assistantship. If they have applied, I have to see if they've been accepted. Any students who have been rejected certainly are not eligible.

After I weed out the applicants who haven't been accepted by the graduate school, I start looking at qualifications. Students with 3.5 undergraduate GPA and a GRE/GMAT score at or above the 90th percentile are eligible for a uni-

versity wide assistantship, which is higher paying and more prestigous than a business school assistantship. Those that don't meet these qualifications but do have GPA's over 3.25 and GRE/GMAT scores at the 80th percentile or higher are eligible for assistantships within the business school. Anyone having a GPA under 3.0 and a GRE/GMAT score below the 60th percentile is not eligible at all. I then look at the records of student's whose qualifications fall between the automatic accept and reject criteria, and if they have some special abilities or job experience, I send their applications to the Assistantship Committee for a final decision.

The other group of applications I have to consider comes from currently enrolled students. These students have to be divided into those that have assistantships already and those that don't have one. Students in either group are eligible for university wide assistantships if they have a 3.5 graduate GPA and a GRE/GMAT score at the 90th percentile or higher. Applicants that don't qualify for these can still get a business school assistantship.

In order to be eligible for one, the students who don't already have an assistantship must have a graduate GPA of at least 3.25 and a GRE/GMAT score of at least the 70th percentile. Students who have an assistantship must have made at least a 3.0 GPA in the first quarter they held the assistantship and at least a 3.25 every quarter after that. They must also have been rated in one of the top two categories on their professor's graduate assistant evaluation sheet.

(a) Develop a decision tree that models the procedure used by the academic coordinator in deciding who is eligible for a graduate assistantship.

(b) What conditions should exist for the automation of this decision-making process to be practical? Be specific in your response.

9.10. Based on your business training and experience, identify decision-making tasks not mentioned in this chapter that might be simulated. Provide a carefully thought out analysis of the usefulness of automating the tasks mentioned.

REFERENCES

Betaque, N. E., and G. A. Gorry, "Automating Judgmental Decision-Making for a Serious Medical Problem," *Management Science* (April 1971): 421–434.

Clarkson, Geoffrey P. E., *Portfolio Selection: A Simulation of Trust Investment* (Englewood Cliffs, N.J.: Prentice-Hall, 1962).

Crosson, Frederick J., and Kenneth M. Sayre, "Modeling: Simulation and Replication," *The Modeling of Mind*, Kenneth M. Sayre and Frederick J. Crosson, eds. (South Bend, Ind.: University of Notre Dame Press, 1963), pp. 3–24.

Dickson, Gary W., "A Generalized Simulation Model of Vendor Selection," in *Management Action: Models of Administration Decisions*, C. E. Weber and G. Peters, eds. (Scranton, Pa.: International Textbook, 1969), pp. 115–136.

Dreyfus, Hubert L., *What Computers Can't Do: A Critique of Artificial Reason* (New York: Harper & Row, 1972).

Ernst, G. W., and Allen Newell, *GPS: A Case Study in Generality and Problem Solving* (New York: Academic Press, 1969).

Feigenbaum, E. A., and Julian Feldman, *Computers and Thought* (New York: McGraw-Hill, 1963).

Gere, William S., "Heuristics in Job Shop Scheduling," *Management Science* (November 1966): B167–B190.

"How Smart Can Computers Get?" *Newsweek* (June 30, 1980): 52–53.

Howard, John A., and William Morgenroth, "Information Processing Model of Executive Decision," *Management Science* (March 1968): A416–A428.

Hunt, Earl B., *Artificial Intelligence* (New York: Academic Press, 1975).

Keuhn, Alfred A., and Michael J. Hamburger, "A Heuristic Program for Locating Warehouses," *Management Science* (July 1963): B643–B666.

Newell, Allen, and Herbert A. Simon, *Human Problem Solving* (Englewood Cliffs, N.J.: Prentice-Hall, 1972).

Parks, Michael S., Nicolai Siemens, and Hugh J. Watson, "A Generalized Model for Automating Judgmental Decisions," *Management Science* (April 1976): 841–851.

Robinson, Art, "The Master's Voice," *Science 80* (March–April 1980): 52–55.

Smith, Robert D., and Paul S. Greenlaw, "Simulation of a Psychological Decision Process in Personnel Selection," *Management Science* (April 1967): B409–B419.

Tonge, Fred M., *A Heuristic Program for Assembly Line Balancing* (Englewood Cliffs, N.J.: Prentice-Hall, 1961).

Turing, Alan M., "Can A Machine Think," *The World of Mathematics*, James R. Newman, ed. (New York: Simon & Schuster, 1956), pp. 2099–2123.

Watson, Hugh J., Ted F. Anthony, and William S. Crowder, "A Heuristic Model for Law School Admissions Screening," *College and University* (Spring 1973): 195–204.

Watson, Hugh J., and H. William Vroman, "A Heuristic Model for Processing Overdrafts," *Journal of Bank Research* (Autumn 1972): 186–188.

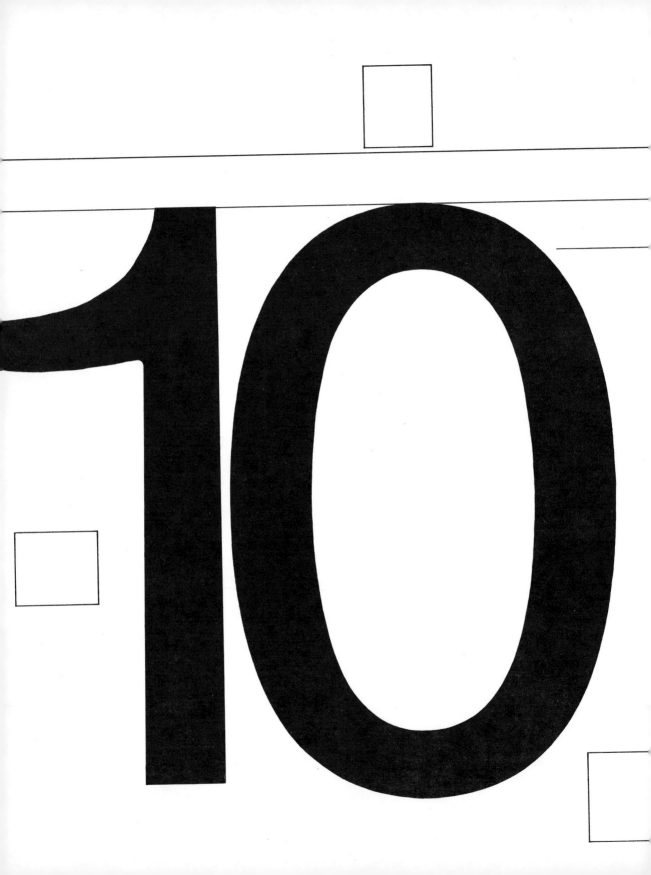

CHAPTER TEN   **MANAGEMENT GAMES**

A Brief History of Games

Types of Games

    General Management Games

    Functional Games

    Specific Industry Games

    Simple Versus Complex Games

    Interactive Versus Noninteractive Games

    Deterministic Versus Probabilistic Games

    Team Versus Individual Played Games

    Computer Versus Manual Scored Games

Purposes of Games

Advantages of Games

Limitations of Games

The Administration of Games

Concepts in Game Design

    Game Equations

The Validation of Games

Adding More Flexibility to Games

Recent Trends in Games

The Credit Union Management Game

    Background on Game Participants

    Game Objectives

    Game Play

    Game Decisions

    The Model

    Game Output

Summary

Assignments

References

It is common for *management games* to be referred to as "simulations." Indeed, the model that is at the "heart" of a management game typically fits our definition of a simulation model. But the model is just part of what is considered a management game. The following definition is given by Dill, Jackson, and Sweeney:

A business (management) game is a contrived situation which imbeds players in a simulated business environment, where they must make management-type decisions from time-to-time, and their choices at one time generally affect the conditions under which the subsequent decisions must be made."[1]

A good distinction between management games and simulation models is provided by Shim:

The distinction between a simulation and a game is a subtle one. Both are mathematical models, but they differ in purpose and mode of use. Simulation models are designed to simulate a system and to generate a series of statistical results regarding system operations. Games are also a form of simulation, except that in games human beings play a significant part. In games, human beings make decisions at various stages and games are distinguished by a sense of play. Major goals of game play are to improve decision-making skills and to facilitate an understanding of the game environment simulated by participation of the players."[2]

The structure of a typical management game is shown in Figure 10.1. For every period of play, there are inputs of game data from previous periods, economic data, and the players' decisions. These inputs are processed through a game model that contains built-in game parameters. The game then outputs various financial documents, summary reports, game data for the next period of play, and data for evaluating the players' performance. This process is repeated for each player or team of players for each period of play.

In this chapter we will consider many aspects of management games. Our exploration will include a brief history of games, the different types of games that have been developed, the purposes that games serve, the advantages and limitations of games, the administration of games, concepts in game design, the validation of games, the addition of more flexibility to games, recent trends in games, and an in-depth examination of a currently used game.

A BRIEF HISTORY OF GAMES

All of us have grown up playing games. They are fun and perhaps even add to our analysis capabilities. Some of the games still played today such as *chess* and the oriental game of *go* date back many centuries. In addition to these games, which are played largely for fun, games that are used for serious purposes have a lengthy history. War games were introduced as early as the seventeenth and eighteenth centuries in the Prussian army for

---

[1] William R. Dill, James R. Jackson, and James W. Sweeney, *Conference on Business Games* (New Orleans: School of Business Administration, Tulane University, 1961), p. 7.

[2] Jae K. Shim, "Management Game Simulation: Survey and New Direction," *University of Michigan Business Review* (May 1978): 26.

Figure 10.1   The structure of a typical management game.

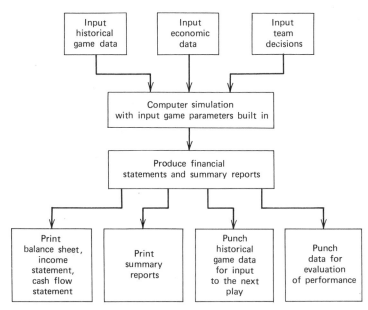

Source. Jae K. Shim, "Management Game Simulation: Survey and New Direction," University of Michigan Business Review (*May 1978*), *p. 27.*

training and planning purposes. But is was not until 1956 that the first true "management" game was created.

The pioneer effort was the "Top Management Decision Simulation" developed by the American Management Association. This team-played game required the players to manage a company that produced a single product that competed with products of other teams.

The A.M.A. game was the forerunner of many similar games that followed. In 1957 Schreiber introduced the "Top Management Decision Game," which was patterned after the A.M.A. game. It was the first game used on a university campus (the University of Washington) and took the players through a series of four increasingly complex phases.

Early participants in the development of management games were IBM and Remington Rand UNIVAC. Undoubtedly, a major factor in their interest was the opportunity to showcase the capabilities of computers in general, and theirs in particular. The A.M.A. game was first programmed to run on an IBM 650.

An early contributor to the popularity of management games was the "Business Management Game" developed by Andlinger, which was described in a 1958 *Harvard Business Review* article.[3] Because of the wide circulation of the *HBR* and the manual scoring feature of Andlinger's game, it was used in many companies as a first gaming experience.

Three different games were developed at UCLA during the late 1950s. Like the A.M.A. game, games number 1 and number 2 simulated a multifirm, single-product indus-

[3]G. T. Andlinger, "Business Games—Play One!," *Harvard Business Review* (March–April, 1958): 115–125.

try. However, game 3 allowed the participants to manufacture and sell up to three differ-ent products that differed in quality and price. The trend in the late 1950s and early 1960s was to more complex games.

The epitome of the movement to complexity was seen in the "Carnegie Tech Manage-ment Game," which is still one of the most complex games in use today. Participants are placed on teams of five to ten players and are required to make between 100 and 300 de-cisions for every month of simulated play. The Carnegie game involves a specific industry (the detergent industry) in which each company can market up to three products in four regional markets.

By 1961 it was estimated that there were over 100 games in existence and over 30,000 executives had played them.[4] Many of the games had been developed by private compa-nies such as General Electric, Westinghouse, Caterpillar Tractor, and Pillsbury. A study by Dale and Klasson in 1962 found that two thirds of the major collegiate schools of business were using games.[5]

Since the mid-1960s, the trend has been away from the development of games requir-ing broad decision making in a hypothetical industry, to games that focus on decision making in a specific functional area and/or a specific industry. This development has taken place for two main reasons—(1) concern over whether general management games are the best way to develop decision-making skills; (2) specific skills are more likely better learned in a game with more limited scope and directed learning objectives. When the game depicts a system with which the players can readily identify, the players usually have greater interest, and the learning is more directly transferable to their specific jobs.

A prolific developer of functional area games since the mid-to-late 1960s has been Paul Greenlaw. In 1964, MARKSIM, a marketing decision simulation was introduced.[6] The year 1967 saw the appearance of FINANSIM, a financial management simulation, which was subsequently revised in 1979.[7] PROSIM, a production management simulation, be-came available in 1969.[8] All three simulations are still widely used in university settings.

Games in the 1970s continued to be popular. In a follow-up to Dale and Klasson's 1962 study, Strauss in 1974 found that 95 percent of the responding *major universities* were using games and that the average percentage of course time devoted to gaming had increased from 20 to 32 percent.[9] These figures should not be taken to be applicable to *all* schools of business. In a broader 1974 survey that included nonaccredited schools, Clark found that approximately 60 percent of the respondents were using games.[10] Clark

---

[4] Joel M. Kibbee, Clifford J. Craft, and Burt Nanus, *Management Games* (New York: Reinhold, 1961), p. 165.

[5] Alfred G. Dale and Charles R. Klasson, "Business Gaming: A Survey of American Collegiate Schools of Business" (Austin: Bureau of Business Research, The University of Texas, 1964).

[6] Paul S. Greenlaw and Fred W. Kniffin, *MARKSIM: A Marketing Decision Simulation* (Scranton, Pa.: International Textbook, 1964), with rights subsequently acquired by Harper & Row, New York.

[7] Paul S. Greenlaw and M. William Frey, *FINANSIM: A Financial Management Simulation* (Scran-ton, Pa.: International Textbook, 1967) and Paul S. Greenlaw, M. William Frey, and Ivan R. Vernan, *FINANSIM: A Financial Management Simulation*, 2nd. ed. (St. Paul, Minn.: West Publishing, 1979).

[8] Paul S. Greenlaw and Michael P. Hottenstein, *PROSIM: A Production Management Simulation* (Scranton, Pa: International Textbook, 1969), with rights subsequently acquired by Harper & Row, New York.

[9] Lance J. Strauss, "Recent Trends in Management Gaming—A Comparative Survey of Management Gaming Practices in American Collegiate Schools of Business in 1962 and 1974," unpublished Mas-ter's thesis (Monterey, Cal.: Naval Postgraduate School, 1974).

[10] J. Daniel Couger, "Computer and the Schools of Business, *Decision Line* (September 1977): 6.

Table 10.1   THE 20 MOST POPULAR GAMES

Game	Area of Application	Publisher
Executive Game	Top management	Richard D. Irwin, Inc.
Business Management Lab	Marketing and management	Business Publications, Inc.
Finansim	Financial management	International Textbook Co.
Marketing in Action	Marketing and management	Richard D. Irwin, Inc.
Tempomatic IV	Management	Houghton Mifflin Co.
The Management Game	Management	The Macmillan Co.
Markism	Top management	Intext Educational Publishers
Intop	International management	The Free Press
GPSS[a]	Simulation language	Wiley/Hamilton and others
Purdue Supermarket Game	Management	Educational Methods, Inc.
Compete	Marketing and management	Business Publications, Inc.
Imaginit	Management	Active Learning Co.
Stanford Bank Management	Finance	Robicheck Publishing
Starting a Small Business	Starting a small business	Not known
Integrated Simulation	Management, finance, and marketing	Southwestern Publishing Co.
Marketing Strategy	Marketing	Didactic Systems, Inc.
AMA General Management Business	Top management	American Management Association
Computer Augmented Accounting	Accounting	Southwestern Publishing Co.
SimQ	Management	Brian Schott, Georgia State Univ.
Sales Management	Sales Management	General Learning Press

Source: J. Daniel Couger, *Computing Newsletter* (November 1977), p. 1.

[a]Not a game, but a special-purpose simulation language.

repeated her survey in 1977 and identified the 20 most popular games. Her findings are shown in Table 10.1.

It has been realized that games have to be as carefully designed and used as any effective teaching device. They have their limitations. Consequently, games are being more selectively used with specific, concrete learning objectives in mind. Game developers are also giving thought as to how to make games more flexible so that their limitations are reduced. These points will be discussed further later in the chapter.

TYPES OF GAMES

Given the multitude of games that have been developed, obviously they vary in many different ways. For example, some games are complex, whereas others are simple; some are computer scored, whereas others rely on manual scoring; some are deterministic, whereas others are probabilistic; and so on. The characteristics of any game are selected so as to meet game objectives and to be compatible with the environment in which they are to be used. Consider now some of the types of games that have been developed.

General Management Games

The earliest management games illustrate what are referred to as "general management" or "total enterprise" games. In these games the players are required to make relatively high-level decisions, which span the various functional areas. For example, the players are frequently required to set production schedules, budget for research and development expenditures, establish pricing and promotion strategies, determine dividend policies, and the like. Working from documents such as income and expense statements, balance sheets, and marketing reports, top-level decisions are made. Perhaps the greatest value of general management games is that they require players to view their company as a total system rather than a set of separate functional areas. For this reason, universities frequently use general management games in their capstone business policy course.

Functional Games

Whereas general management games require decisions covering the activities of the entire organization, *functional games* simulate the activities of only a single functional area and strive to improve the players' decision-making skills in that area. For example, in a production game only production decisions are required.

Functional games usually require middle management level decisions. Because at this level there is often no readily identifiable revenue function, many functional games have cost minimization as their objective. Functional games do not tend to be competitive except in the sense that players attempt to outperform one another according to game criteria.

Specific Industry Games

Some games are designed for *specific industries*. For example, the "Credit Union Management Game," which is discussed in detail later, presents to the players a credit union decision-making environment. Although the "Credit Union Management Game" is of a general management nature, it requires management decisions in a specific industry. However, not all industry games require top management decisions; some are functional games for a particular industry. Specific industry games are among the "most serious" in that they are often developed by a specific company for training purposes. In many instances there is little difference between an industry game and corporate simulation models.

Simple Versus Complex Games

Games vary considerably in their complexity. Some games require only several decisions, whereas games such as the "Carnegie Tech Management Game" can require between 100 and 300 decisions for every period of play. In general, *simple games* attempt to impart only one or two basic concepts or principles, whereas *complex games* attempt to impart broader managerial skills.[11]

Interactive Versus Noninteractive Games

The decisions made by game participants *may or may not interact* to affect other player's output. For example, in the A.M.A.s "Top Management Decision Simulation," decisions are made on selling price and marketing expenditures. The decisions arrived at by the competing teams interact within the model to determine values for competitive variables such as dollar sales.

When there is no interaction among player's decisions, the quality of a set of decisions is much more dependent on the application of analytical thought processes than on the attempt to outguess the opposition. Consequently, noninteractive games are often used to teach basic concepts, principles, and methods of analysis.

Deterministic Versus Probabilistic Games

Most games present a *deterministic* decision-making environment wherein the outcome of a set of decisions is uniquely determined by the decisions rather than by chance elements. In interactive games the uncertainty created by other players' decisions usually creates a sufficiently realistic situation without introducing randomness. In games that impart basic concepts and principles, it is often advisable to exclude randomness so that full attention can be devoted to the concepts and principles. However, it is sometimes the *probabilistic* nature of the system that the game designers want the the players to grow to understand. Consequently, this leads to probabilistic games. Some of the variables that are treated in a probabilistic manner include strikes, acts of God, materials shortages, and so on.

Team Versus Individual Played Games

Some games, because of their complexity and the number of decisions that must be made, are *team played*. Care must be exercised in deciding on how many players to assign to a team. If there are more players than roles to be assumed or work to be accomplished, players tend to lose interest. However, when there are too few players to a team, there tends to be too little discussion about the decisions, because the available time is devoted to necessary analysis.[12]

In team-played games it is common for the players or the game administrator to create an organizational structure with separate functional areas of decision-making responsibility. As discussed later, these organizations are sometimes used by researchers for the purpose of studying small group behavior.

Simpler games are often *individual played*. This is often the case when the game has the teaching of basic concepts and principles as its objective.

---

[11] For a current discussion of the merits of simple versus complex games, see Joseph Wolfe, "The Effects of Game Complexity on the Acquisition of Business Policy Knowledge," *Decision Sciences* (January 1978): 143–155 and Richard J. Butler, Thomas F. Pray, and Daniel R. Strang, "An Extension of Wolfe's Study of Simulation Game Complexity," *Decision Sciences* (July 1979): 480–486.

[12] E. M. Babb and L. M. Eisgruber, *Management Games for Teaching and Research* (Chicago, Ill.: Educational Methods, 1966), p. 20.

Computer Versus Manual Scored Games

Computer scored games can accommodate many decision inputs, complex functional relationships, and detailed output. Most of the complex, general management games are computer scored. However, the costs of developing and operating a computerized game can be large. In addition to cost considerations, an advantage of a *manual scored game* is that more flexibility is afforded; for example, qualitative factors can be directly included in the evaluation of player performance, or the decisions that are required can be varied. Another advantage of manual games is that they can be used in settings where access to a computer is not readily available.

PURPOSES OF GAMES

The purpose of most games can be placed in one of the following categories.

1. Teaching.
2. Operational gaming.
3. Research into human and group behavior.
4. Evaluating personnel.

Most games in use today are employed for *teaching* purposes. Many of them are used in university courses, executive development programs, or in-house company training programs. The development of a game is itself a tremendous learning experience. Not only must the game developer possess technical skills, he or she must also have a fundamental understanding of the decisions, processes, and responses of the represented system.

Operational gaming is another use of games. Its purpose is to find optimal solutions or strategies that can be applied in the real world. With operational gaming, the game provides a realistic representation of a real-world system, and the players experiment in the game environment with alternative decisions. Strategic war games are examples of operational gaming.

Games can be used to conduct *research into group and human behavior*. By placing players on teams with different organizational structures, communication flows, leadership styles, and the like, one can investigate what effect such factors have on behavioral variables such as motivation, satisfaction, and performance. The game provides a laboratory for studying group interaction. This use of games has been increasing over time.

Games are sometimes used in *evaluating personnel*. The evaluation can take the form of identifying areas of weakness where individual or group improvement is needed, or as an input to the selection of personnel for possible organizational advancement. This latter use must be performed with great care, because a game is not the real world and is not always a good indicator of actual performance potential.

ADVANTAGES OF GAMES

Given the popularity of games, many users obviously perceive them as being worthwhile. McGehee suggests the following list of what games can do.[13]

[13]William McGehee, "Business Games—Where They Fit into Training," *Textile World* (January 1966): 68–71.

1. Make certain abstract ideas more meaningful (planning, organizing, and controlling).
2. Give specialists (accountants, personnel managers) an understanding of how other parts of the business function.
3. Increase an individual's awareness of his or her part as a member of a management team in a real-life role.
4. Give participants an understanding of how companies must allocate limited resources to attain various goals and objectives.

Other advantages commonly mentioned include:

5. Create an environment where participants are highly motivated to take part and learn.
6. Provide an opportunity for self-analysis and introspection.
7. Impart specific decision-making skills.

Certain business concepts remain somewhat abstract until actually practiced. For example, the need for careful cash management planning is typically considered to be much more important after difficulties arise from poor planning efforts. A game provides a risk-free environment for experiencing new situations.

Particularly in large organizations, it is common for personnel to identify more with the objectives of their own functional area than with the organization's objectives. However, it is important to have employees view their role as being part of a total system. General management games illustrate the roles and responsibilities of personnel in other functional areas and how the efforts of all organizational subsystems must be integrated to ensure organizational success.

Total system rather than functional area performance should be the focal point of attention to avoid suboptimization. In a game where decisions that cut across the various functional areas are required, an understanding is gained as to how scarce resources must be allocated in light of total system rather than of subsystem objectives.

An almost universal constant with games is that they create an atmosphere of high interest and motivation. Rare is the player who does not become both intellectually and emotionally involved when playing a game. Carlson has stated that "management games work because they get the total involvement of the participant."[14]

Games provide quick feedback on the quality of decision-making. The feedback is not filtered by long time passages and other external factors. Consequently, game participants are in an excellent situation to be reflective on their decision-making processes, skills, and ability. The atmosphere is conducive to favorably influencing decision-making behavior.

Some games are designed to teach or illustrate the importance of specific concepts, principles, or methods of analysis. Typically, functional games are designed to serve these purposes.

These are obviously strong reasons for using games. But in fairness, it should be pointed out that not everyone accepts these advantages as necessarily being valid. Others point out that there is little empirical evidence to support the claims of many game designers and users.[15] Consequently, before using a game, one should carefully consider

[14] Elliot Carlson, "The Versatile Business Game: Its Growing Use in Industry," *Management Review* (September 1966): 45.

[15] John J. Neuhauser, "Business Games Have Failed," *Academy of Management Review* (October 1976): 124–129.

whether a game will satisfy the desired objectives or whether another alternative should be chosen.

LIMITATIONS OF GAMES

Despite the widespread popularity of games, disadvantages or limitations exist. The following criticisms of games have been expressed.

1. Games are often unrealistic, if not misleading, in their representation of the business world.
2. Games omit many of the factors that lead to success in the business world.
3. Games discourage originality in decision making.
4. Games focus on more easily scored quantitative than qualitative factors.
5. Games do not provide sufficient emphasis on the human element.
6. Games are costly and time consuming to develop and operate.

The mathematical relationships that underlie some games are potentially misleading about how the real-world functions. Increased promotion, increased spending on research and development, and lower prices do not always have the effect that some games imply. It is potentially dangerous to have players leave the gaming environment with the belief that the strategies that were effectively employed in playing the game are directly transferrable to the real world.

However, Stewart has pointed out that "lectures, discussion sessions, and critiques can alert the game player to the artificiality of the assumptions in the model and help him to discriminate wisely between what can and cannot safely be applied to real-life situations."[16]

Many events take place in the real world that influence business success, which are omitted or are treated on a random basis in a game. These include such important events as mergers, diversification, product and process innovation, strikes, antitrust suits, and the like. Also most games do not permit companies to enter or leave the market once play has begun.

Some games are developed with built in constraints, which limit the range of decisions that can be made. Consequently, the ability to make daring, original decisions is sometimes limited. For example, in many games it is not possible to drop and/or add new products.

Games often ignore important qualitative factors. All marketing effort is often assumed to be equally effective, all products are equally desirable, and all customers are equally well informed.

Most games assume that the human element in the business world is completely efficient and rational. There are no missed deadlines, information flows are completed without errors, company personnel support the organization's objectives, and customers behave in a rational manner. Obviously, this is not the case.

Games, especially complex, computerized ones, are time consuming and costly to

[16] R. Stewart, "A Survey of Business Games," *Simulation and Gaming: A Symposium*, Management Report No. 55 (New York: American Management Association, 1961).

build. The benefits to be derived from a game must be carefully compared against the costs of developing and using the game. Even running an existing game must be compared to nongaming alternatives.

Many of the criticisms of games are valid. However, considering the widespread usage of games, many people must have decided that for their situation the advantages of games outweigh their disadvantages. And, of course, some of the limitations of games may not actually be a limitation given the purposes and way a particular game is used. Also, games can often be designed so as to reduce or eliminate many of their disadvantages.

THE ADMINISTRATION OF GAMES

How teaching methods are used is as important as the methods themselves. This is certainly the case with management games. The game administrator has important responsibilities before, during, and after game play. For now, our discussion will assume that a previously developed game is being used. In the next section we will discuss concepts in game construction.

A game should be selected for use only after concrete learning objectives have been established and alternative teaching methods have been explored. Sufficient lead time should be included to cover getting the game on the computer, completing a "dry run" to discover problem areas, and preparing sufficient quantities of game materials. From a teaching point of view, little is more disastrous than having unforeseen problems emerge when actually using a game.

Several things should be accomplished at the opening session. The players should be told that while the game will be fun to play, it is being used for serious purposes. It is useful to discuss the game's learning objectives thoroughly with the participants. Obviously, the players must become familiar with the decision-making environment created by the game, the types of decisions that will be required, and the quantifiable indicators of effective decision making. If specific analytical techniques are to be employed to assist in arriving at decisions, they should also be discussed. In team-played games the players must be placed into groups. Usually the instructions for the game administrator provides recommendations as to how many players should be on a team. Players on a team can either be assigned specific roles or left to evolve their own organization structure.

It is often useful for the game administrator to begin play by providing the participants with a set of decisions and the resultant output. This practice shows what a typical set of decisions will look like and what type of output will be forthcoming. Game play can also include a "warm-up" period. With this approach the first set of decisions and the resulting output do not count. After the trial run, the game administrator simply reinitiates the game. It is psychologically frustrating for players to be far behind after the first round of decisions because they did not fully understand the functioning of the game.

Once game play is underway, the decision-output process typically falls into a stable pattern. However, the administrator should always be available to answer questions of a clarifying nature. Furthermore, the administrator should be willing to discuss some of the fundamental forces that impact the decision-making environment. Resentment can result, however, from both those receiving the advice and competing teams if too much help is given. Obviously, teams that are floundering require special attention.

Care must be taken in processing decisions once they have been made. In manual games, arithmetic computations must be carefully checked, whereas in computerized games, keypunch errors must be avoided. The game administrator should always check the decision sheets prior to processing for careless mistakes such as decimal points being incorrectly placed.

The time that is available between when decisions are made and when the output is returned to the players can be used for several purposes. New materials that improve the player's analysis capabilities can be introduced. This is particularly appropriate in university courses where game play often extends over a long period. It is also possible to reorientate the teams. For example, players' roles on the teams can be changed or perhaps even game rules can be modified. The players can be required to present reports during the slack time. The reports might take the form of discussion of decisions that have been made or reports on the condition of the company, such as those that might be given at a Board of Director's meeting. And, of course, the time can be used for relaxation. This practice is sometimes followed in executive development programs where game play is highly intensive.

When game results become available, they should be examined by the game administrator in order to keep abreast of the teams' progress. Teams that are having special problems can be identified and counseled. General comments about game play can be communicated to the entire group. It is interesting for the players to see up-to-date selected summary statistics on the various teams's performance.

A problem that sometimes occurs near the end of a game is that some teams begin making decisions that are intended to make their end-of-the-game financial statements look good rather than making sound long-run decisions. For example, research and development expenditures, which in many games have a lagged effect, may be cut to improve the current profit picture. This "end effect" can be handled to some extent by stressing that the logic behind the decisions as well as the output will be considered at the evaluation stage and that the evaluation of the team's performance will be made on multiple criteria, including the firm's potential for future growth, earnings, productive capacity, and so on.

A management game should always end with a critique or summary session. At this session it is often useful and interesting to have the teams explain, justify, and defend their decision-making policies. The presentations are also helpful in identifying "winning" teams; however, it should be stressed that everyone has won in the sense that they have learned from the gaming experience. Fun can be introduced into the final session by awarding small prizes. The summary session also provides the game administrator with the opportunity to make any final points about the decision making that has taken place.

CONCEPTS IN GAME DESIGN

An early question that arises in developing a game is how much complexity to include. Of course, the answer depends on factors such as game objectives, how much time is available for game play, and the background of the participants. In general, it is best to develop simple games and to add complexity only as needed. Normally, adding more complexity increases the game's computational requirements in a nonlinear manner.

Striving for complete realism is an unrealistic, unattainable goal. It is impossible to develop a game that exactly duplicates a decision-making environment for any but trivial situations. Rather, a game designer should strive for *verisimilitude*, which is the appearance of reality as perceived by the game players. From the players' point of view, the model that underlies the game is little more than a "black box." If the model processes players' decisions into logical output, the game is perceived as being realistic. In order to achieve verisimilitude, the game must be *stable*, include reasonable *elasticities*, and guard against *gimmick policies*.[17]

In real life, conditions usually do not vary drastically from period to period. Likewise a game should be sufficiently stable so that consistently good decisions lead to success rather than to a single set of "fluke" decisions.

A game should be appropriately sensitive to the decisions that are made. This sensitivity is captured in the elasticities that are included in the game. For example, changes in sales should realistically occur in response to changes in price and promotion.

A game should not reward gimmick policies, which would obviously be unsuccessful in real life. However, it is often difficult to anticipate all of the extreme policies that will ultimately be tried in a game. Consequently, safeguards must usually be added over time. It is often easier to include an artifical protection mechanism later than it is to include the actual mechanism that performs the function in the real world.

Game Equations

In designing management games one of the most interesting and important challenges is developing the equations that underlie the game. The equations must present to the players a realistic environment, yet one that supports the game's objectives. If operational gaming is the game's purpose, great care must be taken to ensure that the game accurately describes a real-world system. For other gaming purposes it is usually sufficient that the game provides verisimilitude.

Most games are composed of a large number of equations. However, most of them are *definitional*, usually of an accounting nature, and pose few difficulties for the game developer. It is the *empirically based* equations that pose the greatest problems, for it is here that much of the game's realism is either gained or lost.

Noninteractive Games. Noninteractive games are easier to design than interactive ones for obvious reasons. Specifically, there is no need to include other players' decisions as independent variables in the equations. Taking a simple example, the dollar sales, S_i, generated by the *i*th team's product might be assumed to be functionally related only to price, p_i; see Equation 10-1.

$$S_i = f(p_i) \qquad (10\text{-}1)$$

A typical demand curve might take a functional form, as shown in Equation 10-2; see Figure 10.2.

$$f(p_i) = c_1 - c_2 p_i + c_3 p_i^2 \qquad \text{for} \quad f(p_i) \geq 0 \qquad (10\text{-}2)$$

[17]Richard Bellman et al., "On the Construction of a Multi-Stage, Multi-Person Business Game," *Operations Research* (August 1957): 469–503.

Figure 10.2   Dollar sales as a function of price.

Taking a specific example, if $f(p_i)$ is as shown below, dollar sales would be $550,000 when the price equals $5.

$$S_i = f(p_i) = \$1,000,000 - 100,000p_i + 2000p_i^2$$

$$S_i = f(p_i = 5) = \$1,000,000 - 100,000(5) + 2000(5^2)$$

$$= \$550,000$$

Obviously, factors other than price also affect the sales of most products and would be included as independent variables. Let us now consider how additional factors might be included as we next consider the development of equations that include the interaction of players' decisions.

Interactive Games. One of the first discussions of how to include the interaction of players' decisions was provided by Bellman et al.[18] Alternative approaches do exist, but they possess many similarities.[19] The following discussion is patterned after Bellman et al.

In our discussion the objective will be to generate dollar sales figures for the competing teams. The independent variables are the teams' marketing expenditures, research and development outlays, and the price charged for the product. A constraint on satisfying the simulated demand is that last period inventory plus current production must cover the demand. When this is not the case, demand is set equal to the sum of the two sources of supply.

A starting point is to compute the *relative* impact of the teams' marketing and research and development expenditures. This objective can be realized through computations based on Equations 10-3 and 10-4.

If m_i is the marketing expenditure of the ith team, its relative expenditure, m_i', is given by the following equation.

$$m_i' = \frac{m_i}{\sum m_i} \tag{10-3}$$

[18]Ibid.
[19]See for example, Paul S. Greenlaw, "Designing Parametric Equations for Business Games," *Academy of Management Journal* (June 1963): 150–159.

When r_i is the research and development expenditure of the ith team, its impact relative to other teams, r_i', is given by the following equation.

$$r_i' = \frac{r_i}{\sum r_i} \qquad (10\text{-}4)$$

The attractiveness, A_i, of the ith teams' product is then assumed to be a function of m_i', r_i' and its selling price, p_i.

$$A_i = f(m_i', r_i', p_i) \qquad (10\text{-}5)$$

Different types of functional relationships can be conceptualized, but a linear one as presented in Equation 10-6 provides a simple example.

$$f(m_i', r_i', p_i) = c_1 + c_2 m_i' + c_3 r_i' - c_4 p_i \qquad (10\text{-}6)$$

The constant c_1 is included to add stability to the model. The coefficients c_2 through c_4 determine the impact of the independent variables.

The relative attractiveness of a teams' product (actually its market share) is found through Equation 10-7.

$$A_i' = \frac{A_i}{\sum A_i} \qquad (10\text{-}7)$$

If N is the total market size (in units), a firm's total dollar sales, S_i, is found as follows.

$$S_i = NA_i' p_i \qquad (10\text{-}8)$$

These concepts are perhaps most easily seen by considering an example. Assume that there are four teams and their marketing and research and development expenditures and selling prices are as shown in Table 10.2. Also shown are the results of computations of the relative expenditures for marketing and research and development. Given the following functional relationship, the A_i's and then the A_i''s are computed.

$$A_i = 35 + 50m_i' + 10r_i' - 4p_i$$

Assuming a total market size of 1,000,000 units, dollar sales for each team are determined.

Table 10.2   AN ILLUSTRATION OF INTERACTIVE DECISIONS

Team	Marketing Expenditures, m_i	Research and Development Expenditures, r_i	Price, p_i	m_i'	r_i'	A_i	A_i'	$NA_i'p_i$
1	$ 200,000	$ 0	$3.00	0.1538	0.000	30.69	0.2325	$ 697,500
2	400,000	150,000	5.00	0.3077	0.4286	34.67	0.2627	1,313,500
3	400,000	100,000	4.50	0.3077	0.2857	35.24	0.2670	1,201,500
4	300,000	100,000	4.50	0.2308	0.2857	31.40	0.2379	1,070,550
	$1,300,000	$350,000		1.000	1.000	132.00	1.000	

More complexity, and probably more realism, could have been built into the model. For example, previous periods' market shares for the teams could have been included as independent variables in the computation of A_i. The total market size, N, could have been made functionally related to marketing and research and development expenditures. The appropriateness of such inclusions depend, however, on the type of marketing environment that the model builder wants to create and the desired amount of complexity.

THE VALIDATION OF GAMES

One of the continuing problems and sources of criticism of games involves their validation. One study conducted in the 1970s, which surveyed research on the validation of both general management and functional games used in collegiate schools of business, found a relatively small number of rigorous validation studies, and only one that clearly indicated that learning of importance had taken place in game play.[20] Indeed, validation is a problem with any simulation, but it is particularly acute with management games. How should a game be validated? Answers depend, of course, on the game's purpose. If the game is used for teaching, it should satisfy learning objectives. When the game is employed for operational gaming, it should accurately describe the decision-making and response characteristics of the real-world system. Games used for studying human and group behavior typically depend less on the model that underlies the game than on the interaction environment created by the researcher. Evaluating personnel through gaming requires more of the evaluator than the game. We will discuss the validation of games for teaching purposes next, postpone the validation of real-world models for a later chapter, and leave the validation of the last two uses of games for research courses in organization behavior and personnel selection, respectively.

Kibbee, Craft, and Nanus provide some suggestions for validating games used for teaching purposes.[21] Their first suggestion is for an objective evaluation of the game by the game administrator and/or observers. The extent to which the players assume an active role in analyses and decision making, the time and effort put into decisions, the ability of the players to relate their past experiences to the game, and the participants' ability to identify and deal with fundamental forces and interrelationships in the game are all indicators of the game's effectiveness.

The game participants can be surveyed as to their reactions to the game. Usually such surveys are best conducted several weeks after the gaming experience when the participants have gotten over their initial enthusiasm. The survey should attempt to identify if there were any specific changes in decision-making behavior as a result of playing the game.

In university settings, it is sometimes possible to conduct a controlled experiment. One section of a course might play the game, while another section is taught without benefit of the game. Common tests might be given at the end of the term to determine if the game aided course learning objectives.

---

[20]Paul S. Greenlaw and F. Paul Wyman, "The Teaching Effectiveness of Games in Collegiate Business Courses," *Simulation and Games* (September 1973): 259–294.

[21]Kibbee, Craft and Nanus, op. cit., pp. 80–90.

ADDING MORE FLEXIBILITY TO GAMES

Criticisms of games, such as they omit factors that lead to success in the business world, discourage originality in decision making, concentrate only on quantifiable factors, and provide insufficient emphasis on the human element, can be resolved to some extent by including more flexibility in the game.[22] More flexibility places, however, considerably higher demands on the game administrator and often requires additional personnel.

The additional flexibility can be included in many ways. Consider, for example, what might happen when an expanding firm desires additional capital. Instead of automatically receiving the funds at a predetermined rate from a predetermined source, the players might be told they can seek funds from any source. The team then prepares a report supporting the request for funds and meets with a human "representative." Based on appropriate negotiations with the representative, the additional request for capital is either granted or denied.

During game play a team might be informed that a court order has been issued to close down one of its plants for violating environmental standards. Not only must this factor be taken into consideration in planning production, but a media campaign must be planned to offset adverse public reaction to the plant closing.

Instead of having labor and labor costs assume a passive role as in most games, more realism as well as additional dimensions can be added. Periodically, the teams can be required to meet with "labor leaders" to negotiate a new contract. As a result, wage rates are set, or possibly even a strike occurs.

These examples illustrate that by taking a more flexible approach to game design, many of the criticisms of more conventional games can be reduced or eliminated. The problem, of course, is that they require substantially more time, effort, and resources.

RECENT TRENDS IN GAMES

Several trends in game development can be identified. These trends include:

1. A larger number and variety of games.
2. Conversational games that utilize modern data processing technology.
3. The use of games as vehicles for learning about human and organization behavior.

The number and variety of games continues to grow. As suggested earlier, this growth has been especially great for functional and specific industry games. For example, OPRAD has been created to develop decision-making skills for research and development managers.[23] HOTMAMA has recently been created to develop management skills in the hotel industry.[24] The purposes for which games are used have also been expanding. A

[22]See Kalman Cohen and Eric Rhenman, "The Role of Management Games in Education and Research," *Management Science* (January 1961): 131–166.

[23]Klaus Truemper and Burton V. Dean, "The OPRAD Research and Development Game," *Management Science* (February 1974): 999–1099.

[24]Eric B. Orkin, "HOTMAMA: A Computer Simulation Exercise to Sharpen Management Skills," *The Cornell H.R.Q. Quarterly* (February 1979): 10–17.

game has been used to develop collective bargaining skills in labor–management negotiations.[25] A gaming approach has been suggested for improving on the implementation of management science projects.[26]

Another trend is toward conversational games. With this type of game, players enter their decisions from a computer terminal and receive their output on a real-time basis. With this approach, participants can play the game on their own and make as many plays as they wish. Results are immediate, and the player can replay some decisions if he or she wishes, correcting earlier mistakes. This feature allows the players to investigate the sensitivity of operating results to changes in input decisions, while the decisions of other players are held constant. Examples of conversational games include RISKM for developing risk management decision-making skills[27] and the "Conversational Executive Game," a conversational version of the "Executive Game."[28]

A third trend is the increased use of games for studying human and organization behavior. Because a gaming environment affords a good opportunity to control certain factors while allowing others to vary, it is not surprising that games are used to explore a variety of individual and group decision-making situations. For example, the game presented in assignment 9.10 was used to evaluate alternative methods of obtaining probabilistic data inputs from managers.[29]

The number, variety, technology, and uses of games will continue to expand. Although descriptions and discussions of games are published in many journals, several publications routinely discuss current gaming developments. These publications include *Computing Newsletter*, *Simulation and Games*, and *Simulation/Gaming/News*.

THE CREDIT UNION MANAGEMENT GAME

For a detailed look at a management game, let us consider the "Credit Union Management Game," which was conceptualized by Howard E. Thompson and programmed by LeRoy J. Krajewoki. The game was developed for use in executive development programs for credit union managers. Consequently, it is an example of a specific-industry game. Furthermore, it illustrates a deterministic, noninteractive, team played, computerized game. Because credit unions seldom face other credit unions as competitors, the game involves credit unions "playing against the environment." Its primary focus is on financial decision making.

Background on Game Participants

The participants in the game are all employed by credit unions. There are, however, substantial differences in the credit union environments that the players come from.

[25]Peter A. Veglahan, J. Ronald Frazer, and Michael R. W. Bommer, "Computer Simulation–Training Tool for Collective Bargaining," *Personnel Journal* (November 1978): 614–617.

[26]K. Roscoe Davis and Bernard W. Taylor, III, "Addressing the Implementation Problem: A Gaming Approach," *Decision Sciences* (October 1976): 677–688.

[27]Brian Schott, "Using a Business Game to Teach Risk Management," *Journal of Risk and Insurance* (September 1976): 526–532.

[28]Shim, op. cit.

[29]Carl D. McDevitt and Hugh J. Watson, "An Assessment of Probability Encoding Using a Probabilistic, Noninteractive Management Game," *Academy of Management Journal* (September 1978): 451–462.

At one extreme are single-person credit unions where the manager assumes the role of secretary, loan officer, collections officer, and so on. Some of the participants come from larger credit unions (e.g., military credit unions), which have many employees and are organized by functional specialization. A common weakness of the participants, however, regardless of their background, is a lack of top management perspective, because most policy decisions are made at the Board of Directors' level.

In most instances the participants are not formally trained in credit union or business management. They frequently have "fallen" into credit union management rather than through a formal educational program of study. Consequently, although the participants understand the day-to-day functioning of credit unions, they are often lacking in financial, accounting, marketing, and management theory. These conditions led to the creation of the game objectives.

Game Objectives

The major objectives of the game are to:

1. Provide a top management viewpoint of credit union management.
2. Develop an appreciation of how key variables interact.
3. Provide experience in using standard financial statements.
4. Create a relatively risk-free environment for experimenting with alternative policies.

Game Play

Prior to game play, the game administrator creates the credit union and industry environment. This is accomplished by inputting to the game model information on economic conditions and decisions made by a previous credit union management group (actually the game administrator). From the players point of view, they see a set of previously made decisions, the consequences of these decisions, and the current condition of the credit union. This information provides the basis for the teams' first set of decisions, which from the game model's point of view are actually second-period decisions; see Figure 10.3.

Before receiving any output from the game, the players are placed into teams of three to six players each. They are told to assume the role of the Board of Directors for their credit union. After receiving the output from the first set of decisions (which were made

Figure 10.3   The decision-output sequence in the "Credit Union Management Game."

| Industry and credit union history is created | 1st period decisions (same for all teams) | Decisions are processed in light of past history | Updated history and 1st period output (same for all teams) | 2nd period decisions | Decisions are processed in light of past history | Updated history and 2nd period output |

by the game administrator), the teams establish objectives for their credit union. Their performance is later critiqued against these objectives.

Normally, the game administrator creates a highly unfavorable, identical set of initial conditions for the teams. For example, most of the organizations' assets are in cash rather than in investments. Consequently, careful planning and insightful decision making are required to put the credit unions on sound financial ground before game play ends.

Against this background, game play begins and the players make their first set of decisions. These decisions are input to the computerized model that underlies the game. These second-round decisions result in second-round output, which forms a basis for decision making in the next period. Each period simulates 6 months of activity in the credit union. This decision-output process continues throughout game play. The game is structured for six decision periods but can be modified to accommodate additional play; see Figure 10.3.

At the close of the game, team performance is critiqued. First, the objectives of the teams are discussed. Second, the measurement of the attainment of these objectives is reviewed. And finally, it is interesting to have each team make a presentation supporting its management practices. It is also entertaining to close with a vote for the outstanding team and to award small prizes to the winning team members.

Game Decisions

The game requires decisions in several areas. Upper limits, if any, must be established for the amount loaned for new personal loans, new auto loans, and new mortgage loans. Interest rates must also be set for these new loans and for loans that are covered by shares held in the credit union by borrowers. Investment decisions must also be made on purchasing or selling government securities, shares and certificates of deposit of savings and loan associations. Loans can also be made to other credit unions, and loans can be secured or repaid to banks and other credit unions. Dividends to stockholders must also be specified. Money can be spent on promotion to increase the demand for loans or shares in the credit union. And finally, interest can be refunded to those who have borrowed from the credit union. All these decisions are entered on the decision sheet shown in Figure 10.4.

The Model

The "Credit Union Management Game" processes decisions into outputs in the following sequence.

1. Exogenous factors are input.
2. History data are input.
3. Players decisions are input.
4. Check is made to ensure that undistributed earnings are sufficient to pay the declared dividends.
5. Demand for loans is computed.
6. Computation of the cash flow report is begun.
7. Loan demand for various types of loans is computed.

Figure 10.4 International Conference for Credit Union Executives "Credit Union Management Game"–Decision Sheet.

1. CREDIT UNION NUMBER .... ☐☐☐
    1   3

2. PERIOD NUMBER .... ☐☐
    4 5

ASSET MANAGEMENT

Loans to Members

3. MAXIMUM AMOUNT OF FUNDS TO BE USED FOR NEW PERSONAL LOANS .... ☐☐☐☐☐☐☐☐☐
    6   14

4. MONTHLY RATE CHARGED ON NEW PERSONAL LOANS .... ☐☐☐☐ %
    15   18

5. MAXIMUM AMOUNT OF FUNDS TO BE USED ON NEW AUTO LOANS .... ☐☐☐☐☐☐☐☐☐
    19   27

6. MONTHLY RATE CHARGED ON NEW AUTO LOANS .... ☐☐☐☐ %
    28   31

7. MAXIMUM AMOUNT OF FUNDS TO BE USED FOR NEW MORTGAGE LOANS .... ☐☐☐☐☐☐☐☐☐
    32   40

8. MONTHLY RATE CHARGED ON NEW MORTGAGE LOANS .... ☐☐☐☐ %
    41   44

9. MONTHLY RATE ON LOANS COVERED BY SHARES .... ☐☐☐☐ %
    45   48

Investments

10. AMOUNT OF FUNDS USED FOR THE PURCHASE OF NEW GOVERNMENT .... ☐☐☐☐☐☐☐☐☐
    SECURITIES   49   57

11. TERM TO MATURITY OF NEW SECURITIES (PERIODS) .... ☐☐
    58 59

12. AMOUNT OF SECURITIES TO BE SOLD .... ☐☐☐☐☐☐☐☐☐
    60   68

13. SAVINGS & LOAN SHARES AND CERTIFICATES OF DEPOSIT .... ☐☐☐☐☐☐☐☐☐
    PURCHASED (OR SOLD)   69   77

                    (IF SHARES AND CERTIFICATES OF DEPOSIT ARE SOLD
                    PLACE A MINUTS SIGN (–) IN BOX 69)

14. AMOUNT OF FUNDS TO BE LOANED TO OTHER CREDIT UNIONS THIS .... ☐☐☐☐☐☐☐
    PERIOD   4   12

LIABILITIES, DIVIDEND AND PROMOTION MANAGEMENT

15. AMOUNT OF FUNDS BORROWED FROM BANKS OR OTHER CREDIT............... ☐☐☐☐☐☐☐☐☐
    UNIONS (OR REPAID)   13   21
                    (IF REPAYMENTS ARE DESIRED PLACE
                    A MINUS SIGN (–) IN BOX 13)

16. THE SEMI–ANNUAL DIVIDEND RATE PAID .... ☐☐☐☐ %
    22   25

17. AMOUNT SPENT TO INCREASE SHARES PURCHASED .... ☐☐☐☐☐☐
    26   31

18. AMOUNT SPENT TO INCREASE LOAN DEMAND .... ☐☐☐☐☐☐
    32   37

19. INTEREST REFUND .... ☐☐ ☐☐ %
    38   41

Figure 10.5 Output from the "Credit Union Management Game."

CREDIT UNION NO. 1
BALANCE SHEET

FOR PERIOD 3

ASSETS		LIABILITIES	
Cash	907037.	Shared	9495090.
Loans		Notes payable	0.
Personal loans	3326557.	Reserves for bad loans	506376.
Auto loans	2968287.	Undistributed earnings	89639.
Mortgage loans	1090513.	Net gain this period	
Loans covered by shares	61619.	—after reserve DED—	125123.
Loans to other C. U.	0.		
Government securities	1721319.		
Savings and loan shares and			
certificates of deposit	29677.		
Fixed assets	111223.		
TOTAL ASSETS	10216232.	**TOTAL LIABILITIES**	10216226.

ADDITIONAL FINANCIAL INFORMATION

Effective semi-annual dividend rate this period	0.0
Ratio of notes payable to shares & U.E.	0.0
Ratio of loans to shares	0.77781
Effective rebate on interest this period	0.0
Total interest received from loans this period	334987.
Delinquent loans Personal	94633.
Auto	61983.

CREDIT UNION NO. 1
INCOME AND EXPENSE

FOR PERIOD 3

INCOME		517622.
Interest on loans to members		
Personal loans	156647.	
Auto loans	136464.	
Mortgage loans	39030.	
Loans covered by shares	2845.	
Income from investments		
Government securities	181632.	
Savings and loan shares and C.D.	1004.	
Loans to other credit unions	0.	
EXPENSES		361219.
Salaries	75000.	
Other expense	40031.	
Insurance—loans and shares	41519.	
Interest on borrowed money	201817.	
Promotion expense	0.	
Depreciation	2852.	
NET INCOME THIS PERIOD		156404.

Figure 10.5 *(Continued)*

CREDIT UNION NO. 1
STATEMENT OF CASH POSITION AND FLOW

FOR PERIOD 3

PREVIOUS CASH POSITION		189842.
CASH INFLOW		
Net increase in shares purchased by members	3000.	
Loan repayments—including interest		
Personal loans	1499178.	
Auto loans	708563.	
Mortgage loans	77400.	
Loans covered by shares	47517.	
Loans to other credit unions	0.	
New borrowings from banks or credit unions	0.	
Government securities sold and maturing	4179744.	
Savings and loan and C.D. withdrawn	0.	
TOTAL CASH INFLOW		6515399.
CASH OUTFLOW		
New loans made		
Personal loans	1590909.	
Auto loans	1136363.	
Mortgage loans	300000.	
Loans covered by shares	38250.	
Loans to other credit unions	0.	
Government securities purchased	0.	
Savings and loan shares purchased	0.	
Repayment of loans from banks or credit unions	2374316.	
Expenses—less depreciation	358367.	
TOTAL CASH OUTFLOW		5798203.
NEW CASH POSITION		907037.

8. Computation of the cash flow report is completed.
9. Computations for the income and expense report are made.
10. Computations for the balance sheet are made.
11. Computations for the government securities portfolio report are made.
12. Computations for the financial industry and credit union forecasts are made.
13. All reports are output.

Game Output

After each decision period, the players receive the following output.

1. Balance sheet.
2. Income and expense statement.
3. Cash flow report.

4. Government securities portfolio report.
5. Financial industry and credit union forecast.
6. Financial analysis report.

The balance sheet shows the status of the credit union in terms of its assets and liabilities, plus information such as the ratio of loans to shares and the amount of delinquent loans. The income and expense statement indicates the income and expenses that occurred during the past time period. The government securities portfolio report provides information on securities currently held as well as a perfect forecast of the future market value of securities held by the credit union. The financial industry and credit union forecast presents a perfect forecast of the rates to be paid and to be charged by "competing" financial institutions during the next period. The financial analysis report provides important financial information on the condition of the credit union. Examples of some of the output are shown in Figure 10.5.

SUMMARY

Many people think of management games as simulations. Management games do involve a model that describes a hypothetical or real-world system; however, it is the making of management-type decisions and receiving information on the consequences of the decisions that best characterizes management games. Management games vary tremendously. They include general management games, functional games, and specific industry games. They can be simple or complex, interactive or noninteractive, deterministic or probabilistic, team or individual played, and computer or manual scored.

Games have been played for serious purposes for many years, but it was the A.M.A.s "Top Management Decision Simulation" in 1956 that triggered the use of management games. Today, games are used for teaching, operational gaming to discover optimal strategies, research into human and group behavior, and evaluating personnel. Games have many advantages but possess limitations as well. The use of any game should be carefully weighed against other alternatives and be selected with specific objectives in mind.

Games must be carefully administered in order to be successful. The game administrator has definite responsibilities, beginning with the development or selection of the game through the final game session.

In game design, the game developer strives for verisimilitude, the appearance of reality. This orientation is used in helping decide which variables to include in the game. Also important is developing appropriate equations to describe the represented system. Games can be designed in such a way to minimize the limitations of games. This frequently requires employing a more flexible structure. Any game should be carefully tested and validated to ensure that it satisfies game objectives.

There are several trends in the development of games. These trends include a growth in the number and variety of games, the emergence of conversational games, and the continuing and expanding use of games as vehicles for studying human and organization behavior.

ASSIGNMENTS

10.1. In producing copper, one has to make decisions on a daily basis as to what ingredients should be thrown into the smelter. Many different ingredients can be used and still produce copper. The objective of this *production blending* is to minimize production costs yet satisfy constraints that the ingredients placed in the smelter produce copper. This problem is solved in some companies by using linear programming.

    Assume your objective is to develop a management game to instruct company personnel on how to apply linear programming to the copper blending problem. Describe the characteristics of a game that might serve this purpose.

10.2. A large number of management games have been developed. Using the following references, prepare a report on one of the following games.

    (a) Kolman J. Cohen, et al, "The Carnegie Tech Management Game," *Journal of Business* (October 1960), pp. 303–321.

    (b) Klaus Truemper and Burton V. Dean, "The OPRAD Research and Development Management Game," *Management Science* (February 1974), pp. 999–1009.

    (c) G. R. Andlinger, "Business Games—Play One!", *Harvard Business Review* (March–April 1958), pp. 115–125.

10.3. There is a continuing discussion of how complex games should be. Develop a list of advantages and disadvantages for simple and complex games.

10.4. Management games are widely used in most business schools. Survey your business school as to what games are being used and describe the games' characteristics.

10.5. In the chapter, the following noninteractive equation that relates total dollar sales to price was shown.

$$S_i = \$2,000,000 - 100,000\, p_i + 2000\, p_i^2$$

Over what range of p_i does this equation hold?

10.6. In the chapter, the following general form noninteractive equation that related total sales to price was presented.

$$S_i = c_1 - c_2\, p_i + c_3\, p_i^2$$

Modify this equation to include a term that shows that a change in marketing expenditures, m_i, from the previous period affects total sales.

10.7. In the chapter, equations for a hypothetical interactive game were given. Using these equations and the following data inputs, generate total dollar sales figures for the competing teams. The total market size is 1,000,000 units.

Team	m_i	r_i	p_i
1	$400,000	$100,000	$4.00
2	300,000	300,000	3.00
3	300,000	350,000	3.50

10.8.   In the chapter, Equation 10-6 described a situation where research and development expenditures have an immediate impact on sales. Revise the equation to show the impact when there is a one-period time lag before the impact is felt.

10.9.   In the chapter, Table 10.2 illustrated the effect of several variables, including competing teams' decisions on total sales. Using these data, compute the elasticity of demand for team 4 in moving from a selling price of $4.50 to $4. This figure can be found by calculating Δ total sales/Δ price.

10.10.   Described below is an inventory game developed by the author and Carl D. McDevitt. It provides an illustration of a functional, probabilistic, manual, individual played game. In preparation for playing the game the class should be divided into three groups: (1) Game developers, (2) Game administrators, (3) Game players.

After the game developers and game administrators have planned for conducting the game, actually play the game in class. This exercise should provide a better appreciation of the responsibilities of game developers and administrators, and the feelings experienced by game players.

Shown in Figure 1 are the introductory background statements given to the players. It describes the role that they are to assume. Figure 2 contains the game instructions. They should be carefully understood before play begins.

Instructions for players: Follow the directions of the game administrators. Your objective is to minimize the cost of carrying the item in inventory.

Instructions for game administrators: Play begins with a discussion of introductory background statements, game objectives, what decisions are required and game instructions. Information on weekly demand in the two markets and delivery times will be provided by the game developers. Your responsibility is simply to coordinate game play, communicate weekly demand levels and indicate when orders placed in previous weeks arrive, and at the close of the game lead a discussion of what inventory policies led to cost minimizing behavior. Be sure that an adequate supply of decision sheets are available.

The players should be told the following. "An initial order of 500 cases was placed by the Buying Committee and arrived after 2 weeks. An initial allocation of two cases per store has been completed. There are 101 stores. There have been no advertising other than 'new item' signs with the price, and current plans do not call for an organized campaign. Orders received from the stores the week following the initial allocation totaled 59 cases. This included 24 cases shipped to retail A stores and 35 cases shipped to retail B stores.

It is now week 2 and time for you, the inventory manager, to take control of the inventory system. The first inventory sheet should be marked to show the beginning inventory to be 239 cases (500 cases initial order, minus 202 initial allocation, minus 59 first week's orders). Enter the cost of carrying 239 cases in inventory as $23.90 (0.10 per case) and decide whether or not you want to place an order. After your ordering decision, you will be informed of any shipment received and given the sales amount for that week. Obviously, there will be no shipment arriving in week 2 since the initial order has already been received. After entering sales and cost data on the inventory form, compute ending inventory by subtracting total sales from beginning inventory adjusted for

Figure 1   Introductory Background Statements.

ALTERMAN FOODS INCORPORATED

An Inventory Game

The Buying Committee of Alterman Foods Incorporated has elected to offer a new laundry detergent under its private label to its retail A (regular) and retail B (discount) stores. This low phosphate detergent will be in tablet form and packed in a 49-ounce box. The company will buy the new product from a recently formed manufacturing firm on a trial basis. The Buying Committee wants to be very cautious about permanently adding this item to inventory until more information can be gathered as to how the product will sell and on the ability of the new manufacturer as a supplier.

As a buyer for Alterman Foods, you have been asked to personally manage the warehouse inventory for this new item during its trial period. There has been no previous test marketing, thus there is virtually no information available about either the demand for this product or about the ability of the new manufacturer as a supply source. This is the major reason for the cautious approach taken by the Buying Committee. One of your primary duties will be to become familiar with the demand and supply characteristics of this product through your experience in managing its inventory. In fact, you will be expected to assist the Buying Committee in evaluating this product for possible addition to the regular inventory.

Inventory policy for all Alterman's products stresses good service to the customer, while minimizing cost. Specifically, company policy directs you to:

1. Keep inventory at a level as low as possible to avoid carrying costs, breakage, and product obsolesence.
2. Minimize paper work of ordering, receiving, shipping, and so on. Don't order too often, it costs too much.
3. Never run out of stock. A disappointed customer may never return.

The company has developed cost figures to aid in measuring the success of each of its buyers in achieving low cost inventory service. The costs for the new detergent have been set as follows.

1. Cost of order processing: $10.00 per order.
2. Inventory carrying cost: 0.10 per case.
3. Stockout cost (lost sales): 10.00 per case.
4. Shipping cost: 0.50 per case.
    (from manufacturer to warehouse)

Sales in both retail A and retail B markets will be reported to you weekly and you may order each week to maintain the proper inventory level. Your goal is to maintain inventory such that both markets can be adequately serviced, but without incurring excessive costs. Your performance in dealing with the uncertainty in this situation will have an important impact on the future opportunities you will have with the company.

Figure 2   Game Instructions.

Week #_____   Name_____

Beginning Inventory _____   _____ Carrying Cost
                                                              ($0.10 per case)

Order_____ cases

Cases Received + _____   _____ Ordering Cost
                                                              ($10.00 per order)

from week _____   _____ Shipping Cost
                                                              ($0.50 per case)

Sales:

Retail A _____

Retail B _____

Total Sales _____

Ending Inventory _____   _____ Stockout (Lost sales)
                                                              ($10.00 per case)

                                     _____ Total Cost

This form will be used each week to record inventory transactions. The following sequence of steps describes the use of this form.

1. Enter your name.
2. Enter the beginning inventory level, based on the preceding week's ending inventory. Compute the cost of carrying that inventory at the rate of $0.10 per case.
3. Order the number of units you feel will be required for future sales in both markets. Enter the cost of placing this order. Cost is fixed for any size order at $10.00.
4. The game administrator will inform you of any orders received. Enter the number of cases received and compute the shipping cost at $0.50 per case.
5. The game administrator will inform you of sales in retail A and retail B stores. Enter these sales data and add to determine total sales. Compute ending inventory as beginning inventory plus cases received minus total sales. Compute stockout cost as $10.00 per case short.
6. Compute total cost as the sum of carrying, ordering, shipping and stockout costs.
7. Enter any positive ending inventory as the beginning inventory for the next week of play.

any arriving shipment. Ending inventory for week 2 becomes beginning inventory for week 3 (if positive) and the process starts all over again. Your goal throughout the process will be to provide adequate inventory without undue cost."

Instructions for game developers: The weekly demand in the two markets and the delivery times can be generated by the sampling procedures employed in a Monte Carlo inventory simulation. First develop demand and delivery time probability distributions. Then sample from these distributions and create a table for the game administrators along the lines suggested in the following table.

| | Demand | | Order Received |
Week	Retail A Demand	Retail B Demand	from Week N
1	24	35	—
2	.	.	—
3	.	.	.
.	.	.	.
.	.	.	.

It is your joint responsibility with the game administrators to decide on the number of weeks of play.

REFERENCES

Andlinger, G. T., "Business Games—Play One!," *Harvard Business Review* (March–April 1958): 115-125.

Babb, E. M., and L. M. Eisgruber, *Management Games for Teaching and Research* (Chicago, Ill.: Educational Methods, 1966).

Bellman, Richard et al., "On the Construction of a Multi-Stage, Multi-Person Business Game," *Operations Research* (August 1957): 469-503.

Butler, Richard J., Thomas F. Pray, and Daniel R. Strang, "An Extension of Wolfe's Study of Simulation Game Complexity," *Decision Sciences* (July 1979): 480-486.

Carlson, Elliot, "The Versatile Business Game: Its Growing Use in Industry," *Management Review* (September 1966): 45-47.

Cohen, Kalman, and Erich Rhenman, "The Role of Management Games in Education and Research," *Management Science* (January 1961): 131-166.

Dale, Alfred G., and Charles R. Klasson, "Business Gaming: A Survey of American Collegiate Schools of Business" (Austin: Bureau of Business Research, University of Texas, 1964).

Davis, K. Roscoe, and Bernard W. Taylor, III, "Addressing the Implementation Problem: A Gaming Approach," *Decision Sciences* (October 1976): 677-688.

Dill, William R., James R. Jackson, and James W. Sweeney, *Proceedings of the Conference on Business Games* (New Orleans: School of Business Administration, Tulane University, 1961).

Greenlaw, Paul S., "Designing Parametric Equations for Business Games," *Academy of Management Journal* (June 1963): 150-159.

Greenlaw, Paul S., and M. William Frey, *FINANSIM: A Financial Management Simulation* (Scranton, Pa.: International Textbook, 1967), and Paul S. Greenlaw, M. William Frey and Ivan R. Vernon, *FINANSIM: A Financial Management Simulation*, 2nd ed. (St. Paul, Minn.: West Publishing, 1979).

Greenlaw, Paul S., Lowell W. Herron, and Richard H. Rawdon, *Business Simulation in Industrial and University Education* (Englewood Cliffs, N.J.: Prentice-Hall, 1962).

Greenlaw, Paul S., and Michael P. Hottenstein, *PROSIM: A Production Management Simulation* (Scranton, Pa.: International Textbook, 1969). Rights subsequently acquired by Harper & Row, New York.

Greenlaw, Paul S., and Fred W. Kniffin, *MARKSIM: A Marketing Decision Simulation* (Scranton, Pa.: International Textbook, 1964). Rights subsequently acquired by Harper & Row, New York, N.Y.

Horn, Robert E., *Guide to Simulations/Games for Education and Training*, 3rd ed. (Cranford, N.J.: Didactic Systems, 1978).

Kibbee, Joel M., Clifford J. Craft, and Burt Nanus, *Management Games* (New York: Reinhold, 1961).

McDevitt, Carl D., and Hugh J. Watson, "An Assessment of Probability Encoding Using a Probabilistic, Noninteractive Management Game," *Academy of Management Journal* (September 1978): 451–462.

McGehee, William, "Business Games—Where They Fit into Training," *Textile World* (January 1966): 68–71.

Meier, Robert C., William T. Newell, and Harold L. Pazer, *Simulation in Business and Economics* (Englewood Cliffs, N.J.: Prentice-Hall, 1969).

Neuhauser, John J., "Business Games Have Failed," *Academy of Management Review* (October 1976): 124–129.

Orkin, Eric B., "HOTMAMA: A Computer Simulation Exercise to Sharpen Management Skills," *The Cornell H.R.A. Quarterly* (February 1979): 10–17.

Schott, Brian, "Using a Business Game to Teach Risk Management," *Journal of Risk and Insurance* (September 1976): 526–532.

Shim, Jae K., "Management Game Simulation: Survey and New Direction," *University of Michigan Business Review* (May 1978): 26–29.

Shubik, Martin, "Gaming: Costs and Facilities," *Management Science* (July 1968): 629–660.

Stewart, R., "A Survey of Business Games," *Simulation and Gaming: A Symposium*, *Management Report No. 55* (New York: American Management Association, 1961).

Strauss, Lance J., "Recent Trends in Management Gaming—A Comparative Survey of Management Gaming Practices in American Collegiate Schools of Business in 1962 and 1974," unpublished Master's thesis (Monterey, California: Naval Postgraduate School, 1974).

Thompson, Howard E., "Credit Union Management Game" (Madison: Graduate School of Business, University of Wisconsin, 1968).

Veglahan, Peter A., J. Ronald Frazer, and Michael R. W. Bommer, "Computer Simulation—Training Tool for Collective Bargaining," *Personnel Journal* (November 1978): 614–617.

Watson, Hugh J., and Carl D. McDevitt, "A Probabilistic, Noninteractive Management Game for Probability Encoding Studies," *Simulation and Games* (December 1977): 493–504.

Wolfe, Joseph, "The Effects of Game Complexity on the Acquisition of Business Policy Knowledge," *Decision Sciences* (January 1978): 143–145.

CHAPTER ELEVEN

CORPORATE SIMULATION MODELS

The Growing Use of Corporate Models

Applications of Corporate Models

Benefits of Corporate Models

Problems with Corporate Models

The Structure of Corporate Models

    Financial Models

    Marketing Models

    Production Models

Equations in Corporate Models

An Illustration

Programming Corporate Models

Developing Corporate Models

Teleglobe Canada's Corporate Model

    General Objectives, Applications and Development of the Model

    General Overview of the Model

    The Demand Module

    The Model's Computerization

    Implementation of the Model

    User's Interaction with the Model

    Validation

Summary

Assignments

References

Managing organizations in today's rapidly changing world is becoming increasingly complex. The availability of basic raw materials can no longer be taken for granted. Foreign competition is increasingly keen. Government regulations are assuming an ever growing role in organizational decision making. The fluctuating value of the dollar in international markets complicates foreign trade. In partial response to such complexities, many organizations are now developing and operating *corporate simulation models* (sometimes called *corporate models* or *corporate planning models*). These models attempt to provide *a link between decision making within the organization and conditions in the firm's environment.* As an illustration of this capability, William E. Scott, executive vice president with Public Service Electric Gas Company of New Jersey, has said of their corporate simulation model, "If an oil embargo were announced tomorrow, within 24 hours we would be able to know the major impact of it and begin reacting,"[1]

The purpose of this chapter is to examine the increasing use of corporate models by organizations, the applications for which corporate models are being used, their benefits and problem areas, their structure and types of equations required, and how corporate models should be developed. Then, in order to illustrate corporate models fully, a detailed description of one currently being used by Teleglobe Canada is presented.

THE GROWING USE OF CORPORATE MODELS

The future of corporate models seems especially bright. Lawrence Galitz has made the following prediction:

> *The day is not too far away when a meeting of a company's board of directors will be incomplete without the presence of a computerized model of the firm, whether the firm is a financial institution or a manufacturing company. As matters are raised and discussed, the suggestions will be fed to the model which will present, on a large display screen, their varied effects. The final judgments will naturally be left for the human decision-makers, but use of the model should improve the quality of those decisions.*[2]

Although it can be debated whether corporate models will actually be used *during* a board of directors meeting, it is significant that such a possibility has been seriously suggested.

Growth in the number of corporate simulation models has been rapid. In 1969, Gershefski was able to identify only 63 firms from a sample of 1900 that were actually using corporate models.[3] Five years later, Naylor and Gattis surveyed 1881 organizations that were thought to be either using, developing, or planning to develop a corporate simulation model. They found that "Of the 346 corporations that responded to the survey, 73 percent were either using or developing such a model. Another 15 percent were planning to develop a corporate planning model, and only 12 percent had no plans to develop

---

[1] "Computer Games that Planners Play," *Business Week* (December 1978): 66.

[2] Lawrence Galitz, "Modeling for Bankers," *The Banker* (December 1978): 36.

[3] George W. Gershefski, "Corporate Models—The State of the Art," *Managerial Planning* (November–December 1969): 1–6.

a planning model."[4]   All current indications are that corporate models are now playing an important role in corporate planning and decision making in many large organizations.

APPLICATIONS OF CORPORATE MODELS

Corporate models are being used for a number of applications in a variety of industries. Several examples illustrate this point.[5]   At Ralston Purina, whose food business is subject to the fluctuations of the commodities markets, a corporate model was used to determine what effect the sharp increase in corn and soybean prices, which occurred in the early 1970s, would have on the overall corporate plan.   Inland Steel credits its corporate model with stopping the company from spending $1.5 billion on an expansion program that would have been a financial disaster.   Memorex used a corporate model to negotiate a more favorable line of credit with a bank.   A Swedish shipyard employs a corporate model to determine which currencies to use when buying raw materials to build ships and which currencies to use when the ships are sold.   At United Air Lines a model is used to explore the effects of increases in the price of jet fuel.

In their 1974 survey, Naylor and Gattis investigated the applications of corporate models.[6]   As can be seen from Table 11.1, financial applications such as cash flow analysis, financial forecasting, and balance sheet projections are the most common.   This is not sur-

Table 11.1   APPLICATIONS OF CORPORATE MODELS

Applications	Percentage
Cash flow analysis	65
Financial forecasting	65
Balance sheet projections	64
Financial analysis	60
Pro forma financial reports	55
Profit planning	53
Long-term forecasts	50
Budgeting	47
Sales forecasts	41
Investment analysis	35

Source.   Thomas H. Naylor and Daniel R. Gattis, "Corporate Planning Models," *California Management Review* (Summer 1976): 71.

[4]Thomas H. Naylor and Daniel R. Gattis, "Corporate Planning Models," *California Management Review* (Summer 1976): 69–79.
[5]See "Computer Games that Planners Play," and Naylor and Gattis, op. cit., pp. 69–70.
[6]Naylor and Gattis, op. cit.

Table 11.2   APPLICATIONS OF CORPORATE MODELS

Applications	Percentage
Long range/strategic planning	24
Annual planning/profit planning/budgeting	30
Financial/economic/project analysis	46
	100

Source. G. R. Wagner, paper presented at the Thirteenth Hawaii International Conference on System Sciences, Honolulu, Hawaii, 1980.

prising, because most proposed organizational activities are analyzed in financial terms. However, as we will see later, corporate models often contain submodels that describe systems other than financial systems—such as marketing and production systems.

A more recent look at the applications of corporate models is provided by Wagner in a 1979 study.[7] He investigated the applications of corporate models in organizations using IFPS, a special-purpose planning language that was briefly described in Chapter 8. His findings, shown in Table 11.2, further support the notion that corporate models have a heavy financial emphasis.

BENEFITS OF CORPORATE MODELS

Organizations are deriving a variety of benefits from their corporate models. When used for strategic planning, corporate models provide "a tool for developing long-range plans, testing the effects of various planning strategies, preparing annual corporate budgets and short-term profit plans, and measuring the impact of changing conditions on various facets of the organization."[8]

Naylor and Gattis investigated the benefits and uses of corporate models in their study.[9] The data presented in Table 11.3 show the percentage of respondents who indicated the listed benefits were being realized. The ability to explore more alternatives, better quality decision making, and more effective planning headed the list.

PROBLEMS WITH CORPORATE MODELS

It is important to recognize that some users have reservations about their organization's corporate model. This was the finding of a 1977 survey directed to chief executive

[7]G. R. Wagner, paper presented at the Thirteenth Hawaii International Conference on System Sciences, Honolulu, Hawaii, 1980.
[8]Kuang-Chiau Chen, "Models-based MIS for Top Management," *Data Management* (November 1977): 25.
[9]Naylor and Gattis, op. cit.

Table 11.3   BENEFITS OF CORPORATE MODELS

Benefit	Percentage
Able to explore alternatives	78
Better quality decision making	72
More effective planning	65
Better understanding of the business	50
Faster decision making	48
More timely information	44
More accurate forecasts	38
Cost savings	28
No benefits	4

Source. Thomas H. Naylor and Daniel R. Gattis, "Corporate Planning Models," *California Management Review* (Summer 1976): 77.

officers in over 400 major corporations.[10]   Forty percent of the responding chief executives indicated that the effectiveness of their corporate model was no better than average, and only 6 percent claimed to be completely satisfied.

There is evidence, however, that some of the earlier problems with corporate models are being reduced or eliminated as greater experience in corporate modeling is gained and more organizations are using special-purpose planning languages in their modeling efforts. Naylor and Gattis in their 1974 survey found lack of flexibility, poor documentation, excessive data input requirements, inflexible output format, long development times, high development and operating costs, and users being incapable of understanding the model as problems with some organizations' corporate models.[11] Wagner's 1979 survey, however, found a smaller incidence of such problems.[12]

THE STRUCTURE OF CORPORATE MODELS

A corporate simulation model can be conceptualized as a model that describes the major functional areas of an organization, the interrelationships among the functional areas, and the organization's relationship to its external environment.[13] Figure 11.1 provides a schematic of this conceptualization. For many organizations there is a need to model the finance, production, and marketing areas. Econometric models may be used to obtain information about the external environment. The models are used on either a stand-alone basis or in an integrated manner.

[10] Ephraim McLean, UCLA, unpublished 1977 study on chief executive attitudes toward computer-based planning models.

[11] Naylor and Gattis, op. cit., p. 78.

[12] Wagner, op. cit.

[13] This conceptualization is suggested by Naylor and Gattis, op. cit.

Figure 11.1   The structure of a corporate model.

```
+---------------------------------------------------------+
|                                                         |
|   +-------------+           +-------------+             |  External
|   | Marketing   |           | Production  |             |  environment
|   | model       |           | model       |             |
|   +------+------+           +------+------+             |
|          |                         |                    |
|          +-----------+-------------+                    |
|                      |                            ----> |
|               +------+------+                           |
|               | Financial   |                     <---- |  Econometric
|               | model       |                           |  models
|               +-------------+                           |
|                                                         |
+---------------------------------------------------------+
```

In a multidivision company there may be models for each division.[14]   Figure 11.2 shows models for each division, with financial models at each division being linked to an overall corporate financial model. Financial models serve an integration role, because dollars are the common denominator for division activities. Once again, econometric models may be used to supply information about the external environment.

Figures 11.1 and 11.2 reflect an ideal. In actuality, many organizations do not have all the component models shown and/or do not have the amount of integration indicated. For example, some organizations have only a single overall financial model. Many do not have econometric models and rely instead on other sources of information about the external environment. Some models can only be used on a stand-alone basis rather than as part of an integrated modeling system.

Figure 11.2   A corporate model in a multidivision company.

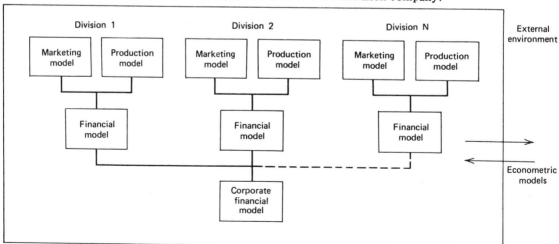

[14] Naylor and Gattis, op. cit., p. 72.

Let us now consider each of the component models in greater detail. We will refer to the conceptualization shown in Figure 11.2, even though it is more comprehensive and integrative than that which exists in many organizations. It represents an ideal for which many organizations might appropriately strive.

Financial Models

Financial models exist at both the division and corporate level. The division models describe financial activities in each division, whereas the corporate model consolidates all financial activity.

The overall corporate model has the capability for generating typical financial statements—pro forma income statements, cash flow statements, and balance sheets. It is through such statements that top management is able to assess the overall impact of changes in economic conditions, tax laws, and the like. The corporate model may require more than the simple addition of inputs from division models, for there may be complex transfers of funds between divisions.

Financial models at the division level tend to be less complex. They may explore division profits but other types of financial statements such as balance sheets may not be meaningful at this level. The division financial models require inputs from the marketing and production models. The marketing model provides unit and dollar sales figures. The production model generates production costs for alternative levels of output.

Marketing Models

The division *marketing models* provide unit sales, dollar sales, and market share forecasts by product or product group. Their use with the division financial model has already been mentioned. They can also be used on a stand-alone basis. For example, they might be used to evaluate the effect of promotion plans or price changes. The models may be relatively straight forward time series analysis models such as trend analysis, or more sophisticated econometric models that relate conditions in the external environment to internal variables of importance.

Production Models

The division *production models* are used to estimate operating costs and cost of goods sold when supplied with unit sales forecasts from the marketing models. These costs can then be supplied to the financial model for further consolidation. The model of the production system can also be used on a stand-alone basis. For example, alternative production schedules might be evaluated using the production model.

EQUATIONS IN CORPORATE MODELS

Having considered the overall structure of corporate models, let us now consider some of the details of their construction. A good starting point is to reconsider the distinction between definitional and empirically based equations, because both types play an important role in corporate modeling.

Definitional equations reflect relationships that have been defined to exist. For example, an important accounting relationship is that total costs equal total variable costs plus fixed costs ($TC = TVC + FC$). Accountants in developing their systems for analyzing cost data have found this to be a useful relationship. In Chapter 4, which discussed financial planning models, we used many definitional equations. Since financial models are critical components of corporate models, it is easy to see the importance of definitional equations to corporate models.

Empirically based equations are derived from empirical (historical) data. The model builder begins with some initial conceptualizations about the relationship between the dependent (forecast) and independent (predictor) variables. Data are then collected and analyzed using appropriate multivariate analysis methods (e.g., multiple regression analysis). Based on this analysis, a forecasting equation is developed. Empirically based equations can be thought of in terms of two different types: equations that show the relationship among variables completely *internal* to the organization and equations that relate *external* variables to internal variables of interest. Econometric models are this latter type of equation.

Definitional equations are usually far greater in number than empirically based equations because of the financial nature of most corporate models. This is fortunate, because empirically based equations are much more difficult to develop. The creation of empirically based equations requires a quantitatively trained model builder, good data, and computer software to perform the required analysis. Space and scope limitations do not allow us to explore the methods used in developing such equations and some of the problems that can be encountered. Naylor's book, *Corporate Planning Models*, provides a good coverage of the subject.[15]

Econometric equations can be especially troublesome to develop. In particular, they tend to demand a data base that many organizations do not have and do not care to develop. Some organizations respond by obtaining needed econometric-type inputs from organizations that provide such a service. A number of time-sharing service companies such as Data Resources, Inc., Lionel D. Edie, Interactive Data Corp., and Rapidata provide econometric modeling services on their network. Many companies do not use econometric models at all. The inputs that would be provided by econometric models are replaced by management's subjective beliefs about future conditions. In this situation the quality of any resultant analysis is dependent on management's judgment.

Equations in corporate models usually *describe* the modeled system rather than suggest optimality conditions. The reasons for this are well expressed by Galitz:

> *At first sight, it might seem that optimising models are superior to descriptive ones, because they actually produce decision strategies rather than merely evaluate them. However, optimising models have the drawback that the decisions they produce are very sensitive to the exact formulation of the criterion to be optimised and the constraints imposed. Yet it is extremely difficult to quantify these accurately. Moreover, the decisions produced by optimising models must be considered carefully, since most of these models assume certainty and produce no hedging strategies other than those forced by specific constraints ... Descriptive models can themselves be used to*

---

[15] Thomas H. Naylor, *Corporate Planning Models* (Reading, Mass.: Addison-Wesley, 1979), Chapters 5–7.

generate decision strategies by using a trial and error process, and subjective judgments and assessments can be made as the user goes along.[16]

Most corporate models are also typically used in a *deterministic* rather than a probabilistic manner. Although methods are available for probabilistic corporate modeling, this type of usage is not yet prevalent, for several reasons. First, probabilistic models are somewhat more difficult, costly, and time consuming to develop and operate. Also, they have greater data input requirements. In addition, there is the potential problem of interpreting the data output, because not all managers feel at ease working with probability concepts. Instead of a probabilistic analysis, management often performs a deterministic analysis and presents a variety of scenarios to the model for analysis. By exploring best, worst, and most likely conditions through the model, management can at least have insights as to the range of possible outcomes. This approach does not allow probability statements to be made, but does at least provide some measure of risk for the situation being analyzed.

Naylor and Gattis in their survey found the smallest number of equations in corporate models to be 20 and the largest number to be several thousand. The average number was 545.[17] Wagner in his study found the mean number to be 360.[18] Both these studies serve to show that corporate models do not need to contain a voluminous number of equations to be useful. In fact, a corporate model should not be a number crunching duplicator of an organization's accounting system. That much detail is not needed, is too costly to create and operate, has excessive data requirements, and probably creates managerial "information indigestion." On the other hand, too little detail may not foster user confidence. Benson states it this way:

There is a fine line between the detail required to generate confidence, and the detail that will encumber the model with an unmanageable data maintenance problem. The corporate model design that is too broad-brushed, and the design that is too detailed, have something in common: neither will serve more than one or two planning cycles before being shelved.[19]

The model builder is faced with the challenge of reducing the detail contained in financial documents, yet maintaining sufficient detail that the resulting documents are still meaningful and useful.

An Illustration

In order to illustrate the creation and use of equations in a corporate model, let us consider the Medical-Surgical Department budget from Chapter 4. Recall that it was used to show the application of simulation to financial planning. It clearly does not represent a large, complex or complete corporate model, but it is appropriate for our current purposes. The budget in its original form is shown in Table 11.4*a*; a reduced version is pre-

[16]Galitz, op. cit., pp. 33–34.
[17]Naylor and Gattis, op. cit., p. 75.
[18]Wagner, op. cit.
[19]Fred S. Benson, "The Corporate Model: Has Management Met the Challenge," *Managerial Planning* (November–December 1978): 16.

Table 11.4a   ORIGINAL MEDICAL-SURGICAL DEPARTMENT BUDGET

Salary and wages = $14,000 + 3.00 × patient-days + 100 × time
Payroll taxes and benefits = 1000 + .30 × patient-days + 10 × time
Operating supplies = 400 + .20 × patient-days + 5 × time
Laundry and linen = 800 + .45 × patient-days + 10 × time
Dietary transfers = 100 + .10 × patient-days + 1.00 × time
Education and travel = education and travel
Maintenance of equipment = 100 + 5 × time
Equipment rental = 300
Total expense = sum of all component expenses

sented in Table 11.4b. Note that many items have been combined. For example, salary and wages and payroll taxes and benefits have been aggregated into a line item called personnel costs. A similar aggregation has been used with many of the other items. For our purposes the aggregation shown in Table 11.4b is deemed appropriate; however, it might vary depending on the intended application of the model.

Our example involving a hospital's Medical-Surgical Department can also be used to show the potential integration between econometric and other types of equations. A look at the budgeting model in Table 11.4b reveals the need for a patient-days estimate. Recall that patient-days is the total number of days that patients spend in the Medical-Surgical Department. It is this type of input that we might expect from an econometric model. It is analogous to a unit sales estimate that might be provided by an econometric model. Our sample equation follows.

$$\text{Patient-days}_t = 1.01 \times \text{patient-days}_{t-1} + 0.002 \times \Delta \text{population} + \text{seasonal adjustment}$$

The model indicates that the patient-days in any time period t can be forecast by adding: (1) 1.01 times the patient-days in time period $t-1$, (2) 0.002 times the change in population in the area served by the hospital, and (3) a seasonal adjustment based on the month of the year. Table 11.5 illustrates the integrated functioning of the various equations. The analysis assumes that the patient-days in the current month is 900, next month's change in population is anticipated to be +500, and the seasonal adjustment for the next month is +100. Furthermore, the next time period is time = 4, and discretionary ex-

Table 11.4b   REDUCED MEDICAL-SURGICAL DEPARTMENT BUDGET

Personnel costs = 15,000 + 3.30 × patient-days + 110 × time
Operating costs = 1300 + .75 × patient-days + 16 × time
Discretionary expenses = discretionary expenses
Equipment costs = 400 + 5 × time
Total expense = sum of all component expenses

Table 11.5 INTEGRATION OF AN ECONOMETRIC MODEL WITH THE MEDICAL-SURGICAL DEPARTMENT BUDGET

$$\text{Patient-days} = 1.01(900) + 0.002(500) + 100$$
$$= 909 + 1 + 100$$
$$= 1010$$

- -

$$\text{Personnel costs} = 15,000 + 3.30(1010) + 110(4) = 18,773$$
$$\text{Operating costs} = 1300 + 0.75(1010) + 16(4) = 2121.5$$
$$\text{Discretionary expenses} = 300$$
$$\text{Equipment costs} = 400 + 5(4) = 420$$
$$\text{Total expense} = 18,773 + 2121.5 + 300 + 420 = \$21,614.50$$

penses of $300 are planned. Using these inputs, one calculates an estimated cost of $21,614.50.

PROGRAMMING CORPORATE MODELS

Corporate models can be programmed in virtually any procedure-oriented language. For example, BASIC, FORTRAN, or COBOL might be used. By selecting a language already available and used on the organization's computer, one avoids the cost of obtaining new software and then training personnel in the use of the software. However, although this is an option, many organizations elect to go with a language designed specifically for corporate modeling (e.g., IFPS, SIMPLAN, BUDPLAN, etc.). These languages generally have features that make them especially attractive. First, they are typically interactive, which provides users with fast response time. They tend to be sufficiently simple that even managers with little data processing and management science experience can use them. They have data analysis capabilities (e.g., regression, time series analysis) that are useful in creating and updating the corporate model. They have data management features that facilitate entering, maintaining, and extracting data from the data base. They have "what if" capabilities that allow alternative scenarios to be easily investigated. They often permit probabilistic and optimization analyses. Because of such features, we are really talking about a modeling language or system rather than a typical programming language.

The contrast between using a batch processing approach and the newer online languages such as IFPS for corporate modeling is shown in Figures 11.3 and 11.4. The batch processing approach is depicted in Figure 11.3 and contains many delays while the models are being developed and later operated. Also, note the nature of the interaction between the manager and the systems analyst. Instead of working concurrently in developing and operating the model, they function in a serial manner. The online approach is shown in Figure 11.4. Because it is online, there are fewer delays. In addition, the systems analyst and manager work as a team in developing and using the model. This approach not only speeds up the development of the corporate model, but also facilitates communication and understanding between the manager and the systems analyst.

Figure 11.3   The older batch processing approach to corporate modeling.

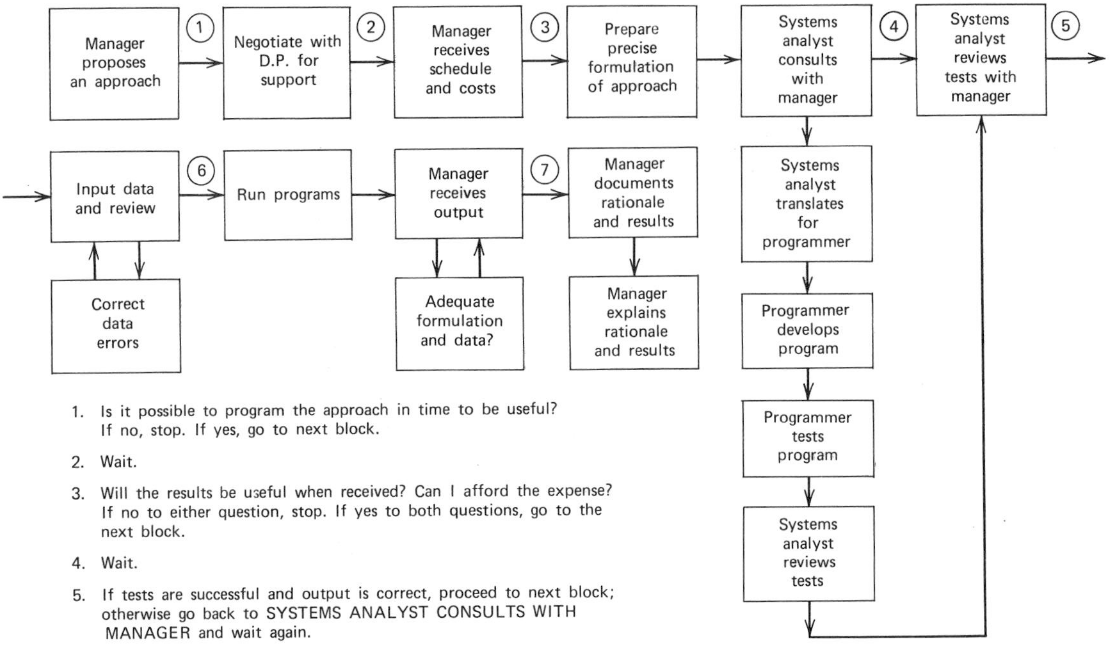

1. Is it possible to program the approach in time to be useful?
    If no, stop. If yes, go to next block.

2. Wait.

3. Will the results be useful when received? Can I afford the expense?
    If no to either question, stop. If yes to both questions, go to the
    next block.

4. Wait.

5. If tests are successful and output is correct, proceed to next block;
    otherwise go back to SYSTEMS ANALYST CONSULTS WITH
    MANAGER and wait again.

6. If data are correctly entered, proceed to next block; otherwise
    wait.

7. If outputs are reasonable, use them; if altered relationships, go to
    SYSTEMS ANALYST CONSULTS WITH MANAGER; if altered data,
    go to INPUT DATA & REVIEW and wait again.

*Source.   G. R. Wagner, "Enhancing Creativity in Strategic Planning Through Computer
Systems,"* Managerial Planning (*July–August 1979*), p. 13.

Access to a corporate modeling language can be obtained in several ways.[20] One alternative is to purchase the necessary software and implement it on the organization's computer. There are a number of companies that aggressively market their systems. The typical software cost is around $50,000. A method used by some companies that are evaluating different modeling languages is to create simple test data and relationships and to invite vendors to demonstrate their system in action.

Another option is to use a time-sharing network that offers a modeling language as part of its services. For example, Boeing Computer Services offers its Executive Information Services (EIS) on its network. Other languages offered by time-sharing vendors include EXPRESS on Tymshare, EPS on Data Resources, FCS on Comshare, XSIM on Interactive Data, NOMAD and EMS on National CSS, and SIMPLAN and RAMIS on Informatics. This approach is attractive for companies that at least initially want to avoid introducing a new language on their computer system. If the corporate model proves successful,

[20]Kenneth Ashcroft, "Selecting Modeling Packages," *Management Accounting* (April 1979): 107–108.

Figure 11.4   The newer online approach to corporate modeling.

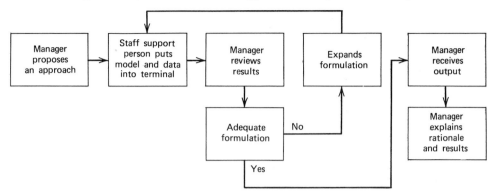

Source. G. R. Wagner, "Enhancing Creativity in Strategic Planning Through Computer Systems," Managerial Planning (*July–August 1979*), p. 13.

many companies ultimately obtain the required software to bring their model in-house. This normally encourages usage, provides greater security, and eliminates what can grow to be expensive time-sharing charges as use of the model grows.

DEVELOPING SUCCESSFUL CORPORATE MODELS

Experience has shown that the process followed in developing corporate models is closely related to the success of the modeling effort.[21] The primary focus should be on integrating the corporate model into the organization's planning processes. This means that the model builder must first understand the environment in which planning takes place. Included in this understanding is a knowledge of the organization's structure, management's philosophy and style, the external environment in which the organization competes, and how planning is carried out in the organization. Given this broad-based understanding, the specifications for the corporate model can then be established. This requires the joint efforts of end users and the model developers. Based on his experiences, Mann sees two golden rules for model development. The first is:

> *The model must be related to the real needs of the managers who are responsible for the running of the business. The model-builder must work closely* with *the manager, to understand his problems, to find a solution for use* within *the existing planning processes.*[22]

Once the specifications for the corporate model are determined, attention then turns to the resources required in order to meet the specifications. This concern must extend to

[21]See T. H. Naylor, "Integrating Models into the Planning Process," *Long Range Planning* (December 1977): 11–15.

[22]Chiu W. Mann, "The Use of a Model in Long Term Planning—A Case History," *Long Range Planning* (October 1978): 55.

required data bases, forecasting methods, models, reports, hardware, software, and human resources. Mann's second golden rule deals with the actual corporate model:

The model must be simple, it must avoid the pit of size. This can be achieved by constructing a system on the modular approach, building a step at a time.[23]

Keeping the model simple helps increase the chances that management will feel comfortable using it. When a modular approach is taken, successful early models create a constituency that is supportive of further model development. The development process for simulation models is discussed further in Chapter 13.

TELEGLOBE CANADA'S CORPORATE MODEL

Let us close this chapter with a detailed look at an actual corporate simulation model. The model described is being developed by Teleglobe Canada and some major components are currently in use. This model is representative of the kind of models found in a growing number of organizations.[24]

Teleglobe Canada is a corporation with a government charter to provide international telecommunication services between Canada and almost every other country in the world. It interfaces with domestic telecommunication carriers to provide facilities such as transoceanic cables and telecommunication satellites for a large variety of telecommunication services, both public and private, in areas such as voice, message, and data communications.

In 1977 Teleglobe began developing a corporate model to support the formal planning process. The purpose was to answer questions such as:

- How are the corporation's costs related to the growth in the demand for telecommunication services?
- Are the prices paid for labor, materials, and capital consistent with productivity, required rate of return, and developments in the external environment?
- How would profits be affected if the rates for a major service were reduced by 10%?

Answers to such questions were not readily available from the existing planning system.

General Objectives, Applications and Development of the Model

The general objectives of the corporate simulation model of Teleglobe Canada were defined as follows.

1. To analyze alternative scenarios and generate business plans based on varying assumptions regarding business policies and the external environment.
2. To relate the demand and supply for telecommunication services to socioeconomic variables and internal, controllable variables.

These objectives called for a model that related corporate revenue, expense, and profitability to two main sets of variables: (1) a set of *exogenous* variables over which the corporation has no control, such as those of the external economic environment, and (2) a

[23] Mann, op. cit., p. 55.

[24] The author would like to thank Ramin Khadem and Alain Schultzki for writing this description of Teleglobe Canada's corporate model. Both have played major roles in its development.

set of *endogenous* variables that are internal to the corporation and therefore controllable within certain boundaries. An example of the latter type of variable would be the price structure of the services offered to the public.

Teleglobe Canada's model functions using a top–bottom approach. More specifically, the estimation of revenues and expenses is done directly through a set of equations, and the estimated corporate position is then derived directly through the processing of these equations for a given set of assumptions. Therefore the model concentrates initially on the "big picture." This means, for example, that the total revenues from all services, or from each individual service, are analyzed directly.

The following analyses are typical of simulations that can be performed.

- Assess the impact of changing external environment variables on total service revenues.
- Assess the impact of strategic decisions such as a large price decrease in one of the services.
- Assess the cross-impact of various corporate decisions on different areas of the corporation.

The model has been a powerful research tool, which allows corporate analyses, allows testing of different scenarios and contingency plans, and supports the planning process.

The model was implemented on a computer in order to encourage widespread usage and to maintain low operating costs. An immediate answer, at minimal cost, then became possible for a large quantity of analyses. Furthermore, this implementation had to be such that the model was easily accessible to the average user and simple to use. Such computerization was accomplished through the use of a sophisticated corporate modeling software package named FCS/EPS.

Given the discussion of the objectives, general applications, and development of the model, an overview of the model itself is appropriate.

General Overview of the Model

A basic modeling assumption was that demand is determined more by the state of the economy than by the supply of services. It assumes, therefore, that demand is derived from economic factors external to the company rather than purely from policies set by the corporation.

A system of equations was developed to interrelate explicitly demand, supply, and the resulting financial position by drawing from and relying mainly on existing bodies of economic theory. These equations consider the influence of the national and international economy, as well as other environmental factors along with company and industry variables. From these equations, viable policy options open to the corporation can be examined and quantitative measurements of the impact of alternative policies can be evaluated. The diagram in Figure 11.5 summarizes this concept.

As can be seen, operating revenues are derived from the demand module and operating costs from the supply module. The difference between the two is the operating income.

The model is structured in three phases representing three different areas. These areas are seen in the general structural diagram presented in Figure 11.6.

PHASE I, the demand module, is composed of the following submodules: economic environment, prices and tariffs of services, demand, and revenues.

Figure 11.5   The model's concept.

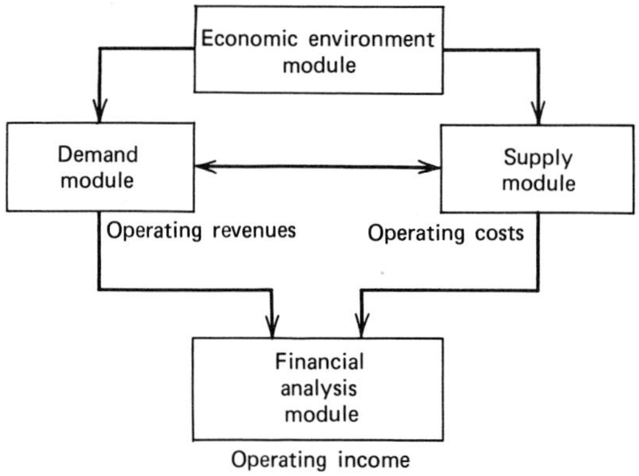

Economic environment module

Demand module ⟷ Supply module

Operating revenues   Operating costs

Financial analysis module

Operating income

PHASE II, the supply module, is composed of capital outlays and labor expenses, supply, and expenses submodules.

PHASE III is a comprehensive financial analysis module, which uses as inputs the outputs from the other phases.

Although phase I relates primarily to the function of the Marketing Department, phases II and III relate more specifically to Engineering and Operations, and Finance,

Figure 11.6   General structural diagram.

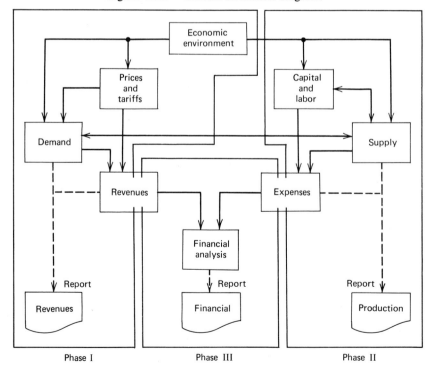

respectively. Phases I and II are independent modules in the sense that they can be operated independently of one another and generate their own reports, such as various traffic and revenue reports for phase I and production factors and expenses reports for phase II.

To give further insight into some of these submodules, the demand module has been selected for further discussion.

The Demand Module

The Demand Module is composed of the submodules shown in Figure 11.7. The forecasting approach used in the module is one that takes external forces directly into account. Another approach would have been to use extrapolative methods such as moving averages, exponential smoothing, or trend analysis. However, because extrapolative techniques essentially ignore the external environment, they were not deemed appropriate. Instead, an econometric approach was employed.

Two basic sets of equations are contained in the demand module: the real demand (traffic) type of equations, which are based on econometric modeling, and the revenue type of equations, which are definitional. These two types of equations are represented in Figure 11.8.

The economic environment consists of variables such as income, trade, immigration, and inflation, as well as institutional and structural variables such as number of telephones installed, habits, postal strikes, prices of substitute services, and so on. A forecast of the value of these economic and structural factors is stored in the economic environment submodule. The users can avail themselves of these prestored data when performing an analysis or can override them by entering user-supplied assumptions. The price vari-

Figure 11.7 The demand module.

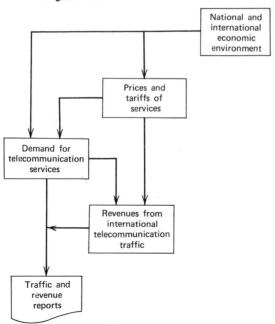

Figure 11.8   Demand and revenue equations.

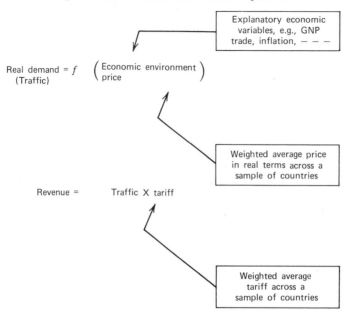

able of the traffic equation is a weighted average of the rate charged to the consumer for a specific service. Finally, the tariff variable is a weighted average of the rates across a sample of major countries representing the majority of telecommunication traffic with Canada. The price and tariff variables are stored in the prices and tariffs submodule. The user can vary these data, and thus analyze the impact of a proposed new tariff structure on traffic and revenue. The result of an analysis is formulated into an appropriate report submodule. The report can be standard or customized for a specific application. Figure 11.9 is a typical telephone traffic report showing the number of minutes of telephone communication originating in Canada and destined for other major countries.

Figure 11.9   A typical report.

	1979	1980	1981	1982	1983	1984
Great Britain	21,866	26,677	31,746	36,088	41,862	48,560
West Germany	4 774	5 827	7 164	9 113	10 844	12 796
Italy	5 568	7 016	8 665	11 114	13 448	16 138
France	3 538	4 316	5 179	6 423	7 451	8 643
Greece	2 493	2 992	3 590	4 452	5 209	6 042
Switzerland	1 258	1 503	1 946	2 392	2 775	3 191
Australia	1 001	1 161	1 335	1 517	1 699	1 886
Japan	945	1 200	1 500	1 869	2 224	2 602
Belgium	698	852	1 039	1 310	1 559	1 840
Total	42,141	51,589	62,164	74,278	87,071	101,698

Figure 11.10   Structure of the system.

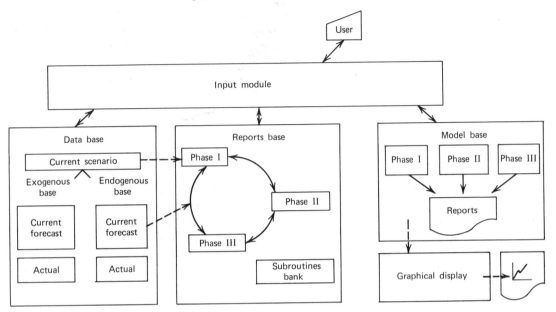

The Model's Computerization

Three main computer software components were required of the corporate model. These include: a data base, a model base, and a report base. In addition, an input module was required to ensure the proper interactive interface with the user. This general structure is represented in Figure 11.10.

The data base is used to store all values of variables, current and projected, and is organized in such a way that an analysis can be undertaken by varying predefined subsets of these variables. For instance, it is possible to see the impact of a 10 percent rate increase for telephone service to a specified group of European countries in the person-to-person class. The relevant data have to be sorted from the data base and the 10 percent increase has to be applied to it. The result is then stored temporarily in the current scenario base, from which it is made available to the model base. Directed by the input module, the appropriate equations in the model base are then activated and the result is made available to the report base. The user then selects the desired outputs from the report base in the form of a table or graph.

Implementation of the Model

From the outset, it was decided that one of the key features of the model should be simplicity of use by management as well as by analysts and technically oriented people. Its development was carried out by a team of specialists from different functional areas. This was done through regular consultation by the specialists. The users were given up-to-date presentations each time a working stage was completed in order to record comments and generate feedback essential before proceeding further.

Regarding the model's programming, it was decided to use a specialized modeling package instead of a conventional procedure-oriented language such as FORTRAN. Some of the main factors that led to the decision were: the programming time was estimated to be much lower; the programming could be done by nonprofessional programmers, thus allowing the specialists to concentrate on the model itself; easy modification and updating could be conducted on very short notice; customized applications could be devised by linking different blocks of the model in various ways at the user's command; and finally, overall implementation costs would be less expensive.

The decision to use a specialized modeling language was concurrent with the decision to use a computer service bureau instead of in-house processing facilities, because the service bureau selected offered specialized outside support in the development of the model. The FCS/EPS system was chosen after exploring many other special-purpose language and modeling systems. The package offers a user-oriented programming language that is powerful enough to be used by a beginner yet able to meet the needs of an experienced analyst. It also met the previously described required structure. In addition, the support offered by the service bureau was found to be good and the system allowed the possibility, if required, to be transferred in-house at the end of the development phase. In fact, such a transfer has recently been completed.

Users' Interaction with the Model

Let us now consider a typical user interaction sequence with the model. The sequence is indicated in Figure 11.11, which along with Figure 11.12 shows the various main options offered to the user. It can be seen that the user is directed in a tree-diagram fashion

Figure 11.11   Sample user-model interaction.

\>   Do you want an explanation of how to use the system?

*NO

\>   What analysis do you want to perform?

*7

\>   What level?

*1

\>   Do you want to perform a lookup or a scenario?

*2

\>   What scenario assumptions?

*2

\>   Is your scenario completed?

*YES

\>   What report do you want?

*6

Figure 11.12   Users' interaction options.

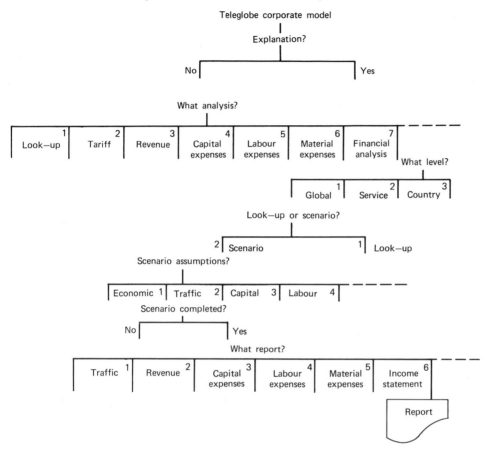

through a sequence of questions. Each particular answer steers the analysis toward a particular submodule. A complete interaction of questions and answers has the effect of interlinking all the requested submodules in the appropriate fashion followed by sequential step calculations.

Validation

In the final analysis, the proof of any model is found in its predictive powers. The model's validity was assessed, for example, by using the set of demand equations estimated over the period 1960 to 1975 to forecast and compare with actual demand values for the years 1976 to 1978. Results showed that the forecasted demand volumes were fairly close to what was actually experienced; for example, errors no larger than approximately 2 to 3 percent per annum for voice and message communications were found.

Also, insofar as the corporate model is ever evolving, it attempts continually to represent and simulate the changing aspects of the company's business within the industrial structure and the economy at large. In order that it meets this objective, the model is continually being validated for its performance versus actual occurrences.

SUMMARY

The external environment is becoming increasingly turbulent for many organizations. In partial response, corporate simulation models are increasingly being developed and used to support managerial planning and decision-making. These describe the functioning of the organization and its relationship to the external environment. The day is quickly approaching when virtually all larger organizations will have some type of corporate model.

Corporate models are being used for a variety of purposes and applications. Most of the applications are financial in nature—cash flow analysis, financial forecasting, balance sheet projections, and so on. This is not surprising because most organizational activities are eventually expressed in financial terms.

Corporate models offer a variety of benefits, including the ability to explore more alternatives, better quality decision-making, and more effective planning. Some corporate models do have problem areas, but many of these problems are being overcome as more corporate modeling experience is gained and the availability and use of special-purpose planning languages is expanding.

Corporate models vary in their structure, but many have marketing, production, and financial submodels that describe the internal functioning of the firm. Econometric models can be used to link the organization to its external environment. In the case of a multidivision company, the financial models at each division may be consolidated into an overall financial corporate model. Corporate models typically consist of definitional and empirically based equations, with the former dominating. Corporate models are usually operated in a descriptive, deterministic manner. The availability of special-purpose modeling languages has done much to encourage and facilitate the development of corporate models.

To enhance the chances of success, one should develop corporate models in a way so that they are integrated into the organization's planning processes. Two important points to remember are that the model builder must work closely with the manager during the development process and that the initial temptation to develop monolithic models should be resisted.

To illustrate a typical corporate model, Teleglobe Canada's has been described. It contains an economic environment module consisting of econometric equations that link the organization to the demand for telecommunication services. The demand module is used to forecast revenues, whereas the supply module estimates operating costs. The financial and economic analysis module receives inputs from the demand and supply modules and provides consolidated financial analyses and documents. Teleglobe Canada's model was computerized using a special-purpose modeling language available on a time-sharing network. Just recently the model has been moved in-house. The model is simple and easy to use and provides valid information to support managerial planning and decision-making.

ASSIGNMENTS

11.1.   Shortages of raw materials, foreign competition, government regulations, and the fluctuating value of the dollar were all suggested as occurrences in the external environment that are motivating organizations to develop corporate simulation models. Suggest other environmental forces that are also causing organizations to develop corporate models.

11.2. Lawrence Galitz has suggested the possibility that corporate models might be used during a board of directors meeting. Do you see this development taking place in organizations? Why? What factors might hinder such a development?

11.3. Assume that you are part of the top management group of a large textile firm and are advocating the development of a corporate simulation model. What reasons might you give for developing such a model?

11.4. Naylor and Gattis found lack of flexibility, poor documentation, excess data input requirements, inflexible output format, long development times, high development and operating costs, and users not being able to understand the model as potential problems with corporate models. To what extent are these problems reduced or eliminated with some of the newer online languages such as IFPS, when compared to predominantly batch-processing languages such as FORTRAN?

11.5. Corporate models frequently contain subsystem models for the finance, marketing, and production areas. For each of these areas, indicate information about the external environment that might be useful for planning and decision-making purposes.

11.6. The following is a financial model used by Contemporary Time Pieces. Identify the equations in the model as being definitional or empirically based.

$\text{Total revenue}_t = \text{selling price}_t \times \text{unit sales}_t$

$\text{Cost of goods sold}_t$

$\quad = 1.05 \times \text{fixed cost of goods sold}_{t-1}$

$\quad\quad + 1.10 \times \text{per unit cost of goods sold}_{t-1} \times \text{unit sales}_t$

Selling expense_t

$\quad = 1.10 \times \text{fixed selling expense}_{t-1} + 1.10 \times \text{per unit selling expense}_{t-1}$

$\quad\quad \times \text{unit sales}_t$

General and administrative expense

$\quad = 1.15 \times \text{fixed general and administrative expense}_{t-1}$

$\quad\quad + 1.05 \times \text{per unit general and administrative expense}_{t-1} \times \text{unit sales}_t$

$\text{Profit before taxes}_t$

$\quad = \text{total revenue}_t - \text{cost of goods sold}_t - \text{selling expense}_t$

$\quad\quad - \text{general and administrative expense}_t$

$\text{Profit after taxes}_t = 0.52 \times \text{profit before taxes}_t$

11.7. TAPPI is the Technical Association of the Pulp and Paper Industry. For its members it provides services such as sponsoring an annual meeting, trade shows, short courses, home study courses, and publishing a trade journal. Each of its major activities is treated as a project center with its own revenue and expense budget. The line item budget for short courses follows.

Income		
Short courses registration fees		*XX*
Expenses		
Salaries	*X*	
Benefits	*X*	
Rent	*X*	
Telephone	*X*	
Office postage	*X*	
Office printing	*X*	
Travel	*X*	
Computer services	*X*	
Meeting supplies	*X*	
Word processing	*X*	
General and administrative	*X*	*XX*
Net Position		*XXX*

Assume that you are an analyst assigned to develop a corporate model for TAPPI. If you were to develop an econometric model to forecast total enrollment in short courses for the year, what independent variables would you consider using? For the expense items, what type of equations would you use and how would you develop them? What aggregation of expense items would you consider?

11.8.   The total expenses for a Medical-Surgical Department were calculated in Table 11.5 to be $21,614.50 based on a patient-days forecast of 1010. Management is interested in how high the expenses might go if actual patient-days are 1200. Provide this estimate for management.

11.9.   Century Products wanted to explore the profitability of a proposed new product. In order to assess the product's potential, Marketing Research Associates (MRA) was hired to analyze the proposed product. The following is a portion of MRAs report:

It is difficult to assess with certainty how any new product will do. The best that can be done is to quantify the uncertainty that exists. We believe that the proposed product has an economically useful lifetime of five years. The total market for the product at the time of introduction should be 500,000 units per year and this market should grow at a rate of 10 percent per year. At a price of $9 per unit, we believe that the product can capture a significant share of the total market. We believe that the market share at that price can be estimated to be normally distributed with a mean of 5 percent and a 95 percent probability that it is between 3 and 7 percent.

In order to incorporate this information into an analysis, the following planning model was prepared:

New Product Planning Model

Total market = 1.10 × previous total market
Sales volume = market share × total market
Gross sales = 9.00 × sales volume
Cost = overhead + sales volume × unit costs
Net profit = gross sales − cost
Initial investment = initial investment
Discount rate = 0.15
Net discounted present value = NDPV (net profit, discount rate, initial investment)

Century Products estimates that overhead costs for the proposed product are described by the triangular distribution with most optimistic, most likely, and most pessimistic costs of $10,000, $12,000, and $15,000, respectively. Unit costs are also believed to be described by the triangular distribution with most optimistic, most likely, and most pessimistic costs of $6.50, $6.75, and $7.25, respectively. The initial investment is thought to be uniformly distributed between $90,000 and $100,000. For analysis purposes, Century Products uses a discount rate of 15 percent.

(a) Does the new product planning model fit within the category of a corporate model? Why or why not?

(b) Identify the external, probabilistic, deterministic, policy, lagged output, and output variables in the model.

(c) What is the data source for the external variables? Could econometric models have been used? Explain.

(d) Create and run a computerized model that prepares a probabilistic estimate of the proposed product's net discounted present value. Base your analysis on 100 iterations. Place the output in a probability distribution with 10 classes.

(e) Do you recommend introducing the proposed new product? How much risk is involved?

REFERENCES

Ashcroft, Kenneth, "Selecting Modeling Packages," *Management Accounting* (April 1979): 107–108.

Benson, Fred S., "The Corporate Model: Has Management Met the Challenge," *Managerial Planning* (November–December 1978): 13–16.

Ben-Yaacov, G. Z., "A Computer-Based Modeling System for Electric Utility Planning," *Long Range Planning* (December 1978): 30–36.

Chen, Kuang-Chiau, "Models-based MIS for Top Management," *Data Management* (November 1977): 23–27.

"Computer Games That Planners Play," *Business Week* (December 1978): 66.

Galitz, Lawrence, "Modeling for Bankers," *The Banker* (December 1978): 33–36.

Gershefski, George W., "Corporate Models—The State of the Art," *Managerial Planning* (November-December 1969): 1-6.

Howard, K., and B. V. Wagle, "A Modeling System for Local Government Resource Planning," *Long Range Planning* (August 1978): 77–83.

Jackson, Barbara B., and Benson P. Shapiro, "New Way to Make Product Line Decisions," *Harvard Business Review* (May-June 1979): 139–149.

Jenkins, D. Terry, "Playing Games with Your Mix," *Pension World* (April 1979): 20-22.

Naylor, Thomas H., *Corporate Planning Models* (Reading, Mass.: Addison-Wesley, 1979).

Naylor, Thomas H., and Daniel R. Gattis, "Corporate Planning Models," *California Management Review* (Summer 1976): 69-78.

Rodriguez, Jaime I., and William R. King, "Competitive Information Systems," *Long Range Planning* (December 1977): 45–50.

CHAPTER TWELVE   # ADDITIONAL SIMULATION TECHNOLOGY

Experimental Design

Time Advance Methods

Variance Reduction Techniques

    Antithetic Variates

    Correlated Sampling

    Use of Variance Reduction Techniques

Planning the Run Time

    Transient and Steady-State Conditions

    Obtaining the Desired Statistical Precision

Validation

    Intended Use

Benefits and Costs

Type of Simulation Model

Scientific Philosophy

Simulation-like Methods

Statistical Analysis of Output

Summary

Assignments

References

Simulation as a method of analysis is somewhat deceptive. With very little study it is possible to build models for interesting and useful applications. This characteristic undoubtedly partially accounts for simulation's popularity. The deception occurs if one is led to believe that all of the applications and technology can be easily and quickly mastered. This is simply not the case. There always seems more to learn—more applications, more probability distributions and process generators, more random number generation methods, more special-purpose simulation languages, and more statistical analysis methods.

This chapter presents additional technology useful in developing simulation models. We will look at experimental design, time advance methods, variance reduction techniques, planning the run time, validation, and statistical analysis of simulation output. The order of presentation will roughly correspond with the way these topics are encountered in the model development process.

EXPERIMENTAL DESIGN

A model is developed to supply needed information or to analyze a specific problem. That is, a simulation model is used with some purpose in mind. Three common purposes are to:[1]

1. Compare means and variances for output variables under different system conditions.
2. Determine the importance or effect of different variables.
3. Identify optimal conditions for a set of variables.

The design of a simulation experiment must include a multitude of considerations, which vary all the way from the broad managerial to the highly technical. In the most global use of the term, *experimental design* encompasses the entire spectrum of considerations. However, in this chapter we will explore the technical aspects of experimental design and postpone the discussion of the broader, more managerial aspects until the next chapter.

There are many technical aspects of experimental design. Some have already been discussed. For example, we have considered random number generation, process generators, and special-purpose simulation languages. Others such as statistical analysis of simulation output and variance reduction techniques are covered later in this chapter. Now, however, we are going to consider experimental design as it is sometimes used in a more restricted sense. In this context, experimental design is concerned with efficiently and effectively determining the importance or effect of different variables on system behavior.

Obtaining information about the importance or effect of variables, especially in large simulation models, can be quite expensive. Each iteration through a large model can consume a large amount of machine time. And when there are many variables whose impact are to be explored, simply "running the machine" may not be practical or feasible.

A study of a highway paving operation provides a good case in point.[2] The contractor

---

[1] Robert E. Shannon, *Systems Simulation* (Englewood Cliffs, N.J.: Prentice-Hall, 1975), p. 150.

[2] E. L. Bidewell, "Simulation in GPSS/360 of a Highway Paving Operation Using a Mobile Control-Mix Plant with Different Haul Truck Speeds and Fleet Size Combinations," *Proceedings of Winter Simulation Conference* (1971).

was considering 19 different fleet sizes (1–18 and 21 trucks), 4 different rates of progress ($\frac{1}{2}$, 1, 1$\frac{1}{2}$, and 2 miles per day), and 3 average truck speeds (15, 30, and 45 mph). The total number of combinations that could have been simulated was 19 $\times$ 4 $\times$ 3 = 228, which would have required 200 hours of computer time.

Problems of this type are not limited to simulation modeling. For example, agricultural experiments are often concerned with determining crop yields with different soil, temperature, and fertilization conditions. Because of the wide-spread nature of experimental design problems, many statistical methods have been developed to maximize the information yield from a given experiment. Although these methods in general go beyond the scope of this book, many excellent references cover this topic.[3] Most involve the use of regression and analysis of variance techniques in their functioning.

Experimental design (in the more limited use of the term) focuses attention on two types of variables—*factors* and *responses*. They can be thought of in terms of input and output variables, respectively, although a factor can also be a different configuration of a system. In the highway paving model previously mentioned, the fleet size, rate or progress, and average truck speed would be factors. The time to complete the project would be a response.

Experimental designs can be either *single* or *multiple-factor* experiments, depending on the number of factors that are allowed to vary. In the highway paving example, a multiple-factor design was obviously required, because fleet size, rate of progress, and average truck speed could all be varied.

Experiments can employ either a *full* or *fractional* factorial design. With a full factorial design, all the factors are allowed to vary over their entire range. Simulating the full 228 combinations of the factors in the paving example would involve a full factorial design. Obviously, however, full designs can be prohibitively expensive and a fractional design is sometimes required. For example, in the paving illustration, if fleet sizes of 1, 11, and 21 trucks, paving rate of $\frac{1}{2}$, 1$\frac{1}{2}$, and 2 miles per day, and average truck speeds of 15, 30, and 45 miles per hour were simulated, the number of combinations would be reduced to 3 $\times$ 3 $\times$ 3 = 27. Obviously, this approach provides less information than a full factorial design but is frequently adequate for identifying the factors with the greatest impact.[4]

We have only briefly considered the nature and some of the terminology associated with experimental design. Full courses are devoted to the subject at many universities. It illustrates an earlier point—as one gets deeper and deeper into the study of simulation, a desire develops for a greater knowledge of modeling, mathematics, statistics, and computer science.

TIME ADVANCE METHODS

When developing a simulation model, one must give thought to the time advance method used. As mentioned previously, simulation models can move through time on either a next-event or a fixed-time increment basis. With a *next-event* simulation, the clock is al-

---

[3] W. J. Dixon and E. J. Massey, Jr., *Introduction to Statistical Analysis* (New York: McGraw-Hill, 1957) and C. R. Hicks, *Fundamental Concepts in the Design of Experiments*, 2nd ed. (New York: Holt, Rinehart and Winston, 1973).

[4] Shannon, op. cit., p. 150.

Figure 12.1   Next-event and fixed-time increment simulations.

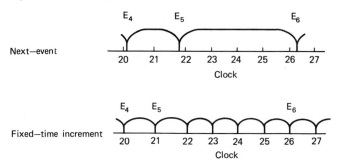

ways updated to the time of the next event. This time advance method was seen in the queuing model presented in Chapter 7. With a *fixed-time increment* simulation the updating of the clock always involves adding a fixed-time amount to the current clock reading. The Monte Carlo inventory simulation in Chapter 3 used a fixed-time advance.

The two methods of moving a simulation model through time are illustrated in Figure 12.1. With the next-event time advance, the clock moves from 20.1 to 21.8 to 26.3 as events E_4, E_5, and E_6 occur. With the fixed-time increment advance, the clock moves forward in fixed-valued time units.

Sometimes the type of simulation model being developed strongly influences or dictates the time advance method. For example, financial planning simulations call for a fixed-time increment, because plans are commonly made on a daily, weekly, monthly, or annual basis. On the other hand, a simulation of a fire-fighting system would probably employ a next-event time advance, because there may be relatively long intervals between fire occurrences.

The use of a special-purpose simulation language typically determines the time advance method employed. Most special-purpose languages such as GPSS, SIMSCRIPT, and GASP employ next-event time advances. However, special-purpose financial planning languages such as IFPS use a fixed-time increment advance.

There are situations where either time advance method can be employed. For example, in a Monte Carlo inventory simulation it is possible to simulate on a next-event basis when and how much demand occurs and when orders are placed and received. Likewise, in a queuing simulation, it is possible to employ a fixed-time increment advance and after each advance determine whether a service arrival, service completion, or end of simulation has taken place.

Several factors need to be taken into consideration when there is some freedom in selecting a time advance method. One is the ease of incorporating the required logic into a computer program. In general, fixed-time increment models require simpler logic than next-event models. This point can be seen by recalling the detailed logic that went into the FORTRAN-based queuing model of Chapter 7.

Another factor in the selection decision is computer running time. A next-event simulation model requires more running time to execute its time advance logic. On the other hand, a fixed-time increment model typically has advances to points in time where no events have occurred. This possibility can be seen in Figure 12.1. Although it is difficult to be specific on whether a next-event or fixed-time increment method will minimize computer running time, the attractiveness of a fixed-time increment advance obviously increases when the probability of an event happening in a time unit is high.[5]

Another factor that should be mentioned is the precision of the information provided by the alternative time advance methods. Information about the behavior of a system is lost, no matter how small the time unit, when a fixed-time increment advance is used. The intuitive logic of this statement can be seen by once again considering Figure 12.1. Note that with the fixed-time increment method the occurrence of events is by necessity rounded off to the next-time interval. Such is not the case with next-event simulations. Gafarian and Ancker provide quantifiable suggestions as how to select the time unit in fixed-time increment models so that the loss of information is controlled.[6]

VARIANCE REDUCTION TECHNIQUES

When computers were much slower than they are today, considerable thought went into planning *probabilistic* simulation experiments. This planning sometimes resulted in the use of methods that are now referred to as *variance reduction techniques.*[7] When correctly applied, these techniques provide variance-reduced estimates of a system's properties. Stated differently, the use of variance reduction techniques makes it possible to improve the statistical precision of the information gained from the output of a simulation experiment.

There are a variety of variance reduction techniques. Some of the more popular ones include stratified sampling, importance sampling, Russian roulette and splitting, antithetic variates, and correlated sampling.[8] In order to provide insights into the functioning and potential value of variance reduction techniques, we will now describe antithetic variates and correlated sampling.

Antithetic Variates

One of the more useful variance reduction techniques involves employing *antithetic variates.* To illustrate, assume that we are interested in estimating the properties of a probabilistic output variable called Z. In order to estimate Z's properties, we create two estimators of Z, call them X_1 and X_2. Each estimator is comprised of a series of statistically independent observations; however, there is a negative correlation between the observations for the two estimators. The mean estimate of Z is then given by Equation 12-1,

$$\overline{Z} = \frac{\overline{X_1}}{2} + \frac{\overline{X_2}}{2} \tag{12-1}$$

[5]An approach to quantifying the time advance decision is presented in R. W. Conway, B. M. Johnson, and W. L. Maxwell, "Some Problems of Digital Systems Simulation," *Management Science* (October 1959): 92–110.

[6]A. V. Gafarian and C. J. Ancker, "Mean Value Estimation from Digital Computer Simulation," *Operations Research* (January–February 1966): 25–44.

[7]Originally these techniques were referred to as "Monte Carlo methods" but use of this rather all-inclusive term caused confusion and led to the current terminology.

[8]An introductory discussion of these techniques can be found in Shannon, op. cit. pp. 197–205. More detailed treatments are available in J. Hammersley and D. Handscomb, *Monte Carlo Methods* (New York: Wiley, 1964) and Jerome Spanier and Ely M. Gebbard, *Monte Carlo Principles and Neutron Transport Problems* (Reading, Mass.: Addison-Wesley, 1969).

with a variance given by Equation 12-2.

$$\sigma_Z^2 = \frac{\sigma_{X_1}^2}{4} + \frac{\sigma_{X_2}^2}{4} + \frac{1}{2} \text{Cov}(X_1, X_2) \tag{12-2}$$

Notice in Equation 12-2 that when X_1 and X_2 are negatively correlated, the covariance term causes the estimate of the variance of Z to be reduced. Variables X_1 and X_2 are referred to as "antithetic variates," because they mutually compensate for each other's variations.

The most common way of providing a negative correlation between two estimators is by controlling the random numbers used with the input variables. As Fishman describes it, "the objective is to induce negative correlation between corresponding elements of the random number streams used to generate input variates. . . . The intuitive feeling is that some of the negative correlation between inputs finds its way to the corresponding output, and hence a variance reduction is realized."[9]

An application of this technique was employed by Page in the simulation of a single-channel, single-phase queue of the type described in Chapter 7.[10] First, arrival times and service times were simulated using the random number streams A_i and B_i, respectively. Next, the simulation was rerun using $1 - A_i$ and $1 - B_i$ for the arrival and service times. Each run provided an estimator of the queuing system's properties, but the observations for each estimator tended to be negatively correlated.

Page also realized a variance reduction using a second approach. First, estimates of the system's properties were obtained using random number streams C_i and D_i, respectively, for the arrival and service times. Then the simulation was rerun using D_i's for the arrival times and the C_i's for the service times. This flip-flopping of the random number streams resulted in negatively correlated output and, consequently, a variance reduction.

Correlated Sampling

Another useful variance reduction technique is *correlated sampling*. It is used when the purpose of the analysis is to compare alternatives. The alternatives might be, for example, different policy decisions or configurations of a system. In such comparisons, attention typically focuses on a difference in means between the alternatives.

To illustrate, assume that there are two alternatives and their attractiveness is measured by the output variable X_1 for the first alternative and X_2 for the second alternative. Of interest, then, is the difference between X_1 and X_2. Call this difference Z. The mean difference is given by Equation 12-3,

$$\bar{Z} = \bar{X}_1 - \bar{X}_2 \tag{12-3}$$

and the variance of Z is given by Equation 12-4.

$$\text{Var}(Z) = \text{Var}(X_1) + \text{Var}(X_2) - 2\,\text{Cov}(X_1, X_2) \tag{12-4}$$

[9]George S. Fishman, *Concepts and Methods in Discrete Event Digital Simulation* (New York: Wiley, 1973), p. 319.
[10]E. S. Page, "On Monte Carlo Methods in Congestion Problems: II. Simulation of Queuing Systems," *Operations Research* (March–April 1965): 300–305.

It is possible to reduce the variance of Z by having the values for X_1 and X_2 positively correlated. The more positively correlated the output, the greater is the covariance between X_1 and X_2, and the smaller is the variance of Z. As with antithetic variates, the correlation is controlled through the random number streams used with the input variables. However, with correlated sampling a positive correlation is introduced, whereas with antithetic variates the correlation is kept negative.

The Monte Carlo inventory simulation of Chapter 3 provides a good illustration of the use of correlated sampling. Recall that various Q and R combinations were simulated in order to identify the least cost combination. Of fundamental interest was the difference in mean costs for the various combinations. Although our justification at the time was based on intuition, it was suggested that it was useful to use the same random number streams when generating the demand and delivery time patterns. When the same random numbers were used, the weekly cost figures for the alternative Q and R combinations tended to be positively correlated. Now we can see that this procedure increased the precision of our experiments.

Use of Variance Reduction Techniques

Despite the intuitive appeal of variance reduction techniques, in practice they do not appear to be widely used for several reasons. First, today's fast computers have somewhat negated their importance. Second, many analysts may not be aware of the existence of the techniques, because they are usually given minimal coverage in most simulation courses and books. Third, even if the techniques are known, the analyst may be uncertain as to how to apply them in a particular situation. Many of the most impressive applications of variance reduction techniques have been with simple models. However, with more complex models, application of the techniques is not always clear. It has even been cautioned that if the analyst's intuition is faulty in applying certain techniques, the variance in the model's output can actually be greater than had the technique not been applied.[11] Fortunately, faulty intuition is unlikely to worsen the situation when antithetic variates and correlated sampling are used. Fourth, it is not simple to estimate in advance how much savings the variance reduction technique will cause. Such an analysis is complicated by the fact that most simulation output are not independent observations. Also the analyst is typically uncertain as to how much of the negative correlation induced into the input variables will filter through to the output. For these reasons it is not too surprising that many analysts ignore the application of variance reduction techniques and simply increase the number of iterations.

PLANNING THE RUN TIME

Before operating a simulation model, one must plan in advance the period of time to be simulated and analyzed. This decision depends heavily on whether the analyst is interested in transient, steady-state, or both conditions. In the case of probabilistic models, care must also be taken to control sampling error to the desired level.

---

[11]Herman Kahn, "Use of Different Monte Carlo Sampling Techniques," *Symposium on Monte Carlo Methods*, H. A. Meyer, ed. (New York: Wiley, 1956).

Transient and Steady-State Conditions

Simulation models must be started with some *initial conditions*. Recall, for example, the need to establish an initial balance in the Monte Carlo inventory simulation. In a queuing simulation, it is necessary to specify how many elements, if any, are in the queue when the simulation begins. These initial conditions are frequently referred to as *starting conditions*. The selection of starting conditions depends primarily on which aspects of a system's behavior are being investigated.

The analyst may be interested in transient, steady-state, or both conditions. *Transient conditions* refer to temporary behavior of a system when it first starts. For example, the first customers entering a bank in the morning find all of the tellers and bank officers available for service. This condition is transient in that it will only last until the queues begin to fill up. Eventually the banking system reaches *steady state* as typical operating conditions evolve. Transient and steady-state conditions are illustrated in Figure 12.2.

When transient conditions are of interest, starting conditions that reflect how the real-world system appears at start-up should be selected. For example, in a production system there may be an interest in how long after start-up it takes for the system to reach the desired production rate. Depending on the system, this may involve a completely empty system or perhaps one with some work in process. After the simulation reaches steady-state conditions, it can be stopped because the desired information has been obtained.

In some cases, only steady-state conditions are of interest. For example, at a fast food hamburger operation there may be little interest in how demand for service builds up to the noon rush hour. Rather, the concern may be over how well the system can hold up to steady-state lunch hour operating conditions.

Two approaches can be used to gather information on steady-state behavior. The first is to select starting conditions for the system that are reflective of how the system appears in steady state. With this approach the simulation should not have any transients. In some cases, however, appropriate starting conditions may not be known in advance. This is typically the case when a new system is being designed. An approach that can be used is to simulate the system's behavior from start-up to steady state, but postpone the collecting of any statistics until after transient conditions have passed.

When both transient and steady-state conditions are of interest, the simulation is run

Figure 12.2   Transient and steady-state conditions.

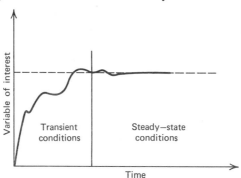

for a sufficiently long time so that both can be observed. Starting conditions reflective of the real-world system at start-up are used. Statistics at several points in time are gathered and output so that the analyst has information on both transient and steady-state system behavior.

Obtaining the Desired Statistical Precision

With probabilistic simulation models the analyst must also think about obtaining the desired statistical precision. The duration of the simulation must be long enough so that the possibility of sampling error is controlled to the desired level. There are several approaches to this problem.

One possibility is to make the run time sufficiently long so that any possible sampling error is obviously controlled. For very simple simulation models this approach is sometimes justifiable. However, for many simulation models this approach causes needlessly excessive machine costs. In fact, an important reason that a deterministic rather than a probabilistic model is often used is simply to keep the costs of the modeling effort down. Consequently, simply "running the machine" is normally not a recommended procedure.

A preferred alternative is to specify the allowable amount of error and the desired level of statistical precision, and then solve for the length of the run. This approach is normally possible when the simulated observations are statistically independent, or nearly so, because the simulation's output is equivalent to randomly sampled observations. Just as in simple random sampling one can solve for the sample size, likewise it is possible to determine the number of iterations to perform.

As an example, assume that management wants to simulate the firm's mean annual profit for some future year within ±$25,000 with a 95 percent degree of confidence. The population standard deviation is $100,000. This situation is visually presented in Figure 12.3. The required computations shown in Table 12.1 reveal that 61 iterations should be run.

Our previous example was somewhat unrealistic in that the population standard deviation was provided as given information. Unfortunately, this is not usually the case. If it were, it is likely that the entire distribution is well understood and there would be no

Figure 12.3   Determining the number of iterations.

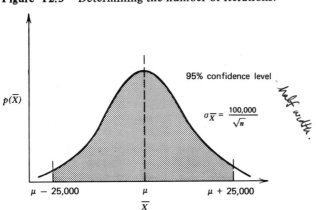

Table 12.1   DETERMINING THE NUMBER OF ITERATIONS

$$Z = \frac{X - \mu}{\sigma/\sqrt{n}}$$

$$Z = 1.96 = \frac{(\mu + 25{,}000) - \mu}{100{,}000/\sqrt{n}}$$

$$1.96 = \frac{25{,}000}{100{,}000/\sqrt{n}} \qquad \text{for a 95\% confidence interval}$$

$$\sqrt{n} = \frac{1.96\,(100{,}000)}{25{,}000}$$

$$n \cong 61$$

need for a simulation. The more common situation is one where the population standard deviation must be estimated. In some cases an intelligent subjective estimate is possible, whereas in others it is hard to estimate in advance the dispersion on the distribution of interest. In the former case a subjective estimate can be used. Then after the simulation has been run, a check can be made to see if the estimate of the standard deviation was indeed a good one. Only if the standard deviation has been underestimated should the simulation be rerun with more iterations.

Pilot study. When no intelligent estimate of the standard deviation is possible, the model can be run for a short period of time to obtain an estimate of the standard deviation. This estimate is then used in determining how many iterations to run.

An alternative that does not require stopping the model is to build an *automatic termination condition* into the computerized model. This is a mechanism that automatically stops the simulation when a preprogrammed condition occurs. In our case, it would terminate the simulation when the desired statistical precision has been obtained. Here is how it might work. After every iteration the standard deviation on the output variable of interest would be recalculated. Then the standard error of the mean would be determined based on the number of iterations that have been run. If the standard error has been reduced enough to give the desired precision, preprogrammed logic shuts off the simulation with appropriate output being provided. The macrologic for an automatic termination condition of this type is shown in Figure 12.4.

Solving for the number of iterations by the methods just illustrated assumes that the output observations are statistically independent. As mentioned previously, many simulation models generate output that is autocorrelated. If an estimate of the population standard deviation is inferred from the output of autocorrelated data, the tendency is to *underestimate* the true population standard deviation. The consequence is that fewer iterations are run than is actually necessary. It is beyond our scope to discuss statistical methods for determining the number of iterations when output observations are autocorrelated, but a rule-of-thumb can be suggested: simply *double* the standard deviation estimate and solve for the number of iterations using the methods described in this section.

Figure 12.4 Flowchart of the macrologic for an automatic termination condition.

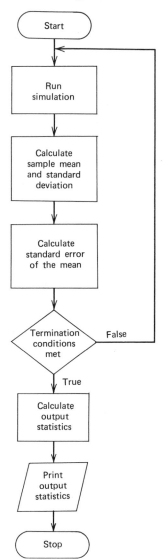

VALIDATION

The validation of a model must include two groups—the *model builders* and the *end users*. The model builders must be certain that the model is valid from a technical perspective. Furthermore, they must work with users in such a way that the users are convinced that the model is valid. These are different, yet clearly interrelated concerns. In this chapter we will discuss the technical aspects of validation and save for the next chapter the discussion of how to develop valid models from the users' perspective.

Because there are a number of considerations, the validation of a model can be time consuming and difficult. The model builder must take into account the model's intended use; the benefits and costs associated with various degrees of validation; the type of simulation model developed; and, to a limited extent, the model builder's philosophy on scientific inquiry. These are important, interrelated, and potentially trouble-laden considerations. They make validation, as Naylor and Finger describe it, "the most elusive of all the unresolved methodological problems associated with computer simulation techniques."[12]

Intended Use

A simulation model is developed with some intended use in mind. Possible uses include, but are not limited to:

1. Assisting in the design of a system.
2. Evaluating proposed plans and policies.
3. Improving decision-making skills.
4. Freeing a human decision maker.

Given this wide variety of uses, obviously there are differences in validation procedures. Instead of a "total" validation, a logical approach is to validate the model only in terms of its intended use. For a model that simulates human decision making, it may be satisfactory to validate only the model's output rather than the way the model generates the output. In a management game that teaches the use of standard financial statements, it may be relatively important that the game model is a great simplification of reality. In a financial planning model used to support strategic decision making, it is often unimportant when variables are aggregated in a way that would never appear on a profit and loss statement. In other words, validation procedures depend on the model's intended use.

Benefits and Costs

In general, the more resources dedicated to a model building and validation effort, the better should be the model that is developed. But from a benefit-cost point of view, incremental expenditures to increase model validity may not be justified by incremental benefits. Anshoff and Hayes have suggested that the benefit-cost curves often look like those shown in Figure 12.5.[13] The maximum benefit-cost ratio is reached at some point before an absolutely valid model. With this benefit-cost orientation to validation, much of the validation problem becomes an optimization problem. Van Horn states it as, "in concept at least, validation reduces to a standard decision problem—to balance the cost of each action against the value of increased information about the validity of an insight."[14]

---

[12] Thomas H. Naylor and J. M. Finger, "Verification of Computer Simulation Models," *Management Science* (October 1967): B92.

[13] H. I. Anshoff and R. L. Hayes, "Role of Models in Corporate Decision Making," *Proceedings of IFORS Sixth International Conference*, Dublin, Ireland (August 1972).

[14] Richard L. Van Horne, "Validation of Simulation Results," *Management Science* (January 1971): 248.

Figure 12.5   Benefit-cost curves relative to model validity.

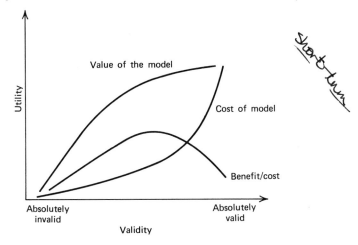

Type of Simulation Model

Because there are so many different types of simulation models, validation procedures must often vary from model to model. For example, probabilistic simulation models require validation procedures not needed with deterministic models. Games used for studying human behavior place the validation effort more on the gaming environment than on the game itself. The validation of simulation models of existing systems differ from the validation of models for proposed systems. Given the large variety of simulation models, then validation procedures must also vary.

Scientific Philosophy

Historically, there have been disagreements between *rationalists* and *empiricists* as how to best conduct scientific inquiries. However, both philosophies have contributions to make when considering the validation of simulation models. First, let us briefly consider the basic tenets of rationalist and empiricist thought and then see how they can be jointly used in validating simulation models.

A rationalist (as does an empiricist) begins by observing the world about him or her. Based on observations, the rationalist formulates what the philosopher Immanuel Kant (1724–1804) called the *synthetic a priori*. These are premises of unquestionable truth.

> *We do not need controlled experiments to establish their validity: they are so much the stuff of our everyday experience that they have only to be stated to be recognized as obvious.* [15]

Given these premises, model building becomes an exercise in logic and mathematics. Validation procedures consistent with this philosophy involve examining the basic assump-

---

[15] Lionel Robbins, *An Essay on the Nature and Significance of Economic Science* (London, England: Macmillan, 1935), p. 80.

tions underlying the model and other relationships that are logically derived from the basic assumptions.

Empiricists, on the other hand, reject the notion of synthetic a priori. Nothing is taken as given. Everything should be subject to empirical verification.

They insist that observation is the primary source of the ultimate judge of knowledge, and that it is self-deception to believe the human mind to have direct access to any kind of truth other than that of empty logical relations.[16]

From a modeling perspective, an empiricist demands that all relationships and equations be based on empirically based observation and testing. Validation procedures focus on empirically testing the relationships in the model with real-world data.

In actuality, there are few, if any, pure rationalists or empiricists. Most scientific inquiries depend at least somewhat on empirical data in the model development process. Likewise, almost all modeling efforts assume certain relationships as "givens."

Just as rationalism and empiricism usually come together in model development, they also make joint contributions to model validation. As a first step in validation, the assumptions that underlie the model should be examined. This step calls for objective introspection on the part of the model builder, perhaps consultation with outside experts, and reading literature relevant to the model-building effort. This is the rationalist approach to validation.

The second step is empirically to test relationships used in the model. For example, χ^2 tests might be used to compare theoretical distributions used in the model with data recorded from the system in operation. This is the empiricist approach to validation.

Both of these steps require ensuring that the model is correct in a logic and a programming sense. For example, Meier, Newell, and Pazer suggest the following checks.[17]

1. Run the computerized model for a short time period so that results can be compared with hand calculations.
2. Run separate segments of complicated models alone so that results can be verified.
3. Eliminate random elements from stochastic models and run them as deterministic models.
4. Replace complex probability distributions with elementary ones so that results are more easily verified.
5. Construct simple test situations that test as many combinations of circumstances in the model as is feasible.

When a simulation model's output is ultimately compared with the behavior of the real-world system, we have the final step in what is called *multistage validation.*[18] With this approach, we rethink the assumptions underlying the model, test relationships used in the model against empirical data, and compare the model's output with output from

[16] Hans Reichenback, *The Rise of Scientific Philosophy* (Berkeley: University of California Press, 1951), pp. 73–74.

[17] Robert C. Meier, William T. Newell, and Harold L. Pazer, *Simulation in Business and Economics* (Englewood Cliffs, N.J.: Prentice-Hall, 1969), p. 294.

[18] Thomas H. Naylor, et al., *Computer Simulation Techniques* (New York: Wiley, 1966), p. 314–315.

the real-world system. A variety of statistical tests can be used with the final stage and care must be taken when selecting which ones to use.

Simulation-Like Methods

In previous chapters we have seen simulation-like methods that do not generate time series data. In most cases their validation requires as much in terms of ingenuity as statistical expertise. Let us briefly consider the validation of simulation-like methods.

Model sampling can involve difficulties in that the model's output is a probability distribution, whereas the real-world system provides only the single actual occurrence. Even when the actual outcome was predicted as having only a small probability of occurrence, it is incorrect to assume that the model is invalid. Unlikely things do happen in the real world. Likewise, just because the actual occurrence was close to the mean of the probability distribution, it is not safe to assume automatically that the model is valid. Only after the model has been used for a while and a number of occurrences of the real-world system have been recorded can the model's predictive powers be tested. Then it is possible to apply regression analysis to the actual occurrences and the means of the predicted probability distributions. The test involves seeing whether the regression of the means against the actual occurrences has a slope and intercept significantly different from 1 and 0, respectively. Prior to the availability of a sufficient quantity of historical data, all the analyst can do is check the validity of the assumptions that underlie the model, explore the relationships captured in the model, investigate the correctness of the data inputs being used with the model, and perform "face validity" on the model's output (check its reasonableness).

Simulations of human decision making create unique validation problems. A most obvious validation procedure is to test the model's output against the decisions made by the human. But even this relatively straightforward procedure is complicated by the fact that human decision makers are usually inconsistent and the modeling effort normally does not intend to capture this inconsistency. Consequently, subjectivity enters into the validation procedure as the analyst attempts to decide when the decision maker might have been inconsistent. When the model also attempts to replicate the human's thought processes, the validation problem intensifies. The most common approach involves comparing traces from the simulation with the decision maker's protocol. Not only is this comparison often difficult to make, our current knowledge of how the brain processes data into decisions makes it uncertain whether the protocols verbally expressed accurately reflect human cognitive processes.

A management game represents another simulation-like method with interesting validation problems. The validation of a game depends heavily on the game's use. When the game is employed for instructional purposes, the validation should focus on whether the game is satisfying its stated learning objectives. When a game is used for operational gaming, validation should ensure that the game provides an accurate representation of the real-world system. Games used for studying human and group behavior should create a realistic environment for conducting the study. When a game is employed for evaluating personnel, there is a strong responsibility to ensure that game performance is closely related to actual performance in the real world.

From this brief discussion it should be obvious why the validation of simulation models creates methodological problems. Because of differences in the model's intended use, benefit and cost considerations, type of simulation model developed, and beliefs as to the best way to conduct a scientific inquiry, every validation effort becomes a somewhat unique experience.

STATISTICAL ANALYSIS OF OUTPUT

References have been made at several points to the statistical analysis of the output from simulation models. In particular, caution has been expressed in regards to the analysis of autocorrelated data. There are also potential problems when the output includes data from both transient and steady-state conditions. In this section we will explore these two areas in greater detail and suggest some appropriate analysis procedures.

Earlier we discussed transient and steady-state conditions. In a probabilistic simulation, transient conditions present a *nonstationary stochastic sequence*, because the system's statistical properties are changing over time. The analysis of certain aspects of nonstationary sequences is more complex than with stationary ones.[19] If the property of interest is a mean, such as for waiting time, there are no problems as long as it is remembered that the mean represents a performance measure of a nonstationary system. The difficulties arise when a variance is estimated. This might be the case when the analyst wants to prepare a confidence interval around a mean waiting time. Estimating the population variance in this case requires advanced statistical methods.[20]

Another source of difficulty in the analysis of simulated data is that the output from simulation models is often *autocorrelated*. Queuing systems, for example, usually generate autocorrelated output. As with nonstationary processes, the mean estimate creates no special problems. It is primarily variance estimates that pose analysis difficulties. Several approaches can be used in this situation.[21]

1. Independent replications.
2. Spectrum analysis.
3. Autoregression analysis.
4. The batch method.

The *independent replications* approach requires repeating the simulation a number of times with all conditions the same except for the random numbers used. The performance measures from each replication are then taken as independent observations. Each one can then be used in estimating a variance for that performance measure. Although this approach is neither conceptually nor statistically difficult, it can require massive amounts of computer time, which can make its use infeasible.

Spectrum and autoregression analysis are two other alternatives. Unfortunately, both require the analyst to be highly skilled in time series analysis.

The *batch method* involves breaking a simulation run into a number of separate periods

[19] See George S. Fishman, *Concepts and Methods in Discrete Event Digital Simulation* (New York: Wiley, 1973), Chapter 10.

[20] Ibid.

[21] George S. Fishman, "Grouping Observations in Digital Simulation," *Management Science* (January 1978): 510–521.

or batches. System performance measures are then recorded for each batch. The objective is to have each performance measure in each batch be an independent observation from every other batch. Statistical tests such as runs tests can be used to ensure that they are indeed independent observations. Each observation can then be used in making a variance estimate. An advantage of the batch method over the independent replications approach is that it does not require reinitializing starting conditions.

As an example of the statistical analysis of autocorrelated output, let us consider the batch method. It will be applied to the single-channel, single-phase queuing model presented in Chapter 7. The system performance characteristic of interest will be the steady-state average time in the waiting line when the arrival and service rates are Poisson distributed at 15 and 18 workers per hour, respectively. These are the same data inputs and characteristic of interest that were used in Chapter 7 and led to Figure 7.6.

A review of Figure 7.6 shows that the average time in the waiting line approaches the steady-state time of 0.2766 hours after about 6 hours of simulated time. Consequently, it is safe to say that after 8 hours the transient conditions are gone and the system is in steady state. Consequently, batches beginning after 8 hours can be assumed to include only steady-state conditions.

Each batch should be sufficiently long so that the average time in the waiting line for each batch is independent from the average times for the other batches. As a rule-of-thumb, this objective is best realized by having fewer batches of longer duration than more batches of shorter length. In our example, each batch will be 8 hours long and a total of 20 batches will be analyzed.

Appropriate changes to the FORTRAN-based queuing model must be made, in order to collect data on each batch. These changes include: collecting no statistics until after 8 hours, computing the average time in the waiting line for each batch, and reinitializing the statistics-gathering variables after each batch. Running the model with these changes led to the 20 average waiting times that are shown in Figure 12.6.

The next step is to test whether the 20 batch means are statistically independent. A variety of tests can be used for this purpose, but we will employ only a runs up and down test. This and other appropriate tests were described in Chapter 6 when the testing of random number generators was considered.

Figure 12.6   The means for each eight-hour batch.

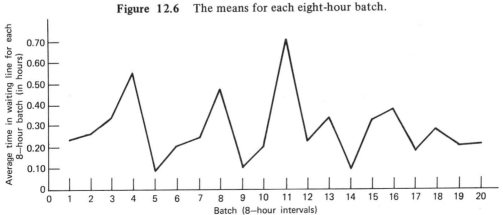

Table 12.2   RUNS UP AND DOWN TEST FOR THE MEANS OF THE 20 BATCHES

$\overline{w}_i$'s: 0.2383, 0.2595, 0.3425, 0.5617, 0.0947, 0.2082, 0.2664, 0.4919, 0.1067,
             +   −   +   −

0.2107, 0.7207, 0.2446, 0.3565, 0.1014, 0.3654, 0.4117, 0.1946, 0.3129,
   +   −   +   −   +   −   +

0.2095, 0.2235
   −   +

Number of runs = 13

$$\mu = \frac{2N - 1}{3} = \frac{2(20) - 1}{3} = 13$$

$$\sigma^2 = \frac{16N - 29}{90} = \frac{16(20) - 29}{90} = 3.23$$

$$\sigma \cong 1.8$$

For a 95% confidence interval

$$R_1 = 13 - 1.96(1.8) \cong 9.5$$

$$R_2 = 13 + 1.96(1.8) \cong 16.5$$

Table 12.2 shows the calculations for the runs up and down test. The actual number of runs up and down was 13, which was also the expected number. Consequently, the 20 mean waiting times easily pass this test of independence and we continue to assume that the means are statistically independent.

We are now close to our objective—an unbiased estimate of the variance of the means on which a confidence interval on the mean waiting time in the line can be based. We

Table 12.3   MEAN AND VARIANCE CALCULATION FOR THE MEANS OF THE 20 BATCHES

$$\overline{\overline{w}} = \frac{\sum\limits_{i=1}^{20} \overline{w}_i}{n} = \frac{(0.2383 + 0.2595 + \cdots + 0.3129)}{20} = 0.2961$$

$$s_{\overline{w}}^2 = \frac{\sum\limits_{i=1}^{20} (\overline{w}_i - \overline{\overline{w}})^2}{n - 1} = \frac{(0.2383 - 0.2961)^2 + (0.2595 - 0.2961)^2 + \cdots + (0.3129 - 0.2961)^2}{19}$$

$$= 0.02496$$

$$s_{\overline{w}} = 0.158$$

Figure 12.7   A 95% confidence interval for mean time in the waiting line.

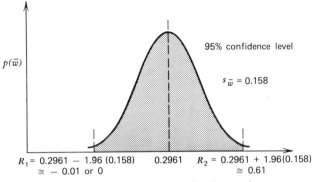

$R_1 = 0.2961 - 1.96\,(0.158)$ 0.2961 $R_2 = 0.2961 + 1.96\,(0.158)$
$\cong -0.01$ or 0 $\cong 0.61$

Average time in waiting line (in hours)

move in this direction by making a variance calculation using the means from the 20 batches. This calculation, along with an overall mean calculation, is shown in Table 12.3. Figure 12.7 graphically shows a 95 percent confidence interval for the average time in the waiting line using the results of the calculations from Table 12.3.

As a practical matter when deviations from statistical independence are believed or found through testing not to be too great, the formulas for simple random sampling can be used with some trepidations. However, as Fishman states in discussing a confidence interval for a mean estimate, "When we suspect that the assumption of independent disturbances is false we should regard the confidence interval that it provides to be at best, a 'ball-park' interval estimate of μ."[22]

SUMMARY

Interesting and useful simulation models can be developed after only limited exposure to the technology of simulation. One quickly discovers, however, that there is much that can and should be learned in order to become a skilled builder of simulation models.

In the broadest use of the term, experimental design includes the entire spectrum of considerations involved in designing an experiment. In a more restricted use of the term, experimental design is involved with the efficient and effective design of an experiment in order to determine the effect of different variables on a system's behavior. It is concerned with a system's responses to different factors. Depending on the number of factors that are allowed to vary, the experiment is either single or multiple factor. Depending on whether the factors are or are not varied over their entire range, the experiment is either a full or fractional factorial experimental design.

Simulation models employ either a next-event or fixed-time increment advance, depending on whether the clock is updated to the time of occurrence of the next event or by a fixed amount. The selection of the time advance method depends on factors such as the application, the programming language being used, computer running time, and the required precision of the information being generated.

[22] Fishman, *Concepts and Methods in Discrete Digital Simulation*, op. cit., p. 290.

Variance reduction techniques can be used to obtain variance-reduced estimates of a system's properties. There are a number of techniques that can be used, but antithetic variates and correlated sampling are among the most popular. Antithetic variates introduce a negative correlation into sampled values for the input variables, whereas correlated sampling uses positively correlated values.

Before operating a simulation model, one must give thought to the period of time to be simulated and analyzed. The analyst may be interested in transient, steady-state, or both conditions depending on which characteristics of a system's behavior are of interest. This in turn influences what initial or starting conditions are used and the period of time over which data are collected and analyzed. In probabilistic simulation models, attention must also be given to controlling the possibility of sampling error. When the simulation's output observations are statistically independent or nearly so, the formulas and methods from simple random sampling can be used to determine the number of iterations.

Validation is perhaps the most vexing of methodological problems associated with simulation. Appropriate validation procedures depend on the intended use of the model, benefit-cost considerations, type of model, and, to a limited extent, one's philosophy on scientific inquiries. Whenever possible, multistage validation is recommended. The required steps include questioning the basic assumptions that underlie the model (the rationalist approach), empirically testing the relationships used in the model (the empiricist approach), and comparing the model's output with data recorded from the real-world system. Validation procedures for simulation-like methods such as model sampling, gaming, and simulation of human decision making vary tremendously because of their somewhat unique nature and use.

The statistical analysis of output from simulation models becomes complex when preparing variance estimates if the output contains data for both transient and steady-state conditions or if the output is autocorrelated. Methods such as independent replications, spectrum analysis, autoregression analysis, and the batch method can be employed with autocorrelated data.

ASSIGNMENTS

12.1. An inventory control manager wants a Monte Carlo inventory simulation run on an expensive inventory item. It is believed that the optimal order quantity and reorder point lies somewhere between 50 to 100 and 25 to 50 units, respectively. Using experimental design concepts and terminology:
  (a) What are the factors and responses in this situation?
  (b) Describe a full experimental design.
  (c) Describe a fractional experimental design.

12.2. In Chapter 2 the following simulation applications were described. What type of time advance was probably employed and why?
  (a) Air Canada's cash budget simulation.
  (b) Bethlehem Steel's machine shop planning and scheduling simulation.
  (c) the advertising media simulation model.
  (d) the simulation of tar sands mining operations.
  (e) the affirmative action simulation model.
  (f) the simulation model for valuing a property-liability insurance agency.

(g)   the simulation model for real estate investment analysis.

(h)   the fire-fighting system simulation model.

(i)   The Georgia econometric model.

(j)   the Club of Rome's world dynamics model.

12.3.   Antithetic variates as a variance reduction technique can be employed in the simulation of queuing systems. First, the arrival and service times are simulated using random number streams A_i and B_i, respectively. Then the simulation is rerun using $1 - A_i$ and $1 - B_i$ for the arrival and service times. The characteristic of interest is then estimated by computing the mean from the output of the two runs. Modify the single-channel, single-phase tool crib operation model given in Table 7.5 of Chapter 7 so that antithetic variates can be used with it. This will require creating separate random number streams for the arrival and service times. Run the modified model twice using antithetic variates with a Poisson arrival rate = 8/hour, a Poisson service rate = 16/hour, for a duration of 4 hours on each run.

12.4.   Management is interested in assessing next year's income before taxes. A preliminary model sampling study suggests an income before taxes of $400,000 with a standard deviation of $200,000. How many iterations must be run in the final study if management wants a mean estimate within ±$30,000 with a 95 percent confidence level?

12.5.   A mathematical model has been developed that simulates the behavior of a mechanical system. Of particular interest is the system's mean time to failure. The analyst wants to estimate this mean ±30 hours with a 90 percent degree of confidence. Write a program segment for an automatic termination condition to control the number of simulated failures.

12.6.   Simulation models of the following systems have been built with the stated objectives in mind. In each case indicate whether the analyst is most likely interested in transient, steady-state, or both conditions.

(a)   A model of an electrical system that will have to withstand a high voltage pulse at system start-up.

(b)   A model of an assembly line employed to evaluate the efficiency of alternative line balancing schemes.

(c)   A demographic model used to analyze the effect that population growth will have on available health service facilities.

(d)   A model to simulate and evaluate the effectiveness of a head-start learning program.

(e)   A model of the national economy used to evaluate the stimulus provided by a tax cut.

12.7.   The FORTRAN-based model of a single-channel, single-phase tool crib operation presented in Chapter 7 utilized the same source of random numbers in determining the arrival and service times. However, this approach does not lend itself to replicating experimental conditions. Modify the program shown in Table 7.5 so that separate strings of random numbers are available for the arrival and service times. This objective might be accomplished in one of two ways: (1) Before running the simulation, store separate random number streams in two arrays, and (2) use a second random number generator. Using one of these approaches, rerun the queuing simulation of Chapter 7 with the same data inputs employed there (arrival rate = 15/hour, service rate = 18/hour, hours simulated = 8).

12.8.   In this chapter the batch method for analyzing correlated output was illustrated. The FORTRAN-based single-channel, single-phase queuing model of Chapter 7 was modified to produce average waiting times for 20 batches of 8 hours' duration. Repeat the analysis described in the chapter except make the batches 4 hours instead of 8. If your batch means are statistically independent, proceed with the analysis until you have a 95 percent confidence interval on the mean time in the waiting line.

12.9.   In this chapter it was mentioned that the weekly total cost figures for a Monte Carlo inventory simulation tend to be autocorrelated. An estimate of first-order autocorrelation can be obtained by calculating the correlation between total cost(week(t)) and total cost(week$(t-1)$). Estimate the first-order autocorrelation contained in the weekly total cost figures of Table 3.4 in Chapter 3. Use the following equation where the X_i's represent total cost(week(t)) and the Y_i's the total cost(week$(t-1)$):

$$r = \pm \frac{n \sum X_i Y_i - \sum X_i \cdot \sum Y_i}{\sqrt{\left[n \sum X_i^2 - \left(\sum X_i \right)^2 \right]\left[n \sum Y_i^2 - \left(\sum Y_i \right)^2 \right]}}$$

12.10.   In Chapter 3 a Monte Carlo inventory simulation was run in order to estimate the mean cost associated with a particular Q and R combination. The worksheet for the simulation was presented in Table 3.4. At that time it was pointed out that the weekly total cost figures were autocorrelated. This condition complicated establishing a confidence interval about the mean because of the problem of determining an unbiased estimate of the population standard deviation. A possible solution to the problem described in this chapter involves employing independent replications. Replicate the simulation shown in Table 3.4 four additional times using different random numbers. The five means can be averaged into a final mean estimate. A standard deviation of the five means can be computed to estimate the standard error of the mean. Based on this approach, prepare a 95 percent confidence interval for the mean cost.

REFERENCES

Cochran, W. G., and G. M. Cox, *Experimental Design*, 2nd ed. (New York: Wiley, 1957).

Conway, R. W., B. M. Johnson, and W. L. Maxwell, "Some Problems of Digital Systems Simulation," *Management Science* (October 1959): 92–110.

Dixon, W. J., and E. J. Massey, Jr., *Introduction to Statistical Analysis* (New York: McGraw-Hill, 1957).

Emshoff, James R., and Roger L. Sisson, *Design and Use of Computer Simulation Models* (New York: Macmillan, 1970).

Fishman, George S., "Estimating Sample Size in Computing Simulation Experiments," *Management Science* (September 1971): 21–38.

Fishman, George S., *Concepts and Methods in Discrete Event Digital Simulation* (New York: Wiley, 1973).

Fishman, George S., "Statistical Analysis for Queuing Simulations," *Management Science* (November 1973): 363–369.

Fishman, George S., "Grouping Observations in Digital Simulation," *Management Science* (January 1978): 510–521.

Hammersley, J., and D. Handscomb, *Monte Carlo Methods* (New York: Wiley, 1964).

Hicks, C. R., *Fundamental Concepts in the Design of Experiments*, 2nd ed. (New York: Holt, Rinehart and Winston, 1973).

Kleijnen, J. P. C., *Statistical Techniques in Simulation, Part I* (New York: Marcel Dekker, 1974).

Kleijnen, J. P. C., *Statistical Techniques in Simulation, Part II* (New York: Marcel Dekker, 1975).

Meier, Robert C., William T. Newell, and Harold L. Pazer, *Simulation in Business and Economics* (Englewood Cliffs, N.J.: Prentice-Hall, 1969).

Naylor, Thomas H. et al., *Computer Simulation Techniques* (New York: Wiley, 1966).

Naylor, Thomas H., and J. M. Finger, "Verification of Computer Simulation Models," *Management Science* (October 1967): B92–B101.

Reichenback, Hans, *The Rise of Scientific Philosophy* (Berkeley: University of California Press, 1951).

Robbins, Lionel, *An Essay on the Nature and Significance of Economic Science*, 2nd ed. (London, Eng.: Macmillan, 1940).

Shannon, Robert E., *Systems Simulation* (Englewood Cliffs, N.J.: Prentice-Hall, 1975).

Spanier, Jerome, and Ely M. Gebbard, *Monte Carlo Principles and Neutron Transport Problems* (Reading, Mass.: Addison-Wesley, 1969).

Van Horne, Richard L., "Validation of Simulation Results," *Management Science* (January 1971): 247–258.

13

CHAPTER THIRTEEN   DEVELOPING SUCCESSFUL SIMULATION MODELS

The Model Development Process

    Problem and/or Information Identification

    Data Collection

    Model Building

    Model Validation

    Model Implementation

    Model Operation

Problems in Model Development

    The Management Scientist's Perspective

    The Manager's Perspective

Differences Between Managers and Management Scientists

Structural and Other Considerations

Summary

Assignments

References

At this point in your study of simulation, you have been exposed to considerable simulation technology and a wide variety of simulation applications. You now have the requisite skills to build reasonably sophisticated simulation models and an understanding and appreciation of potential simulation applications. Only a few additional topics need to be explored before you are ready to go into an organization and build simulation models. Yet these are especially important topics, for instance, knowing how to develop simulation models using a *model development process.* Successful completion of this process requires an understanding of *behavioral and structural considerations* and some of the *problems* that can occur. This concern over successful model development is not limited to simulation modeling. It is crucial to any quantitative analysis and, consequently, the chapter's discussion should help you when developing any kind of mathematical model.

THE MODEL DEVELOPMENT PROCESS

The development of a simulation model should follow a logical, systematic process; that is, a series of steps should be followed. For our purposes it is useful to describe the steps as *problem and/or information identification, data collection, model building, model validation, model implementation,* and *model operation.* Although these steps are generally followed in the sequence mentioned, it is important to understand that the model development process is usually iterative in nature with loops back to previous steps. For example, model validation may show that changes in the model are needed. This in turn may require additional data collection. The steps and iterative nature of the model development process are shown in Figure 13.1.

It is also important to recognize that the steps are not performed in isolation. The execution of any step must be carried out with other steps in mind. For example, the building of a model must be performed based on an understanding of how it will ultimately be operated.

Two groups of people are involved in the development of a model. One group consists of *managers* or *end users* who have a need for the model. The other group consists of *management scientists, model builders,* or *analysts* who are specialists in the creation of models. Each group has responsibilities throughout the model development process, although the amount and nature of their responsibilities vary with the steps in the process.

Table 13.1 provides an indication of the amount of involvement required when de-

Figure 13.1   The model development process.

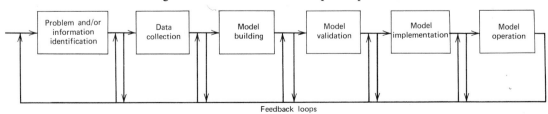

Table 13.1   NEED FOR INVOLVEMENT WHEN DEVELOPING A SIMULATION MODEL

	Upper Management	User Department Management	User Department Personnel	Management Science Staff	Data Processing Staff
Problem and/or information identification	M[b]	H[a]	H	H	L
Data collection	L[c]	M	H	H	L
Model building	L	L	M	H	M
Model validation	M	H	H	H	L
Model implementation	M	H	H	H	M
Model operation	M	H	H	M	M

[a]H = Heavy involvement
[b]M = Moderate involvement
[c]L = Light or no involvement

veloping a simulation model.[1]   The rows in the table identify the steps in the model development process. The columns show the organizational personnel who should be involved in developing a simulation model. In the body of the table are indicators of whether heavy (H), moderate (M), or little or no involvement (L) is required. Obviously, the table entries vary with the model being built, but the amount of involvement indicated should be approximately correct for most simulation models.

It is almost impossible to overemphasize the importance of user involvement. Many management scientists describe "champions" who were important to their most successful model development efforts. These were the managers (or manager) who believed in the project, supported it, and did whatever was necessary to see it completed. Research has shown over and over again the importance of management support and user involvement to the successful completion of management science projects.

Management scientists must view their involvement in the model development process as being more than model building. There is a tendency for the management science group to leave the project before it is really implemented. That is, their job is viewed as being finished once a working model is produced. Actually, it is only after the model is integrated into the user's work environment that the management science group is free to move on to other projects.

A growing body of research has shown the usefulness of viewing the development of a model as being a change process.[2] Two theoretical bases can be used for this conceptualization: the planned change approach and the innovation process approach.

[1]This table is patterned after one presented in Victor B. Godin, "The Dollars and Sense of Simulation," *Decision Sciences* (April 1976): 337.

[2]Michael J. Ginzberg, "Steps Toward More Effective Implementation of MS and MIS," *Interfaces* (May 1978): 57–63.

The *planned change approach* is based on the Lewin/Schein theory of change.[3] This approach suggests that any change effort should consist of three distinct phases: unfreezing, moving, and refreezing.

In the unfreezing phase, existing behavior patterns are disconfirmed. All parties become aware of the need for change. An atmosphere is created where change can be introduced with minimal resistance.

The moving phase sees the introduction of what is new. In the model development process, it is the building of the model. This phase also requires that organizational personnel learn new attitudes and behaviors.

Refreezing requires the stabilization of the change and the integration of new attitudes and behaviors into existing patterns and relationships. These attitudes and behaviors will not be frozen forever, because change is a constant process. Over time there may be changes to the model or possibly even the creation of new models.

The *innovation process approach* involves the delineation of a series of steps that are followed in adopting an innovation.[4] In the case of developing a simulation model, the model is the innovation. The steps we have identified in the model development process are what we are recommending as an innovation process approach for creating a successful model.

The planned change and innovation process approach provide useful perspectives on the development of models. They cause us to view modeling from a broader viewpoint than simply the actual construction of a model. This perspective will be enhanced as the steps in the model development process are described.

Problem and/or Information Identification

A model should be created only in response to an important need of the intended users. A variety of research has demonstrated the importance of the end user perceiving a need for any model that is developed.[5] The need may be the result of some organizational problem or for information to support decision making. Ginzberg expresses the importance of user need this way:

> *All (management science) projects imply some degree of organizational change. If the users do not believe that the project addresses a real and important problem that they are facing, they are unlikely to make the changes necessary to accommodate and use the new system. If the management scientist wants his project to have an impact, he must insure that there are users who believe the project addresses their problems.*[6]

Identifying the correct problem is not always easy. As Charles J. Hitch of the Department of Defense has said:

[3]Kurt Lewin, "Group Decision and Social Change," in *Readings in Social Psychology*, Newcomb and Hartley, eds. (New York: Holt, 1952); Edgar H. Schein, "Management Development as a Process of Influence," *Industrial Management Review* (May 1961): 59–77; and Edgar H. Schein, *Professional Education: Some New Directions* (New York: McGraw-Hill, 1972).

[4]Francis W. Wolek, "Implementation and the Process of Adopting Managerial Technology," *Interfaces* (May 1975): 59–77.

[5]See, for example, Ginzberg, op. cit., p. 61.

[6]Ibid., p. 60.

It is my experience that the hardest problems for the systems analyst are not those of analytic techniques. . . . What distinguishes the useful and productive analyst in his ability to formulate (or design) the problem. . . .[7]

It is vitally important that the analyst and the end user work closely together in exploring the problem and/or information needs. The end user probably understands best what the information needs are. The model builder understands best what information can be provided with varying degrees of difficulty.

It is imperative that the analyst take the time to understand fully the system being modeled and the terminology employed by the personnel who operate the system. It is only from this in-depth understanding that the model builder can differentiate the problem from its symptoms, define systems boundaries for analysis purposes, identify system and subsystem relationships, and the like. And unless the model builder bases the model on conceptualizations and terminology employed by the end user, it is unlikely that the model will be fully and effectively used.

In some cases it may be up to the management scientist to show the manager that there is a problem or that certain information can be provided. Not all managers are fully aware of the capabilities of models and computer-based information systems. In these situations, management scientists have educational responsibilities.

The end product of problem and/or information identification are output specifications for the model. These specifications strongly influence the remainder of the model development process. Also emerging are thoughts about what the remainder of the model development process will entail.

Data Collection

Even though data collection is identified as a separate step in the model development process, it should be recognized as an activity that permeates the entire process. To illustrate this point, problem and/or information typically requires a data collection effort. Data are also required to build, validate, implement, and operate the model. Consequently, data collection plays an important role in the entire model development process.

The type of data needed depends on the nature of the modeling effort. This point is easily seen by considering the different simulation models described in this book and their data requirements; see Table 13.2. The data may be of an accounting nature. It may have come from observing the system in operation and recording observations. It may come from the minds of organizational personnel. Or as in the case of econometric data, it may have to be obtained from sources outside of the organization.

Data collection is a major problem with many modeling efforts, as will be seen later when we discuss the problems of developing and operating models. The data may not be available; it may be expensive to collect; it may be difficult to quantify. All these factors must be kept in mind by the management scientist when developing a model.

---

[7]Charles J. Hitch, *Decision Making for Defense* (Berkeley: University of California Press, 1967), p. 54.

Table 13.2 EXAMPLES OF DATA USED WITH DIFFERENT TYPES OF SIMULATION MODELS

Type of Simulation Model	Examples of Data Requirements
Inventory	Demand data, delivery time data, carrying costs, ordering costs, stockout costs
Financial planning	Demand data, revenue data, cost data, data on the relationships among variables
Queuing	Arrival time data, service time data, waiting time costs, service time costs, data on queue discipline and priorities
Human decision making	Decision maker protocol data, data on decisions made and the variables that led to the decision
Management games	Revenue data, cost data, data on the relationships among game variables
Corporate model	Financial data, marketing data, production data, data on environmental variables

Model Building

Much of this book has discussed the technology used in building simulation models. In this chapter our concern is with the behavioral, structural, and managerial aspects. As much as other factors, these considerations dictate whether there is a successful model development.

It is worth repeating that the model must meet the needs of the user. As the "Charlie Brown" cartoon illustrates (see Figure 13.2), it is unlikely that a tool will be used (whether it be a baseball glove or a model) unless the tool is perceived to be useful. As a result, the educational background, experiences, and preferences of the user are of paramount importance in building a model. For example, a highly sophisticated model, no matter how powerful and potentially useful, is probably wasted on a user whose training and experiences have not prepared him or her to use it. As Francis F. Bradshaw, former president of the Society for the Advancement of Management, has said, "Most managers would rather live with a problem they can't solve than use a solution they don't understand."[8]

A recent article by Gene Woolsey, the iconoclastic editor of *Interfaces*, makes an appeal for simple and usable simulation models. In his article he describes a simulation model he built.

One of my favorite still-operating simulations is one allocating squad cars for a town in Minnesota. It is made up of a large wheel of fortune (confiscated from a passing carnival), dry fly boxes, buckshot, nails, and rubber bands. It is dumb, it does work, the cops use it, and, best of all, it is jolly cheap. Now, that's my kind of simulation.[9]

[8] Russell L. Ackoff, "Frontiers of Management Science," *The Bulletin* (TIMS) (February 1971): 20.
[9] R. E. D. Woolsey, "Whatever Happened to Simple Simulation," *SIMSNIPS* (February 1979): 1.

Figure 13.2   A tool will not be used unless it meets the user's needs.

Source.   © 1976 United Features Syndicate, Inc. Reprinted by permission.

Although most problems do not lend themselves to a physical simulation, Woolsey's example does point out that simulation models do not have to be complex in order to be useful.

It is wise initially to build simple models and perhaps later expand them. Miles Waugh, Manager of the Management Sciences Department at Phillip Morris, U.S.A., expresses these sentiments this way:

In developing planning models, it pays to think big, but start small. Initial costs should be minimized until the benefits of a model can be demonstrated through some concrete results. The natural initial tendency to incorporate everything one can think of into the model should be avoided. [10]

There are good reasons for initially developing small models. One reason is that they can be quickly developed and shown to end users who can then decide if the models are appropriate for their needs. If the models are not appropriate, changes can be made relatively easily and inexpensively. When models are perceived to be useful, greater interest and support is generated for the modeling effort and more comprehensive models can perhaps be developed over time. User involvement is an important ingredient to model-

[10]Hugh J. Watson and Patricia Gill Marett, "A Survey of Management Science Implementation Problems," *Interfaces* (August 1979): 126.

ing success, and this involvement tends to intensify as users see that they are receiving a tool that will assist them in carrying out their decision-making responsibilities.

The actual building of a simulation model requires a variety of technical skills. The model builder may have to select appropriate process generators, test random number routines, determine an experimental design, and analyze the simulation's output. All these, as we have seen, can be challenging tasks.

The model builder also has to give thought to the way the model will be operated. For example, will the end user run the model or will someone else run the model for the user? This is an important decision, especially for models that are used interactively from a terminal. When the end user runs the model, considerable overhead is typically required in terms of documentation, training, English-like programming languages, and systems software. The advantage is that the user can run the model without the services of an intermediary. If the model builder assumes that an intermediary (sometimes called a "chauffeur") will operate the model for the user, much of this overhead is avoided. The drawback is that the need to call for an intermediary may discourage the manager from using the model.

Plans also have to be made for ensuring that the model will continue to be used once it has been created. Of primary concern is creating and maintaining a data base that supports the model. This concern includes obtaining input data for the model and data for updating the model over time.

Model Validation

Chapter 12 explored the technical aspects of validating a simulation model. It pointed out that the intended use of the model impacts how it is validated, that the benefits and costs associated with various degrees of validation should be considered, that validation procedures depend on the type of simulation model built, and that validation should include examining the assumptions underlying the model, testing with empirical data the relationships used in the model, and comparing the model's output with real-world data. These are all important validation procedures, but validation must not be limited to these concerns.

Shycon emphasizes that there are two different groups that must be satisfied with the validation of the model.

1. *Proof to the* management scientists *that the model and its components are performing properly the functions for which they were designed.*
2. *Proof to the* operating managers, *who are the ultimate users, that the model does, in fact, replicate the real world situation with which they are concerned.*[11]

We have discussed validation from the management scientist's point of view, but management's perspective still needs to be considered. Management is most fundamentally concerned about whether the model accurately describes the real-world situation being investigated. The model should be able to predict what has happened in the past and hold promise for predicting what will happen in the future. Reasons for deviations between reality and the model's output should be explainable. Furthermore, the model

---

[11] Harvey N. Shycon, "All Around the Model: Perspectives on MS Applications," *Interfaces* (February 1978): 36.

should generate its reports and output in terminology that is familiar to management. Management wants to make certain that the model produces output that is consistent with what is known about the system and uses terminology with which management is comfortable.

Model Implementation

After a model has been validated, it is ready to be permanently placed in the organizational setting where it will be used. Close attention must be paid to several items. Users must be fully trained in the operation of the model. Ideally, however, users of the model have been working closely with it during the development process and are already familiar with its functioning. Documentation for the model must be completed. Because documentation is one of the least interesting aspects of developing a model, care must be taken to ensure that this important activity is completed. The model must be placed on the organization's computer system, including the preparation of supporting data bases. Final changes to the model must be made in order to better meet the user's needs. If earlier steps in the model development process have been carefully completed, this should only involve "fine tuning" of the model. Attention must be given to how the model will be updated. Failure to do so frequently results in one of two conditions—both of which are bad. First, the model stops being used. Second, the model continues to be used, but produces unreliable information. Because the model builders move on to new projects, a systematic procedure is needed for permitting the user to update the model or for bringing the management science group back to perform the update.

The implementation of the model is not a step that is left for the user to complete. Instead, it is an important responsibility of the model builders. Harvey, in his study of factors that lead to implementation success and failure, found that ". . . a strong relationship exists between the extent to which implementation occurs and the willingness of the management scientists to assume implementation responsibility."[12]

Model Operation

After a model has been implemented, it is ready to be put into operation. At this time the model's benefits are fully realized. Following the model development process and the principles that have been described here should foster modeling success. Still, however, problems can and do occur.

PROBLEMS IN MODEL DEVELOPMENT

There are many potential pitfalls on the path to developing a model successfully. Experience has shown that many modeling efforts end in failure. Ward estimates that only 40 percent of management science projects are ever fully implemented.[13] During the past few years, however, there has been a growing awareness among management scien-

[12]Allan Harvey, "Factors Making for Implementation Success and Failure," *Management Science* (February 1970): B319.

[13]R. A. Ward, "More Implementation Through an OR/Behavioral Science Partnership and Management Training," *Operational Research Quarterly* 25 (2) (1974): 209–217.

tists that developing management science models demands more than technical skills, and this growing awareness should be improving the success rate. Most observers would agree, though, that considerable room for improvement still exists.

Being aware of the problems that have been experienced by others provides a basis for avoiding the errors made in the past. An examination of the problems should consider the viewpoint of both management scientists and end users, because each has a perspective that is legitimate and important if the success rate of management science modeling is to be improved.

The Management Scientist's Perspective

In Chapter 1 a recent survey of nonacademic TIMS/ORSA members was described.[14] A portion of the survey asked respondents to list up to three problems they encountered in developing management science models. Since membership in TIMS/ORSA is typically held by quantitative specialists, their responses provide one of the prospectives we are seeking.

It was found from analyzing the responses that most of the problems could be classified into ten categories. Table 13.3 presents the survey results.[15] Listed are the problems and the percentage of respondents who listed each as being one of the major problems. We will highlight the most important problems.

Table 13.3   THE PERSPECTIVE OF MANAGEMENT SCIENTISTS ON THE PROBLEMS OF DEVELOPING MANAGEMENT SCIENCE MODELS

Problem	Percentage
1. Selling management science techniques to management meets with resistance	35
2. Neither top nor middle management have the educational background to appreciate management science techniques	34
3. Lack of good clean data	32
4. There is never time to analyze a real problem using a sophisticated approach	23
5. Lack of understanding by those who need to use the results	22
6. Hard to define problems for applications	19
7. The payoff from using unsophisticated methods is sufficient	16
8. Shortage of personnel	12
9. Poor reputation of management scientists as problem solvers	11
10. Individuals feel threatened by management scientists and their techniques	10

[14] Hugh J. Watson and Joan M. Baecher, "A Survey of Industrial Usage of Operations Research Techniques," *Proceedings of the Southeastern Chapter of the Institute of Management Science*, Myrtle Beach, S.C. (October 1979), pp. 233–235.

[15] Watson and Marett, op. cit., pp. 124–28.

Several of the problems are related. For example, problems 1, 2, and 5 are either directly or indirectly related to the educational background of users. Mentioned frequently was that neither top nor middle management have the educational background to appreciate management science methods (problem 2). It follows, then, that there would be problems in selling management science methods to management (problem 1) and having users understand the results from an analysis (problem 5).

Education-related problems are not easily overcome. Many managers currently in middle and top management positions received their formal education prior to the 1960s when quantitative methods first began to be emphasized in colleges of business administration. Although many younger managers have now received better quantitative training in universities and executive development programs, it will take time for them to ascend the organizational ladder in large numbers.

Clearly, it is difficult to sell that which is not understood. Fortunately, the functioning of most simulation models can normally be explained in nontechnical terms. Then, too, the model builder can tailor the model to the user's quantitative sophistication. For example, the educational background of the user may be such that a deterministic model is appropriate rather than a probabilistic one. The burden of proof is largely on the management scientist to show that his or her methods can and should be used.

Problem 3 laments the lack of good clean data. This points out that the data collection step in the model development process is not always easy. In some cases it may be that the management scientists are using a modeling approach with unrealistic or unnecessary data requirements. On the other hand, needed data may simply not be readily available.

Problem 4 is that there is never time to analyze a real problem using a sophisticated approach. The time frame for many decisions is such that there is only a limited amount of time available for building a model. Problem 6 expresses the difficulty of defining the problem. We discussed this important concern earlier. Real problems are not always easy to define and model. Problem 7 is that the payoff from using unsophisticated methods is sufficient. Not all problems require a model; sometimes the application of common sense is all that is needed. Problem 8 is that there is a shortage of management science personnel. Later we will look at the staffing of a typical management science department. Problem 9 is the poor reputation of management scientists as problem solvers. Given the mediocre track record of management scientists as problem solvers, this finding is not surprising. Hopefully, it can be improved on. Problem 10 is that users feel threatened by management scientists and their methods. This may be partially related to the personal characteristics of management scientists and we will say more about this point later.

The Manager's Perspective

In another recent survey, Green, Newsom, and Jones asked vice presidents for production or their equivalent to weight the problems of developing management science models.[16] Respondents rated each problem on a 10-point scale ranging from 1 for not important to 10 for very important. The survey findings are shown in Table 13.4 and provide the second perspective we are seeking.

---

[16]Thad B. Green, Walter B. Newson, and S. Roland Jones, "A Survey of the Application of Quantitative Techniques to Production/Operations Management in Large Organizations," *Academy of Management Journal* (December 1977): 669–676.

Table 13.4   THE PERSPECTIVE OF MANAGERS ON THE PROBLEMS
OF DEVELOPING MANAGEMENT SCIENCE MODELS

Problem	Mean
1. Benefits of using techniques are not clearly understood by managers	6.51
2. Managers lack knowledge of quantitative techniques	6.04
3. Managers are not exposed to quantitative techniques early in their training	5.80
4. Required data are difficult to quantify	5.79
5. Only a small portion of management is trained in the use of quantitative techniques	5.47
6. Management is successful without using techniques	5.43
7. Managers in key positions lack knowledge of quantitative techniques	5.39
8. The cost of developing models and using techniques is too high	5.33
9. The data required in using the technique are not available	4.85
10. Managers are not quantitatively oriented	4.56
11. Recent college graduates with quantitative training have not yet attained positions of influence	4.32
12. Managers are unwilling or unable to use the computer for decision making and/or computers are not available	4.17
13. The expense of employing quantitative specialists is too great	4.16
14. Senior management personnel does not encourage use of techniques by younger management personnel	3.93
15. Management distrusts or fears the use of techniques	3.92

Many of the top problems (1–3, 5, and 7) are education related. It is interesting to note the agreement between managers and management scientists on the importance of educational problems. As previously mentioned, however, these problems are not quickly or easily overcome.

There are other areas of agreement between managers and management scientists. Table 13.4 shows that obtaining the required data is difficult (problems 4 and 9). This was also the feeling of management scientists. Both groups also indicated that management lacks confidence in management scientists and their techniques. This problem, however, is not ranked high by either group relative to other problems.

The most notable difference in perspective involves the time and expense required to develop models. Management scientists indicate that there is insufficient time to perform a sophisticated analysis, that the payoff from simple methods is sufficient, and that there is a shortage of personnel. Managers indicate that they are successful without the techniques (problem 6) and the cost of using the techniques (problems 8 and 13) is too great.

Perhaps management scientists sometimes do not understand the information needs of management. Management frequently requires a "quick and dirty" (and inexpensive) analysis, one that does not have extensive data input requirements and can be supplied within the decision-making time frame. If this explanation is correct, then possibly model development problems could be reduced if management scientists would attempt to understand better what information is needed and how much time and money should be expended on the analysis effort.

DIFFERENCES BETWEEN MANAGERS AND MANAGEMENT SCIENTISTS

Earlier it was suggested that there are important personal differences between managers and management scientists. These differences can create problems when models are being developed. Hopefully, by discussing the differences, a basis is provided for increased understanding with the result that the two groups can work more harmoniously together.

C. P. Snow in a book written two decades ago, entitled *The Two Cultures and the Scientific Revolution*, asserted that there is a gulf that separates the scientist from the rest of society.[17] More recently, C. Jackson Grayson, Jr., picked up on this theme when he stated that "Managers and management scientists are operating as two separate cultures, each with its own goals, languages, and methods."[18]

Lawrence and Lorsch identify four categories where managers and management scientists are likely to differ: (1) goal orientation, (2) time orientation, (3) interpersonal orientation, and (4) formality of organizational structure.[19]

Management scientists are professionals with specific skills that are transferable from organization to organization. Their allegiance is sometimes more to their profession than to the organization that employs them. They prefer to work on projects that allow them to apply and extend the skills of their profession. They frequently recommend organizational change as a result of their analyses. Managers, on the other hand, tend to identify with the goals of the organization that employs them. They prefer quick, simple, and inexpensive solutions to their problems. They tend to avoid the disruptions created by organizational change unless it is clearly necessary.

Bringing the goals of these two groups together is not always easy. Managers must provide opportunities for management scientists to use their talents in meaningful and interesting ways. Management scientists must be made to understand that their performance will be evaluated and rewarded on the basis of how much they contribute to organizational goals.

Management scientists are often satisfied working on long-term projects with only limited feedback. Managers, on the other hand, are often in need of answers now rather than later. Consequently, they do not enjoy the luxury of time and may not understand why certain analyses cannot be performed quickly.

A major responsibility of management is to make clear what time and resources are justifiable on a modeling effort. It is then up to the management scientists either to meet these requirements or to communicate why it is impossible to do so. There should always

---

[17]C. P. Snow, *The Two Cultures and the Scientific Revolution* (New York: Cambridge University Press, 1960).

[18]C. Jackson Grayon, Jr., "Management Science and Business Practice," *Harvard Business Review* (July–August 1973): 41.

[19]Paul R. Lawrence and Jay W. Lorsch, "Differentiation and Integration in Complex Organizations," *Administrative Science Quarterly* (June 1967): 1–47.

be a final understanding before an analysis is undertaken of what is expected, by when, and how much it will cost.

Management scientists tend to be task oriented. Their primary concern is solving the problem under consideration. Their approach to problem solving tends to be highly rationalistic with little interest in behavioral considerations. Managers must be people oriented because humans are a unique, organizational resource, and virtually all organizational undertakings are accomplished by groups of people working together.

Some management scientists do not have good interpersonal skills. In fact, they may have at least in part selected their profession because they perceived that technical skills would be the most important ingredient in professional success. Unfortunately, this lack of concern over the quality of interpersonal interactions can lead to poor relationships between managers and management scientists.

Management scientists must understand that working with people is an important part of their job. Although they may not fully understand why, they must appreciate that managerial decision making is more than an optimizing process. On the other side, managers must strive to work harmoniously with bright, skilled, and talented people who may not fit into the typical organizational mode.

Management scientists prefer and expect a loose organizational structure. They want a freedom of action to pursue in a manner they deem appropriate that which is thought to be important. They are frequently impatient with formal lines of authority and communication. Inhibiting rules and policies are resented. Managers, on the other hand, are usually more accustomed to working through formal, established organizational channels. They understand and accept the way that things are done.

Managers should try to reduce or eliminate unnecessary restrictions on management scientists. On the other hand, management scientists should understand that there are usually valid reasons for most rules and procedures and that problems may be created when rules and procedures are not followed.

To some extent our discussion of the differences between managers and management scientists has been exaggerated. The objective has been to show how different the two groups can be. In any particular setting, probably only a few differences are likely to surface and create problems.

STRUCTURAL AND OTHER CONSIDERATIONS

Until now, little has been said about how the management science group fits into the organization's structure, the size of the group, its educational background, its demographic characteristics, and the time and resources devoted to a typical management science project. These considerations can either aid, hinder, or limit the model development process, and therefore merit our attention.

At one time it was thought that most large organizations would create separate management science departments. These departments would then be responsible for the bulk of the organization's management science activities. To some extent this has happened, but not to the degree once anticipated. A recent survey of large corporations by Thomas and DaCosta found that 48 percent of the organizations have a separate management science department.[20]   Although this is a sizable percentage, it is less than what had been predicted just a few years earlier.[21]   Thomas and DaCosta found that a number of organizations at one time did have a separate department, but phased it out after discovering it was inefficient.

There are logical reasons for decentralizing the management science group by either phasing the department out or at least by spreading a portion of the management science group throughout the organization. First, by placing the management science expertise in the functional areas, the management scientists are better acquainted with the problems they have to solve. Second, the management scientist is more accountable to a functional manager who is immediately responsible for the project than a project leader from an outside department.

By itself, the organizational placement of the management science group will not guarantee modeling success or failure. However, at least a partial decentralization of the group may facilitate the accomplishment of certain key elements in the model development process. It will be interesting to observe during the next few years the experiences of firms with different organizational structures.

The trend in organizations is toward continued growth in the hiring of management science personnel. In their survey, Thomas and DaCosta found the average number of management scientists to be 11, with a planned average expansion of 2.4 new members over the next two years.[22]

As might be expected, management science groups are well educated. Over the years, the percentage of management scientists with bachelor's and master's degrees has continued to rise. Interestingly, however, the percentage of Ph.D.'s has recently declined. This phenomenon has been explained this way:

> *The decline in percentage of Ph.D.'s hired is very closely linked to both the maturity of use of OR/MS and the decentralization of OR/MS. Since the use of OR/MS is no longer a new activity for corporations, the educational background for entry level has decreased. Additionally, the emphasis away from OR/MS specialization towards functional areas of application has decreased the need for highly specialized Ph.D.'s.*[23]

The educational background of management scientists is very diversified. Thomas and DaCosta found that mathematics and statistics are the largest areas of concentration for holders of bachelor's degrees, with a little over 28 percent of the personnel holding bachelor's degrees in these fields.[24]   At the master's level, business administration is the most common area of concentration. Degrees in mathematics and statistics are most common among management scientists with Ph.D.s.

Thomas and DaCosta found the average age of management scientists to be $35\frac{1}{2}$.[25]

---

[20]George Thomas and Jo-Anne DaCosta, "A Sample Survey of Corporate Operations Research," *Interfaces* (August 1979): 103–111.

[21]Efraim Turban, "A Sample Survey of Operations Research Activities at the Corporate Level," *Operations Research* (May–June 1972): 708–721.

[22]Thomas and DaCosta, op. cit., p. 104.

[23]Ibid.

[24]Thomas and DaCosta, op. cit., p. 104.

[25]Ibid.

Eighty-four percent are male. The average length of service as a management scientist has lengthened with the maturity of the field and is now 7.1 years.

From their survey, Thomas and DaCosta found the average number of management scientists assigned to a project to be 1.5[26] This is down from that reported in previous surveys. As management science methods are increasingly being applied to everyday problems, the number of management scientists required to analyze the problems have declined. The increased application of management science models to everyday problems is also seen in the decline in time required to complete an analysis. Thomas and DaCosta report an average project length of 7.4 months.[27]

It is logical to ask about the meaning of all these data. In most general terms, it suggests a maturing of the use of management science methods, at least in larger organizations. Hand in hand with this maturing is an increased acceptance, even if the acceptance involves a lowered set of expectations, of management scientists and their methods. These developments bode well for the future of simulation and other modeling efforts.

SUMMARY

The successful development of simulation models requires more than the mastery of technical skills. The analyst must follow a logical, systematic model development process. He or she must be aware of behavioral considerations and potential problems to avoid. Organizational structure arrangements should facilitate modeling efforts. A management science staff with an appropriate mix of talents is needed.

The steps in the model development process include problem and/or information identification, data collection, model building, model validation, model implementation, and model operation. Following these steps is in keeping with the innovation process approach for bringing about organizational change and the planned change approach of unfreezing, moving, and refreezing. There are a number of important considerations to keep in mind when developing a model. Two of them are user involvement and management support. Each is more likely to exist when the model satisfies a real and important need of the user. Care must be taken when defining the problem and/or information requirements, because experience has shown that this step is more difficult than it might first seem. The design of the model should include a concern for realistic data requirements, a knowledge of the user's decision-making characteristics, and plans for how the model will be operated. A good rule-of-thumb to follow is to build small models initially and later expand them when deemed necessary. It should always be kept in mind that a model will be used only if the end user perceives it to be valid.

The track record for management science modeling is not especially good because of a variety of problems. Management scientists frequently comment on difficulties with management's educational background in regard to quantitative methods, the lack of good clean data, a shortage of time and resources to develop sophisticated models, and poor images and relationships with managers. Managers, on the other hand, recognize the educational problem, but feel that many modeling efforts have excessive data input re-

[26]Ibid., p. 108.
[27]Ibid.

quirements and are too time consuming and expensive. It is only through time and better management training that the education problem will be resolved, but if management scientists attempt to understand better what information management needs and how much time and money should be expended on the analysis effort, the incidence of problems should be lessened.

There are sometimes conflicts between managers and management scientists. The two groups tend to differ in goal orientation, time orientation, interpersonal orientation, and formality of organizational structure. Each group must strive to minimize the possible negative consequences emanating from these differences.

Many large organizations have a separate management science department. The trend, however, is to decentralize the management science talent throughout the organization. This and other indicators point to a maturing of the practice of management science.

ASSIGNMENTS

13.1.   It has been suggested that the need for user involvement varies with the project. Describe a project that would involve extensive user involvement and one that would require minimal involvement.

13.2.   A distinction is sometimes made between a systematic, analytic, or thinking style of problem identification and solution, on the one hand, and an intuitive, heuristic, or feeling style on the other. Which categorization best describes you? Which type best describes most managers and management scientists? Which one is best?

13.3.   What are the planned change approach and the innovation process approach? Which best describes the model development process?

13.4.   A company is receiving complaints from customers that orders are being received late. What might be the source of this problem?

13.5.   A high-level executive of one of the nation's largest corporations suggests that some management scientists are much like ". . . evangelical bearers of the Solution trying to make contact with the Problem." What does this statement mean?

13.6.   When working with end users, management scientists should be careful in their use of jargon. List five simulation terms that would be unfamiliar to the typical manager.

13.7.   Peter Drucker, a noted management scholar, writer, and consultant, has made the following statement about what managers should know about management science tools: "To demand of any tool user that he understand what goes into the making of the tool is admission of incompetence on the part of the toolmaker. The tool user, provided the tool is well-made, need not, and indeed should not, know anything about the tool." Discuss why you agree or diagreee with Drucker's statement.

13.8.   Simulation modeling is linked to computer hardware and software available in the organization. Discuss the linkages that exist.

13.9.   List the major problems in developing management science models as seen by managers and management scientists. Which group is "right" in its perception of the problems?

13.10. Managers and management scientists agree that the biggest barriers to using quantitative methods of analysis are educational in nature. Do you see this problem gradually disappearing? Why or why not?

13.11. Explain why a manager might be threatened by a management scientist and his methods.

13.12. In what ways do managers and management scientists differ? What skills are required of a project manager in order to keep these differences under control?

13.13. Would you recommend the decentralization of the management science group? Why? What are the pros and cons of centralization and decentralization?

13.14. Some organizations with separate management science departments operate them as profit centers. With this arrangement, the management science department charges the user for any services provided. What are the pros and cons of this approach?

13.15. The following situation was described in Harvey N. Shycon, "All Around the Model: Perspectives on MS Applications," *Interfaces* (February 1978), pp. 33–37.

Ben Harris, vice president of manufacturing and longtime boss of production for the National Tool Company, was conducting his monthly production review and planning meeting.

"Dammit," he said with obvious exasperation, "Can't you guys give me a plan I can feel comfortable will work? This is the third time your hundred thousand dollar system has given me a plant product allocation that doesn't seem to match my machine capabilities."

Jeff Clark, the young management scientist turned ashen.

"When will you bright computer-types learn that I want proof that your plan is feasible?" said Ben.

National Tool's new Production and Capacity Allocation System (splitting production requirements among its seven plants) had come onstream three months earlier, and Harris had steadfastly refused to accept it or to consider its manufacturing plan seriously.

"Until you can prove it puts production, product by product, at the right plant, and considers my equipment, tools, and dies, manufacturing capability and capacity constraints, and the geographic market to which the product must ultimately be shipped, I'm not buying," he said over and over. "I want proof it will work—the same thing I demand of my engineers."

The management science group had just completed two years of work, developed a well-crafted model of the National Tool manufacturing system, and now the authoritarian manufacturing vice president refused to accept run results.

"But you've got to believe the proper allocations are being made," Jeff insisted. "I have demonstrated to you several times now, Mr. Harris, that the calculations are correct, and I have presented a seminar describing the technique in detail. This model is correct, and the results that it recommends to you are correct. You've got to have faith."

Ben Harris had been with National Tool for 25 years. He had risen steadily from engineer to manufacturing section supervisor, then to plant manager. For the last five years, he was the most successful manufacturing executive for the whole company. He had made his reputation as a tough taskmaker, ran a tight ship, and met or exceeded cost objectives. During these five years as manufacturing vice president, he had added two new plants and brought them onstream—with a minimum of start-up problems. He was one of top management's mainstays in its fight to hold market share and to keep costs in line in this competitive industry. He refused to accept run results without his concept of proof—duplication of last year's schedules and the attendant costs as he knew them.

Jeff Clark was the bright young management scientist who had come into the company two years earlier and had made his reputation as the individual who finally straightened out the financial planning system. Once he had proven himself, he had been given the task of developing the tool for allocating product requirements among the plants and among the production capabilities of the company. Unfortunately, Jeff has not been able to convince Ben Harris to follow the production allocations recommended by the model.

(a)   Where did Jeff Clark go wrong in the model development process?

(b)   If you were Jeff at this point, what would you do?

REFERENCES

Davis, K. Roscoe, and Bernard W. Taylor, III, "Addressing the Implementation Problem: A Gaming Approach," *Decision Sciences* (October 1978): 677–687.

Fenske, Russell W., "Programming Counterproductive Methods to Insure the Rapid Termination of Operations Research/Management Science Departments," *Interfaces* (January 1972): 30–32.

Gallagher, Charles A., and Hugh J. Watson, *Quantitative Methods for Business Decisions* (New York: McGraw-Hill, 1980).

Ginzberg, Michael J., "Steps Toward More Effective Implementation of MS and MIS," *Interfaces* (May 1978): 57–63.

Grayson, C. Jackson, Jr., "Management Science and Business Practice," *Harvard Business Review* (July–August 1973): 41–43.

Green, Thad B., Walter B. Newsom, and Roland S. Jones, "A Survey of the Application of Quantitative Techniques to Production/Operations Management in Large Companies," *Academy of Management Journal* (December 1977): 669–676.

Harvey, Allan, "Factors Making for Implementation Success and Failure," *Management Science* (February 1970): B312–B221.

Lewin, Kurt, "Group Decision and Social Change," In *Readings in Social Psychology*, Newcomb and Hartley, eds. (New York: Holt, 1952).

Rador, Louis T., "Roadblocks to Progress in the Management Sciences and Operations Research," *Management Science* (February 1965): C1–C5.

Radnor, M., A. H. Rubenstein, and Alden S. Bean, "Integration and Utilization of Management Science Activities in Organizations," *Operations Research Quarterly* (June 1968): 117–141.

Schein, Edgar H., "Management Development as a Process of Influence," *Industrial Management Review* (May 1961): 59–77.

Schein, Edgar H., *Professional Education: Some New Directions* (New York: McGraw-Hill, 1972).

Shannon, Robert E., *Systems Simulation* (Englewood Cliffs, N.J.: Prentice-Hall, 1975).

Thomas, George, and Jo-Anne DaCosta, "A Sample Survey of Corporate Operations Research," *Interfaces* (August 1979): 103-111.

Turban, Efraim, "A Sample Survey of Operations Research Activities at the Corporate Level," *Operations Research* (May-June 1972): 708-721.

Urban, Glenn L., "Building Models for Decision Makers," *Interfaces* (May 1974): 1-11.

Ward, R. A., "More Implementation Through an OR/Behavioral Science Partnership and Management Training," *Operational Research Quarterly* (June 1974): 209-217.

Watson, Hugh J., and Patricia Gill Marett, "A Sample Survey of Management Science Implementation Problems," *Interfaces* (August 1979): 124-127.

Wolek, Francis W., "Implementation and the Process of Adopting Managerial Technology," *Interfaces* (May 1975): 59-77.

Zand, Dale E., and Richard E. Sorensen, "Theory of Change and the Effective Use of Management Science," *Administrative Science Quarterly* (December 1975): 532-545.

APPENDIX A RANDOM NUMBER TABLE

69646	90312	78612	16226	82083	37253	17871	27639	41481	80595
73399	81179	95187	23079	11664	13781	35118	74347	48120	24831
16198	72047	61633	09005	45888	72153	37394	69180	98988	43413
65695	03685	46983	71608	51419	73164	43124	60401	12347	15386
01347	05357	39655	58816	73829	10065	33905	39625	22764	27502
71911	76315	70232	55220	91833	35366	94688	15851	16604	11079
91425	65220	35977	80393	35445	13778	95878	59019	74597	52285
99256	76783	24094	23600	72289	37715	60961	40281	97409	14587
18661	12968	66351	60111	21967	98959	89030	89684	28851	92787
33211	97675	46427	11911	38810	96933	74118	58983	11672	31864
65605	93505	64129	54327	48180	29604	40944	74432	43025	69354
86085	61911	90089	43839	81259	13881	18847	01323	70806	60059
94626	59218	31003	97933	10236	20929	47742	95381	57787	22939
39080	18210	03809	79751	15908	66319	40766	23123	49434	34303
38585	01695	60797	01636	22957	72990	66578	57143	64013	92452
84199	87855	26041	11720	68742	04843	38617	41346	63668	21253
45180	32395	41294	57527	31188	29114	28020	28160	23466	69822
91449	59545	66646	03526	03206	51770	07826	03855	18683	96534
03484	91441	50638	91952	26842	87203	57145	06388	71702	06274
81946	40983	02379	96024	68861	41027	50271	68712	23220	01538
58928	65252	99959	02703	94744	95844	29531	23663	28175	76699
30751	41453	46591	42356	36416	32338	21419	80531	61696	44754
36852	13204	63023	59316	49928	09697	76504	24774	67908	61289
70631	46050	12059	46115	36953	44908	20851	08902	17496	14404
05897	25533	60963	06811	77582	05636	37683	38348	80953	33703
21826	18286	14524	58214	71924	13487	09601	34575	47012	58758
38881	45465	01785	66584	58209	29981	04935	82855	16799	04066
32412	11942	33275	04011	56956	52944	00602	84617	16765	35087
66969	52749	74039	29799	04644	45823	10845	48994	99909	33370
98773	25122	02663	62295	76587	77167	88451	79691	57467	15464
03682	52876	21049	23878	15192	80767	49345	47174	11631	50849
11303	82571	32812	72023	11268	70705	12155	44815	30742	06489
81730	86862	98124	69512	68243	78662	79943	84693	89574	46209
26847	91358	19666	90971	08113	31567	19927	23081	77086	43837
49345	01536	67740	99734	34278	24006	85755	17842	16231	04575
17822	70450	88628	89492	43980	39317	63772	79086	25930	56648
29492	20296	54952	08632	38798	41328	46686	96846	27757	97779
65059	50866	95747	90465	54326	96444	44177	84764	08279	04466
57272	87429	91897	94691	44809	98801	29265	15266	47307	47032
89660	14268	50266	20169	55054	61066	56564	20871	97664	26144
35537	13760	93957	14083	75304	41297	03711	47891	30935	30197
62510	22914	88421	76336	98390	33390	47649	72360	74468	65954

65421	75119	28064	65049	44283	22397	52230	89743	71695	75311
01324	38731	28253	98034	57772	19942	30119	08413	38751	87164
49632	48631	42058	30688	18876	76440	09624	65708	57673	86853
24658	36151	48184	46629	89143	62884	34482	58098	89788	35497
20363	15815	06341	92737	05039	73656	23700	67389	51933	21218
88695	06344	50160	81994	24352	58856	70497	34521	07060	57110
36158	59009	54487	37253	99308	21176	75052	70814	69130	70903
36859	03783	18478	01068	91857	85670	65567	18033	46071	00889

Source.   Rand Corporation, *A Million Random Digits with 100,000 Normal Deviates*, (Glencoe, Ill.: The Free Press, 1955).

APPENDIX B   STANDARD NORMAL TABLE

AREAS UNDER THE STANDARD NORMAL CURVE

To find the area under the curve from 0 to Z, shown shaded as $A(Z)$, calculate $Z = (x - \mu)/\sigma$ and enter the table.

Example: If $Z = 2.22$, $A(Z) = p(0 \leqq Z \leqq 2.22) = .4868$

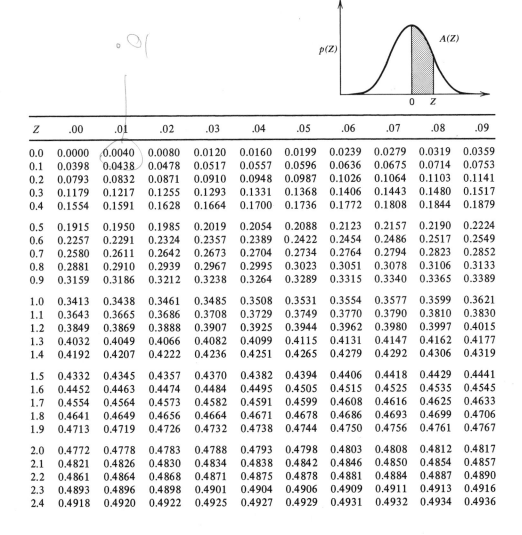

Z	.00	.01	.02	.03	.04	.05	.06	.07	.08	.09
0.0	0.0000	0.0040	0.0080	0.0120	0.0160	0.0199	0.0239	0.0279	0.0319	0.0359
0.1	0.0398	0.0438	0.0478	0.0517	0.0557	0.0596	0.0636	0.0675	0.0714	0.0753
0.2	0.0793	0.0832	0.0871	0.0910	0.0948	0.0987	0.1026	0.1064	0.1103	0.1141
0.3	0.1179	0.1217	0.1255	0.1293	0.1331	0.1368	0.1406	0.1443	0.1480	0.1517
0.4	0.1554	0.1591	0.1628	0.1664	0.1700	0.1736	0.1772	0.1808	0.1844	0.1879
0.5	0.1915	0.1950	0.1985	0.2019	0.2054	0.2088	0.2123	0.2157	0.2190	0.2224
0.6	0.2257	0.2291	0.2324	0.2357	0.2389	0.2422	0.2454	0.2486	0.2517	0.2549
0.7	0.2580	0.2611	0.2642	0.2673	0.2704	0.2734	0.2764	0.2794	0.2823	0.2852
0.8	0.2881	0.2910	0.2939	0.2967	0.2995	0.3023	0.3051	0.3078	0.3106	0.3133
0.9	0.3159	0.3186	0.3212	0.3238	0.3264	0.3289	0.3315	0.3340	0.3365	0.3389
1.0	0.3413	0.3438	0.3461	0.3485	0.3508	0.3531	0.3554	0.3577	0.3599	0.3621
1.1	0.3643	0.3665	0.3686	0.3708	0.3729	0.3749	0.3770	0.3790	0.3810	0.3830
1.2	0.3849	0.3869	0.3888	0.3907	0.3925	0.3944	0.3962	0.3980	0.3997	0.4015
1.3	0.4032	0.4049	0.4066	0.4082	0.4099	0.4115	0.4131	0.4147	0.4162	0.4177
1.4	0.4192	0.4207	0.4222	0.4236	0.4251	0.4265	0.4279	0.4292	0.4306	0.4319
1.5	0.4332	0.4345	0.4357	0.4370	0.4382	0.4394	0.4406	0.4418	0.4429	0.4441
1.6	0.4452	0.4463	0.4474	0.4484	0.4495	0.4505	0.4515	0.4525	0.4535	0.4545
1.7	0.4554	0.4564	0.4573	0.4582	0.4591	0.4599	0.4608	0.4616	0.4625	0.4633
1.8	0.4641	0.4649	0.4656	0.4664	0.4671	0.4678	0.4686	0.4693	0.4699	0.4706
1.9	0.4713	0.4719	0.4726	0.4732	0.4738	0.4744	0.4750	0.4756	0.4761	0.4767
2.0	0.4772	0.4778	0.4783	0.4788	0.4793	0.4798	0.4803	0.4808	0.4812	0.4817
2.1	0.4821	0.4826	0.4830	0.4834	0.4838	0.4842	0.4846	0.4850	0.4854	0.4857
2.2	0.4861	0.4864	0.4868	0.4871	0.4875	0.4878	0.4881	0.4884	0.4887	0.4890
2.3	0.4893	0.4896	0.4898	0.4901	0.4904	0.4906	0.4909	0.4911	0.4913	0.4916
2.4	0.4918	0.4920	0.4922	0.4925	0.4927	0.4929	0.4931	0.4932	0.4934	0.4936

Appendix B   STANDARD NORMAL TABLE

Z	.00	.01	.02	.03	.04	.05	.06	.07	.08	.09
2.5	0.4938	0.4940	0.4941	0.4943	0.4945	0.4946	0.4948	0.4949	0.4951	0.4952
2.6	0.4953	0.4955	0.4956	0.4957	0.4959	0.4960	0.4961	0.4962	0.4963	0.4964
2.7	0.4965	0.4966	0.4967	0.4968	0.4969	0.4970	0.4971	0.4972	0.4973	0.4974
2.8	0.4974	0.4975	0.4976	0.4977	0.4977	0.4978	0.4979	0.4979	0.4980	0.4981
2.9	0.4981	0.4982	0.4982	0.4983	0.4984	0.4984	0.4985	0.4985	0.4986	0.4986
3.0	0.4987	0.4987	0.4987	0.4988	0.4988	0.4989	0.4989	0.4989	0.4990	0.4990

APPENDIX C BINOMIAL TABLE

BINOMIAL PROBABILITIES

To find the probability of x successes in n trials with probability p of success on any one trial, enter the table with the appropriate values for x, n, and p.

Example: If $x = 2$, $n = 5$, and $p = .1$,

$$p(x = 2/n = 5, p = .1) = .073$$

						p						
n	x	0.05	0.1	0.2	0.3	0.4	0.5	0.6	0.7	0.8	0.9	0.95
2	0	.902	.810	.640	.490	.360	.250	.160	.090	.040	.010	.002
	1	.095	.180	.320	.420	.480	.500	.480	.420	.320	.180	.095
	2	.002	.010	.040	.090	.160	.250	.360	.490	.640	.810	.902
3	0	.857	.729	.512	.343	.216	.125	.064	.027	.008	.001	
	1	.135	.243	.384	.441	.432	.375	.288	.189	.096	.027	.007
	2	.007	.027	.096	.189	.288	.375	.432	.441	.384	.243	.135
	3		.001	.008	.027	.064	.125	.216	.343	.512	.729	.857
4	0	.815	.656	.410	.240	.130	.062	.026	.008	.002		
	1	.171	.292	.410	.412	.346	.250	.154	.076	.026	.004	
	2	.014	.049	.154	.265	.346	.375	.346	.265	.154	.049	.014
	3		.004	.026	.076	.154	.250	.346	.412	.410	.292	.171
	4			.002	.008	.026	.062	.130	.240	.410	.656	.815
5	0	.774	.590	.328	.168	.078	.031	.010	.002			
	1	.204	.328	.410	.360	.259	.156	.077	.028	.006		
	2	.021	.073	.205	.309	.346	.312	.230	.132	.051	.008	.001
	3	.001	.008	.051	.132	.230	.312	.346	.309	.205	.073	.021
	4			.006	.028	.077	.156	.259	.360	.410	.328	.204
	5				.002	.010	.031	.078	.168	.328	.590	.774
6	0	.735	.531	.262	.118	.047	.016	.004	.001			
	1	.232	.354	.393	.303	.187	.094	.037	.010	.002		
	2	.031	.098	.246	.324	.311	.234	.138	.060	.015	.001	
	3	.002	.015	.082	.185	.276	.312	.276	.185	.082	.015	.002
	4		.001	.015	.060	.138	.234	.311	.324	.246	.098	.031
	5			.002	.010	.037	.094	.187	.303	.393	.354	.232
	6				.001	.004	.016	.047	.118	.262	.531	.735
7	0	.698	.478	.210	.082	.028	.008	.002				
	1	.257	.372	.367	.247	.131	.055	.017	.004			
	2	.041	.124	.275	.318	.261	.164	.077	.025	.004		
	3	.004	.023	.115	.227	.290	.273	.194	.097	.029	.003	
	4		.003	.029	.097	.194	.273	.290	.227	.115	.023	.004
	5			.004	.025	.077	.164	.261	.318	.275	.124	.041

n	x	0.05	0.1	0.2	0.3	0.4	0.5	0.6	0.7	0.8	0.9	0.95
	6				.004	.017	.055	.131	.247	.367	.372	.257
	7					.002	.008	.028	.082	.210	.478	.698
8	0	.663	.430	.168	.058	.017	.004	.001				
	1	.279	.383	.336	.198	.090	.031	.008	.001			
	2	.051	.149	.294	.296	.209	.109	.041	.010	.001		
	3	.005	.033	.147	.254	.279	.219	.124	.047	.009		
	4		.005	.046	.136	.232	.273	.232	.136	.046	.005	
	5			.009	.047	.124	.219	.279	.254	.147	.033	.005
	6			.001	.010	.041	.109	.209	.296	.294	.149	.051
	7				.001	.008	.031	.090	.198	.336	.383	.279
	8					.001	.004	.017	.058	.168	.430	.663
9	0	.630	.387	.134	.040	.010	.002					
	1	.299	.387	.302	.156	.060	.018	.004				
	2	.063	.172	.302	.267	.161	.070	.021	.004			
	3	.008	.045	.176	.267	.251	.164	.074	.021	.003		
	4	.001	.007	.066	.172	.251	.246	.167	.074	.017	.001	
	5		.001	.017	.074	.167	.246	.251	.172	.066	.007	.001
	6			.003	.021	.074	.164	.251	.267	.176	.045	.008
	7				.004	.021	.070	.161	.267	.302	.172	.063
	8					.004	.018	.060	.156	.302	.387	.299
	9						.002	.010	.040	.134	.387	.630
10	0	.599	.349	.107	.028	.006	.001					
	1	.315	.387	.268	.121	.040	.010	.002				
	2	.075	.194	.302	.233	.121	.044	.011	.001			
	3	.010	.057	.201	.267	.215	.117	.042	.009	.001		
	4	.001	.011	.088	.200	.251	.205	.111	.037	.006		
	5		.001	.026	.103	.201	.246	.201	.103	.026	.001	
	6			.006	.037	.111	.205	.251	.200	.088	.011	.001
	7			.001	.009	.042	.117	.215	.267	.201	.057	.010
	8				.001	.011	.044	.121	.233	.302	.194	.075
	9					.002	.010	.040	.121	.268	.387	.315
	10						.001	.006	.028	.107	.349	.599

APPENDIX D

POISSON PROBABILITIES

To find the probability of x occurrences when there is a mean of μ occurrences per interval, enter the table with x and μ.

Example: If $x = 1$ and $\mu = 1$, $p(x = 1/\lambda = 1) = .36788$

mean (λ)

x \ μ	.1	.2	.3	.4	.5	.6	.7	.8	.9	1.0
0	.90484	.81873	.74082	.67032	.60653	.54881	.49659	.44933	.40657	.36788
1	.09048	.16375	.22225	.26813	.30327	.32929	.34761	.35946	.36591	.36788
2	.00452	.01637	.03334	.05363	.07582	.09879	.12166	.14379	.16466	.18394
3	.00015	.00109	.00333	.00715	.01264	.01976	.02839	.03834	.04940	.06131
4	.00000	.00005	.00025	.00072	.00158	.00296	.00497	.00767	.01111	.01533
5	.00000	.00000	.00002	.00006	.00016	.00036	.00070	.00123	.00200	.00307
6		.00000	.00000	.00000	.00001	.00004	.00008	.00016	.00030	.00051
7					.00000	.00000	.00001	.00002	.00004	.00007
8						.00000	.00000	.00000	.00000	.00001
9								.00000	.00000	.00000

x \ μ	1.1	1.2	1.3	1.4	1.5	1.6	1.7	1.8	1.9	2.0
0	.33287	.30119	.27253	.24660	.22313	.20190	.18268	.16530	.14957	.13534
1	.36616	.36143	.35429	.34524	.33470	.32303	.31056	.29754	.28418	.27067
2	.20139	.21686	.23029	.24166	.25102	.25843	.26398	.26778	.26997	.27067
3	.07384	.08674	.09979	.11278	.12551	.13783	.14959	.16067	.17098	.18045
4	.02031	.02602	.03243	.03947	.04707	.05513	.06357	.07230	.08122	.09022
5	.00447	.00625	.00843	.01105	.01412	.01764	.02162	.02603	.03086	.03609
6	.00082	.00125	.00183	.00258	.00353	.00470	.00612	.00781	.00977	.01203
7	.00013	.00021	.00034	.00052	.00076	.00108	.00149	.00201	.00265	.00344
8	.00002	.00003	.00006	.00009	.00014	.00022	.00032	.00045	.00063	.00086
9	.00000	.00000	.00001	.00001	.00002	.00004	.00006	.00009	.00013	.00019
10	.00000	.00000	.00000	.00000	.00000	.00001	.00001	.00002	.00003	.00004
11		.00000	.00000	.00000	.00000	.00000	.00000	.00000	.00001
12							.00000	.00000	.00000	.00000
13										.00000

μ x	2.1	2.2	2.3	2.4	2.5	2.6	2.7	2.8	2.9	3.0
0	.12246	.11080	.10026	.09072	.08209	.07427	.06721	.06081	.05502	.04979
1	.25716	.24377	.23060	.21772	.20521	.19311	.18146	.17027	.15957	.14936
2	.27002	.26814	.26518	.26127	.25652	.25105	.24496	.23838	.23137	.22404
3	.18001	.19664	.20331	.20901	.21376	.21757	.22047	.22248	.22366	.22404
4	.09923	.10815	.11690	.12541	.13360	.14142	.14881	.15574	.16215	.16803
5	.04168	.04759	.05377	.06020	.06680	.07354	.08036	.08721	.09405	.10082
6	.01459	.01745	.02061	.02408	.02783	.03187	.03616	.04070	.04546	.05041
7	.00438	.00548	.00677	.00826	.00994	.01184	.01395	.01628	.01883	.02160
8	.00115	.00151	.00195	.00248	.00311	.00385	.00471	.00570	.00683	.00810
9	.00027	.00037	.00050	.00066	.00086	.00111	.00141	.00177	.00220	.00270
10	.00006	.00008	.00011	.00016	.00022	.00029	.00038	.00050	.00064	.00081
11	.00001	.00002	.00002	.00003	.00005	.00007	.00009	.00013	.00017	.00022
12	.00000	.00000	.00000	.00001	.00001	.00001	.00002	.00003	.00004	.00006
13	.00000	.00000	.00000	.00000	.00000	.00000	.00000	.00001	.00001	.00001
14				.00000	.00000	.00000	.00000	.00000	.00000	.00000

μ x	3.1	3.2	3.3	3.4	3.5	3.6	3.7	3.8	3.9	4.0
0	.04505	.04076	.03688	.03337	.03020	.02732	.02472	.02237	.02024	.01832
1	.13965	.13044	.12172	.11347	.10569	.09837	.09148	.08501	.07894	.07326
2	.21646	.20870	.20083	.19290	.18496	.17706	.16923	.16152	.15394	.14653
3	.22368	.22262	.22091	.21862	.21579	.21247	.20872	.20459	.20012	.19537
4	.17335	.17809	.18225	.18582	.18881	.19122	.19307	.19436	.19512	.19537
5	.10748	.11398	.12029	.12636	.13217	.13768	.14287	.14771	.15219	.15629
6	.05553	.06079	.06616	.07160	.07710	.08261	.08810	.09355	.09892	.10419
7	.02459	.02779	.03119	.03478	.03855	.04248	.04657	.05078	.05511	.05954
8	.00953	.01112	.01287	.01478	.01686	.01912	.02154	.02412	.02687	.02977
9	.00328	.00395	.00472	.00558	.00656	.00765	.00885	.01018	.01164	.01323
10	.00102	.00126	.00156	.00190	.00230	.00275	.00328	.00387	.00454	.00529
11	.00029	.00037	.00047	.00059	.00073	.00090	.00110	.00134	.00161	.00192
12	.00007	.00010	.00013	.00017	.00021	.00027	.00034	.00042	.00052	.00064
13	.00002	.00002	.00003	.00004	.00006	.00007	.00010	.00012	.00016	.00020
14	.00000	.00001	.00001	.00001	.00001	.00002	.00003	.00003	.00004	.00006
15	.00000	.00000	.00000	.00000	.00000	.00000	.00001	.00001	.00001	.00002
16		.00000	.00000	.00000	.00000	.00000	.00000	.00000	.00000	.00000

x \ μ	4.1	4.2	4.3	4.4	4.5	4.6	4.7	4.8	4.9	5.0
0	.01657	.01500	.01357	.01228	.01111	.01005	.00910	.00823	.00745	.00674
1	.06785	.06298	.05835	.05402	.04999	.04624	.04275	.03950	.03649	.03369
2	.13929	.13226	.12544	.11885	.11248	.10635	.10046	.09481	.08940	.08422
3	.19037	.18517	.17980	.17431	.16872	.16307	.15738	.15169	.14602	.14037
4	.19513	.19442	.19328	.19174	.18981	.18753	.18493	.18203	.17887	.17747
5	.16000	.16331	.16622	.16873	.17083	.17252	.17383	.17475	.17529	.17547
6	.10933	.11432	.11913	.12373	.12812	.13227	.13617	.13980	.14315	.14622
7	.06404	.06859	.07318	.07777	.08236	.08692	.09143	.09586	.10021	.10444
8	.03282	.03601	.03933	.04278	.04633	.04998	.05371	.05752	.06138	.06528
9	.01495	.01680	.01879	.02091	.02316	.02554	.02805	.03068	.03342	.03627
10	.00613	.00706	.00808	.00920	.01042	.01175	.01318	.01472	.01637	.01813
11	.00228	.00269	.00316	.00368	.00426	.00491	.00563	.00642	.00729	.00824
12	.00078	.00094	.00113	.00135	.00160	.00188	.00221	.00257	.00298	.00343
13	.00025	.00030	.00037	.00046	.00055	.00067	.00080	.00095	.00112	.00132
14	.00007	.00009	.00011	.00014	.00018	.00022	.00027	.00033	.00039	.00047
15	.00002	.00003	.00003	.00004	.00005	.00007	.00008	.00010	.00013	.00016
16	.00001	.00001	.00001	.00001	.00002	.00002	.00002	.00003	.00004	.00005
17	.00000	.00000	.00000	.00000	.00000	.00001	.00001	.00001	.00001	.00001
18	.00000	.00000	.00000	.00000	.00000	.00000	.00000	.00000	.00000	.00000
19						.00000	.00000	.00000	.00000	.00000

APPENDIX E

χ^2 **TABLE**

VALUES FOR THE χ^2 DISTRIBUTION

To find a χ^2 value, enter the table with the number of degrees of freedom (df) and the single tail area (α).

Example: If df = 10 and α = .05, then χ^2 = 18.31

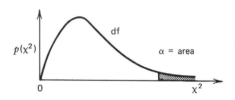

df \ α	.995	.99	.975	.95	.90	.75	.50	.25	.10	.05	.025	.01	.005
1	0.0⁴393	0.0³157	0.0³982	0.0²3	0.0158	0.102	0.455	1.323	2.71	3.84	5.02	6.63	7.88
2	0.0100	0.0201	0.0506	0.103	0.211	0.575	1.386	2.77	4.61	5.99	7.38	9.21	10.60
3	0.0717	0.115	0.216	0.352	0.584	1.213	2.37	4.11	6.25	7.81	9.35	11.34	12.84
4	0.207	0.297	0.484	0.711	1.064	1.923	3.36	5.39	7.78	9.49	11.14	13.28	14.86
5	0.412	0.554	0.831	1.145	1.610	2.67	4.35	6.63	9.24	11.07	12.83	15.09	16.75
6	0.676	0.872	1.237	1.635	2.20	3.45	5.35	7.84	10.64	12.59	14.45	16.81	18.55
7	0.989	1.289	1.690	2.17	2.83	4.25	6.35	9.04	12.02	14.07	16.01	18.48	20.3
8	1.344	1.646	2.18	2.73	3.49	5.07	7.34	10.22	13.36	15.51	17.35	20.1	22.0
9	1.735	2.09	2.70	3.33	4.17	5.90	8.34	11.39	14.68	16.92	19.02	21.7	23.6
10	2.16	2.56	3.25	3.94	4.87	6.74	9.34	12.55	15.99	18.31	20.5	23.2	25.2
11	2.60	3.05	3.82	4.57	5.58	7.58	10.34	13.70	17.28	19.68	21.9	24.7	26.8
12	3.07	3.57	4.40	5.23	6.30	8.44	11.34	14.85	18.55	21.0	23.3	26.2	28.3
13	3.57	4.11	5.01	5.89	7.04	9.30	12.34	15.98	19.81	22.4	24.7	27.7	29.8
14	4.07	4.66	5.63	6.57	7.79	10.17	13.34	17.12	21.1	23.7	26.1	29.1	31.3
15	4.60	5.23	6.26	7.26	8.55	11.04	14.34	18.25	22.3	25.0	27.5	30.6	32.8
16	5.14	5.81	6.91	7.96	9.31	11.91	15.34	19.37	23.5	26.3	28.8	32.0	34.3
17	5.70	6.41	7.56	8.67	10.09	12.79	16.34	20.5	24.8	27.6	30.2	33.4	35.7
18	6.26	7.01	8.23	9.39	10.86	13.68	17.34	21.6	26.0	28.9	31.5	34.8	37.2
19	6.84	7.63	8.91	10.12	11.65	14.56	18.34	22.7	27.2	30.1	32.9	36.2	38.6
20	7.43	8.26	9.59	10.85	12.44	15.45	19.34	23.8	28.4	31.4	34.2	37.6	40.0
21	8.03	8.90	10.28	11.59	13.24	16.34	20.3	24.9	29.6	32.7	35.5	38.9	41.4
22	8.64	9.54	10.98	12.34	14.04	17.24	21.3	26.0	30.8	33.9	36.8	40.3	42.8
23	9.26	10.20	11.69	13.09	14.85	18.14	22.3	27.1	32.0	35.2	38.1	41.6	44.2
24	9.89	10.86	12.40	13.85	15.66	19.04	23.3	28.2	33.2	36.4	39.4	43.0	45.6
25	10.52	11.52	13.12	14.61	16.47	19.94	24.3	29.3	34.4	37.7	40.6	44.3	46.9

α / df	.995	.99	.975	.95	.90	.75	.50	.25	.10	.05	.025	.01	.005
26	11.16	12.20	13.84	15.38	17.29	20.8	25.3	30.4	35.6	38.9	41.9	45.6	48.3
27	11.81	12.88	14.57	16.15	18.11	21.7	26.3	31.5	36.7	40.1	43.2	47.0	49.6
28	12.46	13.56	15.31	16.93	18.94	22.7	27.3	32.6	37.9	41.3	44.5	48.3	51.0
29	13.12	14.26	16.05	17.71	19.77	23.6	28.3	33.7	39.1	42.6	45.7	49.6	52.3
30	13.79	14.95	16.79	18.49	20.6	24.5	29.3	34.8	40.3	43.8	47.0	50.9	53.7
40	20.7	22.2	24.4	26.5	29.1	33.7	39.3	45.6	51.8	55.8	59.3	63.7	66.8
50	28.0	29.7	32.4	34.8	37.7	42.9	49.3	56.3	63.2	67.5	71.4	76.2	79.5
60	35.5	37.5	40.5	43.2	46.5	52.3	59.3	67.0	74.4	79.1	83.3	88.4	92.0
70	43.3	45.4	48.8	51.7	55.3	61.7	69.3	77.6	85.5	90.5	95.0	100.4	104.2
80	51.2	53.5	57.2	60.4	64.3	71.1	79.3	88.1	96.6	101.9	106.6	112.3	116.3
90	59.2	61.8	65.6	69.1	73.3	80.6	89.3	98.6	107.6	113.1	118.1	124.1	128.3
100	67.3	70.1	74.2	77.9	82.4	90.1	99.3	109.1	118.5	124.3	129.6	135.8	140.2

APPENDIX F   KOLMOGOROV–SMIRNOV TABLE

CRITICAL VALUES OF D IN THE KOLMOGOROV–SMIRNOV ONE-SAMPLE TEST

To find a D value, enter the table with the sample size (n) and the level of significance (α).

Example: If $n = 30$ and $\alpha = .10$, then $D = 0.22$

Sample size (n)	Level of significance for D = maximum $\lvert F_o - F_e \rvert$				
	.20	.15	.10	.05	.01
1	0.900	0.925	0.950	0.975	0.995
2	0.684	0.726	0.776	0.842	0.929
3	0.565	0.597	0.642	0.708	0.828
4	0.494	0.525	0.564	0.624	0.733
5	0.446	0.474	0.510	0.565	0.669
6	0.410	0.436	0.470	0.521	0.618
7	0.381	0.405	0.438	0.486	0.577
8	0.358	0.381	0.411	0.457	0.543
9	0.339	0.360	0.388	0.432	0.514
10	0.322	0.342	0.368	0.410	0.490
11	0.307	0.326	0.352	0.391	0.468
12	0.295	0.313	0.338	0.375	0.450
13	0.284	0.302	0.325	0.361	0.433
14	0.274	0.292	0.314	0.349	0.418
15	0.266	0.283	0.304	0.338	0.404
16	0.258	0.274	0.295	0.328	0.392
17	0.250	0.266	0.286	0.318	0.381
18	0.244	0.259	0.278	0.309	0.371
19	0.237	0.252	0.272	0.301	0.363
20	0.231	0.246	0.264	0.294	0.356
25	0.21	0.22	0.24	0.27	0.32
30	0.19	0.20	0.22	0.24	0.29
35	0.18	0.19	0.21	0.23	0.27
Over 35	$\dfrac{1.07}{\sqrt{n}}$	$\dfrac{1.14}{\sqrt{n}}$	$\dfrac{1.22}{\sqrt{n}}$	$\dfrac{1.36}{\sqrt{n}}$	$\dfrac{1.63}{\sqrt{n}}$

APPENDIX G

e^{-x} **TABLE**

VALUES FOR e^{-x}

To find a value of e^{-x}, enter the table with the value for x.

Example: If $x = 5$, then $e^{-5} = 0.00674$

x	e^{-x}	x	e^{-x}
0.0	1.00000	3.1	0.04505
0.1	0.90484	3.2	0.04076
0.2	0.81873	3.3	0.03688
0.3	0.74082	3.4	0.03337
0.4	0.67032	3.5	0.03020
0.5	0.60653	3.6	0.02732
0.6	0.54881	3.7	0.02472
0.7	0.49659	3.8	0.02237
0.8	0.44933	3.9	0.02024
0.9	0.40657	4.0	0.01832
1.0	0.36788	4.1	0.01657
1.1	0.33287	4.2	0.01500
1.2	0.30119	4.3	0.01357
1.3	0.27253	4.4	0.01228
1.4	0.24660	4.5	0.01111
1.5	0.22313	4.6	0.01005
1.6	0.20190	4.7	0.00910
1.7	0.18268	4.8	0.00823
1.8	0.16530	4.9	0.00745
1.9	0.14957	5.0	0.00674
2.0	0.13534	6.0	0.00248
2.1	0.12246	7.0	0.00091
2.2	0.11080	8.0	0.00034
2.3	0.10026	9.0	0.00012
2.4	0.09072	10.0	0.00005
2.5	0.08209	11.0	0.00002
2.6	0.07427	12.0	0.00001
2.7	0.06721	13.0	0.00000
2.8	0.06081	14.0	0.00000
2.9	0.05502	15.0	0.00000
3.0	0.04979		

APPENDIX H

ln x TABLE

VALUES FOR ln x

To find a value of ln x, enter the table with the value for x.

Example: If x = 0.5 then ln 0.5 = -0.69

x	ln x	x	ln x	x	ln x	x	ln x
0.00	$-\infty$	0.25	-1.39	0.50	-0.69	0.75	-0.29
0.01	-4.61	0.26	-1.35	0.51	-0.67	0.76	-0.27
0.02	-3.91	0.27	-1.31	0.52	-0.65	0.77	-0.26
0.03	-3.51	0.28	-1.27	0.53	-0.63	0.78	-0.25
0.04	-3.22	0.29	-1.24	0.54	-0.62	0.79	-0.24
0.05	-3.00	0.30	-1.20	0.55	-0.60	0.80	-0.22
0.06	-2.81	0.31	-1.17	0.56	-0.58	0.81	-0.21
0.07	-2.66	0.32	-1.14	0.57	-0.56	0.82	-0.20
0.08	-2.53	0.33	-1.11	0.58	-0.54	0.83	-0.19
0.09	-2.41	0.34	-1.08	0.59	-0.53	0.84	-0.17
0.10	-2.30	0.35	-1.05	0.60	-0.51	0.85	-0.16
0.11	-2.21	0.36	-1.02	0.61	-0.49	0.86	-0.15
0.12	-2.12	0.37	-0.99	0.62	-0.48	0.87	-0.14
0.13	-2.04	0.38	-0.97	0.63	-0.46	0.88	-0.13
0.14	-1.97	0.39	-0.94	0.64	-0.45	0.89	-0.12
0.15	-1.90	0.40	-0.92	0.65	-0.43	0.90	-0.11
0.16	-1.83	0.41	-0.89	0.66	-0.42	0.91	-0.09
0.17	-1.77	0.42	-0.87	0.67	-0.40	0.92	-0.08
0.18	-1.71	0.43	-0.84	0.68	-0.39	0.93	-0.07
0.19	-1.66	0.44	-0.82	0.69	-0.37	0.94	-0.06
0.20	-1.61	0.45	-0.80	0.70	-0.36	0.95	-0.05
0.21	-1.56	0.46	-0.78	0.71	-0.34	0.96	-0.04
0.22	-1.51	0.47	-0.76	0.72	-0.33	0.97	-0.03
0.23	-1.47	0.48	-0.73	0.73	-0.31	0.98	-0.02
0.24	-1.43	0.49	-0.71	0.74	-0.30	0.99	-0.01
						1.00	-0.01

AUTHOR INDEX

Page numbers followed by an n indicate footnotes.

Ackoff, Russell L., 324n
Adam, Everett E., Jr., 65
Alderson, Wroe, 76, 91
Ancker, C. J., 299n
Andlinger, G. T., 237, 259, 263
Anshoff, H. I., 306n
Anthony, Robert, 227
Anthony, Ted F., 76n, 91, 232
Aquilano, Nicholas J., 49n, 65
Archer, Edward, 23n, 24, 45, 91
Ashcroft, Kenneth, 278n, 291

Babb, E. M., 241n, 263
Baecher, Joan M., 10n, 19, 328n
Balintfy, Joseph L., 204
Baum, Lyman F., 225n
Bean, Alden S., 337
Beggs, Robert I., 4n, 19
Behrens, William S., 204
Bellman, Richard, 247n, 248, 263
Bennett, G. K., 169
Benson, Fred S., 279n, 291
Benson, Tammy, vii
Ben-Yaacov, G. Z., 291
Betaque, N. E., 231
Bidewell, E. L., 296n
Biles, W. E., 11n
Bobillier, P. A., 204
Boere, N. J., 45
Bommer, Michael R. W., 252n, 264
Boughey, Arthur S., 45
Box, G. E. P., 108, 126
Bradshaw, Francis F., 324
Bryant, J. W., 45
Buffa, Elwood S., 65
Burdick, Donald S., 204
Burgess, James S., Jr., 45
Burkhard, Don, vii
Butler, Richard J., 241n, 263

Carlson, Elliot, 243, 263
Cassidy, Henry J., 45
Chase, Richard B., 49n, 65
Chen, Kuang-Chiau, 270n, 291
Chu, Kong, 204
Churchill, Neil C., 45
Clark, Charles T., 126

Clark, Jane, 238, 239
Clarkson, Geoffry P. E., 210-213, 226, 227, 231
Cochran, W. G., 316
Cohen, Kalman J., 251n, 259, 263
Cole, H. S. D., 39n, 45
Conway, R. W., 299n, 316
Cook, Thomas M., 168
Cooper, D. O., 91
Cooper, Robert B., 168
Corbett, Thomas G., 32n, 45
Cosmetatos, George P., 168
Couger, J. Daniel, 238n, 239
Coveyou, R. R., 134, 143
Cox, G. M., 316
Cox, J. Grady, 126
Craft, Clifford J., 238n, 250, 264
Creaven, Gerald, 205
Crosson, Frederick J., 209n, 231
Crowder, William S., 232
Cumpson, Gary, vii

DaCosta, Jo-Anne, 19, 332, 333n, 338
Dale, Alfred G., 238, 263
Davidson, L. B., 91
Davis, K. Roscoe, vii, 33n, 45, 252n, 263, 337
Dean, Burton V., 251n, 259
Denison, W. K., 91
Des Jardines, Larry, vii
Dickson, Gary W., vii, 211, 213, 214, 220, 226, 227, 231
Dill, William R., 236, 263
Dilworth, James B., 65
Dixon, W. J., 297n, 316
Dreyfus, Hubert L., 210n, 231
Drucker, Peter F., 76, 91, 335
Durway, Jerry W., 91

Ebert, Ronald J., 65
Economos, A. M., 45
Eisgruber, L. M., 241n, 263
Emshoff, James R., 173, 174, 204, 316
Ernst, G. W., 210n, 231

Evans, M. K., 37n

Fabian, Henry, vii
Feigenbaum, E. A., 210, 232
Feldman, Julian, 232
Fenske, Russell W., 337
Ferrara, William L., 91
Fetter, R. B., 91
Field, Al, 45
Finger, J. M., 306n, 317
Fishman, George S., 113n, 126, 204, 300n, 310n, 313n, 317
Foote, B. L., 168
Forrester, Jay W., 38, 39, 45, 176, 204
Fox, Phyllis, 176
Frazer, J. Ronald, 252n, 264
Frey, M. William, 238n, 263

Gafarian, A. V., 299n
Galitz, Lawrence, 268n, 274, 275n, 289, 292
Gallagher, Charles A., 66, 168, 337
Gattis, Daniel R., 7, 18, 205, 268, 269n-272n, 275n, 289
Gebbard, Ely M., 299n, 317
Gensh, Dennis H., 28n, 29, 45
Gere, William S., 209n, 232
Gershefski, George W., 268n, 292
Gilliam, Ronald R., 168
Ginzberg, Michael J., 321n, 337
Godin, Victor B., 321n
Gohring, Kenneth W., 176, 204
Gonzalez, Richard F., 18, 126, 130, 144, 169, 204
Gordon, Geoffrey, 182, 183, 204
Gorry, G. A., 231
Grayson, Jackson C., Jr., 331n, 337
Green, Paul E., 76, 91
Green, Thad B., 329n, 337
Greenlaw, Paul S., vii, 211, 215, 217, 220, 221, 226, 227, 232, 238, 248n, 250n, 263
Grimes, A. Ray, 37n
Gross, D., 169

Hamburger, Michael J., 209, 232

Hammersley, J., 299n, 317
Handscomb, D., 299n, 317
Harris, C. N., 169
Harris, F. W., 48
Harvey, Allan, 327n, 337
Hayes, R. L., 306n
Hayya, Jack C., 91
Hendrick, Thomas E., 45
Herlihy, Clifford H., 4n, 19
Herron, Lowell W., 263
Hertz, D. B., 91
Hicks, C. R., 297n, 317
Hill, Marianne, vii
Hillier, Frederick S., 66, 169
Hitch, Charles J., 322, 323n
Horn, Robert E., 264
Hottenstein, Michael P., 238n, 263
Howard, John A., 232
Howard, K., 292
Hunt, Earl B., 208n, 232

Jackson, Barbara B., 292
Jackson, James R., 236, 263
Jaedicke, Robert K., 91
Jain, Suresh K., 25n, 26, 28, 45
Jansson, B., 143
Jenkins, D. Terry, 292
Johnson, B. M., 299n, 316
Jones, Roland S., 329n, 337

Kahan, B. C., 204
Kahn, Herman, 301n
Kant, Immanuel, 307
Kay, Ira M., 176, 204
Keuhn, Alfred A., 209, 232
Khadem, Ramin, vii, 280n
Kibbee, Joel M., 238n, 250, 264
King, William R., 292
Kirkpatrick, Charles A., 169
Kiviat, Phillip, 178, 204
Klasson, Charles R., 238, 263
Kleijnen, J. P. C., 317
Klein, L. R., 37n
Kleinrock, Leonard, 169
Kniffin, Fred W., 238n, 264
Korn, Granino A., 131n, 144
Krajewoki, LeRoy J., 252
Kroeber, Don, vii
Kuzdrall, P. J., 204
Kwak, N. K., 204

LaForge, R. Lawrence, 32n, 45
Lauffer, Arthur C., 66
Lawrence, Paul R., 331n
Ledvinka, James, 32n, 45
Legler, John B., 37n, 38, 45
Lehmer, D. H., 133, 144
Leverett, E. J., Jr., 33n, 45
Levin, Richard I., 169

Lewin, Kurt, 322n, 337
Lewis, T. G., 18, 204
Lieberman, Gerald J., 66, 169
Lord, Robert J., 91
Lorsch, Jay W., 331n
Lubin, John Francis, 12, 19

McCarthy, John, 210, 226
McDevitt, Carl D., 91, 252n, 260, 264
McFadden, Fred, vii
McGehee, William, 242, 264
McLean, Ephraim, 271n
McMillan, Claude, 126, 130, 144, 169, 204
MacPherson, R. D., 134, 143
Mann, Chiu W., 279n, 280n
Marett, Patricia Gill, viii, 325n, 328n, 338
Markowitz, H. M., 204
Massey, E. J., Jr., 29n, 316
Maxwell, W. L., 299n, 316
Meadows, Dennis L., 22n, 38, 45, 204
Meadows, Donella H., 204
Meier, Robert C., 18, 126, 204, 264, 308n, 317
Mesarovic, Mihajlo, 39n
Metropolis, N., 144
Meyer, Herbert A., 132, 144
Miller, Peter J., 45
Minsky, Marvin, 210, 226
Mize, Joe H., 126
Monarchi, David, E., 45
Moore, Lawrence J., 23n, 24, 45, 91
Morgenroth, William, 232
Morse, Philip M., 169
Muller, M. E., 106, 126

Nanda, R., 45
Nanus, Burt, 238n, 250, 264
Naylor, Thomas H., 7, 7n, 18, 126, 169, 204, 205, 268, 269n-272n, 274n, 275n, 279n, 289, 292, 306, 308, 317
Neuhauser, John J., 243n, 264
Newell, Allen, 210, 226, 231, 232
Newell, William T., 18, 126, 204, 264, 308, 317
Newson, Walter B., 329n, 337
Norris, Dwight, vii

Orkin, Eric B., 251n, 264
Orlicky, J., 66

Page, E. S., 300n
Panico, J. A., 169
Parks, Michael S., 225n, 232

Pazer, Harold L., 18, 126, 204, 264, 308n, 317
Pestel, Edward, 39n
Peters, G., 231
Peterson, Clifford C., 66
Phyrr, Stephen A., 35
Plane, Donald R., 45
Plossl, G. W., 66
Pray, Thomas F., 241, 263
Pritsker, A. Alan B., 178n
Prolist, A. R., 204
Pugh, Alexander, III, 176, 177, 205

Radnor, M., 337
Rador, Louis T., 337
Randers, Jorgen, 204
Rawdon, Richard H., 263
Reichenback, Hans, 308n, 317
Rhenman, Erich, 251n, 263
Ritsma, Wybren A., vii
Robbins, Lionel, 317
Robertson, Terry D., 37n, 38, 45
Robichek, Alexander A., 91
Robinson, Art, 211, 232
Rodriguez, Jaime I., 292
Rubenstein, A. H., 337
Russell, Robert A., 168

Saaty, Thomas L., 151n, 169
Saint-Denis, André, 23n, 24, 45, 91
Sanders, Richard L., 176, 204
Sayre, Kenneth M., 209n, 231
Schein, Edgar H., 322n, 337, 338
Schenkel, William M., 34n
Schkade, Lawrence L., 126
Schmidt, J. W., 126, 138, 144, 151n, 155n, 169
Schmitz, Homer H., 204
Schott, Brian, 239, 252n, 264
Schriber, Thomas, viii, 155, 183n, 205
Schultzki, Alain, viii, 280n
Scott, David F., Jr., 23n, 24, 45, 91
Scott, William E., 268
Seila, Andy, vii
Shank, John K., 45
Shannon, Robert E., 11n, 18, 128, 134, 144, 175, 176, 205, 296n, 297n, 317, 338
Shapiro, Benson P., 292
Shaw, J. C., 210, 226
Shim, Jae, 236n, 264
Shore, Barry, 66
Shubik, Martin, 264
Shycon, Harvey N., 326n, 336
Siemens, Nicolai, 232
Simkin, Mark, vii
Simon, Herbert A., 210, 226, 232
Sisson, Roger L., 173, 174, 204, 316

Smith, B. J., 18, 204
Smith, Robert D., 211, 215-217, 220, 221, 226, 227, 232
Snow, C. P., 331n
Sorensen, Richard E., 338
Spanier, Jerome, 299n, 317
Spetzler, Carl S., 76n, 91
Sprague, Ralph, vii
Springer, Clifford H., 4n, 19, 74, 91, 120
Stael von Holstein, Carl-Axel S., 76n, 91
Stewart, R., 244, 264
Strang, Daniel R., 241, 263
Strauss, Lance J., 238, 264
Streveler, Dennis, vii
Swain, Newton D., 176, 204
Sweeney, James W., 236, 263

Taylor, Bernard W., III, 23n, 24 45, 91, 252n, 263, 337
Taylor, R. E., 126, 134, 144, 151n, 155n, 169

Teichroew, Daniel, 12, 19, 144
Tersine, Richard J., 48n, 66
Thomas, George, 19, 332, 333n, 338
Thompson, Howard E., vii, 252, 264
Thompson, J. D., 91
Tippett, L. H. C., 144
Tonge, Fred M., 209, 232
Trieschmann, James S., 33, 45
Trudeau, G. B., 173
Truemper, Klaus, 251n, 259
Turban, Efraim, 333n, 338
Turing, Alan M., 208, 226, 232

Urban, Glenn L., 338

Van Gelden, A., 134, 144
Van Horne, Richard L., 306n, 317
Vatter, William J., 11n, 19
Veglahan, Peter A., 252n, 264
Vernon, Ivan R., 238n, 263
Villanueua, R., 204
Vogel, Myles A., 169
von Neuman, John, 54, 132

Vroman, H. William, 232

Wagle, B. V., 292
Wagner, G. R., vii, 270, 271, 275, 278, 279
Walters, James E., 70n, 91
Ward, R. A., 327n, 338
Watson, Hugh J., 6n, 10n, 11n, 19, 22n, 66, 70n, 76n, 91, 168, 182, 183, 232, 252n, 264, 325n, 328n, 337, 338
Waugh, Miles, 325
Weber, C. E., 231
Wendt, Paul F., 37n, 38, 45
White, J. A., 169
Wolek, Francis W., 322n, 338
Wolfe, Joseph, 241n, 264
Woolsey, R. E. D., 324n, 325
Wright, O. W., 66
Wyman, F. Paul, 30n, 31, 32, 45, 179n, 205, 250n

Zand, Dale E., 338

SUBJECT INDEX

ADvertising MEdia SIMulation
(AD-ME-SIM) model, 28-29
Air Canada, 23-24
Analog models, 4
Analytic mode, 5
Antithetic variates, 299-300
Artificial intelligence (AI), 208-211
Athabasca Tar Sands of Canada,
30-31, 32
Autocorrelation, 310-313
test, 141
Automatic termination condition,
304, 305
Autoregression analysis, 310

Batch method, 310-313
Bernoulli distribution, 113, 114
Bethelehem Steel Corporation,
24-28
Binomial distribution, 113-115
Binomial table, 343-344
Boundaries, of system, 3
Box-Muller method, 106-107
Business application of simulation,
21-45
econometric models, 36-38
engineering, 30-31, 32
finance, 23-24
government, 34, 36
insurance, 33-34
marketing, 28-29
personnel, 31-33
production, 24-28
real estate, 34, 35
systems dynamics, 38-39

Canadian Bechtel Limited, 30
Channels, in queuing systems,
148-150
Chi-square table, 348-349
Chi-square test, 116-118
Clarkson's trust investment model,
210-211, 212-213
Club of Rome, The, 38-39
Computerized financial planning
models, 84-85
Confusion matrix, 221
Congruence relationship, 133
Congruential random number genera-
tion methods, 133-138

Continuous probability distributions,
96-113
Controllable variables, 8
Corporate simulation models,
267-292
applications, 269-270
benefits, 270, 271
developing, 279-280
equations in, 273-277
growing use, 268-269
problems, 270-271
programming, 277-279
structure, 271-273
Teleglobe Canada, 280-287
Correlated sampling, 300-301
Credit Union Management Game,
252-258
Crude approximation method, 96-97
Custom-built models, 5, 6

Decision variables, 8
Definitional equations, 10, 247,
273-274
Dependent demand, 49
Dependent variables, 6-7
Descriptive models, 5
Deterministic models, 5-6
Deterministic variables, 8-9
Dickson's vendor selection model,
211, 213-215
Discrete probability distributions,
94-96

e^{-x} table, 351
Econometric models, 271-277,
283-284
Georgia model, 36-38
Empirically based equations, 10, 247,
273, 274
Empiricist, 307-309
Endogenous variables, 7, 281
Engineering, simulation of tar sands
mining operations, 30-31, 32
Environment, 3
Environmental variables, 8
Exogenous variables, 8, 280
Experimental design, 296-297
External variables, 8

Factors, in experimental design, 297

Feedback, 3
Finance, a cash budget simulation,
23-24
Financial models, 272, 273
Financial planning generations, 70,
86
First-generation financial planning,
70, 71
Fixed-order period, 49-50
Fixed-order quantity, 49-50
Fixed-order quantity model, 50-52
Fixed-time increment time advance,
57, 156, 297-299
Flowchart-oriented languages, 174
FORTRAN-based queuing model,
159-164
Fractional factorial design, 297
Full factorial design, 297
Functional games, 240

Gap test, 141
General management games, 240
General Problem Solver (GPS), 210
General-purpose languages, 172,
173
General Purpose Simulation System,
(GPSS), 182-201
ADVANCE block, 189-190
block diagrams, 184-185
ENTER and LEAVE blocks,
194-197
features, 183
GENERATE block, 187
modeling more complex systems,
199-201
negative exponential processes,
197-199
parallel servers, 194
program output, 192-194
punched card program, 191-192
QUEUE and DEPART blocks,
188
SEIZE and RELEASE blocks,
188-189
stopping the simulation, 190-191
TERMINATE block, 190
Georgia econometric model, 36-38
Goodness-of-fit tests, 116-119
Government, fire department deployment policy analysis, 34-36

Heuristic problem solving or programming, 208-209

Iconic models, 4
Independent demand, 49
Independent replications, 310
Independent variables, 9
Industrial dynamics, 38
Initial conditions, 302-303
Innovation process approach, 321-322
Input variables, 9
Insurance, valuing a property-liability insurance agency, 33-34
Inventory concepts, 48-50
Inventory costs, 48-49
Inverse method, 100-102
Iteration, 82, 303-305

Kolmogorov-Smirnov table, 350
Kolmogorov-Smirnov test, 118-119

Lagged output variables, 8
Linear interpolation method, 97-99
ln x table, 352
Logical Theorist (LT), 210

Management games, 14, 235-264
adding flexibility, 251
administration, 245-246
advantages, 242-244
concepts in design, 246-250
Credit Union Management Game, 252-258
history, 236-239
limitations, 244-245
purposes, 242
recent trends, 251-252
types, 239-242
validation, 250
Management scientists, differences between managers and, 331-332
Marketing, selecting advertising schedules, 28-29
Marketing models, 272-273
Mathematical models, 4-6
Midsquare method, 132-133
Model development process, 13-14, 320-327
data collection, 323-324
model building, 324-326
model implementation, 327
model operation, 327
model validation, 326-327
problem and/or information identification, 322-323
Models, 3-4
Model sampling, 14-15, 85-86

Monte Carlo inventory simulation, 47-66
adding greater realism, 61-62
analysis for optimization, 59-61
Monte Carlo method, 54-55
probability distributions, 53-54
sample size, 58-59
simulation, 55-58
Monte Carlo sampling, 14, 54-55, 78-79
Multiple-factor experiments, 297
Multiplicative congruential random number generators, 133
Multistage validation, 308-309

Negative exponential distribution, 102-105, 115-116
Next-event time advance, 57, 156, 297-299
Nontheoretical probability distributions, 94
Normal distribution, 105-109
Numeric mode, 5

Operational gaming, 242
Optimization models, 4, 5
Output variables, 7

Personnel, affirmative action planning, 31-33
Phases, in queuing systems, 149
Physical models, 4
Planned change approach, 321-322
Poisson distribution, 105, 115-116
Poisson table, 345-347
Poker test, 141
Policy variables, 8
Prescheduled events, 58, 155
Primary events, 155-156
Probabilistic estimates, 76-78
Probabilistic financial planning, 69-91
Probabilistic models, 5-6
Probability distributions and process generators, 93-126
sampling from nontheoretical probability distributions, 94-99
continuous probability distributions, 96-99
discrete probability distributions, 94-96
sampling from theoretical probability distributions, 99
continuous probability distributions, 99-113
discrete probability distributions, 113-116
goodness-of-fit tests, 116
Problem-oriented languages, 174

Problems in model development, 327-332
management scientist's perspective, 328-329
manager's perspective, 329-331
Procedure-oriented languages, 174
Process generator, 94
Production, machine shop planning and scheduling, 24-28
Production models, 272, 273
Product structure, 49
Protocol method, 211
Pseudo random numbers, 132

Queue, 148
Queuing system analysis, 151-166
analytic approach, 151-155, 166
simulation approach, 155-166
trial-and-error approach, 151
Queuing (waiting line) systems, 12, 102, 147-169
basic terminology, 148-150
important characteristics, 154, 155

Random numbers, 54, 78-79, 129-144
digital computer methods, 132-138
generation methods, 131-132
properties of good generator, 130-131
statistical tests for randomness, 138-142
Random number table, 339-340
Random variables, 8
Rationalist, 307-309
Ready-built models, 5-6
Real estate, investment analysis, 34-35
Recursive equations, 36, 132
Rejection method, 108-109
Replicating experimental conditions, 61
Replication, 209
Responses, in experimental design, 297
Response variables, 8, 297
Runs above and below the mean test, 141
Runs up and down test, 138-141, 311-312
Run time, 301-305

Sample size, 58-59, 303-305
Sampling method for normally distributed variates, 107-108
Secondary events, 155-156
Second-generation financial planning, 70, 71-73
Serially correlated variables, 8

358   INDEX

Simulation, 2, 10-13, 85-86
  applications in functional areas,
    22-23
  definition, 2
  model sampling, 85-86
  reasons against, 13
  reasons for, 12-13
  usage, 10-12
Simulation-like methods, 14-15,
    85-86, 207-232, 235-264,
    309-310
Simulation of human decision
    making, 15, 207-232
  artificial intelligence, 208-209
  Clarkson's trust investment model,
    210-211, 212-213
  conditions conducive to modeling,
    221-223
  Dickson's vendor selection model,
    211, 213-215
  history, 210-211
  methodology, 219-221
  potential benefits, 217-219
  processing overdrafts, 223-225
  Smith and Greenlaw's personnel
    selection model, 211, 215-217
Single-factor experiments, 297
Smith and Greenlaw's personnel
    selection model, 211, 215-217
Special-purpose simulation languages,
    171-205

advantages, 172-175
disadvantages, 175
DYNAMO, 176-178
GASP, 178-179
GPSS, 183-201
IFPS, 180-182
popularity of various languages, 182
selection, 175-176
SIMSCRIPT, 179-180
Specific industry games, 240
Spectrum analysis, 310
Standard normal distribution, 106
Standard normal table, 341-342
Starting conditions, 56-57, 302-303
Statistical analysis of simulation out-
    put, 58-59, 83-84, 310-313
Statistical precision, 303-305
Steady-state conditions, 151, 165,
    301-303
Stochastic variables, 8
Subjective probabilities, 76-78
Suboptimization, 3
Symbolic models, 4
Syncrude Canada Limited 30-32
Synthetic a priori, 307-309
System, 2
Systems concepts, 2-3
Systems dynamics, 38-39

Teleglobe Canada's corporate model,
    280-287

Theoretical probability distributions,
    99
Third-generation financial planning,
    70, 73-85
  analytic mode, 74-75
  numeric mode, 75-85
Time advance methods, 57,
    297-299
Traditional line item budgeting, 70,
    71
Transient conditions, 151, 156, 301-
    301-303
Triangular distribution, 110-113

Uncontrollable variables, 8
Uniform distribution, 100-102
Uniformity test, 138-139
Urban dynamics, 38

Validation, 305-310
Variance reduction techniques,
    299-301
Variate, 101
Verbal models, 4
Verisimilitude, 247

Waiting line (queuing) systems, 12,
    102, 147-169
  basic terminology, 148-150
Wharton econometric model, 36-37
World dynamics, 38